A M I S T A D   L I T E R A R Y   S E R I E S

ZORA NEALE HURSTON

**Critical Perspectives
Past and Present**

Also by Henry Louis Gates, Jr.

Figures in Black: Words, Signs, and the "Racial" Self
Signifying Monkey: Toward a Theory of Afro-American Literary Criticism
Loose Canons: Notes on the Culture Wars
Black Literature and Literary Theory (editor)
The Classic Slave Narratives (editor)
Reading Black, Reading Feminist (editor)

Also by K. A. Appiah

Assertion and Conditions
For Truth in Semantics
Necessary Questions: An Introduction to Philosophy
Avenging Angel (fiction)
In My Father's House: Africa in the Philosophy of Culture
Early African-American Classics (editor)

AMISTAD LITERARY SERIES

ZORA NEALE HURSTON

Critical Perspectives
Past and Present

EDITED BY
Henry Louis Gates, Jr., and K. A. Appiah

Amistad

NEW YORK, NEW YORK

Critical Perspectives Past and Present

MICHAEL C. VAZQUEZ, *Project Coordinator*

WAYNE L. APONTE
LISA GATES
SONJA OKUN

Amistad Press, Inc.
1271 Avenue of the Americas
New York, NY 10020

Distributed by:
Penguin USA
375 Hudson Street
New York, NY 10014

Designed by Stanley S. Drate, Folio Graphics Company, Inc.
Produced by March Tenth, Inc.

10 9 8 7 6 5 4 3 2 1

Library of Congress Cataloging-in-Publication Data

Zora Neale Hurston : critical perspectives past and present / edited
by Henry Louis Gates, Jr., and K. A. Appiah.
        p.   cm. — (Amistad literary series)
    Includes bibliographical references and index.
    ISBN 1-56743-015-5 : $24.95. — ISBN 1-56743-028-7 (pbk.) : $14.95
    1. Hurston, Zora Neale—Criticism and interpretation. 2. Afro-
Americans in literature. I. Gates, Henry Louis. II. Appiah,
Anthony. III. Series.
PS3515.U789Z963   1993
813'.52—dc20
                                              92-45759
                                              CIP

Contents

ESSAYS

Preface

◆◆◆◆◆◆◆◆◆◆◆◆◆◆

Zora Neale Hurston
(1891–1960)

Of the various signs that the study of literature in America has been transformed, none is more salient than the resurrection and canonization of Zora Neale Hurston. Twenty years ago, Hurston's work was largely out of print, her literary legacy alive only to a tiny, devoted band of readers who were often forced to photocopy her works if they were to be taught. The Black Arts poet and critic Larry Neal saw to it that *Jonah's Gourd Vine* was reprinted in 1971, just as the scholar Darwin Turner had *Mules and Men* a year before. But these pioneering gestures were rare. In my own case, I recall that in the fall of 1976 an undergraduate student in a seminar at Yale demanded that I add her to our syllabus, and gave me her one dog-eared photocopy so that I could share it with our class. Mary Helen Washington has described an underground network of sharing and exchange that banked the embers of Hurston's literary heritage until they could blaze freely.

Today her works are central to the canon of African-American, American, and Women's literatures. (Last year at Yale alone, seventeen courses taught *Their Eyes Were Watching God!*) Hurston's career thus gives pause to those who would argue for the timelessness of literary judgment and taste. Which is not to say her genius went unappreciated by her peers. A prodigious author of four novels (*Jonah's Gourd Vine*, 1934; *Their Eyes Were Watching God*, 1937; *Moses, Man of the Mountain*, 1939; and *Seraph on the Suwanee*, 1948); two books of folklore (*Mules and Men*, 1935, and *Tell My Horse*, 1938); an autobiography (*Dust Tracks on a Road*, 1942); and over fifty short stories, essays, and plays, Hurston was one of the most widely acclaimed black authors for the two decades between 1925 and 1945.

In May 1925, "Spunk," her short story, won second prize at the annual *Opportunity Magazine* awards ceremony and was published in Alain

Locke's germinal anthology, *The New Negro*, which declared the birth of both the "New Negro" movement and the Harlem Renaissance of black expressive culture. At the age of thirty-four, the wind at her back, Hurston (who had studied at Howard between 1921 and 1924) enrolled at Barnard College to study anthropology, earning a B.A. degree in 1928.

Hurston then enrolled in Columbia's graduate program in anthropology and began to collect black folklore avidly throughout the South between 1927 and 1931; in Jamaica, Haiti, and Bermuda in 1937 and 1938; and in Florida in 1938 and 1939. Hurston seems to have loved listening to and transcribing Negro folktales and myths; as late as 1946, when her own powers of storytelling were on the wane, Hurston found herself drawn to Honduras to gather more folklore. But despite the publication of two widely heralded collections of folklore, it was as a writer of fiction that Zora Neale Hurston would excel.

With the exception of her fourth and final published novel, *Seraph on the Suwanee,* Hurston's fiction was well received by mainstream American reviewers. A few prominent black male writers, on the other hand, thought her work problematic for reasons that will persuade few modern readers. Alain Locke, Richard Wright, and Ralph Ellison, for example, were dismissive of what they took to be the ideological posture inherent in her fiction—her "African-Americanization" of modernism. In the thirties, at least, both Wright and Ellison were more interested in the resources of naturalism as a literary mode than they were in the sort of lyrical symbolism that Hurston would develop.

In later years, however, Ellison himself would embrace the modalities of modernism in a way that would reinforce the counter tradition associated with Hurston. In general, Hurston's black male critics wrote against the majority opinion; Hurston was the most widely acclaimed black woman writer since Phillis Wheatley. When she appeared on the cover of the *Saturday Review of Literature* in 1943, after winning the Anisfield-Wolf Book Award for *Dust Tracks*, she became the first black author to be honored in this way. Unfortunately, Hurston's career had reached its zenith with this event. By 1950 she was working as a maid; at her death in 1960 she had fallen into almost total obscurity.

Thirty years later, however, Zora Neale Hurston is the most widely taught black woman writer in the canon of American literature. Why is this so? While a significant portion of her readership is sustained by her image as a questioning, independent, thoughtfully sensual woman, I believe that Hurston has such a strong claim on a new generation of readers—students and teachers alike—because of her command of a narrative voice that imitates the storytelling structures of the black vernacular tradition. Indeed, no writer in the African-American literary tradition has been more successful than Hurston in registering the range and timbres of spoken black voices in written form. The language of her characters *dances;* her texts seem to come alive as veritable "talking books." Hurston also succeeds where so many of her predecessors failed in shaping a language, and a point of view, that appears to be directed at her black readers, rather than pandering to an imagined white readership responsible for black social mobility or economic and political amelioration. Almost never do we feel Hurston's hand on our shoulders as we read her texts. Given the historical prominence that the propaganda function has, necessarily, been accorded in the black formal arts, this is no mean achievement.

The opening review section presents direct evidence of the controversies surrounding Hurston's work as an Afro-American artist. The reviews, spanning her published work, provide contemporary and immediate—often visceral—interpretations of her emerging work. Culled from a range of magazines, journals, and newspapers from the Afro-American and the popular press, they are snapshots of Hurston and her times.

The fourteen critical essays that follow provide more extensive interpretations of Hurston's literary art. In a sensitive reading of Hurston's first novel, *Jonah's Gourd Vine*, Eric J. Sundquist discusses the preeminence of the preacher in Afro-American culture, an importance based on formal ability, verbal agility, and a resonance with traditions stretching back to African drumming. As in the fictions of James Weldon Johnson and the sermons of C. C. Lovelace, Hurston's preacher documents and transforms folk culture in the act of recording it.

Karla Holloway's piece fastens on the linguistic interiority manifest in the four novels. She sees each text as a frame or context for the emergent black voice, for "signifying" as a linguistic activity. *Seraph on the Suwanee* becomes, for her, an instance of loss of voice, distance from the word, an externalized relationship to language.

Expanding on issues of power and voice, Cheryl A. Wall examines how Hurston's female characters come to full-fledged language, how they learn to fend and speak for themselves in an oral, and predominantly masculine, culture. Reading *Of Mules and Men* alongside the novels, she explores the impact of gender on the folk tradition, on black values, lifestyle, and language.

Mary Helen Washington breaks sharply with affirmative feminist interpretations of *Their Eyes Were Watching God*, finding dominant themes of exclusion and disempowerment. Janie, the heroine, is described as trapped in her status as object, a passive female, lacking an identity independent of the men she loves. Extending Cheryl Wall's discussion of the gendered nature of oral tradition, Washington critiques black oral culture for its pure externality, as a formal game played among men.

In a series of deft close readings, Susan Willis questions the extent to which Hurston's prose succeeds in its ambition to undermine white Northern culture. She finds that Hurston fashions a narratively useful literary language out of a vernacular, a folk tradition tantamount to "name-calling," capable of subversion only through derision. Hurston's triumph, then, consists in her passage from signifying to metaphor, to the condensed and multiply allusive figures of her mature writing.

Having noted the supposed "incongruity" of a white man applying literary theory to a black woman writer, Barbara Johnson, reading "How It Feels to be Colored Me" and *Mules and Men*, suggests that multiple agendas and heterogeneous implied readers are thematized in the texts themselves. Her essay demonstrates the shift of identity, difference, and race representation as revealed in conflicting or overlapping structures of address.

In a carefully delimited discussion of the controversy surrounding dialect, Gayl Jones argues that Hurston's art communicates the full range of human emotion and interaction in the folk language of the masses, as against the deformation and routinization of dialect exemplified by the minstrel tradition. In reading Paul Laurence Dunbar's "The Lynching of Jube Benson" and Hurston's "The Gilded Six-Bits," Jones defends Hurston's subject, the daily life of ordinary people, against charges of frivolity or triviality. My own essay elaborates upon the crucial role of the vernacular structure in Hurston's fictional art, situating her achievement in literary historical perspective.

Building on themes sounded by Susan Willis and Mary Helen Washington, Cynthia Bond claims that Hurston's Janie, in *Their Eyes Were Watching God*, rejects the signifying, "lying" oral tradition normally reserved for men in favor of a figural and written language, the textually transmuted experience of life. Janie's (and Hurston's) writing resolves the split between outside (the external language of the oral tradition) and inside (the dream and emergent self-awareness of the individual woman).

Where Cynthia Bond pursues the displacement of the oral tradition, Maria Tai Wolff attempts to critique it from within. Distinguishing between cruel and playful signifying, she reads *Their Eyes Were Watching God* as a lyrical novel, a large-scale example of tall-tale telling, sportive and affirming. Her reading identifies epiphanic flashes of self-revelation, moments of lyric timelessness that structure the novel.

In a careful reading of Afro-American appropriations of the Moses myth, Deborah E. McDowell argues against the stereotypical image of Hurston as the frivolous "folklorist of Eatonville." She persuasively situates Hurston's *Moses, Man of the Mountain* in the context of the world wars; despite Hurston's evasion of the language and topics of documentary social realism, her treatment of the myth is shown to comment directly on issues of race and racism.

Another voice supportive of Hurston's oblique approach to "serious politics" is Françoise Lionnet-McCumber, who undertakes a Nietzschean defense of Hurston's cultural politics as expressed in the "autobiographical" *Dust Tracks on a Road*. Hurston's skepticism toward racial politics and identity is linked to her wayward discursivity, which signifies without reference to an original or originating story.

Taking issue with a widespread perception that Hurston's final novel represents an abject and disconnected failure, Lillie Howard argues that *Seraph on the Suwanee*, whose main characters are white, nonetheless cleaves to the folk milieu of her earlier works. Her essay suggests that the major themes of the novel—the dynamics of marriage, the search for true love, the individual's struggle for self-knowledge—are vintage Hurston.

In a phenomenologically informed reading of Hurston's compendium of Southern black folklore, *Of Mules and Men*, Houston A. Baker, Jr., presents her ethnographical work as a signal instance of "mythomania," or "hysteric" signifying. In accounting for Hurston's performance, he details the history of "conjure," voodoo and hoodoo, highlighting the spiritual resources it offers to women.

—Henry Louis Gates, Jr.

REVIEWS

JONAH'S GOURD VINE (1934)

◆◆◆◆◆◆◆◆◆◆◆◆◆

MARTHA GRUENING

The New Republic, July 11, 1934

When Miss Hurston's hero ran away from trouble in Alabama and came to central Florida he heard for the first time of a "colored town."

> "You mean uh town uh nothing but colored folks? Who bosses it den?" he asked.
> "Dey bosses it deyself."

This town, Eatonville, was Zora Hurston's birthplace, and some of her happiest qualities are perhaps due to this circumstance. It may well account in part for her zest and naturalness, her freedom from the conventional sentimentality so frequent in writing about Negroes. She handles, incidentally, much the same material as Julia Peterkin; handles it with double authority as a Negro and a student of folklore. An insider, she shares with her hero the touch of "pagan poesy" that made him thrill his hearers when he preached. But she is an insider without the insider's usual neuroses.

This is the story of John Pearson, yellow Alabama fieldhand, and famous preacher. He was a hero and a coward, a magnificent animal following his lusts and a church member praying to be cleansed of his sins. He loved his wife, Lucy, but left her for other women; returned to her, wept for her sorrows and left her again. After Lucy died he married Hattie, but the thought of Lucy so haunted him that he came to hate his second wife. "Whut am I doing married tuh you. . . . It's a hidden mystery to me—what you doin' in Miss Lucy's shoes," he railed at her after seven years, and beat her severely to ease his conscience. But through it all Miss Hurston makes him a credible, human and almost appealing figure. Toward the end, when his troubles are thick upon him, a figure not without tragic dignity.

With white people the book deals only incidentally. Its chief white character is Alf Pearson, the bluff and kindly planter who despised "backwoods whites who live by swindling the niggers." But Miss Hurston is

3

aware also of another side of the Negroes' white folks, as she has indicated in the brief searing paragraphs about the divorce courts where "the smirking anticipation on the faces of the white spectators . . . made John feel as if he had fallen into a foul latrine. . . . 'Now listen close. You're going to hear something rich. These niggers! . . .'" And she is equally vigorous and forthright in her writing about colored people.

Candor like Miss Hurston's is still sufficiently rare among Negro writers. It is only one of the excellences of this book.

♦♦♦♦♦♦♦♦♦♦♦♦♦♦

ESTELLE FELTON

Opportunity, August 1934

From the pen of Zora Neale Hurston comes another story of Negro folklore. Miss Hurston, who has written short stories about Negro Life, now writes a novel of the Negro shortly after the Civil War, placing her story in typical small southern towns in Alabama and Forida. The story concerns the life history of John Buddy Pearson who, through the efforts of his wife, Lucy, rises to be an important Baptist minister in Florida. John's weakness is women, and even his love for his wife cannot guard him from that. After many affairs with women and after having been married twice, John marries Sally, who loves with a mature and unselfish affection. John has a final lapse, but he never lives to see the reproach in Sally's eyes as he is killed by a train on his way home.

Miss Hurston approached her task with a knowledge of Negro dialect and customs that is rare in contemporary writers. She deals with these people, who still cling to the last vestiges of witchcraft, in such a way that the reader wonders at her ability to capture so effectively the emotions of this primitive people. One feels, after reading *Jonah's Gourd Vine,* that one has suddenly been transplanted to the South and given an intimate but exaggerated view of the lives of these people in the latter half of the nineteenth century. Dialect is rather difficult to use successfully, but as a whole the conversations between the characters seem to flow freely and actually without stiffness. Idioms peculiar to the Negro, she uses effectively. Miss Hurston's detailed understanding of the customs and traditions of her people is an invaluable aid in winning for this book the praise some critics have given it.

Although Miss Hurston has the ability to paint clear and vivid pictures of Negro life, her style at times falls flat. Often she brings a new event to the story with a suddenness for which the reader is wholly unprepared. John's fight with his wife's brother, while it serves its purpose to get John out of town, is unnecessary. But still more unwarranted is the brother's treatment of Lucy when she is ill. To show the passage of time, Miss Hurston brings in some opinions about the World War and the migration of the Negroes to the North. These passages are not well done because the material is treated too hastily and because it is unrelated to the rest of the story. However, Miss Hurston rises to great heights when she writes in poetic form the last sermon of John Pearson with such power and emotion that one can almost hear the sermon.

In plot construction and characterization, Miss Hurston is a disappointment. The only thing that holds the series of events together is John Pearson, a strong man physically but weak in character. It seems as if Miss Hurston wished to depict certain phases of Negro life—life in a Negro home, a plantation, and the Negro preacher—and just thrust the characters in them regardless of any connection. Each time the scene changes, there is a formal break with what went on before. Only once does John's mother appear after John, as a young lad, has left his parents' home. John's half-brother disappears from the story at the beginning and is brought back near the end merely so that John will have someone to turn to in his trouble. Miss Hurston does not attempt to maintain any connection between her characters whatever.

It seems as if Miss Hurston has not painted people but caricatures of people. John Pearson, despite the fact that he is a successful preacher and claims to love his wife, cannot resist the temptation to carry on affairs with the prostitutes of his race. This is a weakness in John's character which is emphasized so strongly in contrast to Lucy, John's faithful wife. It is impossible to believe that anyone would take a person's only bed as a payment for three dollars. Still more improbable does this seem when we consider that Lucy's brother does this when Lucy's child is about to be born. Lucy herself seems to possess too much foresight for a girl of her limited experience and age. Langston Hughes in *Not Without Laughter* has presented much more natural characters in Harriet, the impetuous young girl whose fondness for dancing makes her run away from home, and Aunt Hagar, an old woman whose faith in God in unwavering. Compared to Mr. Hughes, Miss Hurston's faults in plot and character appear only the more marked.

Jonah's Gourd Vine is Miss Hurston's first novel, and the weakness which appear in it may be eradicated in future stories. The novel, however, is quite easy to read and entertaining. Some people may object to a minister's having such faults as John Pearson has, but the tolerant person will remember that nobody is perfect and follow John through his numerous escapades. Nevertheless, few will be able to deny Miss Hurston's accomplishments in an effective use of dialogue and traditional customs.

◆◆◆◆◆◆◆◆◆◆◆◆◆◆

ANDREW BURRIS

The Crisis, June 3, 1934

As the author of "Spunk," one of the best short stories in *The New Negro* (edited by Alain Locke, New York, 1925), Zora Neale Hurston was in the vanguard of the movement which took its name from that book. Some of us have had the pleasure of hearing Miss Hurston tell, in her inimitable way, stories about the people in her native village, Eatonville in Florida, or have read and enjoyed the lusty humor, the rich folkways and authentic speech of the characters in her (as yet unproduced) play "Mulebone," done in collaboration with Langston Hughes, or have seen the interesting folk sketches resulting from her anthropological studies that were produced for a brief run at the John Golden Theatre in New York City two years ago; and we have felt that a great delight lay in store for us when finally Miss Hurston committed herself to a book.

We have believed that Zora Hurston was not interested in writing a book merely to jump on the bandwagon of the New Negro movement, as some quite evidently were; but we felt that she was taking her time, mastering her craft, and would, as a result, produce a really significant book.

Now Miss Hurston has written a book, and despite the enthusiastic praise on the jacket by such eminent literary connoisseurs as Carl Van Vechten, Fannie Hust, and Blanche Colton Williams, all sponsors for the *New Negro,* this reviewer is compelled to report that *Jonah's Gourd Vine* is quite disappointing and a failure as a novel.

One must judge Miss Hurston's success by the tasks she has set herself—to write a novel about a backward Negro people, using their peculiar speech and manners to express their lives. What she has done is just the opposite. She has used her characters and the various situations created for them as mere pegs upon which to hang their dialect and their folkways. She has become so absorbed with these phases of her craft that she has almost completely lost sight of the equally essential elements of plot and construction, characterization and motivation. John Buddy emerges from the story through his mere presence on every page, and not from an integrated life with the numerous others who wander in and out and do things often without rhyme or reason. It is disappointing when one considers what Miss Hurston might have done with John Buddy, illegitimate offspring of a white man and a Negro woman, who at an early age leaves the thankless toil and hovel of a home provided by a shiftless, jealous stepfather and a protecting mother, and loves,

prays, preaches, and sings his way up to the eminent position of moderator in the Baptist church. In John Buddy she had the possibility of developing a character that might have stamped himself upon American
life more indelibly than either John Henry or Black Ulysses. But like the
chroniclers of these two adventurers she has been unequal to the demands of her conception.

The defects of Miss Hurston's novel become the more glaring when
her work is placed beside that of contemporary white authors of similar
books about their own people—such as the first half of Fielding Burke's
novel of North Carolina hillbillies, *Call Home the Heart,* or two novels
of Arkansas mountaineers, *Mountain Born* by Emmett Gowen and
Woods Colt by T. R. Williamson. The first two names are, like Miss
Hurston's, first novels, and we feel that it is not asking too much of her
to expect that in writing novels about her own people she give us work
of equal merit to these.

Lest this criticism of *Jonah's Gourd Vine* seem too severe, let us add
that there is much about the book that is fine and distinctive, and enjoyable. Zora Hurston has assembled between the pages of this book a rich
store of folklore. She has captured the lusciousness and beauty of the
Negro dialect as have few others. John Buddy's sermon on the creation
is the most poetic rendition of this familiar theme that we have yet
encountered in print. These factors give the book an earthiness, a distinctly racial flavor, a somewhat primitive beauty which makes its defects
the more regrettable. We can but hope that with time and further experience in the craft of writing, Zora Hurston will develop the ability to fuse
her abundant material into a fine literary work.

Differs with Burris on Jonah's Gourd Vine

May I express my dissent from the judgment of Andrew Burris on *Jonah's Gourd Vine,* as printed in the June number of *Crisis?* His own last
paragraph seems to me to justify the book and explain its success, thus
outweighing his earlier words of dispraise and disappointment.

For this one reader it is a pleasure to record that from the first
to the last word the book held me interested and absorbed. That the
background should be so implicit, never obtruding itself yet never failing
to reveal the sorrowful poverty and backwardness of those conditions in
the Black Belt which produced John Buddy, is one strong point in its
favor. But, over and above that, Miss Hurston has achieved a kind of
power for which any reader may well be grateful; to have made her chief
character so true, so vital and so convincing as he slips from one level
to another in his unintrospective course—or career, if the word may be
stretched to fit this case—and to have retained her reader's understand-

ing and sympathy for her protagonist even though his *acts* distress or revolt, places the book on a high plane—all the more perhaps, that it is in so small a compass. In this short tale the reader enjoys the "sinner" while mourning his weakness and the effects of his unintended cruelties. Surely any book which so brings its chief character to our affections is a boon.

Then, too, think of its continuous ripples or undertow of humor! I may add that those friends to whom I have recommended Miss Hurston's work have been as much impressed by it as I.

♦♦♦♦♦♦♦♦♦♦♦♦♦

MARGARET WALLACE

The *New York Times* Book Review, May 6, 1934

Jonah's Gourd Vine can be called without fear of exaggeration the most vital and original novel about the American Negro that has yet been written by a member of the Negro race. Miss Hurston, who is a graduate of Barnard College and a student of anthropology, has made the study of Negro folklore her special province. This may very well account for the brilliantly authentic flavor of her novel and for her excellent rendition of Negro dialect. Unlike the dialect in most novels about the American Negro, this does not seem to be merely the speech of white men with the spelling distorted. Its essence lies rather in the rhythm and balance of the sentences, in the warm artlessness of the phrasing.

No amount of special knowledge of her subject, however, could have made *Jonah's Gourd Vine* other than a mediocre novel if it were not for Miss Hurston's notable talents as a storyteller. In John, the big yellow Negro preacher, and in Lucy Potts, his tiny brown wife, she has created two characters who are intensely real and human and whose outlines will remain in the reader's memory long after the book has been laid aside. They are part and parcel of the tradition of their race, which is as different from ours as night from day; yet Miss Hurston has delineated them with such warmth and sympathy that they appeal to us first of all as human beings, confronting a complex of human problems with whatever grace and humor, intelligence and steadfastness they can muster.

John was a "yaller nigger," hated by his dusky foster-father because of the white blood in his veins. "His mamma named him Two-Eye John after a preacher she heered, but dey called him John-Buddy for short." When he was too big to be beaten or bullied, the share-cropping Ned Crittenden turned him off the farm. John got a job on Mr. Alf Pearson's place, created with his big young body and rich voice a great stir among the brown maidens in Mr. Pearson's service, and fell in love with Lucy Potts, a bright-eyed little girl who could run faster and recite longer pieces than anybody else in school. In the interests of his ardent courtship, John learned to read and when Lucy attained her fifteenth birthday they were married.

John really loved Lucy and intended to be true to her, but he was totally unable to resist the open and insistent blandishments of other women. Even after he felt a "call" to the ministry, he was always mixed up with some woman or other, frequently to the point of an open breach with his horrified and interested congregation. John's long and futile struggle with his lusty appetites, Lucy's cleverness and devotion in protecting him from the consequences, his entanglement after Lucy's death with the magic-making Hattie, his public ruin, and public regeneration all make an extraordinarily absorbing and credible tale.

Not the least charm of the book, however, is its language: rich, expressive, and lacking in self-conscious artifice. From the rolling and dignified rhythms of John's last sermon to the humorous aptness of such a word as "shickalacked," to express the noise and motion of a locomotive, there will be much in it to delight the reader. It is to be hoped that Miss Hurston will give us other novels in the same colorful idiom.

MULES AND MEN (1935)

◆◆◆◆◆◆◆◆◆◆◆◆◆

HENRY LEE MOON

The New Republic, December 11, 1935

Zora Neale Hurston went South to her native Florida to gather and record the folk tales she had heard in her childhood. She made Eatonville, the Negro town where she was born, a sort of base, from which she prowled about the countryside, living in turpentine camps, railroad camps, a phosphate mining village. Everywhere she went, she inveigled people into telling her all sorts of tales—"big old lies," a townsman called them.

But Miss Hurston did more than record these tales. Alert and keenly observant, she studied the *mores*, folkways, and superstitions, the social and economic life of these people as an essential background for her book. As a result *Mules and Men* is more than a collection of folklore. It is a valuable picture of the life of the unsophisticated Negro in the small towns and backwoods of Florida. To this Miss Hurston has added a revealing section on hoodoo as practiced in New Orleans, where she was initiated into the mysteries of the cult.

Her stories are of wide variety. Some are animal tales of the Uncle Remus stripe. Some attempt to explain everyday social and natural phenomena. Others are rooted in the slave era and bring out the nuances of race relations. Some are fables. Still others are obviously spontaneous creations resembling the exaggerated tales of youngsters engaged in a storytelling contest. In all the stories, the imaginative gift of the Negroes who passed them on is matched by the author's own talent for storytelling. Miss Hurston presents her material with little attempt to evaluate it or to trace its origin. She records things as they were told to her, in an intimate and good style; and the intimacy she established with her subjects, she reproduces on the printed page, enabling the reader to feel himself a part of that circle.

The value of *Mules and Men* is enhanced by the Covarrubias illustrations and by an appendix containing a glossary, work songs, formulas of hoodoo doctors, and paraphernalia of conjure.

♦♦♦♦♦♦♦♦♦♦♦♦♦

LEWIS GANNETT

The *New York Herald Tribune Weekly Book Review*, October 11, 1935

Down in Eatonville, Fla., where Zora Hurston grew up, the men used to gather on the store porch of evenings to swap stories. The women, too, would sometimes stop and break a breath with them. And little Zora, when sent to the store for a pinch of coffee, would drag out her leaving to hear more. . . . But she went away to college; she studied anthropology at Barnard; she acquired a gray Chevrolet and a store dress, and went home to collect what had acquired the dignity of "Negro folklore." The result is *Mules and Men,* and I can't remember anything better since *Uncle Remus.*

Them Big Old Lies

"What you want, Zora, them big old lies we tell when we're jus' sittin' around here on the store porch doin' nothin'?" asked B. Moseley.

That was what she wanted; and night after night the boys came and told her big lies. They took her to the toe-party at Woods Bridge—where the girls hid behind a curtain, with only their toes showing, and the men folk, looking over the toes, bought the privilege of dancing with a toe-owner for an hour; and have to treat her even if they made a mistake; they taught her enough verses of "John Henry" so that her singing served as a passport when she moved down into the swamp log country; they played Florida flip and eleven-card-lay with her; and when she had her hidden notebooks full of Florida stories she moved on to New Orleans and studied hoodoo under the tutelage of Luke Turner, heir to Marie Leveu, the greatest witch doctor in New Orleans's memory, and of Anatol Pierre and Father Watson and Dr. Duke and Kitty Brown. She even earned her Black Cat bone, in a terrifying ceremony; but I like the best the big lies they told her in Florida.

You Can't Read a Black Mind

"We never run outer lies and lovin'," said Gene; and they never did. "Zora, you come to the right place if lies is what you want," said George Thomas. "Ah'm gointer lie up a nation." And he did. They all lied, as only a black man can lie, and only to a dark girl whom he trusts.

"We are a polite people," Zora Hurston, who is dark-skinned herself, explains as she threads her way into the big lies. "We do not say to our questioner, 'Get out of here!' We smile and tell him or her something that satisfied the white person because, knowing so little about us, he doesn't know what he is missing. The Indian resists curiosity by silence. The Negro offers a feather-bed resistance. That is, we let a probe enter, but it never comes out. It gets smothered under a lot of laughter and pleasantries. The white man is always trying to know into somebody else's business. All right, we say, 'I'll leave something outside the doors of my mind for him to play with and handle. He can read my writing but he sho' can't read my mind.'" But Zora Hurston was accepted; she belonged.

Julius, who was little but loud, told Zora Hurston some over-average lies. He told her of the East Coast wind that blowed a crooked road straight and blowed a well up out of the ground and blowed and blowed until it scattered the days of the week so bad that Sunday didn't come back until late Tuesday evening. (Many of these tales are reminiscent of the tall ones of the old Southwest; was it, perhaps, out of the awe-inspired imagination of black Negroes fresh from Africa that a whole tradition of "Mississippi" and "cowboy" tall talk had grown?)

Mosquito-Bone Fertilizer

Black Baby told the story of the Indian River mosquitoes that screwed on their extra-long size bills and bored through three layers of blankets at night; Ulmer remembered mosquitoes so big that his father used their bones for fertilizer; Sack Daddy reminisced about the pumpkins his father grew on mosquito-fertilized land. These pumpkins were so big that Sack's old man built a scaffold inside one, to make it easier to cut out the pumpkin meat, but he dropped his hammer and never could find it, though when he went down to look for it he met another pumpkin-cutter looking for his lost mule team and wagon. Joe Wiley said corn grew still better if you mixed mosquito dust with fertilizer. His brother once tried to sit down on some corn fertilized that way, to keep it from growing too fast, but the next they heard from him was a note dropped from the sky reporting "Passed thu Heben yesterday at 12 o'clock sellin' roastin' ears to de angels."

Some of these "lies" are sheer tall tales; some are Bible legends, scattered, in this book, with liberal dosages of realistic contempt for men who take to preaching because they do not like hard work in the sun; still others are out of that amazing mass of race poetry, still growing in the South, from which Roark Bradford and Marc Connelly got the inspiration for *Green Pastures* and out of which so many white authors have composed good black books. Here is the story of how the woodpecker got his red head (Noah gave it to him with a sledgehammer, to teach him not to drill holes in the leaky ark); why the possum has no hair on his tail; why the rabbit and the dog are friends no longer (in the "Uncle Remus" vein); how come they always use rawhide on a mule; a sermon on Adam and Eve and the rib, which might fit into James Weldon Johnson's resonant "Trumpets of Jubilee"; chain-gang songs; tales of careless love. But the flavor of so rich a book as this can be given only by direct quotation. Here is the story of "How God Made Butterflies":

How God Made Butterflies

He made butterflies after de world wuz all finished and thru. You know de Lawd seen so much bare ground till He got sick and tired lookin' at it. So God tole 'em to fetch "im his prunin" shears and trimmed up de trees and made grass and flowers and throwed 'em all over de clearin's and dey growed dere from memorial days.

Way after while de flowers said, "We'se put heah to keep de world company, but we'se lonesome ourselves." So God said, "A world is somethin' ain't never finished. Soon's you make one thing you got to make somethin' else to go wid it. Gimme dem li'l tee-ninchy shears."

So He went 'round clippin' li'l pieces offa everything—de sky, de trees, de flowers, de earth, de varmints and every one of dem li'l clippin's flew off. When folks seen all them li'l scraps fallin' from God's scissors and flutterin' they called 'em flutter-bys. But you know how it is wid de brother in black. He got a big mouf and a stamblin' tongue. So he got it all mixed up and said "butter-fly," and folks been callin' 'em dat ever since. Dat's how come we got butterflies of every color and kind, and dat's why dey hangs 'round de flowers. Dey wuz made to keep de flowers company.

To read *Mules and Men* is a rich experience.

◆◆◆◆◆◆◆◆◆◆◆◆◆

H. I. BROCK

The New York Times Book Review, November 10, 1935

Here, to put it so, is the high color of Color as a racial element in the American scene. And it comes neither from Catfish Row nor from a Harlem with a jazz tempo affected by the rhythm of Broadway to which contribute so many exotic strains newer to that scene than the African. In this book a young Negro woman with a college education has invited the outside world to listen in while her own people are being as natural as they can never be when white folks are literally present. This is an environment in the deep South to which the Negro is as native as he can be anywhere on this Western Continent.

The writer has gone back to her native Florida village—a Negro settlement—with her native racial quality entirely unspoiled by her Northern college education. She has plunged into the social pleasures of the black community and made a record of what is said and done when Negroes are having a good gregarious time, dancing, singing, fishing, and above all, and incessantly, talking.

The talk (as those fragmentary memories of long ago come back to remind us) runs on such occasions generally to competition in telling what are unashamedly labeled "lies." These "lies" are woven out of the folklore of the black race in the South—with its deeper African background dimmed by years and distance. It is the same folklore, of course, out of which have been rescued for our nurseries in the milder elements— the tales of Br'er Rabbit, Br'er Fox, and the rest of the talking animals that children reared in the South had listened to long before Uncle Remus made them classic for the whole country.

But as the feast is spread here it is not always nursery fare—not by any means. Some of it is strong meat for those who take life lustily— with accompaniment of flashes of razor blades and great gusts of Negro laughter.

The book is packed with tall tales rich with flavor and alive with characteristic turns of speech. Those of us who have known the Southern Negro from our youth find him here speaking the language of his tribe as familiarly as if it came straight out of his own mouth and not translated into type and transmitted through the eye to the ear. This is to say that a very tricky dialect has been rendered with rare simplicity and fidelity into symbols so little adequate to convey its true value that the achievement is remarkable. At the end you have a very fair idea of how the other color enjoys life as well as an amazing round-up of that color's very best stories in its very best manner, which is a match for any storytelling there is in the two qualities of luxuriant imagination and vivid and expressive language.

At the back of the book you find a glossary, the words and music of some of the songs these people sing to the banjo or guitar, and sundry recipes of the hoodoo doctors for success in love or compassing the sudden death of an enemy. Several chapters of the narrative are devoted to the writer's personal investigation of the mysteries of hoodoo or voodoo. Included is the record of her initiation by several eminent witch doctors into the deepest mysteries of their black art and of the part which she took as their assistant in the "conjur" business. No mock modesty is invoked to veil the details of the initiations or the elements and procedure involved in producing for paying clients the death of persons whose living presence is obnoxious—as no-longer-wanted husbands or wives or the like. It is flatly stated that after the conjur work was done, with the writer assisting in the mummery, some of these persons did actually die approximately on schedule. You can think what you please about that.

Descriptions of the preparation of charms and of midnight incantations in the swamp seem to take us all the way back to Africa—and darkest Africa at that. We are told that hoodoo is, in fact, the ancient religion of the Negro race, still carrying on. If that is so and if it does carry on as here reported, we have a revealing account of a very curious personal adventure in a region far on the African side of the color line. That adventure, however, carries to this reviewer no such conviction of solid interest and value as the collection of competitive "lies" from the treasurey of Afro-American folklore.

THEIR EYES WERE
WATCHING GOD (1937)

◆◆◆◆◆◆◆◆◆◆◆◆◆

RICHARD WRIGHT

New Masses, October 5, 1937

It is difficult to evaluate Waters Turpin's *These Low Grounds* and Zora Neale Hurston's *Their Eyes Were Watching God*. This is not because there is an esoteric meaning hidden or implied in either of the two novels; but rather because neither of the two novels has a basic idea or theme that lends itself to significant interpretation. Miss Hurston seems to have no desire whatever to move in the direction of serious fiction. With Mr. Turpin the case is different; the desire and motive are present, but his "saga" of four generations of Negro life seems to have been swamped by the subject matter.

These Low Grounds represents, I believe, the first attempt of a Negro writer to encompass in fiction the rise of the Negro from slavery to the present. The greater part of the novel is laid on the eastern shore of Maryland where Carrie, upon the death of her slave mother, is left to grow up in a whorehouse. After several fitful efforts to escape her lot, Carrie finally marries a visiting farmer, Prince, with whom she leads a life of household drudgery. Having helped Prince become the leading Negro farmer in the country, Carrie rebels against his infidelities and domination and, taking her two young daughters, runs away. Years later Prince discovers her and persuades her to return home. As she is about to make the journey, she is murdered by Grundy, her drunken and jealous lover. The two daughters return to the farm; Blanche remains with her father, but Martha flees North to escape the shame of pregnancy when her lover is killed in an accident. Martha's subsequent career on the stage enables her to send her son, Jimmy-Lew, to college to become a teacher. The novel closes with a disillusioned Jimmy-Lew comforted by his wife because of his bitterness over the harsh and unfair conditions of southern life.

The first half of the book is interesting, for Turpin deals with a subject which he knows intimately. Those sections depicting post-war Negro life in the North do not ring true or full; in fact, toward the conclusion the book grows embarrassingly sketchy, resolving nothing.

Oddly enough, Turpin seems to have viewed those parts of his novel which deal with the modern Negro through the eyes and consciousness of one emotionally alien to the scene. Many of the characters—Carrie, Prince, Martha—are splendid social types, but rarely do they become human beings. It seems that Turpin drew these types from intellectual conviction, but lacked the artistic strength to make us feel the living quality of their experiences. It seems to me, he should strive to avoid the bane of sheer competency. He deals with great characters and a great subject matter; what is lacking is a great theme and a great passion.

Their Eyes Were Watching God is the story of Zora Neale Hurston's Janie who, at sixteen, married a grubbing farmer at the anxious instigation of her slave-born grandmother. The romantic Janie in the highly-charged language of Miss Hurston, longed to be a pear tree in blossom and have a "dust-bearing bee sink into the sanctum of a bloom; the thousand sister-calyxes arch to meet the love embraces." Restless, she fled from her farmer husband and married Jody, a up-and-coming Negro business man who, in the end, proved to be no better than her first husband. After twenty years of clerking for her self-made Jody, Janie found herself a frustrated widow of forty with a small fortune on her hands. Tea Cake, "from in and through Georgia" drifted along and, despite his youth, Janie took him. For more than two years they lived happily; but Tea Cake was bitten by a mad dog and was infected with rabies. One night in a canine rage Tea Cake tried to murder Janie, thereby forcing her to shoot the only man she had ever loved.

Miss Hurston can write; but her prose is cloaked in that facile sensuality that has dogged Negro expression since the days of Phillis Wheatley. Her dialogue manages to catch the psychological movements of the Negro folk-mind in their pure simplicity, but that's as far as it goes.

Miss Hurston *voluntarily* continues in her novel the tradition which was *forced* upon the Negro in the theater, that is, the minstrel technique that makes the "white folks" laugh. Her characters eat and laugh and cry and work and kill; they swing like a pendulum eternally in that safe and narrow orbit in which America likes to see the Negro live: between laughter and tears.

Turpin's faults as a writer are those of an honest man trying desperately to say something; but Zora Neale Hurston lacks even that excuse. The sensory sweep of her novel carries no theme, no message, no thought In the main, her novel is not addressed to the Negro, but to a white audience whose chauvinistic tastes she knows how to satisfy. She exploits the phase of Negro life which is "quaint," the phase which evokes a piteous smile on the lips of the "superior" race.

◆◆◆◆◆◆◆◆◆◆◆◆◆

ALAIN LOCKE

Opportunity, June 1, 1938

And now, Zora Neale Hurston and her magical title: *Their Eyes Were Watching God*. Janie's story should not be re-told; it must be read. But as always thus far with this talented writer, setting and surprising flashes of contemporary folk lore are the main point. Her gift for poetic phrase, for rare dialect, and folk humor keep her flashing on the surface of her community and her characters and from diving down deep either to the inner psychology of characterization or to sharp analysis of the social background. It is folklore fiction at its best, which we gratefully accept as an overdue replacement for so much faulty local color fiction about Negroes. But when will the Negro novelist of maturity, who knows how to tell a story convincingly—which is Miss Hurston's cradle gift, come to grips with motive fiction and social document fiction? Progressive southern fiction has already banished the legend of these entertaining psuedo-primitives whom the reading public still loves to laugh with, weap over and envy. Having gotten rid of condescension, let us now get over oversimplification!

◆◆◆◆◆◆◆◆◆◆◆◆◆

LUCILLE TOMPKINS

The New York Times Book Review, September 26, 1937

This is Zora Hurston's third novel, again about her own people—and it is beautiful. It is about Negroes, and a good deal of it is written in dialect, but really it is about every one, or least every one who isn't so civilized that he has lost the capacity for glory.

"When God made The Man, he made him out of stuff that sung all the time and glittered all over." But, in the name of love, Janie's grandmother took "the biggest thing God ever made, the horizon . . . and pinched it into such a little thing that she could tie it about her granddaughter's neck tight enough to choke her." So it was a long time before Janie found her "shine." Her grandmother had been a slave. So she wanted Janie born in freedom, to have advantages. In Janie, she figured, the Lawd had given her a second chance. "Ah wanted to peach a great sermon about colored women sittin' on high," she said, "but they wasn't no pulpit for me. . . So whilst ah was tendin' you of nights ah said ah'd save de text for you. . . . Ah raked and scraped and bought dis lil piece uh land so you wouldn't have to stay in de white folks' yard and tuck yo' head befo' other chillun at school. . . . Ah don't want yo' feathers always crumpled by folks throwin' up things in yo' face." And she thought she could die easy if she knew neither white men nor black could use Janie the way she'd been used. What she wanted for Janie was protection. So when she saw her kissing a "trashy nigger" over the gatepost she figured Janie had come on her womanhood and married her off straightway to a widower who spelled security.

But Janie found that marriage didn't compel love, neither didn't it "end the cosmic loneliness of the unmated." So she married Jody Sparks and went off with him to a town made all out of colored folks. Jody soon ran the town, and being Mayor went to his head. But being Mrs. Mayor didn't go to Janie's head: it hung around her like a stone. She had had something quite different in her mind's eye when she was 16. She had wanted "flower dust and springtime sprinkled over everything" and all she got on her second try was position and a one-track husband who was so busy being boss to the town and her that he thought of nothing else. All the folks of the town, of course, envied Janie. Her place looked like heaven to them. And as for Jody, he thought he'd done quite enough to make a fine lady out of her. Finally she told him, "all dis bowin' down, all dis obedience under yo' voice—dat ain't whut ah rushed off down de road to find out about you." But Jody, like the Emperor Jones, changed everything, and unlike the Emperor, nothing ever changed him.

So Janie had her old age first, and when shortly before she was 40 Jody died and Tea Cake came along she wasn't too spent and disillusioned to live as sooner or later all creatures ought. How different the story would have been if a sophisticated woman stood, at 40, in Janie's shoes, scores of novels already testify!

The story of Janie's life down on the muck of Florida Glades, bean picking, hunting and the men shooting dice in the evening and how the hurricane came up and drove the animals and the Indians and finally the black people and the white people before it, and how Tea Cake, in Janie's eyes the "son of Evening Son," and incidentally the best crap shooter in the place, made Janie sing and glitter all over at least, is a little epic all by itself. Indeed, from first to last this is a well nigh perfect story—a little sententious at the start, but the rest is simple and beautiful and shining with humor. In case there are readers who have a chronic laziness about dialect, it should be added that the dialect here is very easy to follow, and the images it carries are irresistible.

◆◆◆◆◆◆◆◆◆◆◆◆◆

STERLING BROWN

The Nation, October 16, 1937

Janie's grandmother, remembering how in slavery she was used "for a work-ox and a brood sow," and remembering her daughter's shame, seeks Janie's security above all else. But to Janie, her husband, for all his sixty acres, looks like "some old skull-head in de graveyard,' and she goes off down the road with slick-talking Jody Sparks. In Eatonville, an all-colored town, Jody becomes the "big voice," but Janie is first neglected and then browbeaten. When Jody dies, Tea Cake, with his contagious high spirits, whirls Janie into a marriage, idyllic until Tea Cake's tragic end. Janie returns home, grief-stricken but fulfilled. Better than her grandmother's security, she had found out about living for herself.

Filling out Janie's story are sketches of Eatonville and farming down "on the muck" in the Everglades. On the porch of the mayor's store "big old lies" and comic/serious debates, with the tallest of metaphors, while away the evenings. The dedication of the town's first lamp and the community burial of an old mule are rich in humor but they are not cartoons. Many incidents are unusual, and there are narrative gaps in need of building up. Miss Hurston's forte is the recording and the creation of folk-speech. Her devotion to these people has rewarded her; *Their Eyes Were Watching God* is chock-full of earthy and touching poetry.

> Ah don't want yo' feathers always crumpled by folks throwin' up things in yo' face. And ah can't die easy thinkin' maybe de menfolks white or black is makin' a spit cup outa you. Have some sympathy fuh me. Put me down easy, Janie, Ah'm a cracked plate.

Though inclined to violence and not strictly conventional, her people are not naive primitives. About human needs and frailties they have the unabashed shrewdness of the Blues. It is therefore surprising when, in spite of her clear innocence, all the Negroes turn away from Janie at her murder trial.

But this is not *the* story of Miss Hurston's own people, as the foreword states, for *the* Negro novel is as unachievable as the Great American Novel. Living in an all-colored town, these people escape the worst pressures of class and caste. There is little harshness, there is enough money and work to go around. The author does not dwell upon the "people ugly from ignorance and broken from being poor" who swarm upon the "muck" for short-time jobs. But here is bitterness, sometimes oblique, in the enforced folk manner, and sometimes forthright. The slave, Nanny, for bearing too light a child with gray eyes, is ordered a terrible beating by her mistress, who in her jealousy is perfectly willing to "stand the loss" if the beating is fatal. And after the hurricane there is a great to-do lest white and black victims be buried together. To detect the race of the long-unburied corpses, the conscripted gravediggers must examine the hair. The whites get pine coffins, the Negroes get quicklime. "They's mighty particular how dese dead folks goes tuh judgment. Look lak they think God don't know nothin' 'bout de Jim Crow law."

◆◆◆◆◆◆◆◆◆◆◆◆◆

SHEILA HIBBEN

The *New York Herald Tribune Weekly Book Review,* September 26, 1937

Somewhere in Zora Hurston's book somebody is talking tall about Big John the Conqueror. "Nature and salt, dats what makes a strong man like Big John the Conqueror. He was a man wid salt in him," says this somebody. "He could give uh flavor to anything." Well, that's just what Zora Hurston can give to her writing, and when a book has Nature and salt, it's got a lot.

Not that Miss Hurston has to depend on wit and feeling in *Their Eyes Were Watching God.* Here is an author who writes with her head as well as with her heart, and at a time when there seems to be some principle of physics set dead against the appearance of novelists who give out a cheerful warmth and at the same time write with intelligence. You have to be as tired as I am of writers who offer to do so much for folks as Atlas, Joan of Arc, Faith, Hope and Charity, Numerology, NBC, and Q.E.D. to be as pleased as I am with Zora Hurston's lovely book—sensitive book I might have said, if the publisher's blurb writers had not taken over that adjective for their own.

Readers of *Jonah's Gourd Vine* and *Mules and Men* are familiar with Miss Hurston's vibrant Negro lingo with its guitar twang of poetry, and its deep, vivid humor. If in *Their Eyes Were Watching God* the flowers of the sweet speech of black people are not quite so full blown and striking as in those earlier books, on the other hand, the sap flows more freely, and the roots touch deeper levels of human life. The author has definitely crossed over from the limbo of folklore into the realm of conventional narrative.

As a great many novelists—good and bad—ought to know by this time, it is awfully easy to write nonsense about Negroes. That Miss Hurston can write of them with simple tenderness, so that her story is filled with the ache of her own people, is, I think, due to the fact that she is not too much preoccupied with the current fetish of the primitive.

In a rich prose (which has, at the same time, a sort of nervous sensibility) she tells the tale of a girl who "wanted things sweet with mah marriage, lak when you sit under a pear tree and think." Janie did not get sweetness when her Grandma married her to Mister Killicks with his sixty acres of West Florida land, and his sagging belly, and his toenails that looked like mules' foots; and she didn't get it when she ran off with Joe Starks and got to be the Mayor's wife, and sat on her own store porch. But when Tea Cake came along with his trampish clothes and his easy ways and his nice grin that made even a middle-aged woman like Janie sort of wishful the minute she sets eyes on him, he handed her the keys of the kingdom, and their life together (what there was of it) was rapture and fun and tenderness and understanding—the perfect relationship of man and woman, whether they be black or white.

If I tried to tell you the plot of *Their Eyes Were Watching God* (an inept enough title, to my mind) I would only make a mess of it, so dependent is the story upon Miss Hurston's warm, vibrant touch. There are homely, unforgettable phrases of colored people (you would know, all right, that a man wasn't fooling if he threatened to kill you cemetery daid); there is a gigantic and magnificent picture of a hurricane in the Everglades country of Florida; and there is a flashing, gleaming riot of black people, with a limitless exuberance of humor, and a wild, strange sadness. There is also death—"not the death of the sick and ailing, with friends at the pillow and at the feet," but "the sudden dead, their eyes flung wide open in judgment." Mostly, though, there is life—a swarming, passionate life, and in spite of the Tea Cake's tragic end and the crumbling of Janie's happiness, there is a sense of triumph and glory when the tale is done.

◆◆◆◆◆◆◆◆◆◆◆◆◆

OTIS FERGUSON

The New Republic, October 13, 1937

It isn't that this novel is bad, but that it deserves to be better. In execution it is too complex and wordily pretty, even dull—yet its conception of these simple Florida Negroes is unaffected and really beautiful. Its story comes mostly through the person of Janie, a mulatto girl carefully married off to a proper fellow whom she ran away from shortly because that wasn't love and living as she hoped would be. And her second husband, though he built a town and promoted for himself a main place in its life, cooped her up and smothered her with rectitude until he died, leaving her wiser with middle age and still handsome.

Through these chapters there has been some very shrewd picturing of Negro life in its naturally creative and unselfconscious grace; the book is absolutely free of Uncle Toms, absolutely unlimbered of the clumsy formality, defiance, and apology of a Minority Cause. And when Tea Cake swaggers in with his banter, music, rolling bones, and fierce tender loyalty, there is a lot more picturing of what we would never have known: Darktown and the work on the Everglades muck, the singing and boasting and play-acting, people living the good life but, in the absence of the sour and pretentious and proper, seeming to live it in a different world. It is the time of the Big Blow in Florida, and though Tea Cake and Janie fought through it, the aftermath left the man with hydrophobia, and she had to kill him like a dog. Janie went back to her town after that, her late years to be mellowed with the knowledge of how wide life can be.

If this isn't as grand as it should be, the breakdown comes in the conflict between the true vision and its overliterary expression. Crises of feeling are rushed over too quickly for them to catch hold, and then presently we are in a tangle of lush exposition and overblown symbols; action is described and characters are talked about, and everything is more heard than seen. The speech is founded in observation and sometimes wonderfully so, a gold mine of traditional sayings. "Don't come to *me* with your hair blowing back," someone says. Or "My old woman . . . get her good and mad and she'll wade through solid rock up to her hip pockets"; "She ain't a fact and neither do she make a good story when you tell about her." Or such phrases in their proper place as "Well all right then," and "Got the world in a jug." Or such vivid, simple picture making as a comment on great wind and thunder: "Big Massa draw him a chair upstairs." Or illustrations from natural life, as in the case of the old girl who said you didn't have to worry about her blabbing; she was like a chicken—"Chicken drink water but he don't pee-pee."

But although the spoken word is remembered, it is not passed on. Dialect is really sloppy, in fact. Suggestion of speech difference is a difficult art, and none should practice it who can't grasp its first rule—that the key to difference must be indicated by the signature of a different rhythm and by the delicate tampering with an occasional main word. To let the really important words stand as in *Webster* and then consistently misspell all the eternal particles that are no more than an aspiration in any tongue, is to set up a mood of Eddie Cantor in blackface. The reader's eye is caught by distortions of the inconsequential, until a sentence in the supposedly vernacular reads with about this emphasis: "Dat wuz uh might fine thing fuh you tuh do."

And so all this conflict between the real life we want to read about and the superwordy, flabby lyric discipline we are so sick of leaves a good story where it never should have been potentially: in the gray category of neuter gender, declension indefinite.

TELL MY HORSE (1938)

◆◆◆◆◆◆◆◆◆◆◆◆◆

ELMER DAVIS

Saturday Review, October 15, 1938

Miss Zora Neale Hurston has gone afield from the scenes of her previous work (*Mules and Men* and *Their Eyes Were Watching God*) and turned in the inexhaustible mines of Voodoo and witchcraft in Haiti and Jamaica. *Tell My Horse* is a curious mixture of remembrances, travelogue, sensationalism, and anthropology. The remembrances are vivid, the travelogue tedious, the sensationalism reminiscent of Seabrook, and the anthropology a melange of misinterpretation and exceedingly good folklore.

Jamaica seems to be by way of introduction. Turning at the earliest opportunity to Haiti, Miss Hurston recounts once more, in her own terms, the story of the bloody assassination of President Sam and the entry of the U.S. Naval forces into the private life of Haitian politics; she tells this rather well, having a fine gift for tales. Then she remarks upon the good fortune of the Haitian population in having been, at last, freed from the terror of banditry and tropical politics. Yet this must be more a feeling with her than an idea; she could not have read the late Dr. James Weldon Johnson's articles which appeared in the *Nation* during the summer of 1920. The hardships inflicted by the occupation upon all but the merchants of Haiti have not been forgotten to this day.

Her protest comes in another connection, against the position of women in the Caribbean. That position, she says in effect, is the double standard carried to its furthest possible excess. She discusses the "Black Joan of Arc," Celestina Simon, daughter of President Simon. It is not quite clear why the girl merits the title, but there are stirring tales about her, how she, her father, and her father's pet goat held secret Voodoo rituals in the palace, under the noses of frightened and disapproving guests.

Mostly she writes of Voodoo as she saw it in Haiti and of witchcraft. The Voodoo resolves out of her anthropological training. But it is in her blood and would be inevitable under any circumstances. As one observer said, "She'd find Voodoo in anybody's kitchen." But Haiti is full of the real thing. Seabrook exposed it in sensational, wishful terms. Dr. Herskovits exposed it in its coldest mathematical terms. Miss Hurston tries both. To an extent she is successful, for Voodoo in Haiti is both warmer, possessed of more poetry, than Dr. Hershovits realized, and less wild and orgiastic than Seabrook intimated. *Tell My Horse* is full of fine things. Miss Hurston has an immense ability for catching the idiom of dialogue, of seeing the funniest of exaggeration, of recognizing the essence of a story. And yet, though these qualities do carry through at all times, there is a constant conflict between anthropological truth and taletelling, between the obligation she feels to give the facts honestly and the attraction of (as one of her characters says in *Mules and Men*) the "big old lies we tell when we're jus' sittin' around here on the store porch doin' nothin'."

In dealing with Voodoo rites Miss Hurston is painstaking. There is a good deal of useful material crammed into her eyewitness accounts. But she seems to be at her best with witchcraft. It fires her imagination, gives impetus to the urge to create a story or a scene. The chapter on Zombies is good. She has gone into the subject extensively and, in addition to collecting all the Zombie tales going the rounds in Port-au-Prince, has even seen one and photographed her. "But I saw this case of Felicia Felix-Mentor which was vouched for by the highest authority. So I know there are Zombies in Haiti." The reasoning sounds just a little like that of the lumberjack's explanation that Paul Bunyan's plow made the Grand Canyon: "If you don't believe it, go and look for yourself."

The photographs are exceptionally good. It is unfortunate that it is so generally known that many of the "rituals" portrayed in them were enacted in Port-au-Prince and accessible to the average run of tourists. This does not disqualify them as probably the best available pictorial record of Voodoo, but the pictures Miss Hurston took herself are more honest. It is also a matter of regret that the abundance of Creole was not properly edited before publication. A glossary would have been valuable.

That Miss Hurston loves Haiti is obvious, but there is a general feeling that the material was not completely digested.

MOSES, MAN OF THE MOUNTAIN
(1939)

◆◆◆◆◆◆◆◆◆◆◆◆◆

LOUIS UNTERMEYER

Saturday Review, November 11, 1939

The Old and New Testaments have been radically re-examined during the last year in the light of psychoanalysis, folklore, and fantastic fiction. In "Moses and Monotheism" Freud reappraised the leader of the Jews as a part-Egyptian whose idea of One God was borrowed from the "heretic" Pharaoh Akhnaton—a concept which this reviewer had employed as the basis of a novel published eleven years ago. In *Moses: Man of the Mountain* Zora Hurston has depicted the central figure of the Old Testament not so much as a questioning rebel or an illuminated lawgiver but, chiefly, as the great voodoo man of the Bible.

Miss Hurston's approach is as arresting as it is fresh. In a brief introduction she implies that, to most readers, Moses is merely an old man with a beard—an old man who had some trouble with some Pharoah about some plagues and, thereafter, led the Children of Israel out of the land of bondage toward the Promised Land. The Bible, obviously, was her springboard. But legends about Moses are not confined to Holy Writ; they appear, strangely transmogrified, in Rabbinical literature, in weird forms through the Near East, in various parts of Africa, and in the curious document "The Sixth and Seventh Books of Moses," which many white readers still refuse to accept as a hoax. Miss Hurston has drawn on some of these (as well as Josephus' apocryphal accounts of Moses as an Egyptian general) to present the militant liberator from the point of view of the American Negro. The fancy is whimsical and infectious; the contrasting characters of the shrewdly wise Jethro, the bitterly ambitious Aaron, the voluptuous Zipporah, and the frustrated Miriam are convincing; the setting has the charm of a continually changing panorama. But the whole is less successful than the parts, and the total effect is that of unfulfilled expectation.

The prime disappointment is in the character of Moses himself. The balance between his royal Egyptian breeding and his Hebraic adaptation is insufficiently adjusted; his growth from a warrior-prince to prophet and seer is weakly motivated; the paradox of his violence and his proverbial meekness is scarcely explicated. Such criticism would seem captious had the author decided to depart entirely from reality; but the book is a series of compromises between the plausible and the bizarre, between the legend as we know it and the legend as it has been transplanted and recolored.

Equally disappointing and even more disastrous to the illusion are the compromises which the author had made in idiom. Her books deals largely with magic and to maintain that mood the spell must be complete. Here it is wrecked on inconsistency. Much of the descriptive matter is straightforwardly "correct"—some of it is poetic in the traditional "white" manner—but her conversations are (usually) in broad dialect.

The publishers imply that Miss Hurston's fifth book has the same feeling as *The Green Pastures* in its portrayal of the Negro conception of "our" Christian God. But this is unfair to both volumes. If Miss Hurston's fantasy lacks the combination of humor and poignancy which characterized the Roark Bradford-Marc Connelly collaboration, it has a genre quality of its own. It is not a logically projected work, but it has a racial vitality, a dramatic intensity worthy of its gifted author.

◆◆◆◆◆◆◆◆◆◆◆◆◆

PERCY HUTCHISON

The New York Times Book Review, November 19, 1939

This is the story of Moses as the Negro sees and interprets the "Man of the Mountain." None the less reverent in conception than that of the white man, there is one aspect of the work of the great leader of the Israelites which holds particular fascination for the Negro, so that his view becomes especially interesting, and again, always in a reverent way, entertaining, now and again even amusing. All primitive peoples have an inordinate love of magic, or what appears to be magic, and the African most of all. His descendants in this country may hold that the magic of the radio is more awesome than such relics of voodoo prestidigitation as they may have witnessed or heard about. But even they have traditions that will not die, and one of them, according to Zora Neale Hurston, is that Moses was just about the greatest magician ever in the world. He led his followers out of bondage, because his was better "medicine" than that of Pharaoh's magicians. He talked to God face to face, but he had been singled out by God for this honor because Jehovah recognized the superlative magical power of Moses. Consequently, there comes about almost a transposition of Moses and God in the Negro's point of view of their relationship, or so it would seem from Miss Hurston's pages. Moses seems almost to be greater than God. But this is not irreverence, for it is undoubtedly due to the fact that it was easier for a primitive mind to endow a human being with mystical powers than to grasp a purely rational concept of deity. The author's Man of the Mountain is a very living and very human person.

The narrative begins with a pathetically moving picture of the enslaved Israelites striving to comprehend the cruelty of the decrees suddenly issued against them by the new Pharaoh. They talk in the dialect made familiar by Roark Bradford's books which formed the basis of *The Green Pastures*. When Jochebed, mother of the three-month-old Moses, takes the child in a wicker basket to hide him in the bulrushes, she addresses the river as if it had personality.

> Nile, youse such a big river and he such a little bitty thing. Show him some mercy, please.

For some reason not apparent the author reduces the dialect as she proceeds, and although a more closely knit narrative is the result, the book loses something in flavor. Moses, rescued by Pharaoh's daughter, is brought up as an Egyptian prince, as the leader of an army; not for a long time is he to be the Mountain Man. According to the Book of Exodus Moses was threescore years of age when he delivered the Children of Israel out of their bondage, but little is told of Moses during the intervening years. It is the legendary Moses whom the Negroes have built that Miss Hurston gives us in the first part of the book, a Moses painted in rich imagination.

It is after the plagues get under way that the subtle change from the Biblical relationship between Moses and the Lord becomes noticeable. However, it must not be concluded from this that Moses actually supplants the Lord. No matter how greatly Negro tradition exalts the Israelite leader, it still stands in too much awe of Jehovah to belittle Him.

Moses, a fugitive out of Egypt, has gone up into the hills, where the Lord appears to him for the first time and commands him to go down and liberate his people. Moses retorts that Pharaoh won't listen to him. Answers the Lord,

> Go ahead like I told you, Moses. I am tired of hearing the groaning in my ear. I mean to overcome Pharaoh this time.

Moses objects that he could never make a speech. Then the Lord says:

> You go. I'll go with you. Open your mouth and I'll speak for you.

But if the Lord, as "boss-man," as Moses calls Him, is in control of operations, we presently find Moses acting as Jehovah's adviser, pleading for one more plague after another. Pharaoh remains obdurate, and when the high priest of the Egyptians counsels him to let the Hebrews go because the people are tired of the plagues, Pharaoh replies that they are nothing but tricks, and that Moses is bound to run out of tricks after a while. Thus we see the personal contest waged between Moses and the Egyptian King as represented by his magicians. Then, of course, comes the end of the bondage and Moses leads his people across the Red Sea.

The close of the book is poetic and beautiful with its picture of Moses high up on the slopes of Nebo looking down on the Children of Israel fording the River Jordan into the Promised Land.

It is impossible to say to what extent Miss Huston has woven many legends and interpretations into one and how often she is making verbatim use of given, but, presumably, only orally extant, tradition. But the narrative becomes one of great power. It is warm with friendly personality and pulsating with homely and profound eloquence and religious fervor. The author has done an exceptionally fine piece of work far off the beaten tracks of literature. Her homespun book is literature in every best sense of the word.

DUST TRACKS ON A ROAD (1942)

◆◆◆◆◆◆◆◆◆◆◆◆◆

PHIL STRONG

Saturday Review, November 28, 1942

Zora Neale Hurston's father was the preacher and chief factotum of Eatonville, Fla., one of the few villages of, for, and by Negroes in the United States. The old man was a powerful preacher and also a powerful man and husband; as a slave, says Zora, with the charming practicality which marks the manner of the whole book, he would have fetched a high price for stud stock. He could flatten people to the floor either with his big fists or his hellfire eloquence.

Zora had a good deal of her father's violence and more of her tiny mother's sensitivity, intelligence, and determination. These got her through school, after a bitter struggle, then through Howard University and Barnard, and finally made her what she is, an outstanding anthropologist in the field of Negro folklore and other Negro cultures. She has surveyed everything from Afro-American songs to voodoo and left a mark on modern American music and reasonable accounts of the over-romanticized magics of the Haitians.

This book is more a summary than the autobiography it advertises itself as being. It is a delightful one and a wise one, full of humor, color, and good sense. It is told in exactly the right manner, simply and with candor, with a seasoning—not overdone—of the marvelous locutions of the imaginative field nigger. Miss Hurston explains that there are white niggers and black niggers; being a nigger is a matter of character rather than color among the Negroes.

After Zora's mother died her father married a fat shrew who wanted to make the social jump of being the preacher's wife. The stepmother was jealous of the children and drove them from home, one by one, including Zora who was still in her earliest teens. The girl held "maiding" jobs but very briefly because of her fondness for books and children. These tastes conflicted with her allotted labors virtually to the exclusion of the latter, and Zora moved on and on. Finally, she caught on as maid to the leading in a touring comic opera company, learned manicuring, and manicured her way through Howard.

She had learned that if one wanted to go to school the thing to do was to go to school, so she went on to Barnard, became Fanny Hurst's secretary and a favorite of Franz Boas, and thereafter made her way in research on fellowships and the five books which precede this one. She might have taken either of two attitudes from these experiences; either an arrogant, self-made Negro attitude, or the conventional bitter and downtrodden one. She takes neither because she does not see that she was under any special disadvantage, and in the end she has no reason for bitterness. This text indicates that anyone who tries to downtread Zora Neale Hurston had better wear thick-soled boots.

The race consciousness that spoils so much Negro literature is completely absent here. Miss Hurston is less impressed by her own color than most Aryan redheads. She gives one chapter to "My People"— perhaps the most sensible passage on the subject that has ever been written. She agrees with Booker T. Washington that if the stuff is in you it is likely to come out and that if it isn't it doesn't make any difference whether you are white, black, green, or cerise. Some people, she says, have made a whole career out of moaning, "My people! My people!" She thinks they would have been better engaged in some useful labor. The only thing she claims for the Negro is perhaps a little more capacity for fancy and enthusiasm than the average white man possesses.

The most amusing chapter is Miss Hurston's delightfully frank treatise on love. It makes sense, but few people have had the reckless heroism to come out with it. She has had one "great" love and still has it; she doesn't know yet how it is going to come out, since the chosen gentleman is jealous of her work, as well as of all other gentlemen discovered in even remote proximity to Zora. Miss Hurston, with a prescience of trouble, has tried to break herself of the man several times without success. Occasionally she feels like being in love with someone else, incidentally— and is, briefly. When these unfortunate swains remind her of tender passages she is all too often feeling like "a charter member of the Union League Club" (this may be a slander) and the recalled endearments are "the third day of Thanksgiving turkey hash."

The conclusion is:

> Love is a funny thing; love is a blossom—
> If you want your finger bit poke it at a possum.

It may be judged that the book is rich in humor and that is true; it is real humor—and humor of character, from the old deacon who prays, "Oh, Lawd, I got something to ask You, but I know You can't do it," to Zora's own feud, nourished through the years and beyond all scholarship and honors, with her gross stepmother. The old lady, at last reports, was in the hospital with some malignant growth on her neck—Miss Hurston says, quite frankly and honestly, that she wishes the woman had two necks.

She has, too, a philosophic feeling for the statement of her friend, Ethel Waters, "Don't care how good the music is, Zora, you can't dance on every set."

It is a fine, rich autobiography, and heartening to anyone, white, black, or tan.

◆◆◆◆◆◆◆◆◆◆◆◆◆

BEATRICE SHERMAN

The *New York Times Book Review,* November 29, 1942

Here is a thumping story, though it has none of the horrid earmarks of the Alger-type climb. Zora Neale Hurston has a considerable reputation as anthropologist and writer. When her autobiography begins she is one of eight children in a Negro family with small prospects of making a name for herself. Yet her story is forthright and without frills. Its emphasis lies on her fighting spirit in the struggle to achieve the education she felt she had to have. The uses to which it was put—good uses too— were the fruit of things that cropped up spontaneously, demanding to be done.

Hard work and natural talent were her mainstays. Bad luck and good came in mixed portions. But always Zora Neale Hurston felt that she was a special, a different sort of person—not in any unpleasantly cocky way, but as almost any one does who has energy and ability and wants to use them.

Zora was born in Eatonville, Fla., "a pure Negro town—charter, mayor, council, town marshal and all." Her father was a tall, heavy-muscled mulatto from "over the creek" near a small Alabama town, who came to Florida "resolved to put down roots." Of a landless family, he was looked down upon by the land-owning relatives of Lucy Ann Potts. When Lucy Ann first wondered who he was, she asked "Who is dat bee-stung yaller nigger?" Even though he came from over the creek, she married him. Always in their family she was the hard-driving force forever goading him in and out of his happy, easygoing ways. He was the preacher to a Baptist congregation, and she—tiny and energetic—managed him and the eight children as they came along.

Zora's childhood was happy and carefree. She evolved endless and imaginative games from such simple and enchanting toys as Miss Corn-Shuck, the Reverend Door-Knob, and a tribe of Spool People that increased as she purloined one spool after another from her mother's supply. She liked reading and history at school but abominated arithmetic.

Her happy days were over when her mother died and two months later her father married again. Zora was shifted off to school and then from the home of one friend to another. The second Mrs. Hurston was jealous of the children and did all that a willful woman could to alienate them from their father. They hated her and felt sorry for him. At the earliest possible minute Zora got a job as housemaid, and because that sort of work didn't interest her and she was always getting out of it to read or play with the children, she never kept a job long.

Finally, through sheer nerve and will power, she got a chance at formal education. She went to high school in Baltimore, to Morgan College, to Howard, to Barnard, and Columbia. But before all that she had eighteen months as lady's maid to an actress in a Gilbert and Sullivan troupe, and that association did as much for her as more standardized education in opening up a vista of books and music to be absorbed. Incidentally, she had a happy time and was the pet of the company.

Her whole story is live and vivid. Told in gusty language, it is full of the graphic metaphors and similes that color Negro speech at its richest, sometimes in direct quotations from folk stories—those lying sessions at the village store—and sometimes woven in with her own warm style. There is no "hush-mouth modesty" about the book, for Zora Neale Hurston would not "low-rate the human race" by undue expurgation of her story.

In it there are two terrific fights. One when young Zora came home to Eatonville and could stand no more of her stepmother's tyranny. That was a tooth-and-claw-and-axe battle which almost carried the irate girl to murder. The other fight was a murderous affair, too, in which a Polk County black girl "took a pick at" the unoffending research worker who had come to gather folksongs in the region. Impersonal killing was what she had in mind, but on that occasion Zora Neale Hurston displayed the better part of valor, and when the knives began to fly retired from the scene—100 miles from it—her retreat was covered by her friend Big Sweet.

Further along there are philosophical chapters on books (the Hurston books), love, "My People!" and religion. Then impression simmers down to a feeling that the author regards the Negro race much as she regards any other race—as made up of some good, some bad, and a lot of medium. The problems they face are those of any other race, with the disadvantage of being a younger lot. Anyway, her story is an encouraging and enjoyable one for any member of the human race. Any race might well be proud to have more members of the caliber and stamina of Zora Neale Hurston.

SERAPH ON THE SUWANEE (1948)

◆◆◆◆◆◆◆◆◆◆◆◆◆

FRANK G. SLAUGHTER

The New York Times Book Review, October 31, 1948

"**S**eraph: One of an order of celestial beings conceived as fiery and purifying ministers of Jehova," says *Webster*. Arvay Henson, the heroine of this long novel of the Florida sand barrens and turpentine forests, probably never heard of a seraph, but she set out to be one nevertheless. Arvay never heard of Freud, either, but she's a textbook picture of a hysterical neurotic, right to the end of the novel.

Arvay had reckoned without her "Id," which shortly asserted itself on the appearance of Jim Merserve, dark, handsome turpentine boss from the Alabama River. Before Jim, Arvay had gotten rid of impetuous suitors by having a fit, but the first time she put one on for Jim Meserve, he eyed the performance in critical appraisal, recognized the rather primitive symbolism involved in such hysterical convulsions, and cured it pronto, with a drop of turpentine in one of Arvay's lovely eyes. After that, of course, she was his slave, no matter how much she might protest. Married to Jim Merserve, Arvay should have been over her troubles, but they were only beginning. For Jim was a man with an eye on the future and Arvay was a girl with her eyes on the past. Being neurotic, Arvay could not make up her mind to forget the past and take the exciting ride on a comet that Jim Merserve promised. And when her first child was an idiot, Arvay's guilt over her illicit and hidden passion for a visiting preacher, plus an episode among the turpentine trees with Jim on the afternoon before her wedding, pretty well snowed her under for awhile.

Upon such an uncertain backround, it was inevitable that this chronicle of an unstable woman's search for happiness would be filled with ups and downs. Happy and unhappy by turns, Arvay still helped Jim build a new life for them in southern Florida, but always there was the neurotic's yearnings for the scenes of her childhood. With her children grown and Jim increasingly occupied with business, Arvay's inferiority finally drove her to a break and return to the Suwanee. There, in a sort of self-psychoanalysis, she learns the truth about herself and begins to realize her destiny.

The author knows her people, the Florida cracker of the swamps and turpentine camps intimately, and she knows the locale. One gets the impression that she took a textbook on Freudian psychology and adapted it to her needs, perhaps with her tongue in her cheek while so doing. The result is a curious mixture of excellent background drawing against which move a group of half-human puppets.

◆◆◆◆◆◆◆◆◆◆◆◆◆

WORTH TUTTLE HEDDEN

The *New York Herald Tribune Weekly Book Review*, October 10, 1948

Though *Seraph on the Suwanee* is the love story of a daughter of Florida crackers and of a scion of plantation owners, it is no peasant-marries-the-prince tale. Arvay Merserve, true Cracker in breeding, is above her caste in temperament; James Kenneth Meserve is plain Jim who speaks the dialect and who has turned his back on family, with its static living in the past, to become foreman in a west Florida turpentine camp. Neither is it a romance of the boy-meets-girl school. Beginning conventionally enough with a seduction (a last minute one when Arvay is in her wedding dress), it ends twenty-odd years later when the protagonists are about to be grandparents. In this denouement, the divergent lines of Miss Hurston's astonishing, bewildering talent meet to give us a reconciliation scene between a middle-aged man and a middle-aged women that is erotically exciting and a description of the technique of shrimping that is meticulously exact. Emotional, expository; meandering, unified; naive, sophisticated; sympathetic, caustic; comic, tragic; lewd, chaste— one could go on indefinitely reiterating this novel's contradictions and still end helplessly with the adjective unique.

Incompatible strains in the novel mirror the complexity of the author. Miss Hurston shuttles between the sexes, the professions, and the races as if she were man and woman, scientist and creative writer, white and Negro. She is at her best as a man among men objectively portraying Jim and his workaday life with such verisimilitude that we never doubt "whatever God neglected, Jim Meserve took care of." A fight in a bar complete with appropriate obscenity, a struggle between a man and a diamond back, between a pilot and the sea, are her meat, and, in the speech of her characters, she do know how to cook it. Jim's complaint about Arvay's loving is pure male:

> I feel and believe that you do love me, Arvay, but I don't want that stand-still, haphazard kind of love. I'm just as hungry as a dog for a knowing and

doing love. You love like a coward. Don't take no steps at all. Just stand around and hope for things to happen out right. Unthankful and unknowing like a hog under an acorn tree. Eating and grunting with you ears hanging over your eyes, and never even looking up to see where the acorns are coming from. What kind of satisfaction can I get out of that kind of love?

With Arvay and domestic routine Miss Hurston is less successful, holding her guilt-ridden seraph too consistently in the cloudy sky of the emotions. She knows every intimate detail of Arvay's physical self and reveals it to the point of absurdity, but she has to construct a visible Freudian fretwork to give us understanding of her psychic self. On the other hand, only a woman could animate the adolescent and adult Arvay, now going her wishy-washy unhappy way, now facing facts and courageously burning her past when she burns her house.

How to distill turpentine and "moonshine," grow citrus fruit, catch shrimp, and develop a swamp into a country club area are explained here in an industrial scientist's prose. Motivated by his determination to enhance Arvay's life rather than by personal ambition, these varied enterprises are Jim's steppingstones to success and they advance the plot while they make plausible in realistic fiction the exaggerated devotion of an Augusta J. Evans hero.

The generic life of the Florida Cracker from the cradle to the grave is so documentary in the dramatization of mores and language it seems incredible that one not born to the breed, even though a neighbor and an anthropologist, could be its biographer. Miss Hurston knows her Florida Negro as she knows her Florida white and she characterizes them with the same acumen, but she gives them no more attention than the plot demands. In Jim's relation with the colored workmen whose knowhow has helped him get rich, in Arvay's petulant jealousy of them, in her triumph over her past when she sits at the table with Titty-Nipple and Cup-Cake, the old southern adage that the aristocrat is the darky's best friend is symbolically italicized. "I declare, Miss Arvay, but you sure is folks. Just like Mister Jim. And everybody knows that Mister Him is quality first class. Knows how to carry herself, and then how to treat everybody."

Reading this astonishing novel, you wish that Miss Hurston had used the scissors and smoothed the seams. Having read it, you would like to be able to remember every extraneous incident and every picturesque metaphor. You will not soon forget the vow "if God could fix it so that she got over this greasy log, she would certainly sand the next one," or the articulation of misery: "Her days had nothing in them but hours. Hours that somebody else had got all the light and service out of and chunked them away. Old, worn-out, lifeless marks on time. Like raw, bony, homeless dogs, they took to hanging around her doorway. They were there when she got up in the morning, and still whimpering and whining of their emptiness when she went to bed at night."

ESSAYS

◆◆◆◆◆◆◆◆◆◆◆◆◆◆

"The Drum with the Man Skin": Jonah's Gourd Vine

ERIC J. SUNDQUIST

The spirituals included in volumes such as James Weldon and Rosamond Johnson's first and second *Book of American Negro Spirituals* and the many comparable collections frequently showed pronounced variations resulting not simply from the difficulty of transcription or from historical erosion but rather from the fact that spirituals, in their origins, were fundamentally a communal, improvisatory art. What survives in written, published form depends to some degree upon chance, and the "text" may at that point once again become an occasion for further invention in which communal effort and individual performance are intertwined. Upon a given framework of chord changes, melodic line, and lyric theme, countless variations were created and lost before the late nineteenth century and since, and those elements of early modern black arts that derived from folk culture owe a great deal to an expressive form, both in songs and folktales, that in some respects is antithetical to the notion of a fixed, regulated text. In their landmark 1926 collection, *Blues: An Anthology*, W. C. Handy and Abbe Niles traced Handy's art to African-American worship, where the preacher's lining out of a hymn and the congregation's response formed a dialectic. After the preacher had lined out a portion of the song in his own shout or wail, which was characteristically full of blue notes (a source of Handy's early composition, he recalled), the congregation would adapt the example to their own ceative purposes: "From every note each singer would start on a vocal journey of his own, wandering in strange pentatonic figures, but returning together at the proper moment to the next note of the melody. If one had succeeded in attracting attention by an exceptional note or a striking rhythmic figure, a dozen others would attempt, starting from the next note, to outdo him. To an unaccustomed listener close at hand, the result would be chaos, but at a distance the sounds merged into a strange and moving harmony."

Niles's description of Handy's apprenticeship is striking on several counts. It recapitulates the wealth of commentary that was available, beginning with the earliest studies of slave spirituals and work songs, about the divergence of black American music from the tempered scale and harmonic structure of most European, Protestant music; it indicates a vocal confluence between preaching and singing that elides the registers of speech and music, a central feature of African-American aesthetics; and its description of the call-and-response format underlines the

39

interaction between community and individual performance in black folk culture as it was frequently recorded and then re-created in literary form by Zora Neale Hurston. Indeed, all these elements are bound together in Hurston's most significant writing, which always occupies the abraded border terrain between the oral and the written, between the recorded and the re-created. Unlike Johnson, who highly valued African-American folk culture but argued for its transfiguration into more "sophisticated" forms, Hurston, as we have seen, hyperidealized vernacular, asserting in her famous 1934 essay "Spirituals and Neo-Spirituals" that there never had been a legitimate presentation of "genuine Negro spirituals to any audience anywhere." The true songs, like the true folktales, she said, were "being made and forgotten every day." By the same token, of course, Hurston's career was founded on the premise that the vernacular could be translated, so to speak, into disseminated form—in ethnographic collections, in critical essays, and in fiction.

For this reason, the liminality of her own authorial and professional voice bears an important resemblance to the liminality of her characters' voices—whether those of anthropological subject-informants or fictive protagonists—for all of them frequently inhabit the blurred grounds between folklore and fiction, music and voice. The undervalued "Spirituals and Neo-Spirituals" is most often cited for its rather idiosyncratic elevation of vernacular improvisation in the spirituals. Much of the essay, however, is devoted to Hurston's extremely acute analysis of the intersection between black song and sermonic form, to the "tonal semantics" (to borrow Geneva Smitherman's modern phrase) that lie at the heart of black American expressivity as it was nurtured in the Afro-Christian church and that appear as a primary aesthetic device in her first novel, *Jonah's Gourd Vine* (1936). Perhaps the single most revealing essay in the early theorizing of African-American vernacular culture—leaving aside the more magisterial thesis put forward by Du Bois in *The Souls of Black Folk*—"Spirituals and Neo-Spirituals" is an important gloss on the long-standing debate over dialect verse, the rise of blues and gospel, and the question of community leadership in its relationship to aesthetics—a relationship that is attenuated at best in the Euro-American tradition but can be shown to be central to the African-American tradition.

"As bard, physician, judge, and priest . . . rose the Negro preacher, and under him the first Afro-American institution, the Negro church," wrote Du Bois of the black preacher, in addition styling him "a leader, a politician, an orator, a 'boss,' an intriguer, [and] an idealist." Hurston's early work did not so thoroughly rewrite *The Souls of Black Folk* as had Johnson's *Autobiography of an Ex-Coloured Man*, though her seminal essays for Nancy Cunard's *Negro: An Anthology* (although the essays were written in 1930, the anthology was published in 1934) and *Jonah's Gourd Vine* go a long way toward developing in theoretical detail Du

Bois's central concerns in "Of the Faith of the Fathers": "the Preacher, the Music, and the Frenzy." Although he was modeled in telling ways on Hurston's own father, the preacher John Pearson in her first novel embodied most of the traits of cultural leadership that Du Bois had enumerated, even as he glaringly displayed the faults and sins apparent in the autobiographical figure. More importantly, however, John Pearson became the vehicle for Hurston's testing of the very medium of African-American culture. He is the voice whose "liquefying of words," as she called it, linked sermon to music to communal response; the voice whose tale telling yoked improvisation to a complex allegorical structure, making biblical scripture potently alive with parabolic significance for the African diaspora and the delivery from bondage; the voice whose cadences continually rewrote the languages of resistance and striving carried out of slavery into a modern idiom—what Hurston would refer to in *Their Eyes Were Watching God* (1937) as "words walking without masters; walking altogether like harmony in a song." What is more, it is a voice whose combined power and ambiguity of intention allowed Hurston to find and explore her own voice as an African-American author.

In order to gauge these various interpenetrating elements of vocality that Hurston put at the core of both her ethnographic and fictive work, I will concentrate on the origins of John Pearson's career, Hurston's theory of sermonic language, and the sermon of the Reverend C. C. Lovelace. The Lovelace sermon was first transcribed by Hurston in Eau Gallie, Florida, in 1929, then published along with "Spirituals and Neo-Spirituals" in Cunard's *Negro*, and finally inserted into the text of *Jonah's Gourd Vine* in the mouth of John Pearson when, in a grand sermon, he attempts to redeem himself in the eyes of his congregation, diverting their attention from his marital infidelities and moral weaknesss. Although some readers have lamented that Hurston stretched the plot of her novel incongruously to provide an occasion to display the Lovelace sermon in the mouth of John Pearson, my focus here will be less on the novel's story line and characterizations than on the intersection of its folk and narrative registers. Unlike *Their Eyes Were Watching God*, for example, in which those registers are seamlessly woven together in Hurston's mature narrative discourse—the voices of author and character carefully merged, embedding African-American inflections and figures into a "speaking" text—*Jonah's Gourd Vine* is patently experiental, even jagged in its composition. Virtually stylized moments seem deliberately provided in the novel for Hurston to examine black "talk" (signifying), the issue of African-American metaphor, the work song as a folk source, and most of all, of course, the sermon as performative art. Indeed, the very stylization of these moments is the source of their meaning; they lay bare the process of integration by which Hurston rehearsed the preservation of slave culture in the twentieth century and reconstructed the notion of the novel in an African-American cultural context. Like Johnson in *The Autobiography of an Ex-Coloured Man*, she searched into the survivals of slave culture for the materials of a modern black culture that would properly preserve and extend racial consciousness rather than see it eroded, even erased, by white culture; and like him, she wrote a novel that was principally a metacommentary on novelization. But wherever Johnson was ambivalent or conservative, Hurston was typically daring and unreserved in her indulgent celebration of folk culture as the only undiluted voice of black America.

Hurston's caustic signifying on Johnson in *Dust Tracks on a Road*—that he had for years been "passing for colored"—hardly gives an adequate indication of the admiration she held for him and his work. As suggested in chapter 1, her comic critique provides one way to read her pronounced divergence from him on the issue of the spirituals and "authentic" African-American vocality. For the same reason, it may be read as a reflection of her sincere appraisal not of his aesthetic intentions but of his aesthetic achievement. In the wake of a misinformed review of *Jonah's Gourd Vine*, Hurston complained to Johnson that the reviewer was unwilling to recognize that a Negro preacher like John Pearson "could have so much poetry in him" and failed to understand that the preacher, in order to hold his charge, had to be an "artist": "He must be both a poet and an actor of a very high order, and then he must have the voice and figure. [The reviewer] does not realize or is unwilling to admit that the light that shone from *God's Trombones* was handed to you, as was the sermon to me in *Jonah's Gourd Vine*." As in her theory of the spirituals, Hurston suggested that what went unrecorded was perhaps even more significant: "There are hundreds of preachers who are equalling that sermon weekly."

Hurston's entire characterization of the preacher's leadership and art bears closer examination, but her further remark to Johnson that the two of them "seem to be the only ones even among Negroes who recognize the barbaric poetry in their sermons" elides a profound difference between their mutual understandings and uses of that language (as well as conveniently setting aside other writers and ethnographers who argued for the same importance of the African-American sermon). A further, rather more complicated difference is also elided in Hurston's assertion that both the poetry of *God's Trombones* and the Lovelace sermon were "handed" to the two authors. Johnson, as indicated in chapter 1, based the first of his poems, "The Creation," on a Kansas City preacher who cast aside his formal text in favor of the oratorical vernacular. In all the poems of *God's Trombones*, Johnson composed verse rooted in that experience but hardly replicating it, building in subsequent poems of the sequence on the experience of collecting and analyzing the spirituals for his two published volumes. Hurston, on the other hand, seems virtually to have reproduced the substance of Lovelace's sermon for her Cunard essay, casting it into verse form but preserving its language and cadence, then incorporating it bodily into *Jonah's Gourd Vine*. Her choice of form is significant in both instances, as is, even more obviously, her decision to move the work from one genre to another. In addition, the Lovelace sermon is distinctly more complex in figure and rhetoric than most of the sermons of the period that were being published in journals such as the *Southern Workman* or issued on the race records that flooded the market in the 1920s and 1930s, and the degree of Hurston's intervention may perhaps be a more serious issue than she herself let on. First, however, one can look at Johnson's sermonic verse and his theory of dialect as a way of estimating Hurston's pointed divergence from his model. Dialect writing and the folk sources of its intonations contained within it African sounds propelled into a unique black American vernacular that, as Hurston and Johnson both saw clearly, was to remain a kind of crossroads of cultural languages. As in the case of the spirituals, however, the nuanced difference in their views of dialect is more telling than their points of agreement. On the face of it (although we do not have the original preacher's sermon for comparison), Johnson's is the more composed, the more conventional aesthetic work, demonstrating, as in *his* theory of the spirituals, a "development" of vernacular materials into a more "cultivated," authorial form. Nevertheless, because *God's Trombones* is noticeably less interesting as sermonic language and as poetry, it raises pressing questions about idiom and about the context of publication by which we judge the value of cultural works.

"The old-time Negro preacher is rapidly passing," Johnson writes in his preface to *God's Trombones*, "I have here tried sincerely to fix something of him." The verses of *God's Trombones*, as this passage suggests, are a powerful memorial tribute, a display in Johnson's rather stately language of seven of the major biblical themes of the African-American sermon. His well-known renunciation of dialect (already spelled out in the preface to the *Book of American Negro Poetry* several years earlier and then reiterated in *God's Trombones*) hinges on his view that dialect had typically been the medium of picturesque racism—plantation romance and "darky" humor—even for the black writer. Johnson himself had composed traditional dialect poems—"jingles and croons," as he called them—but in later editions of his own poetry he reprinted such verse as "Ma Lady's Lips Am Like de Honey" and "Brer Rabbit, You's de Cutes' of 'Em All" primarily as archaic data that bore out his own theory. On the other hand, in the 1931 edition of the poetry anthology and in his preface to Sterling Brown's *Southern Road* a year later, Johnson somewhat revised his opinion, allowing that Brown and Langston Hughes had transcended minstrelsy and discovered in dialect the "common, racy, living, authentic speech of the Negro." Such exceptions, however, proved the rule that black authors should, in Johnson's words, seek to "express the racial spirit by symbols from within rather than symbols from without—such as the mere mutilation of English spelling and pronunciation." In *God's Trombones*, then, Johnson sought to re-create the black preacher's "tone pictures," as he called them in describing the folk preacher John Brown in *The Autobiography of an Ex-Coloured Man;* but he did so without recourse to textual markings that would replace conventional dialect with the vernacular signs of blackness and without actualizing a number of the features he had so precisely theorized in his preface. In avoiding the risks of dialect, Johnson at the same time sacrificed its strengths, which are considerable though not simple to specify— or, more accurately, to "hear."

Charles Chesnutt once complained in a letter to Walter Hines Page that it was a "despairing task" to write dialect. The problem was not just orthographic but theoretical. Echoing an increasing tradition of fieldwork, Chesnutt argued that "there is no such thing as a Negro dialect. . . . what we call by that name is the attempt to express, with such a degree of phonetic correctness as to suggest the sound, English pronounced as an ignorant old southern Negro would be supposed to speak it, and at the same time to preserve a sufficient approximation to the correct spelling to make it easy reading." Chesnutt's discomforting detachment from the rural southern folk does not discredit the evaluative importance of his views or his own effective use of dialect for ideological purpose in *The Conjure Woman* (1899) and elsewhere. Moreover, Chesnutt's argument, which posited a black vernacular but said it could not be accurately cast into readable print, would appear to invert the complaint voiced by Howard Odum and Guy Johnson in their important collection of black folksongs, *The Negro and His Songs* (1925), that dialect was hard to record because "there is no regular usage for any word in the Negro's vocabulary," or Newbell Puckett's degrading judgment that the "altiloquent speech" of blacks, satirized in grotesque exaggeration by minstrelsy, showed that "the Negro is constantly being lost in a labyrinth of jaw-breaking words full of sound and fury but signifying nothing." "Signifying nothing," however, might turn out to be a revealing characterization: African-American dialect, in high culture no less than in folk culture, was in a constant condition of signifying on the linguistic power of the masters, appropriating and depleting that power, at least provisionally, by subverting its authority and thus reducing it to "nothing."

Dialect, as Chesnutt saw, was complex semantically and politically, as the significant turn-of-the century debate about it reveals. An anonymous writer for the *Atlantic Monthly* in 1891, arguing that the language of former slaves and their descendants was a mystified jumble of misunderstood English, inadvertantly located the crucial double-terrain of ethnic vernacular when he designated dialect as a language of "word-shadows." African-American dialect, the author argued, is composed of "the shadows cast by words from fairly educated lips into the minds of almost totally ignorant people," the light of civilization thrown into the "dusky realm" of savagery producing "something queer, fanciful, and awkward," a new language it must employ "since it has lost the tongue of its own people." The author goes on to list many examples of highly figurative transformations in black English—for example, a giant is a "high-jinted man"; to keep down grass is to "fight wid Gen'al Green"; to join a church is to "put on a shine-line gyarment"—of the very sort Hurston would later say were characteristic of the "adornment" and "angularity" of black speech. Although his argument is a tissue of commonplace racist assumptions of the post-Reconstruction era, the *Atlantic* author's essay offers important clues to the function of dialect. Because he understood dialect to mean not just accent or intonation but also figurative diction, the writer was somewhat closer than most of his contemporaries to recognizing that African-American language represented a creative as well as a necessary merger, over a number of generations, of native linguistic survivals and the language of Euro-Americans, assimilated in oral forms.

When it was defined in relation to a dominant culture, dialect might therefore function as an index of the power of signs to exclude and oppress; but it might for that same reason indicate a powerful mode of cultural self-determination and self-preservation. As Henry Louis Gates, Jr., has argued, dialect can turn the "metaphor against its master." Located between the two poles of white English and an African language "lost in some mythical linguistic kingdom now irrecoverable," black dialect can be read as the only surviving key to that unknown tongue. Moreover, Gates's view that successful dialect writing is fundamentally musical and approaches the metaphoric richness of black spirituals—a level that dialect poetry or prose has, however, seldom reached, most obviously in the early modern generation in the cases of Hurston and Brown—underlines the necessity that dialect be understood to include the semantic plenitude and singularity of folk speech as well as its oral legends, its material and psychological space, and the implied ancestral sources of its language and beliefs. The "word-shadows" of black dialect may be perceived by whites as a distorted version of correct English or a potentially destructive presence within the master's culture and thus subject to mockery and exorcism through the degrading parody of minstrel stereotypes. In addition, however, dialect must be seen as a signifying alternative, another cultural language historically related to white English while transfiguring it as well.

Whereas ethnologists were prone to characterizing black language as the idiom of a social and cultural world that failed to measure up to civilized standards, there was the counterpossibility, exploited notably by Chesnutt and again more dramatically by Hurston, that black language was also the idiom of a secret world kept out of range to the middle-class mind, much as the coded languages of slavery had been deliberately kept out of the range of the masters. To borrow Ralph Ellison's powerful metaphor, it was a language that spoke on "lower frequencies." Dissembling its communications within a culturally distinct, necessarily private communal language, dialect, like the intonations of the spirituals, may be seen to be governed by hidden semantic constructions and grounded in a signifying response to white culture dating from the origins of slavery. Insofar as it reconstructed slave culture, dialect was both a salvaged speech that pays tribute to those who have gone before and an index of what has been kept alive in the evolving cultural memory of song, folktale, and everyday language. Far from being the obvious sign of regression or the inadequate comprehension of civilized cultural forms, dialect might be the linguistic tool best able to show that the bondage of language could also be liberating.

In this respect in particular dialect bears an important relation to the African-American spirituals. For whites' complaints about the ineffability of black dialect, which led in turn to the grotesque caricatures of minstrelsy and some plantation romance, repeated comparable observations by musicologists, as we have seen in chapter 1, that the intonations of the black spiritual were difficult to transcribe. The opinion of Thomas Fenner, the white arranger of the spirituals sung and published by Hampton Institute, was characteristic: "Another obstacle to [the music's] rendering is the fact that tones are frequently employed which we have no musical characters to represent. . . . These tones are variable in pitch, ranging through an entire interval on different occasions, depending on the inspiration of the singer." As Hurston and others complained, however, the "purification" of African-American spirituals by touring choirs and concert performers eliminated or reconfigured any residual elements of African folk art and the unique sounds forged in slave culture when those characteristic tonalities and rhythms were made to conform more closely to European standards. F. G. Rathbun, writing of Hampton Institute's programs in the *Southern Workman* in 1893, summed up the paradox of the educational process in this way: "After a contact with our sight singing teacher, our English teacher and teacher of elocution, something is missing from these songs, and this goes on as long as the student remains here. Corrected pronunciation and corrected singing make the difference. It is very difficult to teach an educated colored youth to render these songs in the old time way."

In a signifying reversal of the denigration of black dialect as a mere "shadow" of traditional English, Hurston and other early celebrants of African-American language sought to value and preserve the sounds of slave culture threatened with extinction by forced adherence to white educational and artistic standards. As Fenner's caveat suggested, the convergence of musicality and meaning in African-American speech meant that the recorded sign, not the act of signification, would be the "shadow," the inadequate container for a meaning that slid away in the act of performance. The political level of circumspection in black language that slavery entailed has survived on through the twentieth century in the deeply musical vernacular forms of speech, language games, signi- fying, and sermonizing analyzed by Geneva Smitherman, Claudia Mitch- ell-Kernan, Roger Abrahams, and others. The principal strategies and indirection that ethnomusicologists have found to be characteristic of African and African-American music in this way strengthen the tight fusion of tonal and semantic qualities in black vernacular language. In- creasingly in the early twentieth century, black writers, throwing off the post-Reconstruction anxiety about slave culture and seeking to re-create ancestral traditions, recognized that the elaborate metaphoricity and what seemed the unfixed character of African-American language could be construed positively—as a linguistic medium whose fluidity and capac- ity for improvisation was akin to the development of improvisatory arts in black vocal and instrumental music.

It is just here that Hurston diverged from and improved the astute theorizing of Johnson. Even so, she seems, in fact, to have traded on some of the key observations that Johnson made in his preface to *God's Trombones*. Like her, he rightly put oratory and acting on the same plane in the preacher's performance, noting that the biblical text could sometimes serve as a mere starting point for a sermonic flight; he under- lined the centrality of rhythm and intonation in the sermon, placing par- ticular emphasis on the appearance of breathing as a part of the expression and suggesting that the "sense of sound" itself was of such overriding importance that he had seen congregations "moved to ecstasy by the rhythmic intoning of sheer incoherencies"; and he contended that the preacher's language was a "fusion of Negro idioms with Bible En- glish," in which there likely resided "some kinship with the innate gran- diloquence of [the] old African tongues." All of these points reappear in transfigured form in "Spirituals and Neo-Spiritiuals" and *Jonah's Gourd Vine*, but in each case Hurston seems to have articulated better what is specifically African-American in these elments and to have found their natural equivalent in her own rendition of the Lovelace sermon.

In Johnson's taped recordings of *God's Trombones*, the relative for- mality and stateliness is evident in his own vocal "intonation," which, though Carl Van Vechten complimented its emotive power and Johnson's expert delivery, seems rather flat. His elevated tones and extended syl- labic phrasing verge at times on a kind of singsong that seems distant from the experience of the Kansas City preacher that must have been in the back of Johnson's mind (and distant as well from the better recorded sermons of the same or later years). The problem seems to lie less in Johnson's voice, however, than in his verse. S. P. Fullinwider's con- tention that *God's Trombones* is "anthropology, not creativity" is not quite right, nor is Jean Wagner's kinder and more useful judgment that it is a kind of "stylized folklore." The black folk voice, indeed, is what seems most absent. In Johnson's diction and form, vernacular is almost entirely submerged in memorial precision; dialectical invention and altiloquence give way to concertized voicing and diction as he invents a cultivated equivalent to the classic African-American sermon that ran from Creation to Judgment Day in an electrifying pastiche.

Consider, for example, the following lines from Johnson's poem "The Crucifixion":

> And the veil of the temple was split in two,
> The midday sun refused to shine,
> The thunder rumbled and the lightning wrote
> An unknown language in the sky.
> What a day! Lord, what a day!
> When my blessed Jesus died.
>
> Oh, I tremble, yes, I tremble,
> It causes me to tremble, tremble,
> When I think how Jesus died;
> Died on the steeps of Calvary,
> How Jesus died for sinners,
> Sinners like you and me.

Now, Hurston's (or Lovelace's) version of the same scene:

> And about dat time
> De angel of Justice unsheathed his flamin' sword and
>   ripped de veil of de temple
> And de High Priest vacated his office
> And then de sacrificial energy penetrated de mighty strata
> And quickened de bones of de prophets
> And they arose from their graves and walked about in de
>   streets of Jerusalem
> I heard de whistle of de damnation train
> Dat pulled out from [de] Garden of Eden loaded wid cargo
>   goin' to hell
> Ran at break-neck speed all de way thru de law
> All de way thru de prophetic age
> All de way thru de reign of kings and judges—
> Plowed her way thru de Jurdan
> And on her way to Calvary, when she blew for de switch
> Jesus stood out on her track like a rough-backed mountain
> And she threw her cow-catcher in His side and His blood
>   ditched de train
> He died for our sins.

The extraordinary extended figure of the damnation train, to be discussed later for its relevance to other parts of *Jonah's Gourd Vine*, is characteristic of the language Hurston employs in her complex embellishment of the Crucifixion. But even in small tropes—"sacrificial energy" penetrating the "mighty strata" rather than "lightning" writing an "unknown language" in the sky, for example—Hurston's passage calls for contemplation of its far more complicated allegorical layers. This is not Johnson's best passage, but neither is it Hurston's; yet both are representative. To the extent that we are justified in ascribing the language to Hurston, rather than to C. C. Lovelace, the passage no doubt signifies upon Johnson's pallid dramatization, which one might say to paraphrase Hurston, only "passes for colored."

More to the point, however, is the fact that Hurston's orthography, her variations in person and tense, and her lack of grammatical markers or punctuating line stops—that is, her unmistakable but also flexible appeal to dialect—support the vividly inventive metaphors of her scene. Here and elsewhere, her use of enjambment, repetition, assonance, and a metrical scheme based on breathing rather than syllabic count drive the verse into a form that is "readable" only to the degree that it is "heard." The African-American sermon, as she wrote in "The Sanctified Church," an essay unpublished in her lifetime, is "drama with music." The vernacular of the Lovelace sermon, far from suggesting the pathos of humor that Johnson feared it was always in danger of provoking, more exactly realizes the power Johnson himself attributed to the folk preachers when he said: "They were all saturated with the sublime phraseology of the Hebrew prophets and steeped in the idioms of King James English, so when they preached and warmed to their work they spoke another language, a language far removed from traditional Negro dialect." The point here, of course, is not to dismiss Johnson's fine volume or the rationale for his choice to eschew dialect but rather to indicate the manner in which Hurston intuitively grasped the limitations of Johnson's theory and returned directly to the vocal powers of vernacular culture for her inspiration in *Jonah's Gourd Vine* and elsewhere, making herself, as Du Bois might have said, "bone of the bone and flesh of the flesh of them that live within the Veil." Before returning to look in more detail at the Lovelace sermon and its role in Hurston's composition of *Jonah's Gourd Vine*, several other crucial Africanist elements of her theory adumbrated in the novel must be considered.

When the congregation at Notasulga discovers that young John Pearson has a "good strainin' voice," they call on him more frequently to offer prayer, and John responds with some "new figure, some new praisegiving name for God" each time he kneels. Hurston writes: "he rolled his African drum up to the altar, and called his Congo Gods by Christian names. One night at the altar-call he cried out his barbaric poetry to his

'Wonder-working' God so effectively that three converts came thru [to] religion under the sound of his voice." The quality of John's voice becomes Hurston's main focus, but her characterization of it as an African drum and her deliberate fusion of African and Puritan traditions constitute a miniature historical essay on the role of religion in slave acculturation. Likewise, the "barbaric poetry" of his idiom is a virtual quotation from numerous ethnographic essays on black language at the turn of the century. There is no indication that this is conscious on John's part; indeed, the fact that it is unconscious may be crucial, for Hurston was concerned to register African retentions as a powerful, formative undercurrent or syncretism that had been thoroughly absorbed in Afro-Christian practice. Her introduction of a theory of retentions, however, was peculiarly conscious, even forced, according to those readers who have been at a loss to explain Hurston's blunt ethnographic intrusions into her narrative. Yet abrupt though it is, the characterization of John's voice as an African drum goes to the very heart of the leadership and sermonic power that he comes to epitomize.

The more dramatic figuration of the African drum appears in the context of the feast held after the cotton is in. Spurning fiddles, guitars, and banjoes—"us ain't no white folks," they say—the people clap and dance:

> They called for the instrument that they had brought to America in their skins—the drum—and they played upon it. With their hands they played with the little dance drums of Africa. The drums of kid-skin. With their feet they stomped it, and the voice of Kata-Kumba, the great drum, lifted itself within them and they heard it. The great drum that is made by priests and sits in majesty in the juju house. The drum with the man skin that is dressed with human blood, that is beaten with a human shinbone and speaks to gods as a man and to men as a God. Then they beat upon the drum and danced. It was said, "He will serve us better if we bring him from Africa nameless and thingless." So the buckra reasoned. They tore away his clothes that Cuffy might bring nothing away, but Cuffy seized his drum and hid it in his skin under the skull bones. The shin-bones he bore openly, for he thought, "Who shall rob me of shin-bones when they see no drum?" So he laughed with cunning and said, "I am who am borne away to become an orphan, carry my parents with me. For Rhythm is she not my mother and Drama is [he not] her man?" So he groaned aloud in the ships and hid his drum and laughed.

Appearing virtually out of nowhere in the text, this passage is sometimes cited as evidence of Hurston's as yet immature skill at integrating ethnological observation into fictional narrative. Indeed, the passage introduces a flurry of authorial observations about the African roots of black folksinging and dancing, interspersed among the recorded stanzas and ornamented dialogue, and written in what appears to be a kind of fieldwork shorthand: "Hollow-hand clapping for the bass notes. Heel and toe stomping for the little ones. Ibo tune corrupted with Nango. Congo gods talking in Alabama. . . . Too hot for words. Fiery drum clapping." Hurston is frequently an "observer" in the novel, however, and *Jonah's Gourd Vine* a palimpsest of autobiographical and cultural rumination that not only fuses her family history to fieldwork and theory but, in fact, self-consciously extends the attack on the boundary between ethnology and narrative that she had begun in *Mules and Men* (1935), which was written before but published after *Jonah's Gourd Vine*.

Supported by other minor allusions to the rhythm and tonality of drumbeats in the novel, these passages about African drumming are a pointed assertion of African retentions at a moment when the issue continued to be hotly debated. The writers of the Harlem Renaissance, typified by Alain Locke's classic anthology *The New Negro* (1925), frequently argued for the African roots of black art and music; Du Bois had offered clear points of departure in *The Souls of Black Folk* and then again more emphatically in *The Negro* (1915); and Carter Woodson, Melville Herskovits, and others would soon provide invaluable studies of African retentions. At the same time, the dominant view, certainly among most white sociologists and cultural critics, was that African Americans had been divested of their ancestral culture by the ordeal of slavery. The influential sociologist Robert E. Park claimed, for example, that African Americans were entirely estranged from their ancestral land, languages, and cultural traditions; and the eminent historian U.B. Phillips claimed that African Americans were "as completely broken from their tribal stems as if they had been brought from the planet Mars." I am less concerned here with the lines of this debate, however, than with Hurston's deployment of retentions as a particular weapon against the calculated destruction of culture that accompanied slavery. Stripped of the apparent "clothes" of culture, rendered "thing-less," as Hurston's drum passage held, Africans nonetheless carried with them vital traditions figured as the "parents" of Rhythm and Drama, which are central elements of black folk culture as it is analyzed in her essays and in the performance of John Pearson in *Jonah's Gourd Vine*. Although Hurston's fieldwork as it was recorded in *Mules and Men* and especially in her Caribbean volume, *Tell My Horse* (1938), charts linguistic and material survivals with some precision, the passages in the novel, like the essays in Cunard's *Negro*, amount to finely condensed philosophical statements.

What is most notable about Hurston's theory of survivals is that it often dwells especially in the world of the phenomenal rather than the concrete. In her 1943 essay "High John de Conquer," named for the legendary root of black conjure and luck, her personification of High John as a mythic figure accompanying Africans on the middle passage endows him, like the trickster figures of the animal tales, with sacred properties, making him an incarnation of the voice that "has evaded the ears of white people" and borne up black people. The spiritual sustenance and secret powers that he provides his folk—including the signifying power of black laughter and black song—in the new world of enslavement Hurston can trace only to a primordial world of occluded memory, originating existence. Before he is reborn a "natural" man and a trickster who can always get past Old Massa, High John is "a whisper, a will to hope, a wish to find something worthy of laughter and song. Then the whisper put on flesh. His footsteps sounded across the world in a low but musical rhythm as if the world he walked on was a singing-drum." Alongside the "black bodies huddled down there [in the ships' holds] in the middle passage, being hauled across the water to helplessness," High John came "walking on the waves of sound . . . walking the very winds that filled the sails of the ships." The fascinating High John essay, only touched on here, rewrites the drum passage of *Jonah's Gourd Vine* into an allegory of retentions (and physical survival), and it does so by locating the origin of African-American songmaking and storytelling, especially trickster tales and Master-John stories, in *spirit* itself: the wind and the waves of sound that carry High John across the Atlantic yoke the breath of the body, the whisper of life, and the singing sound of African drums. High John, in this configuration, *is* spirit or soul, the rhythm of black life in the voice that links body to drum, mediating between humans and gods, as between language and sound.

The High John essay clarifies Hurston's intentions in *Jonah's Gourd Vine* by demonstrating just how the Lovelace sermon and John Pearson's straining voice are to be read as marked by significant African retentions. Interchangeable figures for one another, drum and body form a single communicative medium that carries African spirit in a New World form, the voice internalizing the rhythm of drumming. The trope of African drums appearing in the work of both black and white writers such as Langston Hughes, Arna Bontemps, Eugene O'Neill, and Vachel Lindsay had nearly been drained of significance by the vogue of primitivism in the 1920s, and one can be certain that Hurston intended to redress the easily misconstrued use of drumming and thereby reanimate the observation of William Arms Fisher in his 1926 collection, *Seventy Negro Spirituals:* "The unseen ghost of the crude African drum walks in the midst of all [the Negro's] poetry and music." Crude of course it was not; but Hurston's contribution was to fuse an awareness of the rhythm and tonality of African drumming in slave culture, where drums were frequently prohibited, to those strategies of subversion, indirection, and secrecy retained in later vernacular culture.

Hurston's drum passage, less so her High John de Conquer allegory, takes for granted the communicative power of drumming—the capacity of African drums to "talk" in a coded language of rhythm and timbre. Although Henry Krehbiel among others had already made tentative associations between the vocalism of African drum language and African-American cultural forms, the considerable debate about the role of African polyrhythms and blue tonality in black American music, and hence the links between drum and voice in the formation of jazz, was not far advanced when Hurston wrote. As in the case of Du Bois, however, her interest in the roots of black music was less musicological than epistemological. That is to say, she wanted to suggest that black folk vernacular was informed, whether with full consciousness or not, by a spirit that broke down boundaries—at extremity the boundaries of consciousness, opening in worship or performance into the ecstasy of possession. The folk spirit, moreover, was closer to ancestral memories, as Hurston contended in: "The Sanctified Church" (an essay that in turn borrowed from *Jonah's Gourd Vine*), where she wrote that "the Negro has not been christianized as extensively as is generally believed. The great masses are still standing before their pagan altars and calling old gods by a new name. As evidence of this, note the drum-like rhythm of all Negro spirituals." The phrase "the drum with the man skin" therefore refers at once to an ancestral drum, held in its sacred precinct and used ceremonially, and to the African-American body in New World slave culture. Although the context of Afro-Caribbean religious practice makes for a symbology distinct from that of the American South, Hurston put it more forthrightly in her later description of a Jamaican dance in *Tell My Horse*: "The drums and the movements of the dancers draw so close together that the drums become people and the people become drums. The pulse of the drum is their shoulders and belly. Truly the drum is inside their bodies." The sign of internalized inheritances that are at once intensely spiritual and practical—with drums lost or prohibited by the slaveholding regime, percussion depended on different instruments: tools, household utensils, hands, and feet—the body as drum becomes the primary site of cultural production, a reservoir of the ancestral and an instrument of re-creation.

The fact that song and drumming together entered so fully into African-American life can be traced to the centrality of music in black labor, beginning in Africa and transformed under slavery. In *Jonah's Gourd Vine* this stands forth in several signal instances, most of all in John's brief experience working on the railroad gang at Sanford. For Hurston, as for other African-American writers, the railroad and train are powerful symbols—powerful in *Jonah's Gourd Vine* to the point of being baroque but not, as some have argued, awkward. Hurston makes the trope of the railroad first of all the crucible of African-American vernacular song—a crossroads of "locomotive energies," as Houston Baker has written in his more general theory of a blues vernacular. The work of lining track makes for a long day of "strain, sweat and rhythm," the men grunting over the lining bar and swinging the nine-pound hammer to drive spike after spike: "Another rail spiked down. Another offering to the soul of civilization whose other name is travel," as Hurston codified the rhythmic labor of the road gang in *Dust Tracks on the Road*. Hurston's repetition of the word "straining," as well as her focus on the hammer's swing and the overt musical punning in her description of the communal labor—"then a rhythmic shaking of the nine-hundred-pound rail by bearing down on the bars thrust under it in concert!"—alert us to the cognate rhythmic labor, straining, and bearing up that will appear in the preacher's sermonic performance, which, like the spirituals, has embedded in it the percussive reminders of ancestral drumming.

The railroad camp, in fact, provides John Pearson a springboard to the pulpit. After hearing the Sanford minister one Sunday, John returns to camp and repreaches the sermon himself, perfectly "marking" the minister; soon he announces his call to preach, is ordained, and moves into his leadership role. The point of this episode, however, is not just to get John Pearson into the pulpit, but to demonstrate the origins—or at least the primary analogues—of his vocal arts in black labor itself. Hurston no doubt drew on the title poem of Sterling Brown's volume *Southern Road* (1932), with its striking connection of work-song rhythm and diction to versified form:

> Swing dat hammer—hunh—
> Steady, bo';
> Swing dat hammer—hunh—
> Steady, bo';
> Ain't no rush, bebby,
> Long ways to go. . . .

The rhythmic iteration of the hammer strike accompanied by the grunting expulsion of breath reappears in Hurston's comparable description of the gang hammering and "singing" the rail into place in a kind of kinaesthetic blues:

> "Oh, Lulu!"
> "Hanh!" A spike gone under John's sledge.
> "Oh, oh, gal!"
> "Hanh!"
> "Want to see you!"
> "Hanh!"
> "So bad!"
> "Hanh!"

Although some of the spirituals derived from or overlapped with work songs—"Michael Row Your Boat Ashore," for instance—James Weldon Johnson distinguished the swing common to each form, and his account of the fusion of labor and aesthetic form in the road gang is particularly insightful:

All the men sing and move together as they swing their picks or rock-breaking hammers. They move like a ballet; not a ballet of cavorting legs and pirouetting feet, but a ballet of bending backs and quivering muscles. It is all in rhythm but a rhythm impossible to set down. There is always a leader and he sets the pace. A phrase is sung while the shining hammers are being lifted. It is cut off suddenly as the hammers begin to descend and gives place to a prolonged grunt which becomes explosive at the impact of the blow. Each phrase of the song is independent, apparently obeying no law of time. After each impact the hammers lie still and there is silence. As they begin to rise again the next phrase of the song is sung; and so on. . . . There are variations that violate the obvious laws of rhythm, but over it all can be discerned a superior rhythmic law.

Such an overarching but unidentifiable law of rhythm, which was to become a central feature of jazz theory, was frequently attributed to the "authentic" spirituals. In his contemporary account of the Fisk Jubilee Singers, *The Story of the Jubilee Singers and Their Songs* (1881), for example, J.B.T. Marsh spoke of the "higher law of rhythmic flow," the broken and irregular but nonetheless exact swaying time, that governed the spirituals. Johnson's analysis is most pertinent because it points both to the intrumentality of the body in labor—its equivalence to tools—and to the regulation of each by song. The hidden rhythmic law is marked by the punctuations of breath: the straining of the road gang is recapitulated in the straining of the preacher when he enters fully upon the labor of his sermon, and the "hanh" of the railroad song becomes the "ha" of the Lovelace sermon, as Hurston first transcribed it and then gave it to John Pearson.

In Dogon belief of West Africa, the hammer of the blacksmith creates primal energy; his anvil was the first drum, and the recreation of the blows of the sacred hammer reminds men of the spiritual beginnings of the world, just as the drums in certain instances are used to summon the ancestors. Other lines might be drawn between hammering, drumming, and oratory—the Bambara, for instance, call the griot the "blacksmith of the word"—but no particular African mythology need be located in order to sense the network of associations bound to John Pearson, the "drum with the man skin," who also speaks "to gods as a man and to men as a God." Hurston's mind, in fact, is fixed as much on the attenuation as on the repetition of Africanisms in black American culture. Noting the great proliferation of railroad themes and railroad sounds in blues and jazz, Albert Murray has argued that "what may once have been West African drum talk" has "long since become the locomotive talk . . . heard by downhome blackfolk on farms, in work camps, and on the outskirts of southern towns." Hurston seems to have apprehended something quite similar in her depiction of the onomatopoeic "chanting" of the train, as she calls it, with which John Pearson is continually fascinated: "Soon in the distance he heard the whistle, 'Wahooom! Wahup, wahup!' And around the bend came first the smoke stack, belching smoke and flames of fire. The drivers turning over chanting 'Opelika-black-and-dirty! Opelika-black-and-dirty.' Then as she pulled into the station, the powerful whisper of steam. Starting off again, 'Wolf coming! Wolf coming! Wolf coming! Opelika-black-and-dirty, Opelika-black-and-dirty! Auh—wah-hoooon'—into the great away that gave John's feet such a yearning for distance." Likewise, the primordial energy of hammer and drum have long since moved into John Pearson's voice, where the sermonic form, with its own incorporation of the rhythms of the work song, carried from the middle passage through slavery and beyond, transfigures the intricate dexterity of song into verbal performance, as the preacher speaks, chants, and sings the story of creation, deliverance, and judgment:

> Jesus have always loved us from the foundation of the world
> When God
> Stood out on the apex of His power
> Before the hammers of creation
> Fell upon the anvils of Time and hammered out the ribs
>   of the earth. . .

John Pearson's delivery of the Lovelace sermon caps his oratorical reha-bilitation of his career. His extraordinary abilities with speech and his fulfilling a function in the community that is both sacramental and per-formative override his moral failings, his indulgence in the sexual plea-sures of a "natchel man." "When Ah speak tuy yuh from dis pulpit," he reminds the congregation earlier, "dat ain't me talkin', dat's de voice uh God speakin' thru me." His sermons mimic God's voice, and if no one believes in such literal prophetism, it is nonetheless true that John Pear-son is the bard of his people, his ability to "talk" encompassing the biblical history of enslavement and delivery in the voice of the black ancestors. Hurston's novelistic delivery of the Lovelace sermon adds to this a con-scious framing of John's role and a conscious appropriation of its power to her own narrative art, as well as a critique of her capacity to represent the sermonic performance in literary form.

Despite his bardic cultural function, John's redemptive role is robbed of its mythic significance by the narrative life in which his sermon is inscribed. The elaborate trope of the "damnation train," whose cow-catcher pierces Jesus' side and releases his sacrificial blood in the Love-lace sermon, is reduced to a burlesque figure in the train that smashes into John's Cadillac after his last act of infidelity. The long-standing reso-nance of the train as a figure of black deliverance in the spirituals ("Same Train," "Get on Board, Little Chillen," and so on), its rich association with movement and migration in modern black history, its embodiment in work songs and the blues of the endless toil of black America—all these associations, which Hurston calls into view over the course of the novel before concentrating their energy into the judgment train of the sermon, are diminished in the comic instrument of reprisal. Hurston thus looked askance at her father, whose moral character is judged harshly in *Jonah's Gourd Vine*, but also at the privileged power accorded the male preacher in the African-American tradition as she had experienced it. By signifying upon that power, however, she also paid tribute to it, joining the preacher's voice provisionally to her own in order to measure the differences between them, to interrogate and preserve the formative power of Afro-Christianity incarnate in the sermonic utterance she sought to rival.

Hurston's interest in the sermon as a vernacular form, then, lay not simply in her sense that it was brilliant verbal art but also in her belief that it contained echoes of African ancestry that were dim but still fundamental and that it offered a continual recomposition of the structuring mythology of black America in which she could participate as a writer and as a woman. The "hammers of creation" in the Lovelace sermon merge an African retention quite explicitly with the work songs of the road gang and a unique mythologizing of the Christian creation. In addition, the "hammers" tie John Pearson, through the medium of his intoning voice, to God's own creativity, a fact further supported by the striking plural—"Jesus have always loved us"—which refers not just to Father and Son or the Trinity but also to John, whose self-serving "wounds of Jesus" sermon is meant to regain the good will of his congregation, who will forgive his marital infidelities—who will even, for that matter, participate in them as they make him the heroic spokesman of their sacred story. Above all, Hurston's adducement of the African source of John's sermonic talent, the most pronounced revision she makes in transferring the Lovelace sermon from the Cunard anthology to *Jonah's Gourd Vine*, is a way to deepen and strengthen the legitimacy and independence of African-American language as an ancestral inheritance capable of transcending slavery and Jim Crow.

If Hurston's novel offers one of the first lengthy dramatizations of black vernacular free from the garbled stereotypes of minstrelsy and plantation mythology, foregrounding black talk about characters and subsuming that same talk into its narrative voice, it also takes its lead from the critical role played by the voice of the preacher throughout the history of African Americans. First analyzed in detail by Du Bois and brought to the fore later in the twentieth century by the national prominence in the Civil Rights movement of Martin Luther King, Jr., and other ministers in the Southern Christian Leadership Conference, the preacher's status as community spokesman was hardly uncomplicated in cultural representations when Hurston came to it. Minstrelsy and nineteenth-century plantation revues such as A. G. Field's "Darkest America" often included burlesque black sermons, full of comically twisted theology and pathetic malapropisms. For many white Americans, such caricatures endorsed Puckett's view that Negro speech was a "laby-

rinth of jaw-breaking words full of sound and fury." (Even well-inten-
tioned white replications of the black sermon went awry. For example,
Vachel Lindsay's "How Samson Bore Away the Gates of Gaza," subtitled
"a Negro sermon" and appearing in *Poetry* in 1917, styled Samson a "bold
Jack-Johnson Israelite," but Lindsay lamented his inability to capture the
language; and Natalie Curtis responded in *Poetry* two months later with
an actual black spiritual version of Samson as a Negro, including a legitimate rendition of "Ride on, Jesus," which Lindsay had alluded to in his
poem.) In addition, black folklore in the early twentieth century increasingly included tales of preacher humor, primarily devoted to corruption
and sexual escapades, indicating a decline in faith and a fragmentation
of the Afro-Christian basis of the black community. At the same time,
however, the *Southern Workman* and other journals had begun by the
turn of the century to feature essays on African-American preachers and
preaching, recognizing it as a grand vernacular art as much deserving
of preservation and study as the spirituals. The nineteenth-century Virginia preacher John Jasper, whose famous sermon "De Sun Do Move an'
De Earth Am Square" had been published as early as 1882 and which
Johnson described in his preface to *God's Trombones*, was the subject of
a biographical and rhetorical study that transcribed a group of his sermons in 1908. Perhaps most important of all in spurring Hurston's decision to feature the sermon, however, was the advent of recorded African-
American sermons. The some 750 sermons recorded between 1926 and
1938 were part of the greater vogue among the black population, North
and South alike, of "race records"—blues, spirituals (or gospel), folksinging, and sermons directed primarily to a black listening audience on
major and minor labels beginning with Okeh in 1923. (The Black Swan
company, the single black-owned label, advertised itself as "The Only
Genuine Colored Record. Others Are Only Passing for Colored.") Among
the many other sermonic themes recorded in the 1920s, one might note
especially the Reverend J. M. Gates's hugely popular "Death's Black
Train Is Coming," as well as the Reverend A. W. Nix's "The Black
Diamond Express to Hell" and its counterpart "The White Flyer to
Heaven." Just this dualism of the damnation train and the salvation train,
a staple in the sermonic tradition, appears in one of Lovelace's most
complex images, near the conclusion of his sermon:

> When we shall all be delegates, ha!
> To dat Judgment Convention
> When de two trains of Time shall meet on de trestle
> And wreck de burning axles of de unformed ether
> And de mountains shall skip like lambs . . .

Any complete account of the significance of Hurston's reproduction of
the Lovelace sermon in her first novel would thus have to place it in

relation to the widespread and complex role that sermons have played in defining the creative limits of African-American expression in many other artistic genres, all of which have drawn power from the preacher's performative eloquence.

The inclusion of African-American sermons on race records is particularly important because sound recording itself had a dual role that facilitated both the collection of folklore and its commercial dissemination. Hurston herself reported to her mentor, Franz Boas, on the prevalence of phonographs among the southern black population; and although her own fieldwork at that point relied on memorization and notebooks (in 1935 she would assist Alan Lomax in recording sermons and songs in Florida), the competition between printed and aural forms of transmission surely entered into her aesthetic as well. Following her own rule, Hurston herself might have designated the Lovelace sermon a "neo-sermon," for the printed sermon stands in much the same relation to its actual performance as did the published "neo-spirituals" to the authentic songs of the folk. The popular Fisk and Hampton collections of spirituals, Jeanette Robinson Murphy noted laconically in a seminal 1899 article, provided no instructions as to the irregular phrasing, "undulations," and "trimmings" common to black singing; nor did they advise the uninitiated how to "sing tones not found in our [European] scale," or indicate that "by some mysterious power, to be learned only from the negro," the singer "should carry over his breath from line to line and from verse to verse, even at the risk of bursting a blood-vessel," at length giving way to "peculiar humming sound—'hum-m-m-m.'" (Murphy's tongue-in-cheek analysis did not undercut her profound admiration for the true style of the spirituals, and her essay was among the first to make a serious case for African retentions in song and folklore.) Likewise, the key for Hurston or other transcribers of sermons was to capture the performative aspects of the sermon and, while avoiding the pitfalls of dialect, to reproduce on the page the vocal characteristics of the sermon that locate it midway between song and speech, as declamation gives way to recitative and "intoning"—those elusive "intonations and delicate variations" that William Allen, as early as 1867 in *Slave Songs in the United States*, had said "cannot be reproduced on paper."

Studies of the African-American sermon have traced its intoning form to African chants of tribal law and communal praise poems; detected in its harmonics the blues tetrachord of the work songs, field hollers, and some spirituals; and associated its tonal improvisations with the beginnings of vocal and instrumental jazz. One may sense all these possibilities in the Lovelace-Pearson sermon, where God's labor from the beginning of time, and Christ's suffering redemption, also present from the beginning of time, are combined into a drama of communal delivery in which the preacher essentially reenacts the entire biblical saga. He does so in order to reenforce the long-standing analogy between the delivery from pharonic bondage and the African-American delivery from slavery; but it is the originality of the story, its improvisation and exposed architectonics, that most fuel the performance. The sermon, that is to say, embellishes both the creation and the Bible, the preacher's labor uniting the hammer and anvil, the drum and shinbone, reinventing the white man's central mythology in each telling. The sign of that labor, as in the structure of the work song, is the preacher's "straining," the irregular but rhythmic inhalations and exhalations marked on the page by "ah!" and "ha!":

> Who shall I make him after? Ha!
> Worlds within worlds begin to wheel and roll
> De Sun, Ah!
> Gethered up de fiery skirts of her garments
> And wheeled around de throne, Ah!
> Saying, Ah, make man after me, ha!
> God gazed upon the sun
> And sent her back to her blood-red socket
> And shook His head, ha! . . .

"Negro singing and formal speech are breathy," Hurston writes in "Spirituals and Neo-Spirituals." "The audible breathing is part of the performance and various devices are resorted to to adorn the breath taking." At length, the embellishment of breathing gives way to a humming or moaning that, in Hurston's apt metaphor, "liquifies" words into a pure vocal music, whose timbre might be traced to the nontempered scale of African music but whose erasure of traditional linguistic structures and sounds is specifically African American. Hurston's own annotations on "straining," in the glossary of *Jonah's Gourd Vine*, is relevant here: "In his cooler passages the colored preacher attempts to achieve what to him is grammatical correctness, but as he warms up he goes natural. The 'ha' in the sermon marks a breath. The congregation likes to hear the preach breathing or straining."

Hurston's characterization at once underscores the performative aspect of the sermon—in its relation to a sort of folk theater and in the audience's choral role—and makes evident the link between sheer tonalities and the altiloquence, the highly figurative, sometimes neological expressions that mark the sermon. Such invention in diction and syntax, as in the acceleration into chant or song, amounts to "recomposing America in terms of Africa," to borrow an idea from Ben Sidran's *Black Talk*. One can see this in a number of phrases, lines, and passages from the sermon that depend on figurative leaps—semantic as well as rhythmic enjambments that reconfigure Protestant mythology, suffusing Bible language with the inventions of the black spirituals and a willful adornment of the text in a speakerly voice, as in the passage following Jesus' appeal to God, "Why hast thou forsaken me?":

The mountains fell to their rocky knees and trembled like a
 beast
From the stroke of the master's axe
One angel took the flinches of God's eternal power
And bled the veins of the earth
One angel that stood at the gate with a flaming sword
Was so well pleased with his power
Until he pierced the moon with his sword
And she ran down in blood
And de sun
Batted her fiery eyes and put on her judgement robe
And laid down in de cradle of eternity
And rocked herself into sleep and slumber
He died until the great belt in the wheel of time
And de geological strata fell aloose . . .
And de orchestra had struck silence for the space of half an
 hour
Angels had lifted their harps to de weepin' willows . . .

Among other remarkable reconfigurations in this passage dramatizing
Christ's Passion, Lovelace, or Hurston, unites the gospels with apposite
prophetic and apocalyptic scripture (Joel 2:30–31, Acts 2:20, and Revelation 6:12); borrows elements from both the powerful imagery of Protestant hymnology and such black spirituals as "My Lord, What a
Morning" or "Stars in the Elements" ("The stars in the elements are
falling / And the moon drips away into blood"), "See How They Done My
Lord" ("They pierced him in the side, / an' He never said a mumbalin'
word / The blood came twinklin' down"), "'Zekiel Saw the Wheel" ("Zekiel saw de wheel of time"), and "O Rocks Don't Fall On Me" ("O, in dat
great great judgment day / Rocks and mountains don't fall on me"); and
personifies a millennial time associated in Afro-Christian thought with
redemption from slavery and its long aftermath.

In this passage as in others, however, the sermon's precise sources
are purposefully obscured by the syntactical slippage and fusion of idea
with incantatory sound, a strategy with African roots but specifically
African-American significance. The Lovelace sermon is an excellent example of the black preacher's creative recomposition of the Bible's narrative, frequently a complex and elusive performance that, as Hortense
Spillers has argued, represents his ambivalent apprenticeship to, and
thus his hermeneutical play with, the central mythos of white culture.
The closer the preacher moves to the tonal semantics of singing, the more
fully he embodies ancestral arts and Africanizes American experience. In
Africa the communal and historical storyteller, the griot, displays an
exemplary command of circumlocution and oratorical wit that are taken
to be extensions of the primal energy of sound itself, the force of *nommo*

harnassed to the medium of communal memory. The form and structure of such talent survive in some instances of the black sermon, put in the service of reimagining America's founding theological mythos. "While he lives and moves in the midst of a white civilization," Hurston remarked in "Characteristics of Negro Expression," everything that [the Negro] touches is re-interpreted for his own use." From this perspective, the movement into a metadiction or into vocalization is a means to reach back toward ancestral tonality, to recite the Christian story in terms of black bondage, and to signify upon the constricting bonds of the master's cultural language.

"Mimicry is an art in itself," Hurston contended in the same essay. Her notion has a range of implications that could include reference to the appearance of African retentions in African-American art; to black dialect as a creative mimicry of white English, as well as the disputed and now generally disavowed belief that the black spirituals and folktales were simply recastings of Euro-American materials; and, in the case of the sermon, to a parallel improvisation upon the text of scripture. Mimicry as Hurston defines it could also encompass her contention that, like the preacher's taking of his text, certain "visions" accompanying conversion in black religion had become virtually formulaic. "I knew them by heart as did the rest of the congregation," she recalled of the visions attested to in her father's church. "Some [converts] would forget a part and improvise clumsily or fill up the gap with shouting. The audience knew, but everybody acted as if every word of it was new." Too, mimicry was integral to the folk arts Hurston recorded: the trickster and Master-John tales of *Mules and Men*, which thrived on signifying combat with the white man, were built by the cyclic tale telling of the "lying" sessions that were the foundation of Hurston's collecting and her own writing. All these elements of mimicry bear on the composition of *Jonah's Gourd Vine* and Hurston's insertion into the novel of the Lovelace sermon, elevating the novel, like the sermon, into the grandest "lying" and further eroding the distinction between fiction and folklore. Indeed, the force of mimicry, in both its aesthetic and ideological contours, appears nowhere more emphatically than in the very fact of Hurston's professional status, straddling the borderline between anthropology and literature.

In both "Spirituals and Neo-Spirituals" and her later essay "The Sanctified Church," Hurston was quick to satirize white singing, prayer, and preaching as dull and predictable, lacking in spontaneity and imagination: A white sermon, she derisively said, was more likely to be a "lecture," just the sort of flat ethnological exhibit she hoped to avoid in her own writing. Notably, that is what the congregation charges against John Pearson's competitor, the Reverend Cozy, who is brought in to unseat John—to cut down "dis Jonah's gourd vine," as they interpret the scripture—after many in the community blame John for Lucy's death, condemning his infidelity and his quick marriage to Hattie. Cozy mistakes his audience, but more than that, Hurston suggests, he mistakes his calling when he competes against John. "Ahm a race man! Ah solves the race problem," Cozy exclaims, and his sermon proceeds to indulge in revisionist statements about black history and black theology. A full five minutes into Cozy's nationalist sermon, one sister whispers to another, "Ah ain't heard what de tex' wuz." Hurston's own cynicism about Race Men no doubt enters into her portrait of Cozy. "The Race Leader is a fiction that is good only at the political trough," she would write in *Dust Tracks on the Road,* and she had already satirized Marcus Garvey in the late 1920s. But more to the point, Cozy's "lecture" lacks the very essence of the sermonic performance. Because his "handlin' de Alphabets" does not spring from scripture, he fails his audience, who demand the formulaic act of the minister heard by John early in his apprenticeship: "Ah takes mah tex' and Ah takes mah time. . . . Ah takes mah tex' 'tween de lids of de Bible. . . . Long ez Ah gives yuh de word uh Gawd, 'tain't none uh yo' business whar Ah gits it from." John Pearson is able to destroy Cozy with a mere rendition of "Dry Bones," his own best sermon but also a highly conventionalized one in the sermonic literature.

The preacher's ritualized act of "taking his text" provides a starting point for his performance—a highly structured moment giving way to a flowing, undulating song-story that, like a controlled improvisation, follows expected chord changes and an identifiable melody but rearranges both. Hurston, it may be said, does much the same thing with the Lovelace sermon, though the question arises: is it Lovelace or Hurston whose sermon we read? and what does her act of appropriation, her mimicry, signify? Hurston's role in the sermon has to be pronounced. Although she drew it more or less directly from her field notes, according to Robert Hemenway, it is Hurston who set the sermon in verse, marking Lovelace's straining, choosing orthographic signals of his dialect, and, quite possibly, modifying his altiloquent diction. The Lovelace sermon, in the Cunard anthology, is pointedly labeled "as heard by Zora Neale Hurston," which, as Robert Stepto has noted, should alert us both to the homage paid to Lovelace's voice and to the likelihood that the sermon was not exactly "recorded" but probably rephrased by its skilled, inventive listener. (In addition, although the sermon is not short compared with those issued on race records, neither is it long by sermonic standards—or by the later recorded standard, for example, of the popular contemporary black preacher C. L. Franklin—and it is therefore probable that Hurston condensed as well as rephrased Lovelace's words.) The transition from prose to verse is at once the moment Lovelace goes "natural," as Hurston puts it, and the moment she herself enters into the creation of the sermon, joining her own authorial voice to his. In that conjunction lies a series of complicated mimetic negotiations that epitomize Hurston's part in the creation and sustenance of African-American cultural expression.

One of Hurston's first articles, an interview with Cudjo Lewis, the only remaining survivor of the last ship to carry African slaves directly to the United States in 1859, was substantially plagiarized from a published book of sketches about the old South. One could suggest that what Hurston discovered in the course of writing *Mules and Men* was how to plagiarize professionally and ethically, so to speak, by utilizing what she called the "spyglass of Anthropology." What is remarkable about *Mules and Men*, however, is the degree of Hurston's personal immersion in the culture she studies; the effectiveness of her collecting lay in her willingness and ability to enter the folk culture of the South, to rely on her own verbal skills and on memory for her record, and finally to participate personally in the tale-telling art she was collecting, to the point of rewriting the context and even the language in which tales were told to give them more clarity and drama. Hurston was clearly capable of careful, painstaking ethnology. Her essays "Conversion" and "Shouting" in the Cunard anthology, for example, resemble case studies to the point of near parody. But it was the liminal terrain between the analytic and the poetic that most engaged Hurston's sympathies, as it was the act of translating from the oral to the written, from black folk culture to the largely white commercial and professional world of her career, that most deserves our attention as an act of mimicry. Just as Lovelace (or John Pearson) "takes his text" from scripture before setting off on an improvised flight that molds the bible to his own inventive use, Hurston "takes her text" from the folkloric record before gathering it into the compass of her personal narrative in *Mules and Men*, or appropriating it to the voice of a fictional character in *Jonah's Gourd Vine*, or in the grandest such gesture of incorporation rewriting the biblical delivery of the Israelites as allegorical black history in *Moses, Man of the Mountain* (1939). Cheryl Wall has convincingly argued that Hurston's use of the "Behold de Rib!" sermon in *Mules and Men*—a sermon that makes woman the equal of man ("God Amighty, he took de bone out of [Adam's] side / So dat places de woman beside us")—represents her own acquisition of a professional storytelling voice. Just so, Hurston's mimicry—her recapitulation of black folklore in the modulation of printed form—stands on the razor-thin line between revelation and preservation, performance and concealment, extending the "lying" of the folk into the domain of white commerce, which, as both her notoriously manipulative patronage by Mrs. Osgood Mason and even her mentoring by Boas taught her, had the ring of neoslavery. In both *Mules and Men* and *Jonah's Gourd Vine*, Hurston provides a glossary of terms and intrudes authorially to explain dialect expressions; but because she does not do so methodically or consistently, such ethnological devices, like her adoption of dialectical figures in her narrative voice, tend to reinforce as much as to lessen the uninformed reader's exclusion from the transcribed world of vernacular. In speaking the dialect of folk culture, she elevated it above ethnological curiosity even as she limited its inherent mutability and freedom; she made it into represented art but left untranscribed its most vital intonations.

Hurston's authorial dualism, to put it another way, reproduces a dualism inherent in African-American expression as it evolved out of slave culture. "The white man is always trying to know into somebody else's business," she writes in *Mules and Men*, paraphrasing the theory of masking that underlines those cultural gestures and folktales intended for a white audience. "All right, I'll set something outside the door of my mind for him to play with and handle. He can read my writing but he sho' can't read my mind." In black arts and language, mimicry includes the parodic signifying on the master's culture and his language, and to that extent it assumes a position of political subordination to the dominant culture. By the same token, however, mimicry folds its object back into itself, recomposing it on its own terms and making it new—as, for instance, Charlie Parker recomposed standard popular tunes in the repertoire of jazz, creating black culture by turning mundane white materials into genius.

As my remarks on dialect have already suggested, the ground of mimicry lies in combined revelation and secrecy, the "indirection" common to theories of slave acculturation and the rise of black dialect. Because of its constant and various pressure of protection, resistance, and dissembling, slave language—the act of talking, the trope of the tongue, borne directly into work and worship songs—came to be riddled with ambiguities and defined by silence or indirection. According to Herskovits and more recent commentators, the principles of subterfuge and concealment that could be found to operate in the language of any oppressed group were strengthened in the case of black America because "indirection" was such a strong part of the language and social etiquette brought by Africans to the New World, where it was transferred, for example, into the animal or Master-John folktales, in which circumlocution and indirection are of paramount importance and constitute the allegorical substructure of the tales themselves. Sustained by a tension between violation and preservation, the "lying" sessions of the folk that Hurston placed at the heart of black communal history, when the stories of the ancestors, in slavery or in Africa, were reiterated and adorned with the verbal pyrotechnics of black talk, made dialect a reservoir of semantic resistance and cultural freedom.

The Eatonville lying sessions, which are re-created in *Mules and Men* and *Their Eyes Were Watching God*, Hurston fondly recalled in *Dust Tracks on the Road* as occasions to hear the storytellers "straining against each other in telling folks tales." Certainly not all the tales are coded with the dynamics of slavery or racial subordination, but many are, and both the alteration of the master's language into the pleasure of tall tales and the construction of allegories of subversion and rebellion employed the survival tactic of verbal economy and indirection, elevating the capacity to carry on secret communication within a disciplinary regime into an expression of culture itself. "Straining," moreover, asks us to think of the lie of the folktale in relation to the straining sounds of the work song and the sermon—the conversion of language into the sheer exertion of sound in those instances acting as a trope of striving under the economic and spiritual burden of racial subordination. Black language might itself be said to be marked by "straining," coded in an alternative sound and diction that, like the motifs of the folktales, can be printed as dialect but cannot be adequately represented by such indices. The very sign of such "straining," dialect therefore cannot be limited to orthography and syntax but includes figuration, rhythm, intonation, indirection, and silence—all the features that might constitute the art of African-American vernacular.

In his divorce trial, John Pearson refuses to testify against the infidelities of Hattie because he does not want whites to hear more about the supposed immorality of blacks: "Dey knows too much 'bout us as it is, but dey some things dey ain't tuh know." The white world, in fact, has a minimal role in the book. At the same time, of course, Hurston's translation of the autobiographical details of her parents' lives, her incorporation of black tales and folklore, and her reproduction of the Lovelace sermon required negotiating the color line between cultural worlds, telling and withholding in the same gesture. Just as she inevitably gave credence to popular folktales of the preacher's sexual prowess and privileged infidelities in the story of John Pearson, she also magnified his power as a community leader and his eloquence as a folk composer. And just as his "wounds of Jesus" sermon is a hypocritical rationalization of his own immorality, it is also an index of the very transfusion into his person of the "hammers of creation"—the artistry and labor of black America dramatized in his ritual theatrical telling of his people's history. Playing the oratorical drum of John Pearson's voice and C. C. Lovelace's sermon, Hurston held African-American vernacular art at a critical point of balance between preservation and erosion, between the transcribed and the unrecordable. She rewrote the foundational arts of slave culture in a modern idiom but left the reader—the white reader in particular, but perhaps the black as well—with an admonition: "He can read my writing but he sho' can't read my mind."

◆◆◆◆◆◆◆◆◆◆◆◆◆◆

The Emergent Voice: The Word within Its Texts

KARLA HOLLOWAY

> When the writer follows languages which are really spoken, no longer for the sake of picturesqueness, but as essential objects which fully account for the whole content of society, writing takes as the locus of its reflexes the real speech of men. Literature no longer implies pride or escape, it begins to become a lucid act of giving information.
>
> —Roland Barthes, *Writing Degree Zero*[1]

In order to perceive the nature of voice as it emerges through text in Hurston's words, the reader can be instructed by an examination of voice in the four novels. The largest body of her work, the novels, offer a revealing insight. My interpretation suggests that the novels are texts related by a lyrical narrative voice that gains enough strength through its practice and through its involvement in the texts to finally "speak itself" into literary being.

This chapter's discussion may be helpful in illustrating the linkage of voices in Hurston's four novels. Each title reveals that the texts are in a state of creation through their structural relationship to a spirit. *Jonah's Gourd Vine* is a literary allusion to God as a maker and destroyer. "One act of malice," Hurston wrote, and the creative act is "withered and gone." *Their Eyes Were Watching God*, her second novel, forces us into an acknowledgment of that power she signaled in *Jonah*, and the symbolic soul's mirror (eyes) are focused on God—an act that the reader must repeat to discover this book. *Moses, Man of the Mountain* unambiguously propels our vision again, this time upward to a mountain where God resides, and this time the journey is not only spiritual, but Moses is "of" the mountain. The identity implicit in this prepositional structure clearly illustrates that we must physically claim the image to meet the text's challenge. *Seraph on the Suwanee*'s angelic title places someone among the elect. Because we are sure (although Hurston may not have been) by the novel's end that it is not Arvay Henson Meserve, the potential remains open to accept the omniscience such sacred company offers and share in its decision that Arvay does not deserve poetic self-awareness. Instead of embedding these texts into sociocultural critical methodology, which has been accomplished for Hurston's texts amply and well, I have looked for semiological significance in her novels, taking the cue from Ellison who warned us to "consult the text."[2]

In sociocultural criticism information from outside the text is applied to textual structures, often without careful regard to the text itself.

Hurston, in writing three novels about black communities and then one about whites, confounded most of the critics who had developed critical structures that worked only when placed onto the black worlds in her first three novels. The result has been that *Seraph* has been examined very little, and, when studied at all, as an aberration.

Semiology and structuralism are related to the degree that they each compel construction metaphors, building linguistic patterns that reveal man's need to build dependent paradigms when visualizing philosophical concepts.[3] Viewing the significance of the sign as linguistic "act," and, therefore, symbol, and viewing the structures of thought and behavior that pattern those acts as visions are perspectives that extend from the recent schools of Euro-American criticism (Barthes, Lacan, Levi-Strauss, Scholes). This theory organizes a structure of word, act and symbol that acknowledges an ancient view of language. British critic Owen Barfield writes of 'langue' when it was close in nature and degree to 'parole'—when the distance between the speaker and speaker's meanings was not unfathomable, when "poetic, and *apparently* 'metaphorical' values were latent in meaning from the beginning." He writes of myth as an "older, undivided 'meaning' from which poetically disconnected ideas have sprung."[4] Barfield has come closest to defining for these Euro-American schools of criticism what I discuss in this book as *nommo*—the creative potential of the word. My point in highlighting Barfield's perspective here is that, in the face of critical methodology that takes us back to text, Barfield takes the Euro-American critic back to an even more primary source—the word. For Hurston, this source is cultural property as the ancient and complex act of "signifying."[5] The black text that signifies takes its impetus from this linguistic activity and internalizes the process until it speaks to itself. This is the perspective under which I feel Hurston's texts deserve scrutiny because she not only shared the signifying participant-structures with her community, but she worked to enclose those structures into her texts. Because of her acknowledgment of the creative structures in her cultural words, we must look to her texts for the networks that inform them.

Hurston's activation of the word *nommo* to represent the mythology of her culture was probably more a natural act than a self-conscious manipulation of linguistic structures. Hurston's literary talent is unassailable, but what provoked that talent was more closely connected to her belonging to a black community than to her literary inventiveness. It seems to me that in Hurston's texts, structure is what defines theme, and voice is what patterns act. This acquiescence to the primary of the word is acknowledgment of *oracy*—the significant codicil to any definition of black words and black linguistic artful acts. The word, as discussed in this book and other black criticism, has an important connection to the natural world. But the critical inquiry that necessarily accompanies those discussions of black literature and language is that which looks to the nature of black words themselves—a view that is inclusive of the physical world, the spiritual universe and the creative power in the alignment of the two. That is why the black word creates; and as it is discussed as the language of the community the imagery of nature and the symbol of the spirit, we must remember that it is all of these things as well as each of them. I propose a look at Hurston's texts as examples of the word complete as complement to the criticism that explores the novels as the collocation of symbols and events that construct their wholes.

I have noted that *Jonah's Gourd Vine* is a novel that foreshadows its own tragedy through its title. Whose gourd vine? John Pearson, as a mulatto, may not be a man who is "tragically colored" in this novel, but he is doomed through his association with that vine and its empty fruit. The novel gathers its massive strength not from its story, nor from the characters, but from the magical words that cause a congregation to enfold its wayward preacher in its compassion and force him back to a pulpit he has threatened to leave. Hurston had determined in this novel that neither the characters nor the events have power equal to the word. In a pastiche that links this preacher's prayer with James Weldon Johnson's "Listen Lord,"[6] John Pearson finds "a prayin' ground," a place for his words: "O Lawd, heah 'tis once mo and again yo' weak and humble servant is knee-bent and body-bowed—Mah heart beneath mah knees and mah knees in some lonesome valley."[7] In this brief prayer, John fulfills the signal of the novel's title. He draws inward toward salvation; but outside of his soul, his spiritual impotence bears his destruction. He pleads for mercy and that the "ranges uh mah deceitful mind" be plucked out before it condemns him. Self-fulfilling, the novel and the character John structure their own outcome. It is possible, certainly, to reference the African images of his spirituality, and it is valuable to recognize his connection to spiritual men in Africa—but the text itself also pleads for a recognition of its intrinsic structure, one that feeds on its own signs and is transformed by its own linguistic activity.

John is a paradox—saint and sinner. This schism is the underlying conflict of the text, and, from its revelation, calls for the destruction of those involved. The prayers uttered by John Pearson should, by rights, be prayers for others—it is for his congregation that his words are meant. His role, ancient or contemporary, is to give life to the community by the enlivening of their spirits. But John is a contradiction and voice takes on its own power to deflate the effects of his physical impotence. His inability to call for the reconciliation of body and soul means that he will eventually lose control of his prayers' power (the word activated), and the spirit he calls on for salvation will destroy him, as it did that gourd vine, in order to extricate itself from this human strayed too far from the creative, nurturing word. The novel builds its own explosive potential through the series of sermons and prayers that climb to a fever pitch, with John's dishonest manipulation of the word at the center of his destruction. He preaches a sermon wittingly structured to move the congregation to forgive him his sins. But John's petition is wrongfully directed and though the church "surged up, a weeping wave about him" and forgives his transgressions, he is struck with a more serious malady—losing the power of the word he has abused. Hurston pictures him feeling as if he were asleep, losing the power that had been in his voice, saying "nothing . . . his words . . . very few" and his spirit calling through him for the power to flee, "oh for the wings, the wings of a dove."[8] The structure of the text, built on words invested with power wrongfully separated from their human conduits, demands that if this flight is realized, it will split the body from the spirit—a sacrifice exacted to assure that the word is no longer threatened by the dishonest preacher. So John loses his life, frees his spirit and its voice to the air.

Hurston leaves this voice airborne and then brings it back as a wind in *Their Eyes Were Watching God*. Here, all the mighty fury of the word unleashed turns the soul inward and forces an acknowledgment of its strength. Hurston leads us, in a novel complicated in ways that make it nearly impossible to leave this text, to her powerful word. "The winds came back," she wrote, "with a triple fury," in a section where the allusion to the voice of God in the whirlwind is clear. The supporting structures of text that dissemble in the fury of this voice are what make it a book that talks to itself.

Hurston develops her character Janie to the point that she is an assertive, self-fulfilled woman. Weaving her maturity through the natural imagery of the pear tree, through a fertile farmland with Logan Killicks where her spirit is spoiled, and into a town grown out of wilderness tamed, Hurston's word destroys sexual and natural fertility. Her word sweeps through with the force of a hurricane destroying all the structures so carefully framed from the opening pages of the novel. Hurston's text has warned the reader from these same early pages of its potential for destruction, teasing itself with the "ships at a distance" puzzle that sets the narrative tone. This often-quoted paragraph (perhaps so much so because its ambiguity invites a variety of critical comment) is a linguistic trope, a tease. It is language used to tell on, to signify upon, itself. It warns the reader through such signification that here is a text that talks its own structures into existence. I think it is less important to try to discover what Hurston's opening paragraphs mean than it is to point out that these paragraphs signal a text with an internal force that will gather strength through its manipulations of language. Gates's observation of the importance of this text's structure clarifies its importance:

> Hurston . . . has made *Their Eyes Were Watching God* into a paradigmatic signifying text, for this novel resolves that implicit tension between the literal and the figurative contained in standard English usages of the term "signi-

fying." *Their Eyes* represents the black trope of signifying both as thematic
matter and as a rhetorical strategy of the novel itself.[9]

I would take Gates' point further and assert that *Eyes* represents a vocal
structure that is something more basic than "strategy." He observes that
Janie, the protagonist, "gains her voice, as it were, in her husband's
store not only by engaging with the assembled men in the ritual of signifying . . . but also by openly signifying upon her husband's impotency."
I support this statement with an amendation important to my thesis
of voice: Jane gains her voice from the available voice of the text and
subsequently learns to share it with the narrator, as I will demonstrate
in the chapters that follow. This is a vital extension of Gates's discussion
of *Eyes*. I must credit the voice gained to the structure itself. Certainly
the traditions of signifying belong to a black community, but Hurston
has made them belong to a literary text in ways that empower them to
take on their own life forms. This is a tradition of voice let loose in *Jonah*
and re-merged to the literary text in *Eyes*. I think it is the same voice
because Hurston uses it as character—investing it with active power.
Sometimes her "word" is a teasing ambiguity; other times, it is an inno-
cent bystander. But lest we fail to take it seriously, it returns in a whirlwind to exact its due on the very world it had created in the beginning.
We know this is so because in the final pages of the novel, which are
really the opening pages because this novel is a flashback (another show
of power by the recursive word), Janie talks to her friend Pheoby, telling
her what she must tell those who criticize what she has done with her
life. "Then you must *tell* [emphasis added] them," Janie says, and if we
have attended to that power of the word to speak itself into being, we
know that Janie too has learned that through telling her spirit will rest
fulfilled. "Love is lak de sea," she tells Pheoby, while the narrative voice
finishes the image that opened the novel and speaks of Jamie pulling "in
her horizon like a great fish-net" and calling her soul "to come and see."
The images of water and air collapse in these final pages; the wind turns
peaceable and waits for its next embodiment.

Having exacted their earthly due in Hurston's first two novels, her
words go on to establish a direct link with god and his magicians, like
Moses and angels on the Suwannee. The word as allegory is the basis of
Moses, Man of the Mountain, and were I to use a more ancient and
intimate term, then I would "tell" that the allegory is Hoodoo. Most
important, *Moses* begins as an oral text, but since the word has developed just about all the strength it can through oracy, it does not end
this way. In this book, characters talk about language, speculating, for
example, that Moses is trying to use some "psychology" by talking the
way they talk.

Characters use language as a means of gaining power as they learn
the spells and incantations that will invest them with the wizardry of

Damballah. But Moses learns his strongest words from the *Book of Thoth*, recommended to him by a palace stableman who taught him the language of animals. This is an important juncture for Hurston's oral texts. Here we know she has acknowledged that within the word's creative potential is the birthing of the literary text, for within the mythology of the *Book of Thoth* is the story of the gift of writing to humankind. The oral word has embraced the written at this juncture, and Hurston's textual explorations of the word face *completio.*

Moses learns from this book the enchantments and secrets of the natural world. Although his teacher Jethro taught him how to free the Israelites, Moses' more important lessons come from that ancient book that facilitates his surpassing the knowledge and abilities of his teacher. To assure that the reader does not miss the power invested in Moses, the novel talks (signifies) to itself in a long passage that repeats the "crossing over" phrase enough to make it litany, chant and incantation:

> Moses had crossed over. He was not in Egypt. He had crossed over and now he was not an Egyptian. He had crossed over. The short sword at his thigh had a jewelled hilt but he had crossed over and so it was no longer the sign of birth and power. He had crossed over, so he sat down on a rock. . . . He had crossed over so he was not of the house of Pharoah. He did not own a palace because he had crossed over. He did not have an Ethiopian princess for a wife. He had crossed over. He did not have enemies to strain against his strength and power. He had crossed over. He was subject to no law. . . . He had crossed over. The sun who was his friend and ancestor in Egypt was arrogant and bitter in Asia. He had crossed over. He felt as empty as a post hole for he was none of the things he once had been. He was a man sitting on a rock. He had crossed over.[10]

Viewed from outside the text, this passage contains all the references and relationships to black sociohistorical experience that are apparent in the patterning of the religious call-and-response, the parody on passing/crossing over[11] and the literary implication of his having been granted, like the convert in that gospel song, a "new life." Within the text, this recursion serves a different function. Highlighted through this repetition of words is the flight of the text after itself, a building of cyclic power like a gyre, tightening and winding its coils into a massive energy and circulating this power into the rock Moses sits on that is an image of the mountain he is to claim. It is a structure at the pinnacle of the semiological relationship between the signifier and that which is signified upon, because, in the coiling, the distinction between the two is lost. The text signifies, speaks to itself and the recursive loops focus back onto the linguistic acts that created the actors. Hurston begins that lengthy passage by telling that Moses' place was not in Egypt. She closes it by telling that he had found his place, and symbolically the place for his word—on a rock. The ground of Egypt, his figurative and literal motherland, became the ground of his being through the text's own incantation in a story about the power of magic words, written and spoken.

Hurston's last published novel, *Seraph on the Suwanee*, is a somber story. Its words are encumbered by clashes of class and gender, and its text is weighted by psychological portaiture. This is a novel that exposes. Its word "reveals" and "tells on" a woman's repression and submission and a family's dissolution. Although Arvay's search for love is "knowing and doing," she has no real idea how to go about this. These words signify her need for spiritual rather than physical activation to replace the emotional lethargy that disables her. I think the appropriate focus in this novel is on the words "knowing and doing" because they embody the elements of Hurston's most powerful linguistic structures. In addition to being a novel of self-actualization, a novel about white people and a novel of contradictory impotence, this is also a novel about direction. The words of its text are tightly controlled and they are quite different from the lyrical modes of Hurston's earlier narration. These are words that refuse to share or alternate perspectives between character, narrator and reader. They are not sheltering words because these white people come to represent distance from the soul rather than nearness to it. Evidence of this evolution into a restricting and exacting word is clear if we admit that Hurston lost control of this text. Although she probably wanted to write a story in which Arvay would assume angelic potential, the text eventually directs itself. Despite or in spite of Hurston's philosophical "stance" on the issues of her story, it became relatively unimportant in the face of a subject who was fatefully destined to lose ownership of the word. I think it entirely possible that Hurston did believe that Arvay Henson Meserve was angelic. She tried to portray her this way when she wrote: "Who shall ascend into the hill of the Lord? And who shall stand in His holy place? Arvay *thought* [emphasis added] that it would be herself,"[12] but it is clear that she never quite reaches this potential and that she remains a servant to the words that craft her. Throughout the text Arvay struggles to *do* and *be* in ways that won't cause her spirit to come back at her, exposing her guilt and causing her pain. But Hurston keeps after Arvay, burdening her with guilt and a deformed child and a husband whose name implies servitude rather than solace. I don't think that Hurston really liked Arvay or that she felt this character could be saved through a discovery of her self. The text reminds us that Arvay "departed from herself" and that time spent with her husband only "appeared" to be like time in Paradise. The seraphim that finally "hovers" over Jim Meserve at the end of the novel is a poor substitute for the potential of that celestial metaphor.

This book, whether it was Hurston's intention or not, works out a theme of inadequacy seeking itself and finding itself, remained earthbound with a distorted vision of Paradise. Contrast, for example, the imagery of *Eyes* where pictures of love and light are vibrant and activated with the acquisition of the human spirit of Janie. In this text, the light and the word are one and they rejoice in her spirit. Thus powerfully invested, Janie "calls" her soul to share her epiphany. But spiritually poor Arvay was still outer-directed and therefore in conflict with a word that pleaded for her internalization. Unlike the assertive Janie, Arvay does what "the big light tells her." Here is no participant-structure. Here is the dominating word, invigorating itself through its directive power and at the same time telling its fate to make modern metaphors that illustrate nothing so much as man's distance from the creative word. Hurston ends this text with the note that Arvay "met the look of the sun with confidence," announcing, in image if not in fact, that she was ready to serve from her distance, but not to own her soul. She is no Janie Starks, and, although Hurston might have intended for her to be, her whiteness, which translates for me as a lack of ownership of language and idea, makes such soulful epiphany impossible. If Hurston was unaware of this as she began the novel, the cautious, controlling word assured that this would be the literary result. The words shift away from the characters of her black universes because her characters are of a world where neither community nor "place" has value. They cannot carry the imagery of her black texts because they are different sorts of vessels. Hurston, in acknowledging the versatility of the word, submits control of her artistry to this restructured text that speaks to itself in a language that manipulates its characters. The rich, complex imagery of the earlier "speaker texts" from which *Seraph* has evolved fits the complexities of those texts' characters. They shuttle between the physical and spiritual worlds in search of themselves. In *Seraph*, Arvay has no world to access but her mother's house (that she later burns) and the swampy outreaches of the home her husband prepared for her. What, then, is the appropriate response of text to such sterility? Probably exactly the wasteland we find in *Seraph*. Hurston has not written a white text, nor has she written a black one in "whiteface," a notion Howard supports in her comment that "Hurston never leaves the folk milieu in *Seraph on the Suwanee*. She does change the color of her characters but she does not change her themes or environment in any significant way."[13]

What has Hurston done in this text? I would argue that she has changed both color and imagery in ways that shout to her readers. The environments are no longer insular, nurturing and fertile. They are deathlike images of dead values, lost ambition and thwarted goals. Her themes have always been various, and rather than looking at the black novels for a shared theme that grows out of their blackness, and lament this one novel because it cannot fit the black aesthetics of the earlier texts, I would suggest we look at these novels for structures that assert themselves as Hurston's craft enables the word to carry the image whatever its color or potential.

It is valuable and important to understand that each of Hurston's novels is related to the degree that they evidence textual structures that speak of themselves. Such a perspective both clarifies and signals the potential of the textual word as it is specifically endowed through texts that are linked by their craftiness and separated in their crafting.

Notes

1. Roland Barthes, *Writing Degree Zero* (1953; reprint, Boston: Beacon Press, 1970), p. 80.
2. Ralph Ellison, "The World and the Jug," in *Shadow and Act* (New York: Vintage Books, 1964), p. 140.
3. Roland Barthes writes of the potential for any graphic representation of signification as a "somewhat clumsy" operation that nonetheless is "necessary" for semiological discourse. He then illustrates the attempts of Saussure, Hjelmslev and Lacan to render graphically the relationship between signifer and signified. See Barthes, *Elements of Semiology* (1964; reprint, Boston: Beacon Press, 1970), pp. 48–49.
4. Barfield's most persuasive discussion on this issue is his text *Poetic Diction* (1928; reprint, Middletown, Conn.: Wesleyan University Press, 1973), especially the chapters "Meaning and Myth" and "The Making of Meaning (I) and (II)." Other references to the nature of meaning are found in his text, *Speaker's Meaning* (Middletown, Conn.: Wesleyan University Press, 1967) and his chapter "The Texture of Medieval Thought" in *Saving the Appearances: A Study in Idolatry* (New York: Harcourt, Brace and World, 1957).
5. I am indebted to Henry Louis Gates's wonderful essay "The Blackness of Blackness: A Critique of the Sign and Signifying Monkey" in *Black Literature and Literary Theory* (New York: Methuen, 1984) for framing my thinking on this issue.
6. Walter C. Daniel, *Images of the Preacher in Afro-American Literature* (Washington, D.C.: University Press of America, 1980). Daniel notes the similarity between James Weldon Johnson's "Listen Lord, A Prayer" and Pearson's prayer in this novel.
7. Zora Neale Hurston, *Jonah's Gourd Vine* (1934; reprint, Philadelphia: J. B. Lippincott, 1971), pp. 50, 51.
8. Ibid., pp. 267, 268.
9. Gates, p. 290.
10. Zola Neale Hurston, *Moses, Man of the Mountain* (1939; reprint, Urbana: University of Illinois Press, 1984), pp. 103, 104.
11. Hemenway (*Zora Neale Hurston: A Literary Biography* [Urbana: University of Illinois Press, 1977], pp. 269–270) and Lillie Howard (*Zora Neal Hurston* [Boston: Twayne Publishers, 1980], pp. 121-122) both spend time discussing this passage. Hemenway's interpretive thrust is directed toward the "pun" on crossing over as "passing"—being a man transformed, spiritually and physically. Howard cites Hemenway's long passage and notes its thematic similarity to James Weldon Johnson's *Autobiography of an Ex-Coloured Man.*
12. Zora Neal Hurston, *Seraph on the Suwanee* (New York: Charles Scribner's Sons, 1948), p. 68.
13. Howard, *Zora Neale Hurston*, p. 134.

◆◆◆◆◆◆◆◆◆◆◆◆◆◆

Zora Neale Hurston: Changing Her Own Words

CHERYL A. WALL

The developing tradition of black women's writing nurtured now in the prose and poetry of such writers as Toni Morrison and Alice Walker began with the work of Zora Neale Hurston. Hurston was not the first Afro-American woman to publish a novel, but she was the first to create language and imagery that reflected the reality of black women's lives. Ignoring the stereotypes, social and literary, that her predecessors spent their energies rejecting, Hurston rooted her art in the cultural traditions of the black rural South. As a daughter of the region, she claimed these traditions by birthright. As an anthropologist, she reclaimed them through years of intense, often perilous, research. As a novelist, she summoned this legacy in her choice of setting, her delineation of character, and most devotedly in her distillation of language. Hers became the first authentic black female voice in American literature.

Despite this achievement, Hurston's work suffered years of obscurity and critical neglect. Ten years ago, outside of that small group of readers and scholars whose primary devotion is to Afro-American literature, few had even heard her name. Still fewer were able to read her work, as it had been out of print since long before her death in 1960. Today Hurston's work has been revived, her reputation restored. She is now considered one of the major writers to have emerged from the Harlem Renaissance. Moreover, hers is the pre-eminent achievement in Afro-American letters during the 1930s; five of her seven books were published in that decade. Two of these, the folklore collection, *Mules and Men* (1935), and the novel, *Their Eyes Were Watching God* (1937), are now recognized classics in the Afro-American canon. The novel is becoming a favorite in American literature and women's studies courses as well. Although very much of its time, *Their Eyes Were Watching God* is timeless. As Sherley Anne Williams has written, its heroine's "individual quest for fulfillment becomes any woman's tale."[1] Other scholars and critics have begun to analyze Hurston's fiction in numerous articles and essays. The fascinating but hitherto fragmented story of her life has been reconstructed in a meticulously researched biography. Although her work is not nearly as well known as it deserves to be, more people have read it in the last few years than in Hurston's lifetime. For general readers and scholars alike, Zora Neale Hurston has emerged as a writer who must be taken seriously.

The black consciousness and feminist movements spurred the rediscovery and reassessment of Hurston's work. Under this impetus, her work began to be reprinted in the 1960s; it garnered little attention initially, overlooked in the flood of books by black writers suddenly returned to print. More of her books became available in the 1970s, often republished with introductions by leading black scholars and critics. By this time, feminists were retrieving works by "lost" women writers, a category for which Hurston was eminently qualified. Hurston's strong, resilient female characters won further favor; the first anthology of her prose, edited by Alice Walker, carried the imprint of the Feminist Press. Walker, whose championing of Hurston has been unselfish and unstinting, surely spoke for others when she wrote, "I became aware of my need of Zora Neale Hurston some time before I knew her work existed."[2] Walker explained that she found in Hurston a conviction of "racial health"; Hurston's characters were invaluable because of their ability to accept and love themselves.

The critical perspectives inspired by the black consciousness and feminist movements allow us to see Hurston's writings in a new way. They correct distorted views of her folklore as charming and quaint, set aside misperceptions of her characters as ministrels caught, in Richard Wright's phrase, "between laughter and tears."[3] These new perspectives inform this re-evaluation of Hurston's work. She asserted that black people, while living in a racist society that denied their humanity, had created an alternative culture that validated their worth as human beings. Although that culture was in some respects sexist, black women, like black men, attained personal identity not by transcending the culture but by embracing it.

Hurston's respect for the cultural traditions of black people is the most important constant in her career. This respect threads through her entire oeuvre, linking the local-color short fiction of her youth, her ethnographic research in the rural South and the Caribbean (an account of her fieldwork in Jamaica and Haiti, *Tell My Horse*, was published in 1938), her novels, and the essays she contributed to popular journals in her later years. In all, she published more than fifty short stories and articles in addition to her book-length works. Because her focus was on black cultural traditions, she rarely explored interracial themes. The black/white conflict, which loomed paramount in the fiction of her black contemporaries, in Wright's novels especially, hardly surfaced in Hurston's. Poet and critic June Jordan has described how the absence of explicitly political protest caused Hurston's work to be devalued. Affirmation, not protest, is Hurston's hallmark. Yet, as Jordan argues, "affirmation of black values and lifestyle within the American context is, indeed, an act of protest."[4] Hurston appreciated and approved the reluctance of blacks to reveal "that which the soul lives by" to the hostile and uncomprehending gaze of outsiders. But the interior reality was what she wished to probe. In that reality, blacks ceased to be "tongueless, earless, eyeless conveniences" whose labor whites exploited; they ceased to be mules and were men and women.

The survival of the spirit was proclaimed first and foremost through language. As a writer, Hurston was keenly sensitive to the richness of black verbal expression. Like Langston Hughes and Sterling Brown, she had no patience with theories of linguistic deficiency among blacks; she ignored racist assumptions that rural blacks spoke as they did because they were too stupid to learn standard English. Hurston, whose father was a Baptist preacher, was well acquainted with the tradition of verbal elegance among black people. From her father's example, she perceived how verbal agility conferred status within the community. His sermons had demonstrated as well the power of his language to convey the complexity of the lives of his parishioners. Early in her career, Hurston attempted to delineate "characteristics of Negro expression." She stressed the heightened sense of drama revealed in the preference for action words and the "will to adorn" reflected in the profusion of metaphor and simile, and in the use of double descriptives *(low-down)* and verbal nouns *(funeralize)*. To her, the "will to adorn" bespoke a feeling "that there can never be enough of beauty, let alone too much." Zora Hurston shared that feeling, as the beautifully poetic prose of her novels attests. The collective folk expression was the soil that nourished the individual expression of her novels. After a lengthy dialogue with her homefolk, Hurston was prepared to change some words of her own.[5]

In one of her first published articles, Hurston declared:

> BUT I AM NOT tragically colored. There is no great sorrow dammed up in my soul, nor lurking behind my eyes. I do not mind at all. I do not belong to the sobbing school of Negrohood who hold that nature somehow has given them a lowdown dirty deal and whose feelings are all hurt about it. . . . No, I do not weep at the world—I am too busy sharpening my oyster knife.[6]

The exuberant tone of the assertions in "How It Feels to Be Colored Me" suggests that they were more strongly felt than reasoned. Hurston locates the source of her feelings in her childhood experiences in Eatonville, Florida, the hometown to which she often returned in fiction and fact. Eatonville was an all-black town, the first to be incorporated in the United States. Hurston remembered it as a place of possibility and promise. She revered the wit and wisdom of the townspeople, admired the originality of their culture and their moral and aesthetic values, saw in their language drama and the "will to adorn." Having been insulated from racism in her early years, unaware of racial distinctions until she was nine, she professed herself "astonished" rather than angered by discrimination. The lingering astonishment accounts perhaps for the shortcomings of the article as self and racial definition; Hurston relied on "exotic primitive" myths popular in the twenties to round out the explanation of herself and her people.

During this time Hurston was studying anthropology at Barnard under the tutelage of Franz Boas. This study complemented by her fieldwork in Florida and Louisiana allowed her to appreciate her past intellectually as well as intuitively. No longer were her homefolk simply good storytellers, whose values were commendable, superstitions remarkable, and humor penetrating. As such, they had been well suited for local-color fiction of the kind Hurston published in the 1920s. Now however, "they became a part of cultural anthropology; scientific objects who could and should be studied for their academic value."[7] The cultural relativity of anthropology freed Hurston from the need to defend her subjects' alleged inferiority. She could discard behavioral explanations drawn from racial mythology. Eatonville blacks were neither exotic nor primitive; they had simply selected different characteristics from what Ruth Benedict, another pioneering anthropologist trained by Boas, called the "great arc of human potentialities."

In possession of these liberating theories, Hurston set forth in 1927 on the first of a series of field expeditions. Not surprisingly her first stop was Eatonville, a site she confidently expected to yield a rich lode of material. When the results of her fieldwork were published in *Mules and Men*, she introduced the book by stating, "I was glad when somebody told me, 'you may go and collected Negro folk-lore.'"[8] Her attitude was not typical of a professional anthropologist and neither was her method. She immersed herself in the culture she studied. Sitting on the porch of Joe Clarke's store in Eatonville, later signing on at sawmill camps and apprenticing herself to hoodoo doctors, she became a member of each community she entered. Clearly her race and personal heritage gave her an entrée previous researchers lacked. Beyond that, Hurston felt herself part and parcel of the culture she investigated. The diligence and skill with which she pursued her studies enabled her to capitalize on these advantages.

Mules and Men holds the distinction of being the first collection of Afro-American folklore published by an Afro-American. It distinguishes itself in other ways. Alan Lomax called it "the most engaging, genuine, and skillfully written book in the field of folklore."[9] Unlike many of its predecessors, it presents the lore not to patronize or demean but to affirm and celebrate. Written for a popular audience, it is highly readable; after nearly half a century, it has lost none of its capacity to delight. *Mules and Men* contains seventy folktales, but it is more than a transcription of individual texts. As her biographer Robert Hemenway points out, Hurston adds an unifying narrative that provides contexts as well as texts. By showing when a story is told, how, and to what purpose, Hurston attempts to restore the original meanings of the tales. Folktales, she understood, serve a function more significant than mere entertainment; "they are profound expressions of a group's behavior."[10] They cannot be comprehended without reference to those whose values and beliefs they embody. Consequently, the tales in *Mules and Men* are not collected from faceless informants, but from real men and women whose lives readers are briefly invited to share. Sharing their lives more profoundly, Hurston was ultimately forced to confront the role of women in rural black life. Her response, necessarily personal and engaged, gave shape to her most successful fiction.

Hurston met the woman who most informed this response soon after she arrived in Polk County, Florida, in January 1928. The sawmill camp where Hurston settled was an even richer repository of the folktales, worksongs, blues and cries, proverbs and sermons than Eatonville had been. And of the people who lived there, Big Sweet was the most memorable. Hurston devoted several pages of her autobiography, *Dust Tracks on a Road* (1942), to her friendship with this woman; the influence of Big Sweet is highly visible in characters in Hurston's novels. Although Hurston gives few details about her appearance, the woman's name, with its suggestions of physical power and sexual attractiveness, of strength and tenderness, aptly sums up her character. Significantly, Hurston hears her before she sees her, and it is her talk that attracts her attention. Big Sweet is "specifying," "playing the dozens" with an outmatched male opponent. Before a large and appreciative audience, she breaks the news to him "in one of her mildest bulletins that his pa was a double-humpted camel and his ma a grass-gut cow." This performance gives Hurston "a measure of this Big Sweet," and her judgment is soon verified by the opinions of others on the job. Though fearsome, Big Sweet is not feared as much as she is respected, because the community draws a distinction between meanness and the defense of one's integrity. Hurston sees the wisdom of acquiring her friendship and hence protection. Big Sweet becomes the author's guardian and guide. She identifies informants, awards prizes in "lying" contests, and eventually saves Hurston's life.[11]

In his article, "Negotiating Respect: Patterns of Presentation among Black Women," folklorist Roger Abrahams notes: "how women assert their image and values as women is seldom found in the folklore literature."[12] In keeping with this premise, Big Sweet contributes only two folktales to *Mules and Men;* neither focuses on female identity. The relative scarcity of woman-centered tales in the oral tradition must have been one of the revelations of Hurston's fieldwork. Although tales created by men about women, many of them virulently antifemale, exist in some quantity, tales about women told from a female point of view are rare.[13] Hurston's narrative strategy permits her to sustain a female perspective in her account of Big Sweet. Her presentation of the context as well as the text of the lore is crucial in this regard. In the general narrative of her experiences in Polk County and in her descriptions of the specific situations in which stories are told, Hurston shows how Big Sweet asserts and maintains her identity. From these descriptions, the reader can take her own measure of this woman.

The dramatic performance of Big Sweet's "specifying" is not recounted in *Mules and Men;* her entrance here is low-keyed. She tells her two tales, "Why the Mocking Bird Is Away on Friday" and "How the 'Gator Got Black," matter-of-factly, but the second is preceded by an exchange that reveals a bit of her mettle. Someone else has recited "How Brer 'Gator Got His Tongue Worn Out" which has reminded Big Sweet of the similar tale she knows. Thus the reader sees one way the lore is transmitted. Before she gets a chance to begin her story, however, Big Sweet is interrupted and must reclaim her place in the discussion. "When Ah'm shellin' my corn, you keep out yo' nubbins" wins her readmission and the tale is told. A bit later, as the others joke and lie good-naturedly, Big Sweet injects a personal and pointed warning to her lover not to repeat his infidelity of the night before. He appeals to the other men for assistance, but they cannot beat her "specifying." Her declaration of independence cuts right to the heart of the matter: "Lemme tell *you* something, *any* time Ah shack up wid any man Ah gives myself de privilege to go wherever he might be, night or day. Ah got de law in my mouth."[14]

Big Sweet's behavior conforms to a pattern Abrahams outlines. Respect in the black community is not a permanent given; it must constantly be earned and negotiated. For women, these negotiations usually occur, as in the scenes described above, when people are "just talking." No one, whatever her reputation, is beyond challenge. "Ideally a woman has the ability to *talk sweet* with her infants and peers but *talk smart* or *cold* with anyone who might threaten her self-image."[15] Big Sweet exemplifies this ideal. She uses "Little-Bit" as a term of endearment for the narrator Zora in *Mules and Men,* warns her that collecting songs from one of the men has provoked his lover's jealousy, and promises to defend her. A conversation between her and Hurston quoted in *Dust Tracks* further evidences her ability to "talk sweet." Not understanding why Hurston wants to collect "lies" (folktales), she pledges to aid her in doing so. Such conversations are held privately; the public smart talking she does earns Big Sweet respect. A crucial incident recounted in *Mules and Men* pits Big Sweet against her arch rival, Ella Wall, a woman whose feats are also chronicled by Leadbelly and other country blues singers. Ella Wall enters the camp "jook" (a combination dance hall, gaming parlor and bawdy house) and sends a bold message to Big Sweet's man. The two women exchange verbal insults and then physical threats, until the conflict is halted by the arrival of the white quarters boss. While Ella Wall is disarmed and thrown off the job, Big Sweets stands up to the white man and refuses to yield her weapon. Her erstwhile lover expresses the admiration of the group in a telling compliment: "You wuz noble! You wuz uh whole woman and half uh man."[16] Big Sweet's increased respect is not earned at the cost of her femininity. Her value as a woman is in fact enhanced by her fierce conduct. After the argument, her lover proudly escorts her home.

Zora Hurston knew that approval of Big Sweet was not shared by the world outside the lumber camp. The life of this hard-living, knife-toting woman was the stuff of myriad stereotypes. And Hurston seemed all too aware of this judgment when she wrote, "I thought of all I had to live for and turned cold at the thought of dying in a violent manner in a sordid sawmill camp." A dramatic revelation follows: "But for my very life I knew I couldn't leave Big Sweet if the fight came. She had been too faithful to me."[17] Hurston vows to stand by her friend. Passages such as this have caused some critics to accuse Hurston of being condescending and self-serving in her presentation of the poor. She does seem to be playing to her audience here; *sordid* voices their opinion of the camp and its people. It does not express Hurston's view. Her problem was to legitimize Big Sweet's conduct without defending it or positing sociological explanations for it. Her solution was to identify the sources of its legitimacy within the folk culture itself. Characteristically, her approach was subtle and easily overlooked by the casual reader; it was deliberate nonetheless. Just before the fight scene, Hurston described the visit of a traveling preacher to the camp. His sermon, "Behold de Rib," is a variant of the creation myth; its text is Genesis 2:21, its subject is female equality.

"Behold de Rib" is one of the book's highlights. It captures the pithy logic of folk wisdom, the rhythmic cadence and vivid imagery of the downhome preacher, and a good measure of folk humor. The preacher begins by defining his terms: he instructs his congregants, "Behold means to look and see," and invites them to "look at dis woman God done made." Before focusing on woman, however, he pauses to consider God's previous handiwork and envisions the acts of creation. A cluster of visual images along with the repetition of the phrase "I can see" unify this section of the sermon/poem, as the preacher bears witness to what can be seen through the "eye of Faith." God emerges as regent and warrior, striding through space, wearing the elements as a helmet, blowing storms through his lips. To make a place for the world, he seizes "de mighty axe of his proving power" and opens a gash in "stubborn-standing space." To light the heavens, ". . . God shook his head/And a thousand million diamonds/Flew out from his glittering crown/And studded de evening sky and made de stars."

This last is a familiar trope in black preaching and brings to mind James Weldon Johnson's poem, "The Creation." One notes that both speakers have an anthropomorphic conception of God, but in "The Creation" He is "lonely"; in his most stirring analogy the speaker compares

Him to a "mammy" bending over her baby. A masculine, even martial, God presides over the world of sexual equality. Johnson's speaker ends his story before getting to what is the central event of "Behold de Rib." Here stars are lit especially to shine on sleeping man and emerging woman:

> So God put Adam into a deep sleep
> And took out a bone, ah hah!
> And it is said that it was a rib.
> Behold de rib!
> A bone out of a man's side.
> He put de man to sleep and made wo-man,
> And men and women been sleeping together ever since.
> Behold de rib!
> Brothers, if God
> Had taken dat bone out of man's head
> He would have meant for woman to rule, hah
> If he had taken a bone out of his foot,
> He would have meant for us to dominize and rule.
> He could have made her out of back-bone
> And then she would have been behind us.
> But, no, God Almighty, he took de bone out of his side
> So dat places de woman beside us;
> Hah! God knowed his own mind.
> Behold de rib!

The preacher has modulated to a comic key, deepening the humor by alluding to that most famous of folk sermons, "Dry Bones." Still, his message is a serious one, as is apparent in the conclusion when he calls on his listeners, male and female, to march to glory side by side "in step wid de host dat John saw."[18]

Its rhythm and imagery place "Behold de Rib" squarely in the tradition of black preaching, but its message is anomalous. Female equality was not, is not, a common subject in black sermons. Hurston had transcribed other sermons in her field notes, including the one that became the centerpiece of her first novel, *Jonah's Gourd Vine*. Her selection of "Behold de Rib" was deliberate and so was its placement in *Mules and Men*. It prepares the reader to accept and approve Big Sweet's actions in the conflict that follows. She is heroic, as any man who similarly defended his honor would be. Although Hurston draws no connection between the sermon and the struggle—here and throughout the book her method is presentational, not analytical—the reader's approbation of Big Sweet is won in part by the juxtaposition of the two scenes.

The portrayal of Big Sweet anticipates the process of self-discovery Hurston's fictional heroines undergo. Like her, they must learn to manipulate language. The novels disclose Hurston's awareness that women, like children, are encouraged to be seen but not heard. She knew that few women had joined the lying sessions on Joe Clark's store porch in Eatonville; Big Sweet was one of a small number of female storytellers in the folklore collection. It was Big Sweet's talk though that first captured Hurston's attention. Her words were emblematic of her power, for they signaled her ownership of self. The ability to back up words with actions was a second indicator of an independent self. The care Hurston took to legitimize Big Sweet's behavior intimated the expected reactions to an assertive woman. Nevertheless, Hurston believed that individual black women could base their personal autonomy on communal traditions. In so doing, her characters achieved their status as heroines.

Lucy Potts Pearson is such a character. Although her husband John is its main protagonist, *Jonah's Gourd Vine* traces Lucy's coming of age as well as his. Loosely based on the lives of Hurston's parents, *Jonah's Gourd Vine* tells the story of Lucy and John's courtship and marriage, John's swift rise to prominence as a Baptist preacher, his equally swift fall resulting from his marital infidelities, Lucy's strength and perseverance, and the family's ultimate dissolution. All this takes place against a background of social and technological change occurring in the South around the turn of the century. These changes are subordinate to the cultural traditions that remain intact: the sermons and sayings, children's games and rhymes, hoodoo beliefs and practices. In the foreground are the experiences of John and Lucy. Lucy dies two thirds of the way through the novel, but her spirit hovers above it until the end.

That talk, and especially women's talk, is a major concern of the book is established on the very first page. Ned Crittenden accuses his wife, John's mother, of "always talkin' more'n yuh know."[19] Amy Crittenden is undaunted, "Ah changes jes ez many words ez Ah durn please!", but her ability to act on her words is limited. An ex-slave whose eldest son John is the child of her former master, Amy has been "freed" to a marriage with a ne'er-do-well sharecropper. Abused by a husband who is unable to "treasure" his children as she does, Amy must watch him hire John out to a white man, the equivalent of selling him into slavery. Amy's resistance is covert: she encourages her son to escape his stepfather's tyranny by seeking work on the plantation owned by his unacknowledged white father. John's return to the town of his birth adheres to the pattern of the young man arriving from the provinces. Every new thing, from shoes to trains, is a source of fascination. But the greatest fascination is with words. The verbal play of the plantation's children, the ribald ditties of youths, and the prayers and sermons of the elders spark John's imagination. To win Lucy's love, he must learn to speak for himself. Both lovers search for words that can express mutual affection and respect.

Their effort is complicated by class distinctions within the community. John is an "over-the-creek nigger" with no prospects. Lucy's father is a land-owner, and her mother has arranged for her to marry a well-to-do farmer when she is of age. John has no education. Lucy is the star pupil in her school, famed for the long recitations she commits to memory. Though attracted to Lucy from the first, John finds her difficult to approach:

> When the opportunity presented itself he couldn't find words. Handling Big 'Oman, Lacey, Semmie, Bootsie and Mehaley merely called for action, but with Lucy he needed words and words that he did not have.

Recognizing that Lucy will not be swayed by the charms that capture other girls' affection, John yearns to master her language. Lucy assures him that he can learn recitations better than she, and he enrolls in school. Neither realizes that the needed words cannot be found in textbooks. They can only be learned from a deeper engagement with the folk culture. John achieves this when he spends a time in a work camp, where "next to showing muscle-power, [he] loved to tell stories." Upon his return, he is prepared to court Lucy in the traditional style. This time she is the one who must master a new tongue.

Robert Hemenway has identified the folkloric origins of the courtship ritual John employs.[20] Organized around the riddle—"are you a flying lark or a setting dove?"—the ritual allows the questioner to ascertain a woman's availability and willingness to pursue romance. A problem arises in the novel because the woman-child Lucy (she is only fourteen) does not know how to respond to the question. She had begun the conversation gaily, coyly matching wits with John. But as John broached more substantive concerns, "Lucy suddenly lost her fluency of speech." John presses this point thus:

> "Lucy, you pay much 'tention tuh birds?"
> "Unhunh. De Jay bird say 'Laz'ness will kill you,' and he go to hell ev'ry Friday and totes uh grain uh sand in his mouf tuh put out de fire, and den de doves say, "Where you *been* so long?""
> John cut her short. "Ah don't mean dat way, Lucy. Whut Ah wants tuh know is, which would you ruther be, if you had yo' ruthers—uh lark uh flyin', uh uh dove uh settin'?'
> "Ah don't know whut you talkin' 'bout, John. It mus'be uh new riddle."
> "Naw 'tain't, Lucy. Po' me, Lucy. Ahm uh one wingded bird. Don't leave me lak dat, Lucy."

Far from new, the riddle is ancient and is meant to elicit a formulaic response. If Lucy wants to encourage John's advances, she should identify herself as a flying lark. Her ignorance of the proper answer imperils the future of the relationship. Lucy is resourceful enough to sift through her memory for plausible replies. She does not hit upon the correct one, but she does keep the conversation going. Her references to the jaybird, for example, demonstrates her awareness that the answer is to be found in folk traditions. The reference is to a familiar folktale, a variant of which, interestingly, is recounted by Big Sweet in *Mules and Men*. Here it is beside the point, as John's quick rejoinder makes clear. He poses the riddle directly. Lucy's continued inability to respond calls forth a plaintive cry: "Po' me, Lucy. Ahm uh one wingded bird."

Although her book learning is commendable, Lucy is clearly not sufficiently conversant with the rituals of her own culture. This suggests an immaturity and lack of experience that would render her an unsuitable wife. The situation is saved only when Lucy helps John improvise a new ritual that can substitute for the old. The instrument is a handkerchief out of which John has crafted what Hurston calls "a love knot." The lovers hold opposite ends of it throughout the conversation, and when Lucy misses the riddle, she points John's attention to the knot. Regaining her ground, she asks John to state what is on his mind. Wary, he asks first for a kiss ("Kiss me and loose me so Ah kin talk.") The kiss unlocks the poetic power that characterizes John's speech for the rest of the novel:

> "Lucy, Ah looked up intuh Heben and Ah seen you among de angels right 'round de throne, and when Ah seen *you*, mah heart swole up and put wings on mah shoulders, and Ah 'gin tuh fly 'round too, but Ah never would uh knowed yo' name if ole Gab'ull hadn't uh whispered it tuh me."

Lucy has reconferred John's wings. Though not as thoroughly grounded in the folk culture as he, she is knowledgeable enough to induce him to state his proposal in terms they *both* can understand. When he does, she accepts.[21] Their acting out of the courtship ritual predicts a marriage between two active partners, both of whom are able to manipulate langauge and negotiate respect between themselves and with others. It does not, however, foretell a marriage between equals. The prerogatives of maleness ultimately undo the balance.

Although he continues to profess and feel love and respect for Lucy, John Pearson does not remain faithful to her. His philandering, which begins shortly after the marriage and continues until her death, not only causes her great emotional pain but frequently jeopardizes the well-being of the entire family. He struggles against his weakness, expresses remorse when he fails, yet lacks all insight into his behavior. A serious flaw in the novel is Hurston's failure to provide a compelling motivation for John's conduct. A reader may infer that John's irresponsibility is, at least in part, a legacy of slavery. The plantation owner's initial reaction to John is, "What a fine stud." He projects all of his sexual fantasies on to John, labelling him at one point "a walking orgasm. A living exultation." John's sexual misadventures never cease to enthrall this man, who aids him in escaping rather than standing up to their consequences. In a period of transition between slavery and freedom, John remains bound by the slaveholder's conception of black men.

Lucy is, by contrast, a new black woman. Whenever John is irresponsible, Lucy is prepared to compensate. What he lacks in ambition and initiative, she is more than able to supply. She had defied her family to marry him and remains steadfast in her love and loyalty. She even looks with compassion on John's struggle to conquer the "brute beast" within, a struggle that intensifies after he is called to the ministry. John's spiritual call is genuine, but his acceptance of it also permits him to design a self-image independent of the white world. His move to Eatonville has further encouraged this possibility. There he can assume his rightful role as leader, his talents can be given free rein. The canker that galls is his recognition that Lucy deserves much of the credit for his success.

John's fellows are not blind to this fact, and they enjoy baiting him with the knowledge: "Aw, 'tain't you, Pearson, . . . iss dat li'l' handful uh woman you got on de place." His resentment of his dependence on Lucy grows and expresses itself in his demand for her total dependence on him. A comparison of the following passage with the courtship ritual discussed above measures the damage the marriage suffers.

> "Lucy, is you sorry you married me instid uh some big nigger wid uh whole heap uh money and titles hung on tuh him?"
> "Whut make you ast me dat? If you tired uh me, jus' leave me. Another man over de fence waiting fuh yo' job."

John's reaction to Lucy's verbal play is a violent threat; he will kill her if she ever repeats that fanciful remark. He stakes out claims of ownership, vowing to be Lucy's first and last man. Calming himself, he asks why Lucy has said such a thing. Her response is telling: "Aw, John, you know dat's jus' uh by-word. Ah hears all de women say dat." Lucy is answering John in terms sanctioned by the folk culture, terms that allow for her autonomy. She is engaging in the same kind of verbal sparring the courtship ritual required. The "by-word" would permit Lucy to negotiate respect in this exchange too, but John is no longer concerned with Lucy's ability to participate in cultural traditions. He concedes that the expression is a common one, but forbids her to use it.

Lucy continues to be supportive of John's career. Through her maneuvering, John becomes pastor of a large church, moderator of the State Baptist Association, and mayor of Eatonville. He can never accept her assistance as a complement to his gifts. He accuses: "You always tryin' tuh tell me whut tuh do. Ah wouldn't be where Ah is, if Ah didn't know more'n you think Ah do. You ain't mah guardzeen nohow." John's real defense against what he perceives to be Lucy's domination is other women. Of course, she cannot retaliate in kind. Words are her only defense, righteous, chastising words that strike fear in John's heart but fail to make him change his ways.

The climactic exchange takes one back to the opening pages of the novel. In his home, though not outside it, John has come to resemble Ned Crittenden, telling his wife to shut her mouth. Like Amy, Lucy refuses to be silenced. Instead she reproaches John severely and claims rights for herself and her children. "Big talk, she tells him, 'ain't changin' whut you doin'. You can't clean yo' self wid yo' tongue lak uh cat." For the first time in their marriage, John strikes his wife. This action, Hurston later suggested, prompted the novel's title. Taken from Jonah 4:6–10, the title refers to the gourd vine which grew profusely and gave the prophet shade. The next morning a worm attacked the vine and it withered. Thus did God punish his disobedient servant. To Hurston the Biblical story represented: "Great and sudden growth. One act of malice and it is withered and gone."[22] Slapping Lucy marks the beginning of the end for John; his public fortunes decline, and his private life falls into disarray. Years later he has no understanding of what has happened to him. It is literally the end for Lucy, who dies of an illness soon after. Unlike John, however, she has learned something from her experiences, a lesson she passes on to her favorite daughter. "Don't you love nobody better'n you do yo'self. Do, you'll be dying befo' yo' time is out."

Though Lucy's insight is personal, she has expressed it in the manner of a folk proverb. Throughout the novel, her speech is aphoristic. Sayings like the still current "God sho' don't like ugly" and the less familiar, more ingenious "God don't eat okra" (in other words, He doesn't like crooked, slick ways) roll easily off Lucy's tongue. She has mastered the language and absorbed much of the wisdom of her culture. In the end, she apprehends some of its limitations. She hears the silence where the sayings affirming female identity should be. She espies the untaught knowledge that no one can live through someone else and begins to teach it. Without her realizing it, the folk culture through her husband had assigned Lucy Pearson a "place"; she warns her daughter to be on guard against such a fate. Loving John too much, she has acquiesced in her own suppression. At her death, she remains on the threshold of self-discovery.

Although Lucy is the character who is given insight, the novel is less hers than John's. He becomes the central character because he serves the author's purposes beyond the demands of the plot. A contemporary reviewer rightly called *Jonah's Gourd Vine* a "talkfest," and a recent critic describes it as "a series of linguistic moments." Both discern that language is Hurston's priority. Published before *Mules and Men* though written afterward, the novel was Hurston's first opportunity to share at length the discoveries of her fieldwork. She incorporated so much of her research that one reviewer objected to her characters being mere pegs on which she hung their dialect and folkways.[23] The objection is grossly overstated, but it does highlight a problem in the book. Too often the folklore overwhelms the formal narrative. The novel is enriched nonetheless by its numerous examples of the Negro's "will to adorn," many of the expressions coming directly from Hurston's notes. She believed resolutely that blacks aspired for and achieved beauty in their verbal expression. With extraordinary care, she sought to reproduce their speech exactly as it was spoken. Given these concerns, John Pearson's was necessarily the key role. As preacher, hence poet, he represented the verbal artistry of his people at its height. He became, in the words of critic Larry Neal, "the intelligence of the community, the bearer of its traditions and highest possibilities."[24] This profound engagement with his culture causes John's struggle to reconcile his physical and spiritual selves to take precedence over Lucy's effort to claim her autonomy. In Hurston's second and most compelling novel, the female quest is paramount. The heroine, through acquiring an intimate knowledge of the folk culture, gains the self-knowledge necessary for true fulfillment.

With the publication of *Their Eyes Were Watching God*, it was clear that Zora Neale Hurston was an artist in full command of her talent. Here the folk material complements rather than overwhelms the narrative. The sustained beauty of Hurston's prose owes much to the body of folk expression she had recorded and studied, but much more to the maturity of her individual voice. The language of this novel *sings*. Unlike Lucy, Janie, the heroine of *Their Eyes*, is a fully realized character. During the twenty-odd years spanned by the plot, she grows from a diffident teenager to a woman in complete possession of her self. Two recurring metaphors, the pear tree and the horizon, help unify the narrative. The first symbolizes organic union with another, the second, the individual experiences one must acquire to achieve selfhood. Early reviewers thought of the novel as a love story, but recent commentators designate Janie's search for identity as the novel's major theme. Following the pattern we have observed, Janie's self-discovery depends on her learning to manipulate language. Her success is announced in the novel's prologue when, as a friend listens in rapt attention, Janie begins to tell her own story.

The action of the novel proper begins when Janie is sixteen, beautiful, and eager to struggle with life, but unable to articulate her wishes and dreams. Her consciousness awakens as she watches bees fertilizing the blossoms of a pear tree. In the following passage, the narrative voice is not Janie's but the scene, like the novel as a whole, expresses her point of view:

> She was stretched on her back beneath the pear tree soaking in the alto chant of the visiting bees, the gold of the sun and the planting breath of the breeze when the inaudible voice of it all came to her. She saw a dust-bearing bee sink into the sanctum of a bloom; the thousand sister-calyxes arch to meet the love embrace and the ecstatic shiver of the tree from root to tiniest branch creaming in every blossom and frothing with delight. So this was a marriage! She had felt a pain remorseless sweet that left her limp and languid.[25]

The lyricism of the passage mutes somewhat its intensely sexual imagery. Still, the image is remarkably explicit for a woman novelist of Hurston's time. Janie's response to the scene and her acceptance of its implications for her own life are instructive: "Oh to be a pear tree—*any* tree in bloom!" Janie acknowledges sexuality as a natural part of life, a major aspect of her identity. Before she has the chance to act on this belief, however, her grandmother interposes a radically different viewpoint.

To Nanny, her granddaughter's nascent sexuality is alarming. Having been unable to protect herself and her daughter from sexual exploitation, Nanny determines to safeguard Janie. Janie must repress her sexuality in order to avoid sexual abuse; the only haven is marriage. Marriage had not been an option for nanny, who as a slave was impregnated by her master; her mistress had forced her to flee with her newborn infant. Her daughter was raped by a black schoolteacher, convincing Nanny that male treachery knows no racial bounds. The world has thwarted her dreams of what a woman should be for herself and her daughter, "Ah wanted to preach a great sermon about colored women sittin' on high, but they wasn't no pulpit for me," but she has saved the text for Janie. She envisions her on the pedestal reserved for southern white women, far above the drudgery that has characterized Nanny's own life—the drudgery that has made the black woman "de mule uh de world." She arranges for Janie to marry Logan Killicks, an old man whose sixty acres and a mule constitute his eligibility. "The vision of Logan Killicks was desecrating the pear tree, but Janie didn't know how to tell Nanny that." So she assents to her grandmother's wish.

Joe Starks offers Janie an escape from her loveless marriage. He arrives just after Logan Killicks, despairing of his efforts to win his wife's affection by "pampering" her, has bought a second mule and ordered Janie to plow alongside him. Perceiving that Killicks's command threatens to reduce her to the status her grandmother abhorred, Janie decides to escape with Joe. Their marriage fulfills Nanny's dreams. Eventually it causes Janie to understand that the old woman's dreams are not her own. Initially though, Joe Starks cuts a fine figure. Stylishly dressed and citified, he is a man of great ambition and drive. He is like no *black* man Janie has ever seen. He reminds her vaguely of successful white men, but she cannot grasp the implications of the resemblance. She can appreciate his big plans and the élan with which he courts her. Tempering her reservations that "he did not represent sun-up and pollen and blooming trees," Janie resolves, "he spoke for far horizon. He spoke for change and chance."

It quickly becomes apparent that, like Nanny, Joe has borrowed his criteria for success from the white world. He takes Janie to Eatonville because there, he believes, he can be a "big ruler of things." His ambition is soon realized. He buys property and opens a store which becomes the town's meeting place. He decrees that roads be dug, a post office established, a street lamp installed, and town incorporation papers drawn. Already landlord, storekeeper, and postmaster, Joe runs for mayor to consolidate his power. After his election, he builds a large white house that is a travesty of a plantation mansion, and then furnishes it in the grand manner right down to brass spittoons. His brashness elicits equal measures of respect and resentment from the townspeople. As much as they admire his accomplishments, they take exception to his manner. One citizen's observation is widely shared: "he loves obedience out of everybody under de sound of his voice."

Everybody naturally includes Janie. Joe assigns her the role of "Mrs. Mayor Starks." She must hold herself apart from the townspeople, conduct herself according to the requirements of his position. Under no circumstances must she speak in public. Starks first imposes this rule during a ceremony marking the opening of the store. The ceremony has occasioned much speechmaking, and toward the end, Janie is invited to say a few words. Before she can respond, her husband takes the floor to announce:

> Thank yuh fuh yo' compliments, but mah wife don't know nothin' 'bout no speech-makin'. Ah never married her for nothin' lak dat. She's uh woman and her place is in de home.

Joe's announcement takes Janie by surprise. Unsure that she even wants to speak, she strongly resents being denied the right to decide for herself. Joe's prohibitions increase. He forbids Janie to participate in the lying sessions held on the store porch; she is hustled inside when they begin. Janie loves these conversations and notes that Joe, while not deigning to join in, stays around to listen and laugh. Being forbidden to speak is a severe penalty in an oral culture. It short-circuits Janie's attempt to claim an identity of her own, robs her of the opportunity to negotiate respect from her peers. Barred from speaking to anyone but Joe, she loses the design to say anything at all. "So gradually, she pressed her teeth together and learned to hush."

After seven years of marriage, Janie recognizes that Joe requires her total submission. She yields. As she does so however, she retains a clear perception of herself and her situation, a perception that becomes her salvation in the end. On one occasion after Joe has slapped her (for naturally, her submission has not slowed his verbal or physical abuse), she experienced the following revelation:

> Janie stood where he left her for unmeasured time and thought. She stood here until something fell off the shelf inside her. Then she went inside to see what it was. It was her image of Jody tumbled down and shattered. But looking at it she saw that it never was the flesh and blood figure of her dreams. Just something she had grabbed up to drape her dreams over. In a way she turned her back upon the image where it lay and looked further. She had no more blossomy openings dusting pollen over her man, neither any glistening young fruit where the petals used to be. She found that she had a host of thoughts she had never expressed to him, and numerous emotions she had never let Jody know about. Things packed up and put away in parts of her heart where he could never find them. She was saving up feelings for some man she had never seen. She had an inside and an outside now and suddenly she knew how not to mix them.

Facing the truth about Joe allows Janie to divorce him emotionally. She accepts her share of responsibility for the failure of the marriage, knowing now that if Joe has used her for his purposes, she has used him for hers. Yet she understands that her dreams have not impinged on Joe's selfhood; they have been naive but not destructive. By creating inside and outside selves, she hopes to insulate the core of her being from the destructive consequences of Joe's dreams. She cannot claim her autonomy, because she is not yet capable of imagining herself except in relationship to a man. Still, she is no longer willing to jeopardize her inner being for the sake of any such relationship.

Janie remains content to practice a kind of passive resistance against Joe's tyranny until he pushes her to the point when she must "talk smart" to salvage her self-respect. For many years, Joe has forced her to clerk in the store, taking every opportunity to ridicule her for minor mistakes. As he grows older, he adds taunts about her age to his repertoire of verbal insults. Sensing that her womanhood as well as her intelligence is under attack, she retaliates: "Humph! Talkin' 'bout *me* lookin' old! When you pull down yo' britches, you look lak de change uh life." So unaccustomed is Joe to hearing his wife "specify" that he imputes nefarious motives to her words. Ill and suspicious, he hires a hoodoo doctor to counteract the curse he believes Janie is putting on him. No curse exists, of course, but Starks is dying of kidney disease and of mortal wounds to his vanity. As he lies on his deathbed, Janie confronts him with more painful truths. Again she reveals how well she comprehends the effect of his domination: "Mah own mind had tuh be squeezed and crowded out tuh make room for yours in me."

The attack on her dying husband is not an act of gratuitous cruelty; it is an essential step toward self-reclamation. Moreover, in terms of the narrative, the deathbed episode posits a dramatic break with Janie's past. She is henceforth a different woman. Independent for the first time in her life, she exults in the "freedom feeling." Reflecting on her past, she realizes that her grandmother, though acting out of love, has wronged her deeply. At base, Nanny's sermon had been about things, when Janie wanted to journey to the horizons in search of people. Janie is able at last to reject her grandmother's way and resume her original quest. That quest culminates in her marriage to Tea Cake Woods with whom she builds a relationship totally unlike the others she has had.

Tea Cake is a troubadour, a traveling bluesman, whose life is dedicated to joyful pursuits. With this character, Hurston explores an alternative definition of manhood, one that does not rely on external manifestations of power, money, and position. Tea Cake has none of these. He is so thoroughly immune to the influence of white American society that he does not even desire them. Tea Cake is at ease being who and what he is. Consequently, he fosters the growth of Janie's self-acceptance. Together they achieve the ideal sought by most characters in Hurston's fiction. They trust emotion over intellect, value the spiritual over the material, preserve a sense of humor and are comfortable with their sensuality. Tea Cake confirms Janie's right to self-expression and invites her to share equally in their adventures. She sees that he "could be a bee to a blossom—a pear tree blossom in the spring." Over the protests of her neighbors, she marries this man several years younger than she whose only worldly expression is a guitar.

They embark on a nomadic existence which takes them to the rich farmland of the Florida Everglades where both Tea Cake and Janie work on the muck and where both share household chores. Their cabin becomes "the unauthorized center of the job," the focal point of the community like the store in Eatonville. Here, however, Janie "could listen and laugh and even talk some herself if she wanted to. She got so she could tell big stories herself from listening to the rest." This is an important and hard-won accomplishment. Even Tea Cake, strongly idealized character though he is, has had difficulty accepting Janie's full participation in their life together. Zora Hurston knew that Tea Cake, a son of the folk culture, would have inherited its negative attitudes toward women. She knew besides that female autonomy cannot be granted by men, it must be demanded by women. Janie gains her autonomy only when she insists upon it. Under pressure, Tea Cake occasionally falls back on the prerogatives of his sex. His one act of physical cruelty results from his need to show someone else who is boss in his home. In the main though, Tea Cake transcends the chauvinistic attitudes of the group. He largely keeps his pledge to Janie that she "partake wid everything."

The marriage of Janie and Tea Cake ends in the wake of a fierce hurricane that is vividly evoked in the novel. In the process of saving Janie's life, Tea Cake is bitten by a rabid dog. Deranged, he tries to kill Janie, and she shoots him in self-defense. Despite these events, the conclusion of *Their Eyes Were Watchin God* is not tragic. For, with Tea Cake as her guide, Jane has explored the soul of her culture and learned how to value herself. This fact is underscored in the prologue and epilogue of the novel, sections set after Janie's return to Eatonville following Tea Cake's death. In the former, she tells her friend Pheoby: "Ah been a delegate to de big 'ssociation of life. Yessuh! De Grand Lodge, de big convention of livin' is just where Ah been dis year and a half y'all ain't seen me." Having been to the horizon and back, as she puts it, she is eager to teach the crucial lesson she has learned in her travels. Everybody must do two things for themselves: "They got tuh go tuh God, and they got tuh find out about livin' fuh theyselves." This is Janie's text; the sermon she preaches is the novel itself. She has claimed the right to change her own words.

Hurston was never to duplicate the triumph of *Their Eyes Were Watching God*. In her subsequent novels, she changed the direction of her work dramatically. *Moses: Man of the Mountain* (1939) is a seriocomic novel which attempts to fuse Biblical narrative and folk myth. *Seraph on the Suwanee* (1948) is a psychological novel whose principal characters are upwardly mobile white Floridians. Although Hurston's willingness to experiment is admirable, the results are disappointing. Neither of her net settings is as compelling as the Eatonville milieu. Though the impact of black folk expression is always discernible, it is diminished and so is the power of Hurston's own voice. In these novels, the question of female autonomy recedes in importance, and when it is posed in *Seraph,* the answer is decidedly reactionary. What is of interest in terms of this essay is Hurston's reworking of themes identified in her earlier work.

Hurston's Moses is a combination of Biblical lawgiver and Afro-American hoodoo man. He is officially a highborn Egyptian, but according to legend, he is a Hebrew; Moses neither wholly rejects nor accepts the legend. The uncertainties about his identity complicate his question for fulfillment. That quest conforms in part to the pattern we have outlined. Moses becomes a great manipulator of language, and much of his authority derives from the power of his words. As an educated man, he has been taught the formal language of the Egyptian elite. He later spends many years with the Midianites in spiritual preparation for his divinely appointed task; this period is somewhat comparable to John Pearson's stay in the work camp and Janie's sojourn on the muck. With the Midianites, Moses adapts to the rhythms of a rural folk culture and learns to speak more colloquial English. The Hebrews speak in the black folk idiom, and when he becomes their leader, Moses masters their tongue. Moses is of course a man of action, and as befits a leader, he fights most often for the rights of those under his stewardship. Though he knows he would be more beloved as a king and more popular as a politician, Moses rejects the accouterments of power. He has as little use for class distinctions as Janie and Tea Cake. In Moses, Hurston developed a character who was already a certified hero, not only in the Judeo-Christian tradition, but according to her introduction, also among the peoples of Asia and Africa. What she adds are new points of emphasis, and these had precedents in her earlier work. The most important is implicit in her attempt to reconcile the Biblical Moses and her conception of Moses as conjurer. Hurston had been the first scholar ever to research hoodoo in America and had studied the more systematic religion of Vodun in Haiti. In both instances, she had noted the coexistence of seemingly antithetical religious beliefs in the lives of her informants. In *Moses: Man of the Mountain,* one looks in vain for a synthesis of the two belief systems to which the hero is heir. Hurston simply allows them to coexist. In a novel whose protagonist seeks and achieves cosmic fulfillment, the failure to explicate the spiritual sources of that fulfillment is serious indeed.

Moses is a very ambitious novel. If it fails in some respects, it succeeds in others. It offers a very effective satire on the transition from slavery to freedom for black Americans. Hurston drew on the long-standing identification of blacks with the enslaved Hebrews, the identification that had inspired the majestic spiritual "Go Down, Moses" and countless other sacred and secular expressions. Most dwelt on the sufferings of bondage and the joys of emancipation. Hurston's concerns were the responsibilities of freedom. In the novel, the people of Goshen are hesitant to rebel against slavery and unable to fully comprehend freedom. Hurston satirizes their ready assent to the commands of their slavemasters and their reluctance to follow Moses. She mocks the vainglory of self-appointed leaders and the failure of the people to understand the need for sacrifice. Their petty bickering and constant backbiting are also objects of her ridicule. Hurston's satirical sallies are invariably good-natured and often very funny. But her novel is not the serious statement about faith and freedom she seems to have intended.

Hurston did not publish another novel for nine years. In the interim, her political instincts grew markedly conservative. World War II and its Cold War aftermath hastened the rightward drift of her thinking. At the suggestion of her publisher, she revised the manuscript of *Dust Tracks on a Road* to eliminate sections critical of the American system; as it was published in 1942, her autobiography seemed a celebration of the American way. Through the decade, Hurston contributed a number of articles to the *American Mercury* and the *Saturday Evening Post* which developed patriotic themes. By the 1950s, her work was welcome in the pages of the *American Legion Magazine*. Not all of Hurston's articles were reactionary. Some applauded the achievements of blacks in various endeavors. Others reaffirmed her belief in the value of black folklore, though she had ceased her research in the field. A few pieces, written for *Negro Digest*, protested racism in diplomacy, publishing, and everyday life. On the whole, however, Hurston's political views, which she expounded more often in the 1940s than at any other time in her life, supported the status quo. The same charge might be leveled at her last work of fiction, *Seraph on the Suwanee.*

This novel restates the major themes of *Their Eyes Were Watching God*, perhaps in a misguided attempt to universalize them. Here the protagonist is Avray Henson Meserve, who like Janie searches for self-identity. She is hindred in her quest by the deep-rooted inferiority she feels about her poor cracker background. For the wrong reason, she has come to the right conclusion. As Hurston depicts her, she is inferior to her husband Jim and the only identity she can attain is through accepting her subordinate role as his wife. Hurston endows Jim Meserve with a mixture of the attractive qualities found in Joe Starks and Tea Cake. He is more crudely chauvinistic than either of them, but this aspect of his character is treated with amazing tolerance. Early in the novel, Arvay reflects that if she married Jim, "her whole duty as a wife was to just love him good, be nice and kind around the house and have children for him. She could do that and be more than happy and satisfied, but it looked too simple."[26] The novel demonstrates that it is much too simple, but at the conclusion the happiness Arvay supposedly realizes is achieved on exactly those terms. The problem is Hurston's inability to grant her protagonist the resources that would permit her to claim autonomy. Although Arvay "mounts the pulpit" at the end of the novel, she has no words of her own to speak.

Ultimately, Arvay's weakness may be less a personal problem than a cultural one. Though black characters play minor roles in the novel, black cultural traditions permeate the narrative. They influence everyone's speech, so much so that at times the whites sound suspiciously like the storytellers in Eatonville. Jim relishes the company of his black employees, whom he treats in a disgustingly condescending manner; and one of his sons, after being tutored by a black neighbor, leaves home to join a jazz band. Unlike the earlier protagonists, Arvay cannot attain her identity through a profound engagement with the folk culture, because she has no culture to engage. The culture of the people Arvay despises has supplanted her own. Seen from this perspective, *Seraph on the Suwanee* is not as anomalous or as reactionary as it otherwise appears.

From any vantage point, however, it represents an artistic decline. Hurston was at her best when she drew her material directly from black folk culture; it was the source of her creative power. Throughout her career, she endeavored to negotiate respect for it, talking smart then sweet in her folklore and fiction, proclaiming its richness and complexity to all who would hear. Her most memorable characters are born of this tradition. In portraying them, she was always cognizant of the difficulties in reconciling the demands of community and the requirements of self, difficulties that were especially intense for women. The tension could not be resolved by rejecting the community or negating the self. Hurston challenged black people to dig deep into their culture to unearth the values on which it was built. Those values could restore the balance. They could give men and women words to speak. They could set their spirits free.

Notes

1. Introduction to *Their Eyes Were Watching God* (Urbana: University of Illinois Press, 1978), p. xiv.
2. *I Love Myself When I Am Laughing . . . and Then Again When I Am*

Looking Mean and Impressive, A Zora Hurston Reader (Old Westbury, N.Y.: The Feminist Press, 1979); the quotation is from Walker's introduction to Robert Hemenway, *Zora Neale Hurston: A Literary Biography* (Urbana: University of Illinois Press, 1977), p. xii.

3. "Between Laughter and Tears," review of *Their Eyes Were Watching God, New Masses* 23 (5 October 1937): 25.

4. June Jordan, "On Richard Wright and Zora Neale Hurston: Notes toward a Balancing of Love and Hatred," *Black World* (August 1974): 5.

5. "Characteristics of Negro Expression," [1934]; in *Voices from the Harlem Renaissance* ed. Nathan Huggins (New York: Oxford University Press, 1976), pp. 224–27. The expression "changing words" appears in several of Hurston's works. I suspect it derives from a form of the word "exchange," in which the weakly stressed syllable has been dropped. J. L. Dillard identifies the dropping of such syllables as a common characteristic of Black English. See *Black English* (New York: Random House, 1972), p. 249.

6. *I Love Myself,* p. 153.

7. Hemenway, *Zora Neale Hurston,* p. 62.

8. *Mules and Men* (1935; reprint ed., Bloomington: Indiana University Press, 1978), p. 3.

9. Quoted in Robert Hemenway, "Are You a Flying Lark or a Setting Dove," *Afro-American Literature: The Reconstruction of Instruction* (New York: Modern Language Association, 1979), p. 132.

10. Hemenway, *Zora Neale Hurston,* p. 168.

11. *Dust Tracks on a Road* (Philadelphia: J. P. Lippincott, 1942; rpt. 1971), pp. 186–91.

12. *Journal of American Folklore* 88 (Jan.–March 1975): 58.

13. Hurston first noted "this scornful attitude towards black women" in "Characteristics of Negro Expression," p. 234. For examples of sexism in folktales, see Daryl C. Dance, *Shuckin' and Jivin': Folklore from Contemporary Black Americans* (Bloomington: Indiana University Press, 1978), pp. 110–42.

14. *Mules and Men,* p. 134.

15. Abrahams, "Negotiating Respect," pp. 58–62.

16. *Mules and Men,* p. 162.

17. *Mules and Men,* p. 160.

18. *Mules and Men,* pp. 148–51.

19. *Jonah's Gourd Vine* (Philadelphia: J. P. Lippincott, 1934; rpt. 1971), p. 9. All further references to this work appear in the text.

20. Hemenway, "Flying Lark or Setting Dove," pp. 134–38.

21. See Hemenway, "Flying Lark or Setting Dove," pp. 139–47, for an extended gloss on this passage. The essay as a whole has influenced my reading of the novel.

22. Hemenway, *Zora Neale Hurston,* p. 192.

23. John Chamberlain, *New York Times,* 3 May 1934, p. 7; Hemenway, *Zora Neale Hurston,* p. 192; Andrew Burris, review of *Jonah's Gourd Vine, Crisis* 41 (1934): 166.

24. Introduction to *Jonah's Gourd Vine,* p. 7.

25. *Their Eyes,* p. 24.

26. *Seraph on the Suwanee* (New York: Scribner's, 1948), p. 33.

◆◆◆◆◆◆◆◆◆◆◆◆◆◆

"I Love the Way Janie Crawford Left Her Husbands":
Emergent Female Hero

MARY HELEN WASHINGTON

In the past few years of teaching Zora Neale Hurston's *Their Eyes Were Watching God*,[1] I have become increasingly disturbed by this text, particularly by two problematic relationships I see in the novel: women's relationship to the community and women's relationship to language. *Their Eyes* has often been described as a novel about a woman in a folk community, but it might be more accurately described as a novel about a woman outside of the folk community. And while feminists have been eager to seize upon this text as an expression of female power, I think it is a novel that represents women's exclusion from power, particularly from the power of oral speech. Most contemporary critics contend that Janie is the articulate voice in the tradition, that the novel celebrates a woman coming to self-discovery and that this self-discovery leads her ultimately to a meaningful participation in black folk traditions.[2] Perhaps. But before bestowing the title of "articulate hero" on Janie, we should look to Hurston's first novel, *Jonah's Gourd Vine*, to its main character, Reverend John Pearson, and to the power that Hurston is able to confer on a male folk hero.[3]

From the beginning of his life, John Pearson's relationship to the community is as assured as Janie's is problematic. Living in a small Alabama town and then in Eatonville, where Janie also migrates, he discovers his preaching voice early and is encouraged to use it. His ability to control and manipulate the folk language is a source of power within the community. Even his relationships with women help him to connect to his community, leading him to literacy and to speech while Janie's relationship with men deprive her of community and of her voice. John's friendship with Hambo, his closest friend, is much more dynamic than Janie and Pheoby's because Hurston makes the male friendship a deeper and more complex one, and because the community acknowledges and comments on the men's friendship. In his Introduction to *Jonah's Gourd Vine*, Larry Neal describes John Pearson's exalted function in the folk community:

> John Pearson, as Zora notes in her letter to [James Weldon] Johnson is a poet. That is to say, one who manipulates words in order to convey to others the mystery of that Unknowable force which we call God. And he is more; he

is the intelligence of the community, the bearer of its traditions and highest possibilities.[4]

One could hardly make such an unequivocal claim for Janie's heroic posture in *Their Eyes*. Singled out for her extraordinary, anglicized beauty, Janie cannot "get but so close to them [the people in Eatonville] in spirit." Her friendship with Pheoby, occurring apart from the community, encapsulates Janie and Pheoby in a private dyad that insulates Janie from the jealousy of other women. Like the other women in the town, she is barred from participation in the culture's oral tradition. When the voice of the black oral tradition is summoned in *Their Eyes*, it is not used to represent the collective black community, but to invoke and valorize the voice of the black *male* community.[5]

As critic Margaret Homans points out, our attentiveness to the possibility that women are excluded categorically from the language of the dominant discourse should help us to be aware of the inadequacy of language, its inability to represent female experience, its tendency not only to silence women but to make women complicitous in that silence.[6] Part of Janie's dilemma in *Their Eyes* is that she is both subject and object—both hero and heroine—and Hurston, apparently could not retrieve her from that paradoxical position except in the frame story, where she is talking to her friend and equal, Pheoby Watson. As object in that text, Janie is often passive when she should be active, deprived of speech when she should be in command of language, made powerless by her three husbands and by Hurston's narrative strategies. I would like to focus on several passages in *Jonah's Gourd Vine* and in *Their Eyes* to show how Janie is trapped in her status as object, as passive female, and to contrast the freedom John Pearson has as subject to aspire to an heroic posture in his community.

In both *Their Eyes* and in *Jonah's Gourd Vine* sexuality is established in the early lives of Janie and John as a symbol of their growing maturity. The symbol of Janie's emerging sexuality is the blossoming pear tree being pollinated by the dust-bearing bee. Early in the text, when Janie is about fifteen, Hurston presents her stretched out on her back beneath a pear tree, observing the activity of the bees:

> She saw a dust-bearing bee sink into the sanctum of a bloom; the thousand sister-calyxes arch to meet the love embrace and the ecstatic shiver of the tree from root to tiniest branch creaming in every blossom and frothing with delight. So this was marriage! She had been summoned to behold a revelation. Then Janie felt a pain remorseless sweet that left her limp and languid.

She leaves this scene of the pear tree looking for "an answer seeking her" and finds that answer in the person of Johnny Taylor who, in her rapturous state, looks like a golden glorious being. Janie's first sexual encounter is observed by her grandmother and she is summarily punished.[7] To introduce such a sexual scene at the age when Janie is about to enter adulthood, to turn it into romantic fantasy, and to make it end in punishment certainly limits the possibility of any growth resulting from that experience.

John's sexual encounters are never observed by any adult and thus he is spared the humiliation and the punishment Janie endures for her adolescent experimentation. In an early scene when he is playing a game called "Hide the Switch" with the girl in the quarters where he works, he is the active pursuer, and, in contrast to Janie's romantic fantasies, John's experience of sexuality is earthy and energetic and confirms his sense of power:

> . . . when he was "it" he managed to catch every girl in the quarters. The other boys were less successful but girls were screaming under John's lash behind the cowpen and under sweet-gum trees around the spring until the moon rose. John never forgot that night. Even the strong odor of their sweaty bodies was lovely to remember. He went in to bed when all of the girls had been called in by their folks. He could have romped till morning.

A recurring symbol Hurston uses to represent John's sexuality is the train, which he sees for the first time after he meets Lucy, the woman destined to become his first wife. A country boy, John is at first terrified by the "panting monster," but he is also mesmerized by this threatening machine whose sides "seemed to expand and contract like a fiery-lunged monster." It looks frightening, but it is also "uh pretty thing" and it has as many destinations as John in his philandering will have. As a symbol of male sexuality, the train suggests power, dynamism, and mobility.[8]

Janie's image of herself as a blossom waiting to be pollinated by a bee transforms her figuratively and literally into the space in which men's action may occur.[9] She waits for an answer and the answer appears in the form of two men, both of whom direct Janie's life and the action of the plot. Janie at least resists her first husband, Logan, but once Jody takes her to Eatonville, he controls her life as well as the narrative. He buys the land, builds the town, makes Janie tie up her hair, and prescribes her relationship with the rest of the town. We know that Hurston means for Janie to free herself from male domination, but Hurston's language, as much as Jody's behavior, signifies Janie's status as an object. Janie's arrival in Eatonville is described through the eyes and speech of the men on the front porch. Jody joins the men, but Janie is seen "through the bedroom window getting settled." Not only are Janie and the other women barred from participation in the ceremonies and rituals of the community, but they become the objects of the sessions on the porch, included in the men's tale-telling as the butt of their jokes, or their flattery, or their scorn. The experience of having one's body become an object to be looked at is considered so demeaning that when it happens to a man, it figuratively transforms him into a woman. When Janie launches her most devastating attack on Jody in front of all the men in the store, she tells him not to talk about her looking old because "When you pull down yo' britches you look lak de change uh life. Since the "change of life" ordinarily refers to a woman's menopause, Janie is signifying that Jody, like a woman, is subject to the humiliation of exposure. Now that he is the object of the gaze, Jody realizes that other men will "look" on him with pity: "Janie had robbed him of his illusion of irresistible maleness that all men cherish."

Eventually Janie does speak, and, interestingly, her first speech, on behalf of women, is a commentary on the limitations of a male-dominated society.

> Sometimes God gits familiar wid us womenfolks too and talks His inside business. He told me how surprised He was 'bout y'all turning out so smart after Him makin' yuh different; and how surprised y'all is goin' tuh be if you ever find out you don't know half as much 'bout us as you think you do.

Speech does not lead Janie to power, however, but to self-division and to further acquiescence in her status as object. As her marriage to Jody deteriorates she begins to observe herself: "one day she sat and watched the shadows of herself going about tending store and prostrating itself before Jody, while all the time she herself sat under a shady tree with the wind blowing through her hair and her clothes."

In contrast to Janie's psychic split in which her imagination asserts itself while her body makes a show of obedience, John Pearson, trapped in a similarly constricting marriage with his second wife, Hattie, experiences not self-division but a kind of self-unification in which the past memories he has repressed seep into his consciousness and drive him to confront his life with Hattie: "Then too his daily self seemed to be wearing thin, and the past seeped thru and mastered him for increasingly longer periods. He whose present had always been so bubbling that it crowded out past and future now found himself with a memory." In this new state John begins to remember and visit old friends. His memories prompt him to confront Hattie and even to deny that he ever married her. Of course his memory is selective and self-serving, and quite devastating to Hattie, but it does drive him to action.

Even after Janie acquires the power of speech which allows her to stand up to Jody, Hurston continues to objectify her so that she does not take action. Immediately after Jody's death she goes to the looking glass where, she tells us, she has told her girl self to wait for her, and there she discovers that a handsome woman has taken her place. She tears off the kerchief Jody has forced her to wear and lets down her plentiful hair: "The weight, the length, the glory was there. She took careful stock of herself, then combed her hair and tied it back up again." In her first moment of independence Janie is not seen as autonomous subject but again as visual object, "seeing herself seeing herself," draping before herself that "hidden mystery" which attracts men and makes her superior to women. Note that when she turns to the mirror, it is not to experience her own sensual pleasure in her hair. She does not tell us how her hair felt to her—did it tingle at the roots? Did she shiver with delight?—no, she takes stock of herself, makes an assessment of herself. What's in the mirror that she cannot experience without it: that imaginary other whom the mirror represents, looking on in judgment, recording, not her own sensations, but the way others see her.

Barbara Johnson's reading of *Their Eyes* suggests that once Janie is able to identify the split between her inside and outside selves, incorporating and articulating her own sense of self-division, she develops an increasing ability to speak.[10] I have come to different conclusions: that Hurston continues to subvert Janie's voice, that in crucial places where we need to hear her speak she is curiously silent, that even when Hurston sets out to explore Janie's internal consciousness, her internal speech, what we actually hear are the voices of men. Once Tea Cake enters the narrative his name and his voice are heard nearly twice as often as Janie's. He walks into Janie's life with a guitar and a grin and tells her, "Honey since you loose me and gimme privelege tuh tell yuh all about mahself. Ah'll tell yuh." And from then on it is Tea Cake's tale, the only reason for Janie's account of her life to Pheoby being to vindicate Tea Cake's name. Insisting on Tea Cake's innocence as well as his central place in her story, Janie tells Pheoby, "Teacake ain't wasted no money of mine, and he ain't left me for no young gal, neither. He give me every consolation in the world. He'd tell 'em so too, if he was here. If he wasn't gone."

As many feminist critics have pointed out, women do get silenced, even in text by women, and there are critical places in *Their Eyes* where Janie's voice needs to be heard and is not, places where we would expect her as the subject of the story to speak. Perhaps the most stunning silence in the text occurs after Tea Cake beats Janie. The beating is seen entirely through the eyes of the male community, while Janie's reaction is never given. Tea Cake becomes the envy of the other men for having a woman whose flesh is so tender that one can see every place she's been hit. Sop-de-Bottom declares in awe, "wouldn't Ah love tuh whip uh tender woman lak Janie!" Janie is silent, so thoroughly repressed in this section that all that remains of her is what Tea Cake and the other men desire.

Passages which are supposed to represent Janie's interior consciousness begin by marking some internal change in Janie, then gradually or abruptly shift so that a male character takes Janie's place as the subject of the discourse; at the conclusion of these passages, ostensibly devoted to the revelation of Janie's interior life, the male voice predominates. Janie's life just before and after Jody's death is a fertile period for such self-reflection, but Hurston does not focus the attention of the text on Janie even in these significant turning points in Janie's life. In the long paragraph that tells us how she has changed in the six months after

Jody's death, we are told that Janie talked and laughed in the store at time and was happy except for the store. To solve the problem of the store she hires Hezikiah "who was the best imitation of Joe that his seventeen years could make." At this point, the paragraph shifts its focus from Janie and her growing sense of independence to Hezikiah and his imitation of Jody, describing Hezikiah in a way that evokes Jody's presence and obliterates Janie. We are told at the end of the paragraph, in tongue-in-cheek humor, that because "managing stores and women store-owners was trying on a man's nerves," Hezikiah "needed to take a drink of liquor now and then to keep up." Thus Janie is not only removed as the subject of this passage but is subsumed under the male-defined category of worrisome women. Even the much-celebrated description of Janie's discovery of her split selves: "She had an inside and an outside now and suddenly she knew how not to mix them" represents her internal life as divided between two men: her outside self exists for Joe and her inside self she is "saving up" for "some man she had never seen."[11]

Critic Robert Stepto was the first to raise the question about Janie's lack of voice in *Their Eyes*. In his critique of Afro-American narrative he claims that Hurston creates only the illusion that Janie has achieved her voice, that Hurston's strategy of having much of Janie's tale told by an omniscient third person rather than by a first person narrator under-cuts the development of Janie's "voice."[12] While I was initially resistant to this criticism of *Their Eyes*, my reading of *Jonah's Gourd Vine* sug-gests that Hurston was indeed ambivalent about giving a powerful voice to a woman like Janie who is already in rebellion against male authority and against the roles prescribed for women in a male dominated society. As Stepto notes, Janie's lack of voice is particularly disturbing in the courtroom scene, which comes at the end of her tale and, presumably, at a point where she has developed her capacity to speak. Hurston tells us that down in the Everglades "She got so she could tell big stories herself," but in the courtroom scene the story of Janie and Tea Cake is told entirely in third person: "She had to go way back to let them know how she and Tea Cake had been with one another." We do not hear Janie speaking in her own voice until we return to the frame where she is speaking to her friend, Pheoby.[13]

There is a similar courtroom scene in *Jonah's Gourd Vine*, and there is also a silence, not an enforced silence, but the silence of a man who deliberately chooses not to speak. John is hauled into court by his second wife, Hattie, on the grounds of adultery. Like the court system in *Their Eyes*, this too is one where "de laws and de cote houses and de jail houses all b'longed tuh white folks" and, as in Janie's situation, the black community is united against John. His former friends take the stand against him, testifying on Hattie's behalf in order to spite John, but John refuses to call any witnesses for his defense. After he has lost the trial, his friend Hambo angrily asks him why he didn't allow him to testify.

John's eloquent answer explains his silence in the courtroom, but more than that, it shows that he has such power over his own voice that he can choose when and where to use it, in this case to defy a hypocritical, racist system and to protect the black community:

> Ah didn't want de white folks tuh hear 'bout nothin' lak dat. Dey knows too much 'bout us as it is, but dey some things dey ain't tuh know. Dey's some strings on our harp fuh us tuh play on an sing all tuh ourselves. Dey thinks wese all ignorant as it is, and dey thinks wese all alike, and dat dey knows us inside and out, but you know better. Dey wouldn't make no great 'miration if you had uh tole 'em Hattie had all dem mens. Dey wouldn't zarn 'tween uh woman lak Hattie and one lak Lucy, uh yo' wife befo' she died. Dey thinks all colored folks is de same dat way.

John's deliberate silence is motivated by his political consciousness. In spite of the community's rejection of him, he is still their defender, especially in the face of common adversary. Hurston does not allow Janie the insight John has, nor the voice, nor the loyalty to her people. To Mrs. Turner's racial insults, Janie is nearly silent, offering only a cold shoulder to show her resistance to the woman's bigotry. In the courtroom scene Janie is divorced from the other blacks and surrounded by a "protecting wall of white women." She is vindicated, and the black community humbled. Janie is the outsider; John is the culture's hero, their "inspired artist," the traditional male hero in possession of traditional male power.

But John's power in the community and his gift for words do not always serve him well. As Robert Hemenway asserts in his critical biography of Hurston, John is "a captive of the community's need for a public giver of words."

> His language does not serve to articulate his personal problems because it is directed away from the self toward the communal celebration. John, the man of words, becomes the victim of his bardic function. He is the epic poet of the community who sacrifices himself for the group vision.[14]

For John, words mean power and status rather than the expression of feeling. When he first discovers the power of his voice, he thinks immediately of how good he sounds and how his voice can be exploited for his benefits:

> Dat sho sound good . . . If mah voice sound *dat* good de first time Ah ever prayed in, de church house, it sho won't be de las'.

John never feels the call to preach until the day on Joe Clarke's porch when the men tease John about being a "wife-made man." One of his buddies tells him that with a wife like Lucy any man could get ahead in life: "Anybody could put hisself on de ladder wid her in de house." The following Sunday in his continuing quest for manhood and power, John turns to preaching. The dramatic quality of his preaching and his showmanship easily make him the most famous preacher and the most powerful man in the area. John's inability to achieve maturity and his sudden death at the moment of his greatest insight suggest a great deal about Hurston's discomfort with the traditional male hero, with the values of the community he represents, with the culture's privileging of orality over inward development. Janie Starks is almost the complete antithesis of John Pearson, "She assumes heroic stature not by externals, but by her own struggle for self-definition, for autonomy, for liberation from the illusions that others have tried to make her live by or that she has submitted to herself."[15]

While Janie's culture honors the oral art, "this picture making with words," Janie's final speech in *Their Eyes* actually casts doubt on the relevance of oral speech:

> Talkin' don't amunt tuh uh hill uh beans when you can't do nothin else . . . Pheoby you got tuh *go* there tuh *know* there. Yo papa and yo' mamma and nobody else can't tell yuh and show yuh. Two things everybody's got tuh do fuh theyselves. They got tuh go tuh God, and they got tuh find out about livin' fuh theyselves.

Janie's final comment that experience is more important than words is an implicit criticism of the culture that celebrates orality to the exclusion of inner growth. The language of men in *Their Eyes* and in *Jonah's Gourd Vine* is almost always divorced from any kind of interiority. The men are rarely shown in the process of growth. Their talking is a game. Janie's life is about the experience of relationships. Logan, Jody, and Tea Cake and John Pearson are essentially static characters, whereas Pheoby and Janie allow experience to change them. John, who seems almost constitutionally unfitted for self-examination, is killed at the end of the novel by a train, that very symbol of male power he has been seduced by all of his life.[16]

Vladimir Propp, in his study of folklore and narrative, cautions us not to think that plots directly reflect a given social order but "rather emerge out of the conflict, the contradictions of different social orders as they succeed or replace one another." What is manifested in the tensions of plots is "the difficult coexistence of different orders of historical reality in the long period of transition from one to the other . . ."[17]

Hurston's plots may very well reflect such a tension in the social order, a period of transition in which the conflictual coexistence of a predominantly male and a more egalitarian culture is inscribed in these two forms of culture heroes. Both novels end in an ambiguous stance: John dies alone, so dominated by the ideals of his community that he is completely unable to understand his spiritual dilemma. And Janie, having returned to the community she once rejected, is left in a position of interiority so total it seems to represent another structure of confinement. Alone in her bedroom she watches pictures of "love and light against the walls," almost as though she is a spectator at a film. She pulls in the horizon and drapes it over her shoulder and calls in her soul to come and see. The language of this section gives us the illusion of growth and development, but the language is deceptive. The horizon represents the outside world—the world of adventure where Janie journeyed in search of people and a value system that would allow her real self to shine. If the horizon is the world of possibility, of journeys, of meeting new people and eschewing materialistic values, then Janie seems to be canceling out any further exploration of that world. In Eatonville she is a landlady with a fat bank account and a scorn for the people that ensures her alienation. Like the heroine of romantic fiction, left without a man she exists in a position of stasis with no suggestion of how she will employ her considerable energies in her now—perhaps temporarily—manless life.

Hurston was obviously comfortable with the role of the traditional male hero in *Jonah's Gourd Vine*, but *Their Eyes* presented Hurston with a problem she could not solve—the questing hero as woman. That Hurston intended Janie to be such a hero—at least on some level—is undeniable. She puts Janie on the track of autonomy, self-realization, and independence. She allows her to put on the outward trappings of male power. Janie dresses in overalls, goes on the muck, learns to shoot—even better than Tea Cake—and her rebellion changes her and potentially her friend Pheoby. If the rightful end of the romantic heroine is marriage, then Hurston has certainly resisted the script of romance by having Janie kill Tea Cake. (Though he exists in death in a far more mythical and exalted way than in life.) As Rachel Blau Du Plessis argues, when the narrative resolves itself in the repression of romance and the reassertion of quest, the result is a narrative that is critical of those patriarchal rules that govern women and deny them a role outside of the boundaries of patriarchy.[18]

While such a critique of patriarchal norms is obvious in *Their Eyes*, we still see Hurston's ambivalence about Janie's role as "hero" as opposed to "heroine."[19] Like all romantic *heroines*, Janie follows the dreams of men. She takes off after Jody because "he spoke for far horizon," and she takes off after Tea Cake's dream of going "on de muck." By the rules of romantic fiction, the *heroine* is extremely feminine in looks. Janie's long, heavy, Caucasianlike hair is mentioned so many times in *Their Eyes* that, as one of my students said, it becomes another character in the novel. A "hidden mystery," Janie's hair is one of the most powerful forces in her life, mesmerizing men and alienating the women. As a trope straight out of the turn-of-the-century "mulatto" novel, *(Clotel, Iola Leroy, The House Behind the Cedars)*, the hair connects Janie inexorably to the conventional romantic heroine. Employing other standard devices of romantic fiction, Hurston creates the excitement and tension of romantic seduction. Tea Cake—a tall, dark, mysterious stranger—strides into the novel and wrenches Janie away from her prim and proper life. The age and class differences between Janie and Tea Cake, the secrecy of their affair, the town's disapproval, the sense of risk and helplessness as

Janie discovers passionate love and the fear, desire, even the potential violence of becoming the possessed are all standard features of romance fiction. Janie is not the subject of these romantic episodes, she is the object of Tea Cake's quest, subsumed under his desires, and, at times so subordinate to Tea Cake that even her interior consciousness reveals more about him than it does about her.

In spite of his infidelities, his arrogance, and his incapacity for self-reflection, John Pearson is unambiguously the heroic center of *Jonah's Gourd Vine*. He inhabits the entire text, his voice is heard on nearly every page, he follows his own dreams, he is selected by the community to be its leader and is recognized by the community for his powers and chastised for his shortcomings. The preacher's sermon as he eulogized John at his funeral is not so much a tribute to the man as it is a recognition that the narrative exists to assert the power of the male story and its claim to our attention. Janie has, of course, reformed her community simply by her resistance to its values. The very fact of her status as outsider makes her seem heroic by contemporary standards. Unable to achieve the easy integration into the society that John Pearson assumes, she stands on the outside and calls into question her culture's dependence on externals, its lack of self-reflection, and its treatment of women. Her rebellion changes her and her friend Pheoby, and, in the words of Lee Edwards, her life becomes "a compelling model of possibility for anyone who hears her tale."[20]

Notes

1. Zora Neale Hurston, *Their Eyes Were Watching God* (Urbana: University of Illinois Press, 1978).
2. Robert Hemenway, *Zora Neale Hurston: A Literary Biography* (Urbana: University of Illinois Press, 1977), p. 239. Hemenway says that Janie's "blossoming" refers personally to "her discovery of self and ultimately to her meaningful participation in black tradition." But at the end of *Their Eyes*, Janie does not return to an accepting community. She returns to Eatonville as an outsider, and even in the Everglades she does not have an insider's role in the community as Tea Cake does.
3. Zora Neale Hurston, *Jonah's Gourd Vine* (Philadelphia: J. B. Lippincott, 1971).
4. Ibid., p. 7.
5. Henry Louis Gates, Jr., "Zora Neale Hurston and the Speakerly Text," in *The Signifying Monkey* (New York: Oxford University Press, 1987). Gates argues that *Their Eyes* resolves the implicit tension between standard English and black dialect, that Hurston's rhetorical strategies create a kind of new language in which Janie's thoughts are cast—not in black dialect per se but a colloquial form of standard English that is informed by the black idiom. By the end of the novel this language (or free indirect discourse) makes Janie's voice almost inseparable from the narrator's—a synthesis that becomes a trope for the self-knowledge Janie has achieved. While Gates sees the lan-

guage of *Their Eyes* representing the collective black community's speech
and thoughts in this "dialect-informed" colloquial idiom that Hurston has
invented, I read the text in a much more literal way and continue to maintain
that however inventive this new language might be it is still often used to
invoke the thoughts, ideas, and presence of men.

6. Margaret Homans, "Her Very Own Howl," *SIGNS* 9 (Winter 1983): 186–205.

7. One of the ways women's sexuality is made to seem less dignified than men's
is to have a woman' sexual experience seen or described by an unsympathetic
observer. A good example of the double standard in reporting sexual behavior occurs in Ann Petry's "In Darkness and Confusion" in *Black Voices: An
Anthology of Afro-American Literature*, ed. Abraham Chapman (New York:
New American Library 1968), pp. 161–91.The young Annie Mae is observed
by her uncle-in-law who reports that her sexual behavior is indecent. In
contrast, his son's sexual adventures are alluded to respectfully as activities
a father may not pry into.

8. The image of the train as fearsome and theatening occurs in Hurston's autobiography, *Dust Tracks on a Road; An Autobiography*, ed. Robert Hemenway
(Urbana: University of Illinois Press, 1984). When she is a young girl on her
way to Jacksonville, Zora, like John Pearson, is at first terrified of its "big,
mean-looking eye" anad has to be dragged on board "kicking and screaming
to the huge amusement of everybody but me." Later when she is inside the
coach and sees the "glamor of the plus and metal," she calms down and
begins to enjoy the ride which, she says "didn't hurt a bit." In both *Dust
Tracks* and *Jonah's Gourd Vine* the imagery of the train is clearly sexual,
but, while Zora sees the train as something external to herself, something
that is powerful but will not hurt her, John imagines the train as an extension
of his own power.

9. Teresa De Lauretis, *Alice Doesn't: Feminism, Semiotics, Cinema* (Bloomington: Indiana University Press, 1984), p. 143. De Lauretis notes that the
movement of narrative discourse specifies and produces the masculine position as that of mythical subject and the feminine position as mythical obstacle, or, simply "the space in which that movement occurs."

10. I am indebted to Barbara Johnson for this insight which she suggested when
I presented an early version of this paper to her class of Afro-American
women writers at Harvard in the fall of 1985. I was struck by her comment
that Jody's vulnerability makes him like a woman and therefore subject to
this kind of attack.

11. Barbara Johnson, 'Metaphor, metonymy and voice in *Their Eyes Were Watching God*," in *Black Literature and Literary Theory*, ed. Henry-Louis Gates,
(New York: Methuen,1984), pp.204–19. Johnson's essay probes very carefully
the relation between Janie's ability to speak and her ability to recognize her
own self-division. Once Janie is able "to assume and articulate the incompatible forces involved in her own division," she begins to achieve an authentic
voice. Arguing for a more literal reading of *Their Eyes*. I maintain that we
hear precious little of Janie's voice even after she makes this pronouncement
of knowing that she has "an insider and an outside self." A great deal of the
"voice" of the text is devoted to the men in the story even after Janie's
discovery of self-division.

12. Robert Stepto, *From Behind the Veil: A Study of Afro-American Narrative*
(Urbana: University of Illinois Press,1979), pp.164–67.
When Robert Stepto raised this issue at the 1979 Modern Language Association Meeting, he set off an intense debate. While I do not totally agree
with his reading of *Their Eyes* and I think he short-changes Hurston by
alloting so little space to her in *From Behind the Veil*, I do think he is right

about Janie's lack of voice in the courtroom scene.
13. More accurately the style of this section should be called *free indirect discourse* because both Janie's voice and the narrator's voice are evoked here. In his *Introduction to Poetics: Theory and History of Literature*, vol. I (Minneapolis: University of Minnesota Press, 1982), Tzvetan Todorov explains Gerard Genette's definition of free indirect discourse as a grammatical form that adopts the indirect style but retains the "semantic nuances of the 'original' discourse."
14. Hemenway, *Zora Neale Hurston*, p. 198.
15. Mary Helen Washington, "Zora Neale Hurston: A Woman Half in Shadow," in *I Love Myself When I Am Laughing . . . And Then Again When I Am Looking Mean and Impressive: A Zora Neale Hurston Reader*, ed. Alice Walker (Old Westbury, N.Y.: Feminist Press, 1979), p. 16. In the original version of this essay, I showed how Joseph Campbell's model of the hero, though it had been applied to Ralph Ellison's invisible man, could more appropriately be applied to Janie, who defies her status as the mule of the world, and, unlike Ellison's antihero, does not end up in an underground hideout.

Following the pattern of the classic mythological hero, defined by Campbell in *The Hero with a Thousand Faces*, (Princeton, N.J.: Princeton University Press, 1968), Janie leaves her everyday world to proceed to the threshold of adventure (leaves Nanny and Logan to run off with Jody to Eatonville); she is confronted by a power that threatens her spiritual life (Jody Starks and his efforts to make her submissive to him); she goes beyond that threat to a world of unfamiliar forces some of which threaten her and some of which give aid (Tea Cake, his wild adventures, and his ability to see her as an equal); she descends into an underworld where she must undergo the supreme ordeal (the journey to the Everglades; the killing of Tea Cake and the trial); and the final work is that of the return when the hero reemerges from the kingdom of dread and brings a gift that restores the world (Janie returns to Eatonville and tells her story to her friend Pheoby who recognizes immediately her communion with Janie's experience "Ah done growed ten feet higher from jus' listenin' tuh you, Janie").
16. Anne Jones, "Pheoby's Hungry Listening: Zora Neale Hurston's *Their Eyes Were Watching God*" (Paper presented at the National Women's Studies Association, Humboldt State University, Arcata, California, June 1982).
17. De Lauretis, *Alice Doesn't*, p. 113. In the chapter, "Desire in Narrative," De Lauretis refers to Vladimir Propp's essay, "Oedipus in the Light of Folklore," which studies plot types and their diachronic or historical transformations.
18. Rachel Blau Du Plessis, *Writing Beyond the Ending: Narrative Strategies of Twentieth-Century Women Writers* (Bloomington: Indiana University Press, 1985). Du Plessis asserts that "it is the project of twentieth-century women writers to solve the contradiction between love and quest and to replace the alternate endings in marriage and death that are their cultural legacy from nineteenth-century life and letters by offering a different set of choices."
19. Du Plessis distinguishes between *hero* and *heroine* in this way: "the female hero is a central character whose activities, growth, and insight are given much narrative attention and authorial interest." By *heroine* she means "the object of male attention or rescue." (*Writing Beyond the Ending*, n. 22), p. 200, Hurston oscillates between these two positions, making Janie at one time a conventional romantic heroine, at other times a woman whose quest for independence drives the narrative.
20. Lee R. Edwards, *Psyche As Hero: Female Heroism and Fictional Form* (Middletown, Conn.: Wesleyan University Press, 1984), p. 212.

♦♦♦♦♦♦♦♦♦♦♦♦♦♦

Wandering: Hurston's Search for Self and Method

SUSAN WILLIS

> I used to climb to the top of one of the huge chinaberry trees which guarded our front gate, and look out over the world. The most interesting thing that I saw was the horizon.

When, as a teenager, Zora Neale Hurston took a job as a lady's maid to a young starlet in a traveling Gilbert and Sullivan troupe, she became an instant success, a new "play-pretty" for the entire company. To explain the fascination the actors and musicians felt for her, Hurston discounts the fact that she was the only black in the group and attributes her popularity, instead, to her Southerness, particularly her use of language:

> I was a Southerner, and had the map of Dixie on my tongue. They were all Northerners except the orchestra leader, who came from Pensacola. It was not that my grammar was bad, it was the idioms. They did not know of the way an average Southern child, white or black, is raised on simile and invective. They know how to call names. It is an everyday affair to hear somebody called a mullet-headed, mule-eared, wall-eyed, hog-nosed, 'gator-faced, shad-mouthed, screw-necked, goat-bellied, puzzle-gutted, camel-backed, butt-sprung, battle-hammed, knock-kneed, razor-legged, box-ankled, shovel-footed, unmated so-and-so! Eyes looking like skint-ginny nuts, and mouth looking like a dishpan full of broke-up crockery! They can tell you in simile exactly how you walk and smell. They can furnish a picture gallery of your ancestors, and a notion of what your children will be like. What ought to happen to you is full of images and flavor. Since that stratum of the Southern population is not given to book-reading, they take their comparisons right out of the barnyard and the woods. When they get through with you, you and your whole family look like an acre of totem-poles.

Aside from the rich array of barnyard epithets, this passage includes another, more subtle feature, all the more suggestive of Hurston's relationship to language and writing. Contrary to the author's own good opinion of her grammar, the paragraph is based on a number of awkward and misleading shifts in the pronouns. This ungrammatical use of pronouns occurs throughout Hurston's autobiography, *Dust Tracks on a Road*, where it articulates the contradictory nature of Hurston's project as a black woman writer and intellectual attempting to mediate two deeply polarized worlds, whose terms include: South/North, black/white, rural/urban, folk tradition/intellectual scholarship. Hurston begins this passage with the first person and positions herself as a Southerner in opposition to the body of Northerners represented by the third-person pronoun "they." "*I* was a Southerner." "*They* were all Northerners."

They did not know how a Southern child uses language. However, at this point, the third-person pronoun abruptly takes on a new referent. "*They* know how to call names." Here the pronoun represents Zora's own Southern neighbors, from whom Hurston now differentiates herself. She might have maintained her identification with the group of Southern speakers had she continued with the first person, using the pronoun "we" instead of shifting to the third person, "they."

The shift in pronouns is significant in relation to the introduction of the pronoun "you" later in the paragraph. "They can tell *you* in simile exactly how *you* look and smell" and so on. Who can this "you" be but the Northern audience, the white patron who financed much of Hurston's research and writing and the basically white, intellectual readership, who, in 1942, might have been expected to buy this book. The pronoun shifts have two functions. They suggest Hurston's inevitable turmoil and ambivalence over being in the middle and being a mediator. And they suggest a certain smugness on the part of the author, "a poor black Southern girl" whose ungrammatical use of English is a deft ploy for turning the tables on the superior Northern establishment. One has the image of Hurston, standing back and chuckling over the "acre of totempoles" she has just thrown in her reader's face, while she remains blameless because the shift in pronouns has separated the authorial "I" from the Southern "they."

Hurston's writing is full of tricks of this sort. As she explains in her introduction to *Mules and Men:*

> You see we are a polite people and we do not say to our questioner, "Get out of here!" We smile and tell him or her something that satisfies the white person because, knowing so little about us, he doesn't know what he is missing. The Indian resists curiosity by a stony silence. The Negro offers a feather-bed resistance. That is, we let the probe enter, but it never comes out. It gets smothered under a lot of laughter and pleasantries.[1]

Again the pronoun shifts enable Hurston to be both Southern and not-Southern, black and not-black, inferior and not-inferior. This is not to say that she assumes a Northern, white identity; rather, she lifts herself, as a writer, out of any possible inscription in the stigmatized view of Southern blackness. Bear in mind that this is the Jim Crow South. The passage is a remarkable example of how grammatical tricks make "feather-bed resistance" a form of subversion, whose deep hostility is masked by the displacement of aggression into "laughter and pleasantries." The entering "probe," and unmistakable image of invasion and male domination, is neatly smothered by a feminine, castrating image, the "feather-bed," notwithstanding all the polite double-talk.

Nowhere is Hurston's subversive intent and smug demeanor more evident than in the conclusion to *Mules and Men*. Here, she tells the story of Sis Cat, who, having let one rat get away while washing her face and hands, decides to eat a second rat straight off. When the rat objects, "Where's yo' manners at, Sis Cat? You going to eat 'thout washing yo' face and hands?" Sis Cat responds:

> "oh, Ah got plenty manners, . . . But ah eats mah dinner and washes mah face and uses mah manners afterwards." So she et right on 'im and washed her face and hands.

Hurston's concluding one-liner is: "I'm sitting here like Sis Cat, washing my face and usin' my manners." Having just served up the body of black Southern folktales to the Northern white readership, Hurston, gloating like the cat who's just devoured a rat, asks her reader, Now, who's swallowed who? In identifying herself with the aggressor, Hurston takes the subversive intent of her writing one step further than she was able to with her use of pronoun shifts. Rather than the displaced "I," lifted above the terrain of struggle between North and South, white and black, she is here the wily predator, using her "manners"—her writing—with confidence and satisfaction.

I'd like to return to the litany of barnyard names that began this essay and so astounded Hurston's traveling companions. From "puzzle-gutted" to "knock-kneed" and "unmated" this is the raw idiom, which Hurston inherits as a Southerner, particularly one born soon after the turn of the century and raised in a rural environment, and which she, as a writer, will have to transform. Full of assertive expressivity, this is basically still an oral idiom; and as such, it is limited both as a means of communication and as the basis for narrative. Notwithstanding their aggressive intent and vivid imagery, these words do not constitute a language for the audience to whom the book is intended. It is, instead a delightful object, a "play-pretty," like Zora Neale herself, who at this point is a fifteen-year-old pretending to be twenty, a flirtatious and talkative lady's maid, who doesn't yet see herself as a writer nor her discourse as the production of narrative.

One of the tasks Hurston will face as a writer is to develop a literary mode of discourse out of a folk tradition whose basic component is name-calling. The task is complicated by the fact that the tradition includes some qualities that an assertive and resourceful writer like Hurston would want to preserve in the course of developing a more properly literary style. When, in her autobiography, Hurston recalls her introduction to Big Sweet, we sense the dramatic strength that name-calling entails. And we get a glimpse of a woman who accomplishes in her outspoken use of the vernacular what Hurston will eventually achieve in writing:

> I heard somebody, a woman's voice "specifying" up this line of houses from where I lived and asked who it was.
> "Dat's Big Sweet" my landlady told me. "She got her foot up on somebody. Ain't she specifying?" . . . She was giving her opponent lurid data and bringing him up to date on his ancestry, his looks, smell, gait, clothes, and his route through Hell in the hereafter . . . his pa was a double-humpted camel and his

ma was a grass-gut cow, but even so, he tore her wide open in the act of getting born, and so on and so forth. He was a bitch's baby out of a buzzard egg.

Although "specifying" may "signify" without the group of "four or five hundred people on the 'job' [who] are listening to Big Sweet's 'reading'," it would not "signify" for an audience outside the rural South as anything more than stereotypically provincial. Big Sweet cannot directly speak her life to the reader, but her image as Hurston describes her, foot up on her opponent's porch, invective in her mouth, can embody something of her experience and gutsy spirit. "Specifying" may be the most self-affirming form of discourse, but it is bound up by its inscription within a specific group of language users. And it is circumscribed, held in check, by the larger system of domination that defines the South and women like Big Sweet as marginal and inferior. As another of Hurston's informants makes clear in his rendition of a folktale, "specifying" is something you do to a neighbor or a fellow camp worker. It's not something you pull on a straw boss or "Ole Massa." As his story goes:

> During slavery time two ole niggers wuz talkin' an' one said tuh de other one, "Ole Massa made me so mad yestiddy till Ah give 'im uh good cussin' out. Man, Ah called 'im everything wid uh handle on it.

When the second man is later upbraided by the master he, too, decides to cuss Old Massa out. But contrary to his friend's experience, "Old Massa had 'im took down and whipped nearly tuh death." When the poor man asks his companion why he wasn't punished for the cussing he gave the master, the friend responds:

> "Man, you didn't go cuss 'im tuh his face, didja?"
> "Sho Ah did. Ain't dat whut you tole me you done?"
> "Naw, Ah didn't say Ah cussed 'im tuh his face. You sho is crazy. Ah thought you had mo' sense than dat. When Ah cussed Ole Massa he wuz settin' on de front porch an' Ah wuz down at de big gate."

If we remember the wily cat who swallowed the rat, then we might say that Hurston's project is analogous to cussing out the master. But because her medium is the narrative, rather than oral language, she can't take refuge down at the gate and do her cussing out in private. Instead, she must do her "specifying" in the form of a book Ole Massa can hold in his hands and read on his very own porch.

Whether or not we decide Hurston's writing achieves the subversion of domination inherent in its bold intent depends largely on how the act of "specifying" is transformed in the process of creating a literary language. As the distance between opponents is foreshortened and finally condensed into the narrative space between writer and reader, barnyard simile becomes metaphor and a lot of the invective is redirected. In line with the relationship between condensed metaphoric images and the raw material of history that I suggested in chapter 1, I want to emphasize that the development of metaphor as a literary language is what differentiates Hurston's writing from that of her more realist contemporaries like Ann Petry and makes her the precursor of today's great modernist writers like Toni Morrison and Paule Marshall. However, because Hurston's work defines the incipient stages of black modernism (which also includes Jean Toomer's unique book, *Cane*), not all of her metaphors are the highly condensed, multireferential figures we have come to associate with Morrison's writing. In fact, many of Hurston's images occupy a midway point between "specifying" and metaphor. These, although drawn from colloquial expression, represent a more complex form of describing than the simple "calling out" and naming. One such example occurs as Hurston continues her account of Big Sweet. Recognizing the importance of befriending Big Sweet, Hurston remarks on her own feeling of insecurity and estrangement in the Polk County mill camp. As she puts it, "I felt as timid as an egg without a shell." And no wonder—with men and women carrying knives and apt to do more than "specify" at each other, Hurston was definitely in a precarious position. Describing herself as a "bootlegger," she showed an inordinate interest in the camp's male population—their songs, stories, and general practice of "woofing" on each other. Big Sweet would prove herself an important ally and lifesaver. In her own advice to Hurston, "You just keep on writing down them lies. I'll take care of all the fighting. Dat'll make it more better, since we done made friends."

When Hurston describes herself as feeling "as timid as an egg without a shell," she evokes absolute vulnerability and she does so in a language that is only one step removed from the barnyard, but on its way to a frame of reference that will no longer be purely animal. "Specifying" equates the opponent with a brute, and, by the very nature of animal existence, cannot give symbolic expression to feelings. In contrast, the colloquial image, even though it is still rooted in a rural system of specification, gives ample space for the expression of emotion. This is possible not only because of the explicit comparison "as timid as," but because the shell-less egg is no longer strictly a part of nature in the same way as a "puzzle-gutted" and "knock-kneed" animal is.

The "egg without a shell" is also a particularly female image. This is true because the egg is the most basic female cell and because eggs—especially shell-less ones, in pans and ready to be fried—summon up the range of women's domestic labor. Hurston often draws from this same register in the creation of images based on colloquial expressions. A good example occurs in her most widely read novel, *Their Eyes Were Watching God*. Janie's grandmother has just finished describing her own life in slavery, the care she lavished on her daughter, who, nevertheless, went astray, abandoning her baby daughter, Janie, into the grandmother's care. In giving this account of her trials and tribulations, the grandmother is attempting to justify the marriage she has arranged between her young granddaughter and a middle-aged, pinch-penny farmer, Logan Killicks. Janie, who dreams of love and self-fulfillment, objects to the arranged marriage, knowing full well that although Killicks might never beat her, he'd sure plan on working her like a mule. But Janie's grandmother wins out. Appealing to Janie to consider her tired bones and old age as well as the hardships she has endured to secure Janie's future, the grandmother pleads, "Have some sympathy fur me. Put me down easy, Janie, Ah'm a cracked plate."[2]

With this expression, the grandmother confronts Janie with all the accumulated years of her domestic toil—both in her own home and in the kitchen of her white employer. She demands that Janie experience guilt for her grandmother's unfulfilled life and recognize her responsibility to care for her grandmother by respecting her decisions. The image evokes self-pity and domestic blackmail—perhaps the two most oppressive aspects of any mother-relationship in this culture. It will be some twenty years before Janie finally comes to realize the awful burden her grandmother placed in her hands the day she called herself a "cracked plate."

What enables Hurston to transcend colloquialisms such as these and write more complex and condensed metaphors is the same element of distance that allows her to look back on and study the folklore she was born into. As she puts it:

> From the earliest rocking of my cradle, I had known about the capers Brer Rabbit is apt to cut and what the Squinch Owl says from the house top. But it was fitting me like a tight chemise. I couldn't see it for wearing it. It was only when I was off in college, away from my native surroundings, that I could see myself like somebody else and stand off and look at my garment.

When Hurston remarks that her culture once fit "like a tight chemise," she describes a situation most women will recognize as their own. Women wear their daily lives like a snug and intimate article of clothing, so familiar it's apt to be taken for granted. Very often only a significant transformation in situation or consciousness will bring women to scrutinize their daily surroundings and relationships. Another great writer of the Southern experience, for instance, is Harriette Arnow, whose documentation of rural Appalachian history and culture equals Hurston's collection of folklore and hoodoo medicine. Arnow (in her novel *The Doll-maker*,[2] first published in 1954) gives an even fuller account than Hurston's autobiography of the sort of changes women must experience in order to see themselves and their culture in critical perspective. For Hurston, the move North, the urban environment, the Barnard education created the distance between herself and the once-tight chemise. For Arnow, migration North included proletarianization and an introduction to mass culture. And for both women, the gift of radical hindsight is paid for by estrangement. Hurston's simple expression of alienation, "I could see myself like somebody else," can be read in two ways. Either she could see herself as if she had become somebody else, or as if she were miraculously split in two, her old self standing there with her new self looking on. In any case, there is a sense of schizophrenia, not only between the self and the cultural garment, but deep within the self as well.

Distance and alienation, then, give rise to some of the most beautiful images set forth in the history of black women's writing. Looking back on her childhood, but seeing it from her perspective as an adult, Hurston describes a memorable dream image:

> for weeks I saw myself sitting astride of a fine horse. My shoes had sky-blue bottoms to them, and I was riding off to look at the bellyband of the world.

This delightful image is Hurston's response to a friend's refusal to join her in a quest for the horizon. Always a wanderer, she recounts many instances of stifled wanderlust in her autobiography. Throughout her childhood, the desire for mobility would very often work its way out in images such as these until the day when, as a teenager, she would make her own "dust tracks on a road" headed North. The image of shoes with "sky-blue bottoms" captures the clarity and mind-stretching creativity of the best surrealist art. It elides a child's vocabulary and boundless desire with a sophisticated notion of the world turned topsy-turvy. With the sky brought down to earth and made accessible, one might easily capture the world's belly-band."

Not all of Hurston's meditations on journey are couched in such positive terms. Very often the desire to wander is described as a compulsion that began in earnest with her mother's death:

> That hour began my wanderings. Not so much in geography, but in time. Then not so much in time as in spirit.

As we so often find in Paule Marshall's writing, journey for Hurston is a quest for self. But as Hurston makes clear, although the self at the end of the road may be articulate, speaking and writing will have been bought at the price of the individual's alienation.

Echoing throughout Hurston's phrases about wandering and writing, both in her autobiography and elsewhere, is the strong influence of time and place. In many ways, the claim for time and place is at odds with the evolution toward alienation. In order to tell her stry, Hurston cautions the reader, "you will have to know something about the time and place where I came from." She goes on to demonstrate that time and place are more than contextual backdrop:

> Like the dead-seeming, cold rocks, I have memories within that came out of the material that went to make me. Time and place have had their say.

This is another seemingly simple statement whose subtle complexities reside in metaphoric allusion. Essentially, Hurston is saying that her becoming a writer is tantamount to a rock learning to talk. In fact, the rocks will talk through her. And who are these "dead-seeming, cold rocks" but the tens of thousands of rural black women, considered less than beasts and denied a voice in history and letters.

In writing, Hurston stakes a claim to time and place for her own sake and for the sake of all the women and men whose stories will not reach our eyes and ears. Her efforts have far-reaching implications. For, in claiming a right to time and place, she contests the essential nature of capitalist society, which inscribes time and place within property relationships. Those who own property and control the means of production control time and place as well (both in the home and the workplace). When black women write to reclaim time and place, they do so outside of property relationships. This is true of Hurston, whose folktales fill the interstices of her informants' workdays and whose taletelling takes place in those areas, like the jooks and the front porches, that are not included in either the system of industrial production or domestic labor. Taletelling, like tale gathering, is something you do on the "job" when there is no job.

In her conception of time and place as self-defining and affirming and in her recovery of temporal and spatial zones outside of property relationships, Hurston lays the basis for Toni Morrison's conceptualization of Pilate in *Song of Solomon*. Pilate is another wanderer whose journey from the mountains of Virginia to Detroit is as much a journey through the geography of spirit as it is through concrete time and space. Pilate makes a point of telling people of her abiding interest in geography as if it were a personal attribute like texture of hair and shape of nose. Pilate, who has no possessions in the capitalist sense, has gathered and saved a rock from every place she has visited; just as Hurston, decades earlier, gathered and preserved folktales from the "dead-seeming, cold rocks" she met in sharecropping villages and turpentine camps. The geography that constitutes Pilate's spirit and the rhythm of her domestic space are, finally, the direct antitheses of her brother's propertied conception of space and time. For Macon Dead, the slumlord, rents are the equivalent of his tenants' spatial allotments in relation to their earning power.

Whereas Morrison's portrayal of Pilate offers an alternative to capitalist society, a household devoted to nonaccumulation, Hurston's claim to time and place fails to project a wholly new and positive reworking of social relationships. Most often, Hurston remains locked into the motif of wandering, trapped in a geography of spirit that is independent of property relationships and domination, but unable to transform the metaphoric geography into an alternative notion of daily life. The image of Hurston, in her dusty Chevy, bouncing over the Florida back roads from camp to camp, translates the spirit of wanderlust but doesn't prefigure an alternative form of society (as will be the case years later in Morrison's depiction of Pilate].

Hurston's lack of an alternative vision informs much of her writing about herself with desolation:

> I had always thought I would be in some lone, arctic waste land with no one under the sound of my voice. I found the cold, the desolate solitude, and earless silences, but I discovered that all that geography was within me. It only needed time to reveal it.

Clearly, the cold and solitude have very little to do with the fear of being exiled to an "arctic wasteland." What Hurston is really worried about is not having anyone "under the sound of [her] voice." Her fear as a teller of tales is the "earless silence." The image captures the dread felt by an untried black women, who would be a writer, of casting her words into a void. This is a fear which has long haunted black peoples' writing in this hemisphere. It goes back into the time of slavery, when many slaves who placed their narratives in the hands of abolitionists sensed that they were casting their words on a sea of uncertainty like messages in a bottle.[4] Although times had changed and so had the publishing industry, Hurston could well appreciate the anxiety of the slave narrator over getting a book published, keeping it in print, and having it well distributed. When she summons up an "arctic wasteland," then tells us "that all that geography was within [her]," we are made to realize in very concrete terms the burden of her uncertainty, to trace as we read the topography of her doubt as she expresses herself in image and metaphor.

However, the process of writing also involves the choice and development of the larger form of the narrative. As I see it, Hurston defined and worked in two very different forms, both of which express a social form as well as an aesthetic mode. The first of these is exemplified by the collection *Mules and Men*, whose narrative topography includes the self-contained islands of the tales themselves, which are then interconnected and defined on a broader grid by the path of Hurston's journey and her conversations with the tale-tellers. The oral tales are the original text, which Hurston contextualizes through her own discourse and work as an anthropologist, finally producing yet another, properly literary, text: the book *Mules and Men*. The most basic formal feature to arise out of these layers of textualization is containment. This is a codifying and concretizing form that allows no room for narrative transformation. It is a text whose form mimetically reproduces the economy and social structures of the rural South. The tales, like the work camps, include great creative and human energies, but both are contained: the tale, by the closure of its form; the camps, by their isolation one from another and by their inscription within a larger economic system of domination. Although the camps were in many ways privileged zones, where men and women could hide from the long arm of white, Southern justice, these zones were included in a larger system, which required cheap labor, and so defined a part of its work force as "criminals."

How, then, does the figure of Hurston relate to the form of narrative containment? Born and raised only miles away from the Polk County work camps, she has returned as an anthropologist trained by Franz Boas and funded by a wealthy patron. As a mediator, her task is to transform the raw material of culture into a form accessible to a Northern, intellectual clientele. As a figure in the narrative, Hurston establishes and articulates links between the closed units represented by the tales. Her discourse creates the web of narrative context while it separates the tales from the bed of social context. Hurston's mobility and the larger text she writes break down the sense of closure that defines each tale told in isolation, but she does not so transform the tales as to make of them some new narrative form.

Part of the reason why the folktales themselves resist transformation resides in their internal structure, which, like the whole of Hurston's text, reflects the economics of an oppressed area as it is contained within a larger capitalist economy. A close reading of a single tale will demonstrate how these narratives partake of economic structures.

The story, which tells of Jack and the Devil, is typical of all the Devil stories in *Mules and Men* even though it is longer than most tales and includes more detail and narrative transitions. It is important to note that the Devil, although he has power and represents authority, is in no way comparable to the Ole Massa. The Devil, a trickster like the Jack or John of the stories, is an alternative representation of the black man, who, because he is an otherworldly figure, is not completely inscribed within the economic and social restraints common to the black population.

The story opens with an inheritance distributed equally between two brothers. The first brother uses his share to buy "a big farm" and "a pair of mules," and to settle down. This is the last we hear of this brother. What follows is all about the second brother, Jack, who "took his money and went on down the road skinnin' and winnin'."

Why is the first brother even mentioned? His part is very small and he's of no interest. Nevertheless, his function in the story is absolutely crucial. For the first brother represents the larger economy, the system of stability based on property ownership within which Jack's "skinnin' and winnin'" is inscribed. Although the whole of the story will focus on Jack's inventive and alternative economics, everything Jack does is contained by the system of capital that is in no way influenced or affected by the forms of exchange employed by Jack.

The first of these modes of exchange is gambling and features Jack pitted against an unbeatable opponent, who, having won all of Jack's money, suggests they keep the game going by staking Jack's life against "all de money on de table." This is a good lesson in the forms of equivalence that evolved under capitalism, which equates a human being with currency. The attachment of exchange value to human beings is, of course, as old as slavery, capitalism's first mode of labor control in this hemisphere.

Jack agrees to the wager, loses, and suddenly finds himself facing a "twelve-foot tall" opponent. "De man looked down on 'im and tole 'im says, 'De Devil is mah name and Ah live across de deep blue sea'." Within the terms of the wager and certainly by reason of his greater power, the Devil could kill Jack on the spot. But that would make a dull story and an unprofitable economics. As the Devil will show, and in keeping with the economics of slavery, Jack is more valuable alive than dead. So the Devil perpetuates the game, but changes its form, and in so doing, lifts Jack out of the economics of slavery and reconstitutes his relationship to him in terms of a system defined by debt peonage, not unlike the sharecropping system of the post-Civil War South.

The transformation to this new economic mode occurs after a transitional interlude in the story during which Jack must journey across the ocean to the Devil's house "befo' the sun sets and rise again." Jack accomplishes the journey on the back of a bald eagle, whom he must feed in midflight "everytime she holler." He has brought along a yearling bull for the eagle's meals. The first time the eagle hollers, "Jack was so skeered dat instead of givin' de eagle uh quarter of de meat, he give her de whole bull." This puts Jack in a terrible fix when the eagle makes a subsequent demand for food. Jack's response is to tear off his own arm and then a leg, so that when he finally arrives at the Devil's house and knocks on the door, he identifies himself as, "One of de Devil's friends. One widout uh arm and widout uh leg." The Devil quickly remedies the situation because, as we shall see, he wants an able-bodied worker, not a cripple:

> Devil tole his wife, says: "Look behind de do' and hand dat man uh arm and leg." She give Jack de arm and leg and jack put 'em on.

What's remarkable about this passage is not Jack's self-mutilation and acquisition of new limbs per se. Such things happen throughout the mythic stories of Africa, the roots of the Afro-American storytelling tradition, as in Amos Tutuola's *The Palm-Wine Drinkard*,[5] which at one point describes a man who, journeying from the market to his own village, returns all the limbs and body parts he borrowed from other people on his way to town. When he finally arrives home he is only a head. The Afro-American folktale, as Hurston records it, regards the loss and acquisition of body parts with the same matter-of-fact attitude we find in Tutuola's mythic writing. These narratives shift the focus away from the notion of a body as it belongs to an individual who might experience pain and loss; they demand that we instead consider the process of transformation itself and what it implies. Broadly speaking, the incident articulates the fluctuations in fortune an individual might experience.

Gambling, sharecropping, and all the conniving schemes anyone like Jack might invent hold out the promise of instantaneous reward and the probability of rapid downfall. One minute, you're on top of the world; the next, you're hobbling around barely able to survive; and then, you're miraculously restored. The story of the eagle is a mythic device for describing the worldview of people whose lives ultimately are in someone else's hands.

Once at the Devil's house, Jack quickly learns his new economic status. Now in the Devil's debt for his arms, legs, and life, Jack is required to perform a number of tasks. With his labor, given in exchange for a debt that can never be paid, Jack now symbolizes another era in the economic history of this hemisphere, an era that assigned the Indians of Latin America to the haciendas and the emancipated blacks of North America to the peonage of sharecropping. First, Jack must clear a hundred acres for the Devil; then he must retrieve a lost ring from the bottom of a well; and finally, he must pluck two geese in a raging gale without losing a single feather. Luckily, Jack, who could never have performed the tasks in the amount of time allotted by the Devil, is aided by the Devil's daughter, who magically completes each of the tasks. It should be noted the women figures in the tales are never portrayed as stereotypically subservient peasant women, but exercise free will, guile, and intelligence. They make their own decisions and form their own alliances, often contrary to the wishes of male figures in positions of authority.[6] The conclusion of the story features a new set of economic relationships. Jack, having fulfilled his obligations to the Devil, marries his daughter and sets up housekeeping. The situation suggests his liberation from bondage and access to a form of freeholding. Although the Devil might be forced to accept Jack's independence as the logical result of their contract, he, as a domineering master, fails to accept the situation emotionally. This is evident one night when the Devil comes looking to kill Jack. As a free man, Jack is now worth more dead than alive. This is the reverse of his economic definition under slavery. Hurriedly, Jack and his wife escape in a buckboard pulled by two of the Devil's horses with the Devil in pursuit on his jumping bull.

The outcome of this section of the story has to do, significantly, with the manipulation of language. It suggests the historical function of black language and writing from slavery to the present, which has often reversed systems of domination. The horses Jack has stolen are booby-trapped. Named "Hallowed-be-thy-name" and "Thy-Kingdom-Come," they've been trained to fall to their knees every time the Devil calls their names. Jack is able to outdistance the Devil only because his wife knows the charm to reverse the Devil's spell each time he calls out. However, the Devil finally catches up with Jack, who has hidden in a hollow log, where he invents his own language trick to turn the tables on the Devil. When the Devil picks up the log, Jack cries out, "O Lawd, have mercy."

His speech act parallels the Devil's use of holy names and has the effect of causing the Devil such a fright that he drops the log and attempts to flee. But in his haste, he orders his bull to turn around with such ferocity that "De jumpin' bull turnt so fast till he fell and broke his own neck and throwed de Devil out on his head and kilt 'im." So the Devil is mastered by himself and by Jack in the use of language.

"Dat's why dey say Jack beat de Devil." The conclusion of the story is a statement of closure. It separates the tale from the workers' daily lives. Although the story's characters and their relationships have spoken for the real-life situation of black people in this country, these lessons do not carry over to the daily life and toil in the camps. The story is a unit whose function is not to transform anyone's thoughts about his or her working and living conditions. Rather, the story and its telling affirm the group as a cohesive unit, whose members' real-life possibilities are just as contained as the form of the stories they tell.

Group definition and affirmation are the positive features of these stories, whose form, like the society in which they occur, denies transformation. Affirmation is their strength, but it is a strength evolved in response to containment. A good example are the stories of one-upmanship. One man begins: "I know land so poor it won't grow rocks." Thereafter, each of the tellers must respond with another, more impoverished and humorous example. The formula is the same in the "I-know-a-man-blacker-than" stories and the "uglier-than" stories.

> "Ah seen a man so ugly till he could get behind a jimpson weed and hatch monkies."
> Everybody laughed and moved closer together. Then Officer Richardson said: "Ah seen a man so ugly till they had to spread a sheet over his head at night so sleep could slip up on him."
> They laughed some more, then Clifford Ulmer said:
> "Ah'm goin' to talk with my mouth wide open. Those men y'all been talkin' 'bout wasn't ugly at all. Those was pretty men. Ah knowed one so ugly till you could throw him in the Mississippi river and skim ugly for six months."

Who wins in a "lying" contest? Is it the best man and the best tale? Or is it group, "Everybody laugh[ing] and mov[ing] closer together?" Telling stories like these affirms the group more than its individual members. It allows each participant to experience the force of cohesion. But it does so on the basis of derision, and this, too, is a feature of the oppressive system that contains the storytellers and their tales. The stories look at blackness like they look at ugliness. They affirm race, but they do not then transcend racial prejudice. This is, instead, the project for our time. The stories Hurston records begin in negativity; seize their negativity; and in so doing, position themselves on the brink of formulating an alternative vision. But they go no further. This is the significance of "lying," the rural black word for storytelling. From the point of view of the dominant white population, "Niggers lie and lie." Seizing the negativity, the black folk tradition affirms the right to "lie"—to tell tales—to give shape to the self and community. But "lying" can go no further because so long as racial domination exists, "lying" cannot transcend the boundary of otherness and inferiority defined from above.[7]

At this point, I'd like to look at Hurston's most remarkable book—remarkable because its narrative form does transcend containment. This is the novel *Their Eyes Were Watching God*. What makes this text so different from Hurston's other, more conventional, novels and at the same time defines it as the precursor for many contemporary novels by black women is its dialectical form. This is the form Paule Marshall develops in *Praisesong for the Widow* and Alice Walker brings to fruition in *The Third Life of Grange Copeland*. I emphasize the importance of the dialectical narrative because this is what enables a vision of the future. As we saw, the rural black narrative tradition was also influenced by a sense of history as dialectical process. This is evident in the tale of Jack and the Devil where Jack's relationship to domination is traced through three distinct economic modes: slavery, debt peonage, and freeholding.[8] Similarly, *Their Eyes Were Watching God* works through three historically produced economic modes. The great difference between the novel and the folktale is the way we experience the novel, for the most part, as a universal process that is not contained or inscribed in some larger oppressive economic system. This is due to the fact that text and context are not separate as they were in Hurston's collection of folk tales. Rather than the sense of closure evoked at the end of each tale and enhanced by the difference between Hurston's mobility and the static isolation of the camps, the novel welds the authorial persona to the figure of the protagonist, Janie Woods, and articulates its dialectic through her movements through geography and through three very different relationships to men. The economics of marriage are, in this novel, the figuration for larger historical forms.

Janie's relationship to her first husband, Logan Killicks, suggests the system of sharecropping. Although Killicks does not himself work on shares, he allows us to perceive how the society itself is locked into a system of debt peonage. Then, too, in what Killicks expects from his wife, he is really no different from the sharecroppers he has managed to rise above. Hurston shows a deft sense for the influence of the forces of history on people's lives in refusing to portray Killicks as a personally mean man. If he regards his young wife as a mule, it is because in this system of backbreaking rural labor, women were expected to bear the burdens of fieldwork as well as domestic toil. Killicks wants a woman who will plow alongside him, cut up "seed taters," move manure, and accept sex whenever and however he wants it. There is no room for frivolity and spontaneity. Spring is not a set of lacy leaf patterns, as Janie would like to see it, but a set of tasks to be performed. The brutality of this system is not necessarily related to physical violence and abuse.

Killicks has never laid a hostile hand on Janie. Rather, it resides in the stifling of dreams; the death of spirit; the denial of art, imagination and creativity.

So when Joe Starks comes whistling down the road, "cityfied" and "stylish," Janie cannot help but see in him the possibility for her self-fulfillment. The problem is that Janie confuses manner and style with creativity and dreams. She doesn't realize that these indicators of success are merely signs for another, equally stifling economic mode. Janie runs off with Joe and the two of them make their way to Eatonville, Florida, an all-black town, which under Joe's leadership, will soon become a model for progress, as it has been defined by dominant, white urban society. Joe gives the town its post office, store, and street lamp, and presides over all in a most paternalistic way.[9]

Again Hurston avoids overpersonalizing the terms of Janie's relationship to Joe and allows us to see the economic factors that condition their life together. Joe Starks represents the nascent black bourgeoisie, hell-bent for progress and ready to beat white society at its own game. In the more cutthroat atmosphere of the urban North where property ownership and land speculating mediate race prejudice, Joe might have more closely resembled Toni Morrison's portrayal of Macon Dead. In the rural South and the racially calm atmosphere of Eatonville, Joe is at his ease to evolve a more provincial model of bourgeois domination. But it is nonetheless oppressive. Joe may glad-hand everybody, but he runs the town with a loud mouth, a big belly, and an iron will.

In this situation, the degree of Janie's oppression is no less than it was on the farm. Only the terms of the oppression have changed. As the wife of the town's leading citizen, Janie is denied self, voice, and sexuality. She must dress in a decorous fashion, taking particular care to tie up her hair, lest any other man share in the sensual pleasure reserved for her husband. She may wait on customers in the store; but she may not speak out of turn, and she may certainly not offer an opinion or join in any rowdy behavior like playing checkers or telling tales. If Janie was a beast of burden in her first life, she has, in her bourgeois life, become a domestic pet. Like Matt Bonner's starved and abused yellow mule, which her husband turns into the town mascot, Janie was freed from brutal labor and turned into an object. And if Logan Killicks rebuked her for her failure to do her share of the work, Joe Starks made Janie bear the weight of constant derision for the inadequacies and stupidity he daily brought to her attention.

In describing Janie's relationship to her third husband, Hurston offers a utopian betrayal of history's dialectic. She chooses not to depict the Northern migration of black people, which brought Hurston herself to New York and a college degree and brought thousands of other rural blacks to the metropolis and wage labor. In this, Hurston sets a precedent in black women's writing that will leave unexplored the possibility of a black working-class culture in this country. By their absence from her novel, industrialization, the city, the black working class are not shown to represent the future for black people.

Instead, Janie and Tea Cake evolve their relationship on the "muck," whose very name suggests something of a primal never-never land, more south than the rural South. Perhaps the "muck," or "glades" as it's sometimes called, articulates the recovery of Caribbean culture. Indeed, Janie learns to sing and dance with the Bahamians who also work on the "muck." Then, too, it summons up images of precapitalist societies: the Seminoles and renegade black slaves who allied with them. The "muck," as Hurston portrays it, is a mythic space with just enough reference to migrant agricultural workers to give it credibility.

We might criticize Hurston for situating the utopian future in an economic reality we know to be highly exploitative, but what's more important here is how the "muck"—and some atypical economic aspects Janie and Tea Cake bring to it—allow Hurston to develop a truly reciprocal relationship between Janie and her husband. This is possible because Janie and Tea Cake are really not inscribed within the economics of the "muck." If they plant and harvest beans, they do so because they enjoy fieldwork and because it allows them to live in the heart of Southern black cultural production. They are not, like many of the other migrant workers, bowed down by debts and kids. In fact, Janie and Tea Cake do not fit into any larger economic model. Janie, with a large inheritance in the bank, need not work at all and Tea Cake, whose forte is gambling, need never accept a job unless he wants it. Lifted out of economic constraints by their atypicality, Tea Cake and Janie are free to experience work as an enjoyable and fulfilling endeavor, whose capacity to give pleasure is only slightly less than sex, music, and a plate of baked beans.

Throughout Janie's three relationships, Hurston demonstrates how a woman's sexuality is defined in relation to the economics of heterosexuality in male-dominated situations. The instant Janie's grandmother catches her kissing a boy over the garden fence, she is defined as a functioning heterosexual woman. The grandmother's immediate decision to contract Janie's marriage clearly shows that a woman's role in this society is to be put into the circuit of male exchange. Janie's value is her virginity and possessability. As an object destined for male ownership, she can have no aspirations for selfhood. These girlish desires must be put on the shelf until her fiftieth birthday, when, if she has outlived her husband, she might once again sit under a springtime pear tree and contemplate what's left of the future.

In her relationship with Killicks, Janie's sexuality is subsumed under her ability to produce. The strength of her back in the field and her arm in the kitchen are worth more than her function in bed. From Killicks's point of view, Janie's sexuality is the place where he puts his penis. Since sex is intended to satisfy his need, rather than Janie's desire, it doesn't matter that he refuses to wash his dirty, stinking body before getting into bed with his wife. Killicks might grant Janie a biology, but he and the economics of rural impoverishment reduce women's sexuality to animal need, with the male animal on top.

With her second marriage, Janie's sexuality enters into a system of display and exchange defined by the market under capitalism. If she was little more than an animal for her first husband, she is essentially a commodity for her second. In this system, Janie's sexuality is lifted out of the economics of production and redefined by consumption. Thus, appearance takes precedence over strength. And this is the basis for the contradiction between male domination and patriarchy on the one hand and the capitalist market system on the other. Hurston clearly senses the contradiction in her depiction of the tension between Joe Starks' possessive domination of his wife and his desire that she be on display and available—but modestly, like the canned goods on his store's shelf. To say simply that such a system makes women into objects does not fully express the fearful double bind that women are forced to live, having to be unquestionably loyal to their husbands, while making themselves accessible to other men's gaze. The system is, however, not without its hazards for the patriarch, whose deepest fear, as Joe Starks knows, is impotence.

With her third marriage, Janie is lifted out of all previously defined economic modes and male domination as well. Since possession and objectification do not define the dynamic of their union, Tea Cake and Janie are free to devote their energy and attention to maintaining reciprocity. When, at their first meeting, Tea Cake teaches Janie to play checkers, he sets the terms of their relationship in which all endeavor will be defined as sport and shared equally. Heterosexuality is neither a basis for power nor a reason for submission, but a mode in which a man and a woman might equally participate. Although Tea Cake and Janie enjoy frequent sex, they also like good food, evenings with friends, and afternoons spent hunting. When sex is not essentialized, sensuality may be found in all aspects of daily life.

Many who read *Their Eyes Were Watching God* for the first time are struck by the fact that Janie's happy relationship with Tea Cake comes to such an abrupt and tragic end. We might even want to accuse Hurston of literary overkill in making Tea Cake the victim of a mad dog's attack, and then portraying Janie confronted by her enraged hydrophobic husband and forced to shoot him down like a stray dog. The only way to avoid turning this otherwise very modernist text into a cliché of naturalism is to read Tea Cake's death in a figural way. The fact that he turns on Janie in his last hour reiterates the death of Janie's previous husband, Joe Starks, who, with his last breath, heaps blame and recrimination on Janie. Although Tea Cake and Joe Starks are worlds apart and in no other way comparable in their treatment of Janie, Hurston is making it clear in her portrayal of their dying moments that women cannot hope to have themselves fully realized in their husbands.

When Janie shoots the maddened Tea Cake, she not only saves her own life, she also steps outside of the male-defined circuit of exchange her grandmother thrust her into with her first marriage. Janie's killing of Tea Cake is the book's strongest statement. In terms of heterosexuality, it provides a far more radical response to potential domination than the utopian fantasy of life on the "muck" suggests in relation to economic exploitation. It demonstrates that no matter if Tea Cake was a truly supportive husband, as long as relationships between men and women are embraced by a larger system in which men dominate, no woman can expect to attain selfhood in marriage. The radical nature of Janie's symbolic claim for her own time and space is apparent in the events immediately following Tea Cake's death. The legal system and public opinion that seek to brand Janie a criminal and the ordeal of the courtroom hearing testify to the forces in this society that view a heterosexual female outside the male circuit as aberrant and in need of punishment.

This, however, is not the book's final moment. Rather, the novel opens and concludes with a back-porch conversation between Janie, who has just returned to Eatonville after Tea Cake's death, and her close friend, Pheoby Watson. Janie, her road-sore feet in a pan of water, a bowl of Pheoby's beans in her stomach, tells her story to her friend. The nucleus of their warm companionship counterbalances the recrimination of Tea Cake's friends who rose up against Janie when they first heard of the shooting, and it offers an alternative to the gossipy chatter of the townspeople who greet Janie's return with hostility born of narrow-mindedness. These are the images of the backward, oppressed, exclusionary community: women held back by men and men acting out of rivalry. In contrast, the image of Janie and Pheoby captures the spirit and hope for some new community based on sisterhood. This is not to suggest that in killing Tea Cake Janie has put an end to her heterosexuality. Rather, Janie has learned that although women must be with men and for men, they must also be with women and for women. Pheoby brings to the sisterhood her care of Janie's fatigued body; Janie supplies the lessons she has learned. Pheoby's exclamation is a vision of the future upon which the book closes:

> "Lawd! . . . Ah done growed ten feet higher jus' listenin' tuh you, Janie. Ah ain't satisfied wid mahself no mo'. Ah means tuh make Sam take me fishing wid him after this."

This is the book's most radical single statement.

Notes

1. Zora Neale Hurston, *Muses and Men* (Bloomington: Indiana Univ. Press, 1978), 4.
2. Zora Neale Hurston, *Their Eyes Were Watching God* (Urbana: Univ. of Illinois Press, 1978), 37.
3. Harriette Arnow, *The Dollmaker* (New York: Macmillan, 1954).
4. The Cuban slave poet, Juan Francisco Manzano, was one such writer, who, in entrusting his narrative to English abolitionist, had little assurance that it ever would be published or that he might one day hold his own autobiography in his hands. For a fuller account of Manzano's narrative and the difficulties surrounding his life as a writer, see Susan Willis, "Crushed Geraniums: Juan Francisco Manzano and the Language of Slavery," in *The Slave's Narrative*, ed. Charles T. Davis and Henry Louis Gates, Jr. (New York: Oxford Univ. Press, 1985), 199–224.
5. Amos Tutuola, *The Palm-Wine Drinkard* (New York: Grove, 1953).
6. Hurston makes many comparisons between the plight of rural black women and animals; in *Their Eyes Were Watching God*, she says: "De nigger woman is de mule uh de world so fur as Ah can see." I feel that the disparity between the strong, positive portrayal of women in the folktales and the potentially demeaning connotations of their comparison with mules, which the title *Mules and Men* cannot help but suggest, represents another of Hurston's back-handed and subtle ttempts to undermine prevailing ideology. It should be noted that there are very few mules in the stories and a great number of assertive women—both in the tales and as tale-tellers.
7. This is the basis for the political aesthetic of negritude poetry as Sartre de-scribes it in his essay, "Orphée Noire," (originally published as the preface to *Anthologie de la nouvelle poésie nègre et malgache de langue française* by L. Sédar Senghor [Presses Universitaires de France, 1948]). What differentiates the poetry of such writers as Léopold Sédar Senghor and Aimé Césaire from the Afro-American tale-telling tradition is that the negritude poets are writ-ing in a very literary and sophisticated form of French while the tale-tellers are working in the oral dialect. As Sartre sees it, when black people rise up and speak—and do so in the language of their oppressor—their act so reverses domination as to put an end to racist society. Extrapolating from Sartre's logic, we might say that the failure of the folktales to be transformative of society resides in their use of dialect and, therefore, their perpetuation of a culture of otherness.
8. In his masterful novel, *Things Fall Apart*, Chinua Achebe describes the last years of traditional, village-based African culture. As he depicts the process of a child's growing up and acculturation, Achebe mentions that as boys enter adolescence they begin to spend more time with their fathers, who narrate very different stories from the ones their mothers would tell—and will go on telling to their girl children. It seems that women's stories pertain to the world of myth—the animal heroes, origins, and cosmology—whereas the men's stories pertain to the world of history–events like battles and tribal genealogy. As the story of Jack and the Devil makes clear, the Afro-American stories compress myth and history. It may well be that when the plantation system leveled the traditional African division of labor, which defined men as hunters and warriors and women as planters, food preparers, and child raisers, it created a situation in which the distinction between a male and a

female discourse no longer obtained. If this is so, the roots of the great American mythic novel (Gabriel García Marquez's *Cien Años de Soledad*) (New York: Avon, 1971) may reside in the combination of myth and history that we find in the Afro-American stories.

9. In her description of Joe Starks, Hurston is paraphrasing the real history of her hometown, Eatonville, and its founding father, Joe Clarke. For her account of Eatonville's inception, see the chapter called "My Birthplace" in *Dust Tracks on a Road*.

◆◆◆◆◆◆◆◆◆◆◆◆◆

Thresholds of Difference: Structures of Address in Zora Neale Hurston

BARBARA JOHNSON

In preparing to write this paper, I found myself repeatedly stopped by conflicting conceptions of the structure of address into which I was inserting myself. It was not clear to me what I, a white deconstructor, was doing talking about Zora Neale Hurston, a black novelist and anthropologist, or to *whom* I was talking. Was I trying to convince white establishment scholars who long for a return to Renaissance ideals that the study of the Harlem Renaissance is not a trivialization of their humanistic pursuits? Was I trying to contribute to the attempt to adapt the textual strategies of literary theory to the analysis of Afro-American literature? Was I trying to rethink my own previous work and to re-referentialize the notion of difference so as to move the conceptual operations of deconstruction out of the realm of abstract linguistic universality? Was I talking to white critics, black critics, or myself?

Well, all of the above. What finally struck me was the fact that what I was analyzing in Hurston's writings was precisely, again and again, her strategies and structures of problematic address. It was as though I were asking her for answers to questions I did not even know I was unable to formulate. I had a lot to learn, then, from Hurston's way of dealing with multiple agendas and heterogeneous implied readers. I will focus here on three texts that play interesting variations on questions of identity and address: two short essays, "How It Feels to Be Colored Me"[1] and "What White Publishers Won't Print,"[2] and a book-length collection of folktales, songs, and hoodoo practices entitled *Mules and Men*.[3]

One of the presuppositions with which I began was that Hurston's work was situated "outside" the mainstream literary canon and that I, by implication, was an institutional "insider." I soon came to see, however, not only that the insider becomes an outsider the minute she steps out of the inside but also that Hurston's work itself was constantly dramatizing and undercutting just such inside/outside oppositions, transforming the plane geometry of physical space into the complex transactions of discursive exchange. In other words, Hurston could be read not just as an *example* of the "noncanonical" writer but as a commentator on the dynamics of any encounter between an inside and an outside, any attempt to make a statement about difference.

One of Hurston's most memorable figurations of the inside/outside structure is her depiction of herself as a threshold figure mediating between the all-black town of Eatonville, Florida, and the big road traveled by passing whites.

> The front porch might seem a daring place for the rest of the town, but it was a gallery seat for me. My favorite place was atop the gatepost. Proscenium box for a born first-nighter. Not only did I enjoy the show, but I didn't mind the actors knowing that I liked it. I usually spoke to them in passing. . . .
>
> They liked to hear me "speak pieces" and sing and wanted to see me dance the parse-me-la, and gave me generously of their small silver for doing these things. . . . The colored people gave no dimes. They deplored any joyful tendencies in me, but I was their Zora nevertheless.

The inside/outside opposition here opens up a reversible theatrical space in which proscenium box becomes center stage and small silver passes to the boxholder-turned-actor.

Hurston's joyful and lucrative gatepost stance between black and white cultures was very much a part of her Harlem Renaissance persona and was indeed often deplored by fellow black artists. Langston Hughes, who for a time shared with Hurston the problematic patronage of the wealthy Charlotte Mason, wrote of Hurston:

> Of th[e] "niggerati," Zora Neale Hurston was certainly the most amusing. Only to reach a wider audience, need she ever write books—because she is a perfect book of entertainment in herself. In her youth she was always getting scholarships and things from wealthy white people, some of whom simply paid her just to sit around and represent the Negro race for them, she did it in such a racy fashion. . . . To many of her white friends, no doubt, she was a perfect "darkie."[4]

"Representing the Negro race for whites" was nevertheless in many ways the program of the Harlem Renaissance. While Hurston has often been read and judged on the basis of personality alone, her "racy" adoption of the "happy darkie" stance, which was a successful strategy for survival, does not by any means exhaust the representation strategies of her *writing*.

Questions of identity, difference, and race-representation are interestingly at issue in the 1928 essay entitled "How It Feels to Be Colored Me," in which the gatepost passage appears. Published in *World Tomorrow*, a white journal sympathetic to Harlem Renaissance writers, the essay is quite clearly a response to the unspoken question inevitably asked by whites of the black artist. Since any student of literature trained in the European tradition and interested in Hurston out of a concern for the noncanonical is implicitly asking her that same question, a close reading of that essay is likely to shed light on what is at stake in such an encounter.

The essay is divided into a series of vignettes, each of which responds to the question differently. The essay begins, "I am colored but I offer nothing in the way of extenuating circumstances except the fact that I am the only Negro in the United States whose grandfather on the mother's side was *not* an Indian chief." Collapsed into this sentence are two myths of black identity, the absurdity of whose juxtaposition sets the tone for the entire essay. On the one hand, it implies that being colored is a misdemeanor for which some extenuation must be sought. On the other hand, it implies that among the stories Negroes tell about themselves the story of Indian blood is a common extenuation, dilution, and hence effacement of the crime of being colored. By making *lack* of Indian blood into an extenuating circumstance and by making explicit the absurdity of seeking extenuating circumstances for something over which one has no control, Hurston is shedding an ironic light both on the question ("How does it feel to be colored you?") and on one possible answer ("I'm not 100 percent colored"). Hurston is saying in effect, "I am colored but I am different from other members of my race in that I am not different from my race."[5]

While the first paragraph thus begins, "I am colored," the second starts, "I remember the very day that I *became* colored" (my emphasis). The presuppositions of the question are again undercut. If one can become colored, then one is not born colored, and the definition of "colored" shifts. Hurston goes on to describe her "pre-colored" childhood spent in the all-black town of Eatonville, Florida. "During this period," she writes, "white people differed from colored to me only in that they rode through town and never lived there." It was not that there was no difference, it was that difference needed no extenuation.

> But changes came in the family when I was thirteen, and I was sent to school in Jacksonville. I left Eatonville, the town of the Oleanders, as Zora. When I disembarked from the river-boat at Jacksonville, she was no more. It seemed that I had suffered a sea change. I was not Zora of Orange County any more, I was now a little colored girl. I found it out in certain ways. In my heart as well as in the mirror, I became a fast brown—warranted not to rub nor run.

In this sea change, the acquisition of color is a *loss* of identity: the "I" is no longer Zora, and "Zora" becomes a "she." "Everybody's Zora" had been constituted not by *an* Other but by the system of otherness itself, the ability to role-play rather than the ability to play any particular role. Formerly an irrepressible speaker of pieces, she now becomes a speaker of withholdings: "I found it out in certain ways."

The acquisition of color, which is here a function of motion (from Eatonville to Jacksonville), ends up entailing the fixity of a correspondence between inside and outside: "In my heart as well as in the mirror, I became a fast brown—warranted not to rub nor run." But the speed hidden in the word "fast," which belies its claim to fixity, is later picked up to extend the "color = motion" equation and to transform the question of race into the image of a road race:

> The terrible struggle that made me an American out of a potential slave said "On the line!" The Reconstruction said "Get set!"; and the generation before

said "Go!" I am off to a flying start and I must not halt in the stretch to look behind and weep.

Later, however, "I am a dark rock surged upon"—a stasis in the midst of motion.

The remainder of the essay is dotted with sentences playing complex variations on the title words "feel," "color," and "me":

But I am not tragically colored.

I do not always feel colored.

I feel most colored when I am thrown against a sharp white background.

At certain times I have no race, I am *me*.

I have no separate feelings about being an American citizen and colored.

The feelings associated with being colored are, on the one hand, denial of sorrow and anger ("There is no great sorrow dammed up in my soul"; "Sometimes I feel discriminated against, but it does not make me angry") and, on the other, the affirmation of strength and excitement ("I have seen that the world is to the strong regardless of a little pigmentation more or less"; "It is quite exciting to hold the center of the national stage"). Each case involves a reversal of implicit white expectations: I am not pitiful but powerful; being colored is not a liability but an advantage. "No one on earth ever had a greater chance for glory. . . . The position of my white neighbor is much more difficult."

There is one point in the essay, however, when Hurston goes out of her way to conform to a stereotype very much in vogue in the 1920s. The passage bears citing in its entirety:

Sometimes it is the other way around. A white person is set down in our midst, but the contrast is just as sharp for me. For instance, when I sit in the draft basement that is The New World Cabaret with a white person, my color comes. We enter chatting about any little nothing that we have in common and are seated by the jazz waiters. In the abrupt way that jazz orchestras have, this one plunges into a number. It loses no time in circumlocutions, but gets right down to business. It constricts the thorax and splits the heart with its tempo and narcotic harmonies. This orchestra grows rambunctious, rears on its hind legs and attacks the tonal veil with primitive fury, rendering it, clawing it until it breaks through to the jungle beyond. I follow those heathens—follow them exultingly. I dance wildly inside myself; I yell within, I whoop; I shake my assegai above my head, I hurl it true to the mark *yeeeeooww!* I am in the jungle and living in the jungle way. My face is painted red and yellow and my body is painted blue. My pulse is throbbing like a warm drum. I want to slaughter something—give pain, give death to what, I do not know. But the piece ends. The men of the orchestra wipe their lips and rest their fingers. I creep back slowly to the veneer we call civilization with the last tone and find the white friend sitting motionless in his seat, smoking calmly.

"Good music they have here," he remarks, drumming the table with his fingertips.

Music. The great blobs of purple and red emotion have not touched him. He has only heard what I felt. He is far away and I see him but dimly across the ocean and the continent that have fallen between us. He is so pale with his whiteness then and I am *so* colored.

"Feeling" here, instead of being a category of which "colored" is one example, becomes instead a *property* of the category "colored" ("He has only heard what I felt"). While the passage as a whole dramatizes the image of the exotic primitive, its relation to expectations and presuppositions is not as simple as it first appears. Having just described herself as feeling "most colored when I am thrown against a sharp white background," Hurston's announcement of having it "the other way around" leads one to expect something other than a description of "feel[ing] most colored." Yet there is no other way around. The moment there is a juxtaposition of black and white, what "comes" is color. But the colors that come in the passage are skin *paint*, not skin complexion: red, yellow, blue, and purple. The "tonal veil" is rent indeed, on the level at once of color, of sound, and of literary style. The move into the jungle is a move into mask; the return to civilization is a return to veneer. Either way, what is at stake is an artificial, ornamental surface.

Hurston undercuts the absoluteness of the opposition between white and black in another way as well. In describing the white man as "drumming the table with his fingertips," Hurston places in his body a counterpart to the "war drum" central to the jungle. If the jungle represents the experience of the body as such, the surge of bodily life external to conscious knowledge ("give pain, give death to what, I do not know"), then the nervous gesture is an alienated synecdoche for such bodily release.

In an essay entitled "What White Publishers Won't Print" written for *Negro Digest* in 1950, twenty-two years after "How It Feels to Be Colored Me," Hurston again takes up this "jungle" stereotype, this time to disavow it. The contrast between the two essays is significant:

> This insistence on defeat in a story where upperclass Negroes are portrayed, perhaps says something from the subconscious of the majority. Involved in western culture, the hero or heroine, or both, must appear frustrated and go down to defeat, somehow. Our literature reeks with it. It is the same as saying, "You can translate Virgil, and fumble with the differential calculus, but can you really comprehend it? Can you cope with our subtleties?"
> That brings us to the folklore of "reversion to type." This curious doctrine has such wide acceptance that it is tragic. One has only to examine the huge literature on it to be convinced. No matter how high we may *seem* to climb, put us under strain and we revert to type, that is, to the bush. Under a superficial layer of western culture, the jungle drums throb in our veins.

There are many possible explanations for Hurston's changed use of this image. For one thing, the exotic primitive was in vogue in 1928, while this was no longer the case in 1950. For another, she was addressing a white readership in the earlier essay and a black readership here. But the most revealing difference lies in the way the image is embedded in a structure of address. In the first essay, Hurston describes the jungle feeling as an art, an *ability* to feel, not a reversion. In the second, the jungle appears as a result of "strain." In the first, Hurston can proclaim "I am this"; but when the image is repeated as "you are that," it changes completely. The content of the image may be the same, but its interpersonal use is different. The study of Afro-American literature as a whole poses a similar problem of address: any attempt to lift out of a text an image or essence of blackness is bound to violate the interlocutionary strategy of its formulation.

"What White Publishers Won't Print" is a complex meditation on the possibility of representing difference in order to erase it. Lamenting the fact that "the average, struggling, non-morbid Negro is the best-kept secret in America," Hurston explains the absence of a black *Main Street* by the majority's "indifference, not to say scepticism, to the internal life of educated minorities." The revelation to the public of the Negro who is "just like everybody else" is "the thing needed to do away with that feeling of difference which inspired fear and which ever expresses itself in dislike." The thing that prevents the publication of such representations of Negroes is thus said to be the public's *in*difference to finding out that there *is* no difference. Difference is a misreading of sameness, but it must be represented in order to be erased. The resistance to finding out that the Other is the same springs out of the reluctance to admit that the same is Other. If the average man could recognize that the Negro was "just like him," he would have to recognize that he was just like the Negro. Difference disliked is identity affirmed. But the difficulty of pleading for a representation of difference *as* sameness is exemplified by the almost unintelligible distinction in the following sentence:

> As long as the majority cannot conceive of a Negro or a Jew feeling and reacting inside just as they do, the majority will keep right on believing that people who do not feel like them cannot possibly feel as they do.

The difference between the difference and sameness can barely be said. It is as small and as vast as the difference between "like" and "as."

Hurston ends "How It Feels to Be Colored Me," too, with an attempt to erase difference. She describes herself as "a brown bag of miscellany" whose contents are as different from each other as they are similar to those of other bags, "white, red, and yellow." The outside is no guarantee of the nature of the inside. The last sentence of the article, which responds distantly to the title, is "Who knows?"

By the end of the essay, then, Hurston has conjugated a conflicting and ironic set of responses to her title. Far from answering the question of "how it feels to be colored me," she deconstructs the very grounds of an answer, replying "Compared to what? As of when? Who is asking? In what context? For what purpose? With what interests and presuppositions?" What Hurston rigorously shows is that questions of difference and identity are always a function of a specific interlocutionary situation—and the answers, matters of strategy rather than truth. In its rapid passage from image to image and from formula to formula, Hurston's *text* enacts the questions of identity as a process of *self*-difference that Hurston's *persona* often explicitly denies.

It is precisely that self-difference, however, that Hurston will assert as the key to her anthropological enterprise in *Mules and Men*. In discussing Hurston's folktale anthology, I will focus less on the tales themselves than on Hurston's multilayered envelope of address, in which such self-differentiations are most obvious and functional. In the opening lines of her introduction to the volume, Hurston writes:

> I was glad when somebody told me, "You may go and collect Negro folklore."
> In a way it would be a new experience for me. When I pitched headforemost into the world I landed in a crib of negroism. . . . But it was fitting me like a tight chemise. I couldn't see it for wearing it. It was only when I was off in college, away from my native surroundings, that I could see myself like somebody else and stand off and look at my garment. Then I had to have the spy-glass of Anthropology to look through at that.

The journey away to school does not confer color and fixed identity as it did in "How It Feels to Be Colored Me" but rather sight and self-division. "Seeing" and "wearing" (significantly, not seeing and being) cannot coincide, and we cannot always be sure which side of the spyglass our narrator is standing on. The ambiguity of the inside/outside opposition involved in "see[ing] myself like somebody else" is dramatized in many ways in which Hurston's collection of folktales, songs, and hoodoo practices, resulting in a complex interaction between the authority of her spy-glass and the rhetorical nature of her material.

Mules and Men is a book with multiple frames: it begins with a preface by Franz Boas, Hurston's teacher, and ends with a glossary and appendix. As we have seen, Hurston's own introduction begins with a paraphrase of Psalm 122 which replaces the Biblical "they" with an unnamed "somebody," and it ends by placing itself geographically just outside the town line of Eatonville:

> So I rounded Park Lane and came speeding down the straight stretch into Eatonville. . . .
> Before I enter the township, I wish to make acknowledgments to Mrs. R. Osgood [Charlotte] Mason of New York City. She backed my falling in a hearty way, in a spiritual way, and in addition, financed the whole expedition in the manner of the Great Soul that she is.

And part 1 begins:

> As I crossed the Maitland-Eatonville township line

That line is the line between the two ends of the spy-glass, but it is also supposed to stand as the line between the theoretical introduction and the tales. Yet Hurston has already told the first tale, a folktale she remembers as she drives, a tale of creation and of the unequal distribution of "soul." Hence, not only does the first tale subvert the opposition between theory and material, but the tale itself comments doubly upon the acknowledgment to Mrs. Mason: what Mrs. Mason backed is called a "falling"—both a postcreational Fall and a losing hand in the "Georgia Skin Game" often referred to in the text. And since the story is about God's promise to redistribute "soul" more equally in the future, it sheds an ironic light on the designation of Hurston's wealthy patron as a "Great Soul."

Hurston does, however, offer some theoretical remarks in her introduction:

> Folk-lore is not as easy to collect as it sounds. The best source is where there are the least outside influences and these people, being usually underprivileged, are the shyest. They are most reluctant at times to reveal that which the soul lives by. And the Negro, in spite of his open-faced laughter, his seeming acquiescence, is particularly evasive. You see we are a polite people and we do not say to our questioner, "Get out of here!" We smile and tell him or her something that satisfies the white person because, knowing so little about us, he doesn't know what he is missing. The Indian resists curiosity by a stony silence. The Negro offers a feather-bed resistance. That is, we let the probe enter, but it never comes out. It gets smothered under a lot of laughter and pleasantries.
>
> The theory behind our tactics: "The white man is always trying to know into somebody else's business. All right, I'll set something outside the door of my mind for him to play with and handle. He can read my writing but he sho' can't read my mind. I'll put this play toy in his hand. and he will seize it and go away. Then I'll say my say and sing my song."

The shifts and reversals in this passage are multiple. Hurston begins as an outsider, a scientific narrative voice that refers to "these people" in the third person, as a group whose inner lives are difficult to penetrate. Then, suddenly, she leaps into the picture she has just painted, including herself in a "we" that addresses a "you"—the white reader, the new implied outsider. The structure of address changes from description to direct address. From that point on it is impossible to tell whether Hurston the narrator is *describing* a strategy or *employing* one. Is her book something set "outside the door" for the white man to "play with and handle," or is the difficulty of penetrating the featherbed resistance being described in order to play up her own privileged skill and access to its inner secrets? In any event, theory is here on the side of the withholder.

The text itself is a frame narrative recounting Hurston's *quest* for folktales along with the folktales themselves. It is a tale of the gathering of tales, or "lies," as they are called by the tellers. Hurston puts herself in a position to hear the tales only to the extent that she herself "lies." When she tells the townspeople that she has come to collect their "lies," one of them exclaims, "Aw shucks, . . . Zora, don't you come here and tell de biggest lie first thing. Who you reckon want to read all them old-time tales about Brer Rabbit and Brer Bear?". Later, when Hurston leaves Eatonville to gather more tales, she is snubbed as an outsider because of her car and expensive dress until she lies and says that she is a bootlegger fleeing from justice. With her loss of difference comes a flood of tales. The strategy to obtain the material becomes indistinguishable from the material obtained.

This is not to say that the anthropolitical frame is entirely adequate to its task of accurate representation. The following tale can be read as a questioning of the framing activity:

> Ah know another man wid a daughter.
> The man sent his daughter off to school for seben years, den she come home all finished up. So he said to her, "Daughter, git yo' things and write me a letter to my brother!" So she did.
> He says, "Head it up," and she done so.
> "Now tell 'im, 'Dear Brother, our chile is done come home from school and all finished up and we is very proud of her.'"
> Then he ast de girl "Is you got dat?"
> She tole 'im "yeah."
> "Now tell him some mo'. 'Our mule is dead but Ah got another mule and when Ah say (clucking sound of tongue and teeth) he moved from de word.'"
> "Is you got dat?" he ast de girl.
> "Naw suh," she tole 'im.
> He waited a while and he ast her again, "You got dat down yet?"
> "Naw suh, Ah ain't got it yet."
> "How come you ain't got it?"
> "Cause Ah can't spell (clucking sound)."
> "You mean to tell me you been off to school seben years and can't spell (clucking sound)? Why Ah could spell dat myself and Ah ain't been to school a day in mah life. Well jes' say (clucking sound) he'll know what yo' mean and go on wid de letter."

The daughter in the tale is in a situation analogous to that of Hurston: the educated student returns home to transcribe what her forebears utter orally. She has learned a notation system that considers itself complete but that turns out to lack a sign for (clucking sound). The "inside" is here commenting on the "outside," the tale commenting on the book as a whole. It is not by chance that this should be a tale precisely about mules and men. The noncoextensiveness of oral signs and written signs is a problem very much at the heart of Hurston's enterprise. But lest one fall into a simple opposition between the tale's orality and the transcriber's literacy, it is well to note that the orality/literacy relation is the very *subject* of the tale, which cannot be appreciated by those who, like the father *in* the tale, cannot write. Its irony is directed both ways.

Despite Boas' prefatory claim that Hurston has made "an unusual contribution to our knowledge of the true inner life of the Negro," the nature of such "knowledge" cannot be taken for granted. Like Hurston's representation of "colored me," her collection of folktales forces us to ask not "Has an 'inside' been accurately represented?" but "What is the nature of the dialogic situation into which the representation has been called?" Since this is always specific, always a play of specific desires and expectations, it is impossible to conceive of a pure inside. There is no universalized Other, no homogeneous "us," for the self to reveal itself *to*. Inside the chemise is the other side of the chemise: the side on which the observer can read the nature of his or her own desire to see.

Mules and Men ends, unexpectedly, with one final tale. Hurston has just been talking not about folktales but about hoodoo practices. Suddenly, after a break but without preamble, comes the following tale:

> Once Sis Cat got hongry and caught herself a rat and set herself down to eat 'im. Rat tried and tried to git loose but Sis Cat was too fast and strong. So jus' as de cat started to eat 'im he says, "Hol' on dere, Sis Cat! Ain't you got no manners at all? You going set up to de table and eat 'thout washing yo' face and hands?"
>
> Sis Cat was mighty hongry but she hate for de rat to think she ain't got no manners, so she went to de water and washed her face and hands and when she got back de rat was gone.
>
> So de cat caught herself a rat again and set down to eat. So de rat said, "Where's yo' manners at, Sis Cat? You going to eat 'thout washing yo' face and hands?"
>
> "Oh, Ah got plenty manners," de cat told 'im. "But Ah eats mah dinner and washes mah face and uses mah manners afterwards." So she et right on 'im and washed her face and hands. And cat's been washin' after eatin' ever since.
>
> I'm sitting here like Sis Cat, washing my face and usin' my manners.

So ends the book. But what manners is she using? Upon reading this strange, unglossed final story, one cannot help wondering who, in the final analysis, has swallowed what. The reader? Mrs. Mason? Franz Boas? Hurston herself? As Nathan Huggins writes after an attempt to determine the sincerity of Hurston's poses and self-representations, "It is impossible to tell from reading Miss Hurston's autobiography who was being fooled."[6] If, as Hurston often implies, the essence of telling "lies" is the art of conforming a narrative to existing structures of address while gaining the upper hand, then Hurston's very ability to fool us—or to fool us into *thinking* we have been fooled—is itself the only effective way of conveying the rhetoric of the "lie." To turn one's own life into a trickster tale of which even the teller herself might be the dupe certainly goes far in deconstructing the possibility of representing the truth of identity.

If I initially approached Hurston out of a desire to re-referentialize difference, what Hurston gives me back seems to be difference as a suspension of reference. Yet the terms "black" and "white," "inside" and "outside," continue to matter. Hurston suspends the certainty of reference not by erasing these differences but by foregrounding the complex dynamism of their interaction.

Notes

1. See Zora Neale Hurston, "How It Feels to Be Colored Me," *World Tomorrow* 11 (May 1928): 215–16; rpt. in *I Love Myself When I Am Laughing and Then Again When I Am Looking Mean and Impressive: A Zora Neale Hurston Reader,* ed. Alice Walker (Old Westbury, N.Y., 1979), pp. 152–155.
2. See Hurston, "What White Publishers Won't Print," *Negro Digest* 8 (Apr. 1950): 85–89; rpt. in *I Love Myself When I Am Laughing,* pp. 169–73.
3. See Hurston, *Mules and Men* (1935; Bloomington, Ind., 1978).
4. Langston Hughes, *The Big Sea: An Autobiography* (New York, 1963), pp. 238–39.
5. This formulation was suggested to me by a student, Lisa Cohen.
6. Nathan Irvin Huggins, *Harlem Renaissance* (London, 1971), p. 133.

◆◆◆◆◆◆◆◆◆◆◆◆◆◆

Breaking Out of the Conventions of Dialect[1]
GAYL JONES

I. MINSTRELSY AND EARLY LITERARY DIALECT.

The history of Afro-American fiction, along with poetry, has represented a tension between oral and literary forms. In his book *Neo-African Literature*, Jahn speaks of "Afro-American folklore making its breakthrough to literature" in the works of Paul Laurence Dunbar and Charles Waddel Chesnutt but he also refers to Dunbar as a "black nigger minstrel."[2]

This points to a dual problem in Afro-American literary history. First, Afro-American folklore did exist as viable and complex literary forms and Afro-American writers from the turn of the century certainly made deliberate artistic use of these forms in their literary creations. Secondly, the distortions (human and linguistic) of minstrelsy also existed as literary models in the language and character of the interlocutor and Mr. Bones and Mr. Tambo. The former was usually white and spoke in formal, standard, "intelligent" and serious language (the beginnings of the "straight man" in American comedy) while the latter spoke in dialect whose subject matter was limited to clownish discourse.[3] Not only then was there the tension between the "pure" oral and literary models as complex forms, but the uses of oral tradition and "black speech" were further complicated by the intrusion of the "artistic models" of the minstrel show and its reduction of the artistic possibilities of Afro-American oral tradition—speech and folklore—through distortion and caricature. It is curious that, not only do American comedic teams continue this pattern but that this is the precedent for the American musical comedy and even the first American talking movie (the 1927 "Jazz Singer") was, without question, in the minstrel tradition.[4]

Minstrelsy, then, contributed to the ambivalent attitudes of the early Afro-American writers toward "the dialect" and fastened the former toward this language as distortion, compounding, molding and securing apparent distortions of character and the relationship between language and character revelation. Because audiences as well were used to hearing "dialect" only in comic contexts, even the writers who used it for other purposes or with different intentions were often accused, as Richard Wright accused Zora Neale Hurston, of "perpetuating the minstrel tradition"[5] even though her own work was not only necessary for the "authentic" representation of the speech of her characters but also contributed to broadening the range of dialect in literature.

Dunbar's short story, "The Lynching of Jube Benson," brings together all of the early problems of dialect and demonstrates the attempts at making the "breakthrough" of folklore into literature. James Weldon Johnson, an Afro-American writer, whose own writings, such as *God's Trombones: Seven Negro Sermons in Verse* (1927), show efforts to resolve the tensions of literary dialect, clarifies the problems of dialect in his Introduction to *The Book of American Negro Poetry* (1931):

> Today, even the reader is conscious that almost all poetry in the conventionalized dialect is either based upon the minstrel traditions of Negro life, traditions that had but slight relation—often no relation at all—to actual Negro life, or is permeated with artificial sentiment. It is now realized both by the poets and by their public that, as an instrument for poetry, the dialect has only two main stops, humor and pathos.
>
> That this is not a shortcoming inherent in the dialect as dialect is demonstrated by the wide compass it displays in its use in the folk creations. The limitation is due to conventions that have been fixed upon the dialect and the conformity to them by individual writers. Negro dialect poetry had its origin in the minstrel traditions and a persisting pattern was set. When the individual writer attempted to get away from that pattern, the fixed conventions allowed him only to slip over into a slough of sentimentality. These conventions were not broken for the simple reason that the individual writers wrote chiefly to entertain an outside audience and in concord with its stereotyped ideas about the Negro. And herein lies the vital distinction between them and the folk creators, who wrote solely to please and express themselves.[6]

Elsewhere in the Introduction, Johnson suggests that, if Afro-American writers had been the first to "fix" their dialect as literature, perhaps these "conventions" of distortion and caricature for the benefit of outsiders could have been superseded. He cites Robert Burns' use of the Scottish dialect as an example of what might have been done. When we consider his poetry, we apprehend its elegance, variety of subjects and range of humanity; it is not the language solely of burlesque or pathos, though even Burns was once "hailed by the literati of Edinburgh as an instance of the natural genius (. . .) whose poems were the spontaneous overflow of his native feelings" (my emphasis).[7]

Of course, this accusation of "artlessness," as observed in the writing of the Canadian Margaret Laurence, continues to be the bane of writers writing outside standard literary conventions in spite of the "intelligence and sensibility" that their efforts bring to, or cull from, their indigenous speech and their "deliberate craft". But both "the Scottish oral tradition of folklore and folk song, and the highly developed Scottish literary tradition" were both parts of Burns' artistic heritage. Perhaps it is this sense of security in both a literary and oral tradition that provided Burns' "sure fix" on intricate poetry in Scottish dialect. However, for the slave in America, literacy was a criminal act. Not only was he denied legal access to the literary heritage of the West but there was no clear continuity with the African oral literatures as an aesthetic alternative in a "highly developed African oral tradition" (Finnegan), including ritual dramas and great epics. The only outlet for his visions, concerns and struggles in the New World were the oral forms developed here: the blues, spirituals and worksongs. Later Afro-American writers drew upon these forms to insure a new connection with tradition but they did not hold the same currency or status in a literary culture to whose access his ancestors were both denied and alien.

Social history thus also compounded the problems of the early Afro-American writers who incorporated Afro-American dialect and folklore into their literatures. There are two of them to be considered here: Paul Laurence Dunbar and Zora Neale Hurston: the first, a turn-of-the-century writer and the second a representative of the Harlem Renaissance period. The questions that may be raised in reviewing the works of these writers are: how does one use in literature a dialect that has already been codified into burlesque? How does one employ the language in order to return it to the elasticity, viability and, indeed, the complexity, "intelligence and sensibility" that it often has when not divorced from the oral modes and folk creators, as it has especially in the grand language of the spirituals and in the complex musical language of jazz, which has been called America's only classical music?

II. PAUL LAURENCE DUNBAR.

Dunbar's "The Lynching of Jube Benson"[8] illustrates the codification of literary dialect in the turn-of-the-century Afro-American fiction and the links between dialect, perspective, character and audience.

At the beginning of the story, three men are seated in Gordon Fairfax's library and Dunbar uses not only Dr. Melville's viewpoint but his indirection to initiate the story. First, through the dialogue of the four white men, the author sets up the popular feeling of the time of the Jim Crow codes and legislation at home and encroachments abroad in the Pacific and Caribbean, extending the convolvulus of white supremacy—a time when lynchings were advertised in newspapers under "amusements". In the conversation, Gay rather callously says "I would like to see a real lynching". And if a real lynching were to come his way, Fairfax admits, "I should not avoid it". "I should" spoke Dr. Melville "from the depths of his chair, where he had been puffing in moody silence," and thus begins the story . . .

This restriction of perspective to Melville's viewpoint and using him as the story-teller is, of course, related to the audience of this turn-of-the-century fiction. Addressed to white audiences, it admonishes them to change their social attitudes and put an end to lynching. Similarly, slave narrators addressed such audiences to change their sentiments to abolitionist ones. Like most literature in that tradition of protest, it is a a white man who argues and authenticates the case of Jube who comes to consciousness and realisation and gives the lynching story its authenticity.

But there are problems. Jube remains essentially invisible. Revealed solely in a frame-story told by Melville, he must be seen only through the stereotypes and cliched metaphors of the latter. The "perfect Cerberus," he is "black but gentle". As the descriptions proceed, Melville reveals more of himself than he does of Jube and, in addition, allows for dramatic ironies when he speaks of recognising his "false education," yet persists in being circumscribed by it:

> Why did I do it? I don't know. A false education, I reckon, one false from the beginning. I saw his black face glooming there in the half light, and I could only think of him as a monster. It's tradition. At first I was told that the black man would catch me, and when I got over that, they taught me that the devil was black, and when I recovered from the sickness of that belief, here were Jube and his fellows with faces of menacing blackness. There was only one conclusion: this black man stood for all the powers of evil, the result of whose machinations had been gathering in my mind from childhood up. But this has nothing to do with what happened.

Melville recognizes but ironically continues to be guided by this false education in his symbolic, linguistic and metaphorical systems. Dunbar compounds the irony, for what happens—the false judgment and the consequent lynching—has everything to do with these machinations.

Melville is in love with Jube's mistress, Ann. When she is sick Jube takes care of her: "He was a fellow whom everybody trusted—an apparently steady-going, grinning sort, as we used to call him (. . .) faithful servitor". Jube not only nurses Ann when she falls victim to the typhoid outbreak but he also nurses Melville "as if I were a sick kitten and he my mother (. . .) a black but gentle demon". He sees him thus in his delirium and "chimerical vision".

This guarantees nothing. When Ann is attacked and murdered by a White masked with soot to resemble a Black and Annie, before dying, exclaims, "that Black," Jube is the first to be suspected. The "black rascal" identification, psycho-sexual myths and "the diabolical reason of his slyness" insure the white mob's ability to see Jube only as a "human tiger" and judge him guilty of the crime without evidence or trial. The white men pursue Jube—"he gave a scream like an animal's"—and lynch him.

Later, when Jube's brother Ben and another Black come with the real culprit, it is too late. Ben accuses fiercely: "You he'ped murder my brothah, you dat was his frien'; go 'way, go 'way! I'll take him home myse'f".

Melville, however, forms the final judgement in calling himself and the others in the mob "blood guilty" and telling the "gentlemen" gathered in Gordon Fairfax's library that that was his last lynching.

Because the story is told from Melville's perspective and much of Jube's dialect is contained within this "frame," we may surmise that many of the restrictions and conventions of literary dialect (like the metaphorical restrictions on Jube's humanity) could be ascribed equally to Melville and the author's concern with the truth and consistency of the narrator's personality. Whether or not this is true, Dunbar's use of dialect clinches the problems in this particular use of conventions.

First, the emotional range is restricted to pathos. We do not rise to the tragic potential of the story and are only allowed to glimpse its possibility near the conclusion when Jube's brother Ben and another Black briefly enter the scene and Ben makes his strong accusation. But, in accordance with Johnson's description, there are elements of minstrel parody in Melville's rendering of Jube's language, gestures and mannerisms although he does not recognize this because he considers he is giving an affective and serious rendering of Jube and expressing genuine sentiment. In his article on Booker T. Washington's *Up From Slavery*, critic Robert Steptoe noted a "real life" example of this situation. Though the white man who describes Washington intends to praise him, he nevertheless resorts to cliched stereotypical descriptions and a symbolic system which does exactly the opposite in which language and perception conspire together:

(. . .) while "the noted war correspondent" James Creelman's *New York World* account of Washington's Atlanta address undoubtedly authenticates both speech and event, it does so while perpetuating certain popular stereotypes of black and, indeed, resorts to clichés in describing Washington. The most offensive passage occurs when Creelman attempts to add a little sentiment and "color" to his story: "A ragged ebony giant, squatted on the floor in one of the aisles, watched the orator with burning eyes and tremulous face until the supreme burst of applause came, and then the tears ran down his face. Most of the Negroes in the audience were crying, perhaps without knowing just why". We needn't labor over Creelman's opinion of the Negroes in the audience, or strain to mime his attitude toward (or anxiety over) the responses of the white women: "The fairest women of Georgia stood up and cheered (. . .) It was as if the orator [Washington] had bewitched them". Of Washington, Creelman writes that he is a "Negro Moses," a "tall tawny Negro" with "heavy jaws, and strong, determined mouth, with big white teeth, piercing eyes (. . .) bronzed neck (. . .) muscular right arm (. . .) clenched brown fist (. . .) big feet (. . .) and dusky hand".[9]

Like Melville's account of Jube, the language says more about the teller's psychology and attitudes than it gives "accurate portraiture".

Secondly, in Dunbar's story, the transcription techniques depend on easy mutilations of spelling and grammar, as well as the use of "eye dialect"—unnecessary orthographic changes such as "tuk" for "took", "a laffin'" for "laughing". Such words do not depend on pronunciation for their changes but add to the visual distortion, increasing the sense of the language as humorous or pathetic aberration.

Finally, literary formulae are used in the place of heard speech but Melville accounts for much of the formulae in his retelling. Since everyone's "rehearing" is somehow distorted by imagination, memory or judgement, and compounded with his "false education", Melville does not surprise us here. Nevertheless, the problems of literary dialect as delineated by Johnson are finely illuminated by this story: the restricted emotional range, the limited range of subject-matter, experience and perception.

Although "The Lynching of Jube Benson" is a frame story, told by Melville to a group of lynching enthusiasts to convince them (and the white reading public) of the moral wrong of lynching and we are not sure how much of the conventions of dialect are due to persona/perspective/ audience or "world-view", it is important to reiterate and clarify that the limitations of literary dialect are not just limitations of language and not just a literary or artistic dilemma, but that language is inseparable from our comprehension and sense of character. By restricting the emotional and experiential ranges, as well as the distractions brought about by transcription techniques, a fully realized, complex character is impossible. We might ask ourselves the following questions: if Jube's brother Ben had told the story would the range of emotions have been extended beyond pathos and parody? What other aspects of Jube's character (unknown to Melville) might have been revealed? Would a broader range and context of subjects and concerns have entered the story? Would Afro-American characters have been moved from the background to the foreground in dramatic scenes? Though there would have still been the use of "eye dialect" and other transcription devices shared by all the turn-of-the-century writers, could the dialect have been made to do more and would it have more to do? How might it have been stretched? These questions lead us again to the problem of audience: the audience that was taken for granted at a time when the "broader perspective" was always white and the significant relationships were always interracial ones of unambiguous conflict and dangerous confrontation. It is only when the folklore tradition gains more of its own authority in literature that such questions will be answered and character, audience, viewpoint and language gain more elasticity.

III. ZORA NEALE HURSTON.

Hurston's "The Gilded Six-Bits" (1933)[10] takes us out of the conventional restrictions observed in Dunbar. This transformation is partly due to the shift in perspective: we are inside rather than outside the black community and there is not the same double-conscious concern with an exclusive white audience. Because there are not the same motives of the anti-lynching story or of the tradition of protest literature in general, Hurston can be concerned with the relationship between a man and woman in "a Negro settlement". She can expand the range beyond "humor and pathos" to a crisis-of-love story; there can be development and recognition, dilemma and resolution, delineated personality.

Critic George Kent has called this a "simple story". In an interview with Bell he says "that one [the story] suggests that really simple people could suddenly resolve all problems by suddenly forgiving each other very easily (. . .) I (. . .) recall that incident being very tediously resolved. I don't recall a really imposing short story by her (. . .)."[11]

Though the story is about "simple people" whose relationship seems to be apparently simply resolved, in view of the problems manifest in Dunbar, it might be reviewed in a more complex light. Its shift in perspective (what Ellison would term "restoring of perspective"), its lack of preoccupation with audience, its sense that Southern rural black speech as dialect may contain any emotion in literature adds degrees of complexity not easily acknowledged or perceived in a cursory reading. Although there certainly is humor in places (as in all her work) it is the spontaneous good humor of fully realized characters in interaction and not that of dimensional minstrel humor. We laugh along with the characters in their happy moments; we go down into the depths with them during the "crisis of love"; we come out with them. We are brought beyond humor and pathos.

The focus is on relationships, interpersonal conflict and conflict of values. There are some elements of sophistication in the story (particularly in its many reversals) but the problem with Hurston (and this perhaps also accounts for Kent's reaction) is how does one write of ordinary people without making the story seem trivial, without making the writer's concerns seem likewise? The subject of Dunbar's story is perhaps a more "significant event"[12] in socio-historical reality but, nevertheless, his Afro-American characters remain in the background in both their physical presence and psychological reality. On the other hand, Hurston's characters are pulled to the foreground in both these respects. Like most literary transitions, this does not appear to be of great note these days with contemporaray Afro-American writers who automatically do the same, notwithstanding certain persistent (or recalcitrant) white critics who may still be asking the former whether they write about "black people or human beings?" and consider the Afro-American character's perspective "the broader perspective" and the significant one. However, it was an important transition and should be seen as an initial link between a literary technique (viewpoint) and its broader humanistic implications in the depiction of black humanity in literature.

* * *

We first meet Missie May and Joe in a ritual scene that occurs every Saturday morning when he throws nine silver dollars in the door "for her to pick up and pile beside her plate at dinner". He also brings her candy kisses. The beginning is full of happiness, "joyful mischief", "mock anger" and the "play fight".

Otis Slemmons, introduced shortly after this payful scene, becomes the center of a conflict of values and the latter, as the subject of much of Hurston's fiction, should be considered a worthy subject or what E.M. Forster would call a "noble" one. Nevertheless, Otis is from Chicago and "spots and places". In the initial dialogue between husband and wife we see the things that interest the couple about him: he has been places, he has gold teeth, he wears "up to date" clothes, his "puzzlegutted" build makes him "look like a rich white man", he has the attention of many women (including white ones up North) and he has gold pieces. These are the things that Joes notices and talks about. Initially, May's concerns seem not to be material but her love for Joe is uppermost; she loves him as he is. Joe, however, feels he "can't hold no light to Otis D. Slemmons" because he "ain't never been nowhere" and "ain't got nothing but you".

At first, May is not taken in by Otis or what he represents. Then there is a reversal. The next time we hear the couple talking together (after they have returned from seeing Otis at the local ice-cream parlor), Joe is expressing her earlier values and she is expressing his. We see then all the things she wants for him "because she loves him". Nevertheless, she wants them:

> Joe laughed and hugged her. "Don't be so wishful 'bout me. Ah'm satisfied de way Ah is. So long as Ah be yo' husband, Ah don't keer 'bout nothin' else".

However, to get the gilded six-bits which the gold coins turn out to be, May betrays Joe with Otis. Joe comes home early from work and finds them together. There is a fine handling of emotional reactions here. He sees them and "opens his mouth and laughs". Because this is not the expected response—the reaction and emotion seem contradictory—it deepens our sense of the emotion as "a howling wind [which] raced through his heart" and he "kept on feeling so much". He fights Slemmons, drives him away and the crisis of love begins. There is no laughter or banter.

Kent calls the resolution easy. I think that it appears easy because Hurston handles all the emotional reversals and complications in narrative summary rather than in active dramatic scenes. One reads them quickly and so it seems that they are done quickly but these are real, subtle and difficult changes. Joe makes love to May then leaves a piece of Slemmon's "gold" with the bit of chain attached under her pillow. She then discovers that "it was a gilded half dollar". After the love making she thinks that "they were man and wife again. Then another thought

CONVENTIONS OF DIALECT • 149

came clawing at her. He had come home to buy from her as if she were any woman in the long house. Fifty cents for her love". She dresses and leaves the house but she encounters her husband's mother and, so as not to "admit defeat to that woman", she returns home. Joe discovers she is pregnant and when she has the child he knows it is his (his mother even confirms that it looks like him so it must be his!) and they reconcile.

The story is perhaps resolved too simply at this point, the "baby chile" being a kind of deus ex machina. Nevertheless, Hurston's handling of their complications and reversals of emotion up to now has been superb and certainly adds more shadings of emotion than revealed in earlier dialect stories. Dialect itself is more complex and shows more literary sophistication. The links with the interior of the characters, the processes of emotional transformation, as well as the foreground presentation make it no "simple story" though it deals with "ordinary folks", yet it poses a challenge because it contains everything that was considered not the stuff of important fiction: it is regional, it focuses on the relationship between a black man and a black woman and it does not make interracial conflict its reason for being.

The problem of the "stuff of important fiction" of course transcends racial lines. A contemporary American white writer, Mary Gordon, has written an article entitled "The Parable of the Cave or In Praise of Water Colors" in which she speaks of Theodore Roethke saying that woman poets were "stamping a tiny foot against God" and that she has been told by male (but not female) critics that her work is "exquisite", "like a water color": "Water colors are cheap and plentiful; oils are costly: their base must be bought. And the idea is that oil paintings will endure".

Because Gordon's remarks are important in cross-sexual and cross-cultural criticism, I will quote her in full:

> There are people in the world who derive no small pleasure from the game of "major" and "minor." They think that no major work can be painted in water colors. They think, too, that Hemingway writing about boys in the woods is major; Mansfield writing about girls in the house is minor. Exquisite, they will hasten to insist, but minor. These people join up with other bad specters and I have to work to banish them. Let us pretend these specters are two men, two famous poets, saying, "your experience is an embarrassment; your experience is insignificant".
>
> I wanted to be a good girl, so I tried to find out whose experience was not embarrassing. The prototype for a writer who was not embarrassing was Henry James. "And you see", the two specters said, proffering hope, "he wrote about social relationships but his distance gave them grandeur".
>
> Distance, then, was what I was to strive for. Distance from the body, from the heart, but most of all, distance from the self as writer (. . .)
>
> If Henry James had the refined experience, Conrad had the significant one. The important moral issues were his: men pitted against nature in moments of extremity. There are no important women in Conrad's novels, except for Victory, which, the critics tell us, is a romance and an exception. Despite the example of Conrad, it was all right for the young men I knew, according to my specters, to write about the hymens they had broken, the diner waitresses

they had seduced. Those experiences were significant. But we were not to write about our broken hearts, about the married men we loved disastrously, about our mothers or our children. Men could write about their fears of dying by exposure in the forest; we could not write about our fears of being suffocated in the kitchen. Our desire to write about these experiences only revealed our shallowness; it was suggested we would, in time, get over it. And write about what? Perhaps we would stop writing.

"And so", the specters whispered to me, "if you want to write well, if you want us to take you seriously, you must be distant, you must be extreme".

I suppose the specters were not entirely wrong. Some of the literature that has been written since the inception of the women's movement is lacking in style and moral proportion. But so is the work of Mailer, Miller, Burroughs, Ginsberg. Their lack of style and proportion may be called offensive, but not embarrassing. They may be referred to as off the mark, but they will not be called trivial.

And above all I did not wish to be trivial; I did not wish to be embarrassing.[13]

Most female writers (black and white) have experienced this from male critics. Black writers (male and female) have experienced it from (white) male critics and, ironically, given Gordon's remarks, from white female critics. The problem of writers dominated by literary standards of "significant events" (national, sexual, racial) is not only finding one's voice but of trusting it when one does find it; then finding the voice or voices that one most values and avoiding destruction of the creative spirit and discovering how one can most (as Kent would term it) "assert one's existence" and the existences of all the characters.

Kent himself feels that black women writers fail to explore real depth: "Often, the problem is that you don't get a deep enough definition of all the things that the woman encounters which are her responses to power (. . .) I would say that black women writers that I've read don't seem to get much into subtle possibilities (. . .) I don't see much possibility and I'm not sure that there is always depth (. . .)". Yet, unlike most critics, he acknowledges that "it might be that male thing you were talking about."[14]

This could be the "elliptical details" in the work for which a male critic would need more "analytical commentary."[15]

But regardless of the "subtle possibilities" (of society, history, gender?) that critics confuse with aesthetics, in the case of Hurston, dialect, as regional vernacular, can and does contain subject, experience, emotion and revelation. Two reasons for this new attitude and sense of possibility in character and dialect might be that she was born in the first incorporated tall-black town of Eatonville, Florida, and that she was a folklorist possessing an exact as well as a creative ear. In her Foreword to *Their Eyes Were Watching God*, Williams speaks of her "command":

She had at her command a large store of stories, songs, incidents, idiomatic phrases, and metaphors; her ear for speech rhythms must have been remarkable. Most importantly, she had the literary intelligence and developed the literary skill to convey the power and beauty of this heard speech and lived experience on the printed page.

Hurston's evocations of the lifestyles of rural Blacks have not been equaled but to stress the ruralness of Hurston's settings or to characterize her diction solely in terms of exotic "dialect" spellings is to miss her deftness with language. In the speech of her characters, black voices—whether rural or urban, northern or southern—come alive. Her fidelity to diction, metaphor and syntax—whether in direct quotations or in paraphrases of characters' thoughts—rings, even across forty years, with an arching familiarity that is a testament to Hurston's skill and to the durability of black speech[16].

In "The Gilded Six-Bits" one sees the folklorist in the metaphors, images and descriptions in the dialogue: "He ain't puzzlegutted, honey"; "God took pattern after a pine tree and built you noble"; "You can make 'miration at it, but don't tetch it"; "Ah reckon dey done made him vast-rich". Certainly there is a difference between the metaphors used here and those in Melville's descriptive evaluation of Jube or Creelman's of Washington because we have individuality, range and elegance.

Oral tradition enters, complements and complicates character in the use of "storytelling" or reported scenes to reinforce the dramatic ones. When May and Joe go to the ice-cream parlor and see Otis, they return and Joe re-tells the encounter:

> On the way home that night Joe was exultant. "Didn't Ah say ole Otis was swell? Cain't he talk Chicago talk? Wuzn't dat funny whut he said when great big fat ole da Armstrong come in? He asted me, "Who is dat broad wid de forte shake?" Dat's a new word. Us always thought forty was a set of figgers but he showed us where it means a whole heap of things. Sometimes he don't say forty, he jes' say thirty-eight and two, and dat mean de same thing. Know whut be told me when Ah wuz payin' for our ice cream? He say, "Ah have to hand it to you, Joe. Dat wife of yours is jes' thirty-eight and two. Yessuh, she's forte!" Ain't he killin'?

This description of the scene is important. Hurston does not take us to the ice-cream parlor directly and dramatically; she skips the scene and lets Joe's storytelling serve as a flashback and the story advances through the character's reactions to the moment. Therefore, the psychology of relationships is explored: there are complicating reversals and confusions of value, then the renewed and stronger affection.

Besides the use of storytelling dialogue, Hurston also moves "folk expressions" into the narrative while in most early fiction, and certainly the turn-of-the-century fiction of both Dunbar and Charles Waddell Chesnutt, it was confined to dialogue: "way after while", "make his market", "mess of honey flowers".

Here, the syntax, lexicon and expressive techniques of oral tradition break though to the narrative and alter it; this enlarges the scope of dialect to the modes of exposition. It is also possible for this extensible language to tell a story and Hurston offers a beginning here as well. Wideman speaks of this important "evolution":

From the point of view of American literature then, the fact of black speech (and the oral roots of a distinct literary tradition—ultimately the tradition itself) existed only when it was properly "framed" within works which had status in the dominant literary system. For black speech, the frame was the means of entering the literate culture and the frame also defined the purposes or ends for which black speech could be employed. The frame confers reality on black speech; the literary frame was a mediator, a legitimizer. What was outside the frame—chaotic, marginal, not worthy of the reader's attention—becomes, once inside, conventionalized into respectability.

The frame implies a linguistic hierarchy, the dominance of one language variety over all others. This linguistic subordination extends naturally to the dominance of one version of reality over others[17].

Hurston, in her use of dialect, was one of the first to initiate this breaking out of the frame—an important initiation for those writers committed to such linguistic explorations in fiction.

In "The Gilded Six-Bits", not only does the dialect have more functions but it is used in a story of greater complexity of character, greater thematic range and literary sophistication. Though the people themselves are "simple" in the sense of being "ordinary folks", their range is more than sentimental or comic emotion. Because the dialect here is given a fuller value and use, we move a step further toward a fuller exploration of black personalities in fiction but it will not be until *Their Eyes Were Watching God* that language, thought, experience, emotion and imagination will break through and add to the text like an apical bud, increasing the length of the stem or, to use Hurston's own image "a peartree bud coming to flower". She fulfills the possibility of what dialect might do when moved beyond the literary conventions and allowed more of the image and flexibility of authentic folk creation.

Notes

1. Essay taken from *Oral Tradition in African American Literature* (unpublished).
2. Janheinz Jahn; *Neo-African Literature: A History of Black Writing* (New York: Grove Press, 1968), pp. 149–151.
3. Camille Yarbrough: "Black Dance in America" in *The Black Collegian* (April/May 1981), pp. 20–21. See also Robert C. Toll's *On with the Show*, Oxford University Press, 1976, ch. 4.
4. Some may argue that the minstrel tradition continues (but without "blackface") through the rock singers.
5. Robert Hemenway: *Zora Neale Hurston: A Literary Biography* (Urbana: University of Illinois Press, 1977), p. 241. Also see Wright's review of *Their Eyes Were Watching God* in *New Masses*, October 5, 1937.
6. New York: Harcourt, Brace and World,Inc., 1959, p. 4.
7. M. H. Abrams (general editor): *The Norton Anthology of English Literature*, 4th ed., Vol. 2 (New York: Norton, 1979), p. 89.

8. In *American Negro Short Stories*, John Henrik Clarke (editor): (New York: Hill and Wang, 1966), pp. 1–8. All quotations from the story are taken from this anthology.
9. In *From Behind the Veil: A Study of Afro-American Narrative* (Urbana: University of Illinois Press, 1979), pp. 43–44.
10. In Clarke: *op. cit.*, pp. 63–74. All quotations from the story are taken from this anthology.
11. Roseann P. Bell, Bettye J. Parker and Beverly Guy-Sheftall (editors): *Sturdy Black Bridges: Visions of Black Woman in Literature* (New York: Anchor, 1979), p. 225.
12. W. E. Abraham: *The Mind of Africa* (Chicago: The University of Chicago Press, 1962), p. 11. Abraham speaks of historical events which "derive their significance from the culture in which they find themselves". His discussion may also raise questions regarding the significance of events in literature and "evaluation of facts and events".
13. In *The Writer On Her Work*, Janet Sternburg (editor): (New York: W.W. Norton, 1980).
14. In *Sturdy Black Bridges* (. . .) pp. 226, 228–229.
15. Lloyd W. Brown: *Women Writers in Black Africa* (Connecticut: Greenwood Press, 1981), p. 140.
16. Sherley Anne Williams: "Foreword" to *Their Eyes Were Watching God*, by Zora Neale Hurston (1937, rpt. Urbana: University of Illinois Press, 1978), p. ix.
17. John Wideman: "Frame and Dialect: The Evolution of the Black Voice" in *The American Poetry Review*, September/October 1976, pp. 34–37.

◆◆◆◆◆◆◆◆◆◆◆◆◆◆

Their Eyes Were Watching God: Hurston and the Speakerly Text

HENRY LOUIS GATES, JR.

Our house stood within a few rods of the Chesapeake Bay, whose broad bosom was ever white with sails from every quarter of the habitable globe. Those beautiful vessels, robed in purest white, so delightful to the eye of freemen, were to me so many shrouded ghosts, to terrify and torment me with thoughts of my wretched condition. I have often, in the deep stillness of a summer's Sabbath, stood all alone upon the lofty banks of that noble bay, and traced, with saddened heart and tearful eye, the countless number of sails moving off to the mighty ocean. The sight of these always affected me powerfully. My thoughts would compel utterance; and there, with no audience but the Almighty, I would pour out my soul's complaint, in my rude way, with an apostrophe to the moving multitude of ships:—

"You are loosed from your moorings, and are free; I am fast in my chains, and am a slave! You move merrily before the gentle gale, and I sadly before the bloody whip! You are freedom's swift-winged angels, that fly around the world; I am confined in bands of iron! O that I were free!"

Frederick Douglass, 1845

Ships at a distance have every man's wish on board. For some they come in with the tide. For others they sail forever on the horizon, never out of sight, never landing until the Watcher turns his eyes away in resignation, his dreams mocked to death by Time. That is the life of men.

Now, women forget all those things they don't want to remember, and remember everything they don't want to forget. The dream is the truth. Then they act and do things accordingly.

Zora Neale Hurston, 1937

I

The eighteenth-century revisions of the trope of the Talking Book that I traced in Chapter 4 and its displacement into tropes of freedom and literacy in the slave narratives published after 1815 help us to understand the remarkable degree to which the quest to register a public black voice in Western letters preoccupied the Afro-American tradition's first century. Writing could be no mean thing in the life of the slave. What was at stake for the earliest black authors was nothing less than the implicit testimony to their humanity, a common humanity which they sought to demonstrate through the very writing of a text of an ex-slave's life. In one sense, not even legal manumission was of more importance to the slave community's status in Western culture than was the negation of the image of the black as an absence. To redress their image as a negation of all that was white and Western, black authors published as if their collective fate depended on how their texts would be received. It is as difficult to judge how effective this tacitly political gesture was as it is to judge how the negative image of the black in Western culture was affected by the publication of black texts. It seems apparent, however, that the abolition of slavery did not diminish the force of this impulse to write the race fully into the human community. Rather, the liberation of the slave community and the slow but steady growth of a black middle class between Reconstruction (1865–1876) and the sudden ending of the New Negro Renaissance (circa 1930) only seem to have made this impulse even more intense than it had been in antebellum America. Perhaps this was the case because, once slavery was abolished, racism assumed vastly more subtle forms. If slavery had been an immoral institution, it had also been a large, fixed target; once abolished, the target of racism splintered into hundreds of fragments, all of which seemed to be moving in as many directions. Just as the ex-slaves wrote to end slavery, so too did free black authors write to redress the myriad forms that the fluid mask of racism assumed between the end of the Civil War and the end of the Jazz Age.

In the writings of black people retained their implicitly political import after the war and especially after the sudden death of Reconstruction, then it should not surprise us that the search for a voice in black letters became a matter of grave concern among the black literati. This concern, as we might expect, led to remarkably polemical debates over the precise register which an "authentic" black voice would, or could, assume. It is also clear that postbellum black authors continued to read and revise the central figures they received from the fragments of tradition that somehow survived the latter nineteenth century's onslaught of de facto and de jure segregation. Zora Neale Hurston's revision of Frederick Douglass's apostrophe to the ships (the epigraphs to this chapter) is only one example of many such instances of a black textual grounding through revision.

Hurston underscores her revision of Douglass's canonical text by using two chiasmuses in her opening paragraphs.[1] The subject of the second paragraph of *Their Eyes Were Watching God* (women) reverses the subject of the first (men) and figures the nature of their respective desire in opposite terms. A man's desire becomes reified onto a disappearing ship, and he is transformed from a human being into "a Watcher," his desire personified onto an object, beyond his grasp or control, external to himself. Nanny, significantly, uses this "male" figure—"Ah could see uh big ship at a distance"—as does Tea Cake, whose use reverses Douglass's by indicating Tea Cake's claim of control of his fate and ability to satisfy Jamie's desire: "Can't no ole man stop me from gittin' no ship for yuh if dat's whut you want. Ah'd git dat ship out from under him so slick til he'd be walkin' de water lak ole Peter befo' he knowed it."

A woman, by contrast, represents desire metaphorically, rather than metonymically, by controlling the process of memory, an active subjective process figured in the pun on (re)membering, as in the process of narration which Janie will share with her friend, Phoeby, and which we shall "overhear." For a woman, "The dream is the truth"; the truth is her dream. Janie, as we shall see, is thought to be (and is maintained) "inarticulate" by her first two husbands but is a master of metaphorical narration; Joe Starks, her most oppressive husband, by contrast, is a master of metonym, an opposition which Janie must navigate her selves through to achieve self-knowledge. The first sentence ("Now, women forget all those things they don't want to remember, and remember everything they don't want to forget") is itself a chiasmus (women/remember//remember/forget), similar in structure to Douglass's famous chiasmus, "You have seen how a man became a slave, you will see how a slave became a man." Indeed, Douglass's major contribution to the slave's narrative was to make chiasmus the central trope of slave narration, in which a slave-object writes himself or herself into a human-subject through the act of writing. The overarching rhetorical strategy of the slave narratives written after 1845 can be represented as a chiasmus, as repetition and reversal. Hurston, in these enigmatic opening paragraphs, Signifies upon Douglas through formal revision.

This sort of formal revision is one mode of tacit commentary about the shape and status of received tradition. A more explicit mode was the literary criticism published by blacks as a response to specific black texts which, despite great difficulties, somehow managed to be published. While this subject demands a full-length study, I can summarize its salient aspects here. The debate about the register of the black voice assumed two poles. By the end of the Civil War, the first pole of the debate, the value of the representation, of the reality imitated in the text, had been firmly established. Black authors wrote almost exclusively about their social and political condition as black people living in a society in which race was, at best, problematical. By the turn of the century, a second and more subtle pole of the debate had become predominant, and that pole turned upon precisely how an authentic black voice should be represented in print. The proper manner and matter of representation of a black printed voice are not truly separable, of course; these poles of concern could merge, and often did, as in the heated issue of the import of Paul Laurence Dunbar's late-nineteenth-century dialect poetry. To understand more fully just how curious were Zora Neale Hurston's rhetorical strategies of revision in *Their Eyes Were Watching God* (1937) and just how engaged in debate these strategies were with the Afro-American tradition, it is useful to summarize the nineteenth-century arguments about representation.

We gain some understanding of this concern over representation by examining *The Anglo-African Magazine*, published in New York by

Thomas Hamilton between January 1859 and March 1860. Hamilton, in his introductory "Apology" to the first number, argues what for his generation was self-evident: "[black people], in order to assert and maintain their rank as men among men, must speak for themselves; no outside tongue, however gifted with eloquence, can tell their story." Blacks must "speak for themselves," Hamilton writes, to counter the racist "endeavor to write down the negro as something less than a man."[2] In the second number, W. J. Wilson, in a poem entitled "The Coming Man," defines the presence of the text to be that which separates "the undefinable present," "the dim misty past," and "the unknown future":

> I am resolved. 'Tis more than half my task;
> 'Twas the great need of all my passed existence.
> The glooms that have so long shrouded me,
> Recede as vapor from the new presence,
> And the light-gleam—it must be life
> So brightens and spreads its rays before,
> That I read my Mission as 'twere a book.[3]

Wilson's figure of life as a text to be read, of the race's life as embodied in the book, Frances E. W. Harper elaborated upon in a letter to the editor later that same year. In this letter, we have recorded one of the first challenges to what was then, and has remained, the preoccupation of Afro-American male writers: the great and terrible subject of white racism. "If our talents are to be recognized," Frances Harper writes,

> we must write less of issues that are particular and more of feelings that are general. We are blessed with hearts and brains that compass more than ourselves in our present plight. . . . We must look to the future which, God willing, will be better than the present or the past, and delve into the heart of the world.[4]

Consider the sheer audacity of this black woman, perhaps our first truly professional writer, who could so freely advocate this position in the great crisis year of 1859, which witnessed both John Brown's aborted raid on the Harper's Ferry arsenal and the U.S. Supreme Court's decision to uphold the constitutionality of the Fugitive Slave Act of 1850. Harper, in this statement about representation and in her poems and fictions, demanded that black writers embrace as their subjects "feelings that are general," feelings such as love and sex, birth and death. The debate over the content of black literature had begun, then, as articulated by a black woman writer.

Whereas Harper expressed concern for a new content or "signifier," a content that was at once black, self-contained, and humanly general, the other pole of the debate about representation concerned itself with the exact form that the signifier should take. This concern over what I am calling the signifier occupied, in several ways and for various reasons, the center of black aesthetic theory roughly between the publication of

Paul Laurence Dunbar's *Lyrics of Lowly Life* in 1895 and at least the publication in 1937 of Zora Neale Hurston's *Their Eyes Were Watching God.* This debate, curiously enough, returns us in the broadest sense to the point of departure of this chapter, namely the absence and presence of the black voice in the text, that which caused Gronniosaw so much consternation and perplexity. It is not surprising that Dunbar's widely noted presence should engender, in part, the turn of critical attention to matters of language and voice, since it is he who stands, unquestionably, as the most accomplished black dialect poet, and the most successful black poet before Langston Hughes. Nor is it surprising that Hurston's lyrical text should demarcate an ending of this debate, since Hurston's very rhetorical strategy, her invention of what I have chosen to call the speakerly text, seems designed to mediate between, for fiction, what Sterling A. Brown's representation of the black voice mediated between for black poetic diction: namely, a profoundly lyrical, densely metaphorical, quasi-musical, privileged black oral tradition on the one hand, and a received but not yet fully appropriated standard English literary tradition on the other hand. The quandary for the writer was to find a third term, a bold and novel signifier, informed by these two related yet distinct literary languages. This is what Hurston tried to do in *Their Eyes.*

Critics widely heralded Dunbar's black poetic diction, and poets, white and black, widely imitated it. It is difficult to understand the millennarian tones of Dunbar's critical reception. The urgent calls for a black "redeemer-poet," so common in the black newspapers and periodicals published between 1827 and 1919, by the late 1880s were being echoed by white critics. One anonymous white woman critic, for example, who signed herself only as "A Lady from Philadelphia," wrote in *Lippincott's Monthly Magazine* in 1886 that "The Coming American Novelist" would be "of African origin."[5] This great author would be one "With us" but "not of us," one who "has suffered everything a poet, a dramatist, a novelist need suffer before he comes to have his lips anointed." "When one comes to consider the subject," this critic concludes, "there is no improbability to it." After all, she continues, the African "has given us the only national music we have ever had," a corpus of art "distinctive in musical history." He is, moreover, "a natural story-teller,"[6] uniquely able to fabricate what she calls "acts of the imagination," discourses in which no "morality is involved."

> [Why] should not this man, who has suffered so much, who is so easy to amuse, so full of his own resources, and who is yet undeveloped, why should he not some day soon tell a story that should interest, amuse us, stir our hearts, and make a new epoch in our literature?[7]

Then, in a remarkable reversal, the writer makes an even bolder claim:

> Yet farther: I have used the generic masculine pronoun because it is convenient; but Fate keeps revenges in store. It was a woman who, taking the

wrongs of the African as her theme, wrote the novel that awakened the world to their reality, and why should not the coming novelist be a woman as well as an African? She—the woman of that race—has some claims on Fate which are not yet paid up.

It is difficult to discern which of this critic's two claims is the bolder: that the great American writer would be black or that she would be a black woman. It is not difficult, however, to summarize the energizing effect on our literary tradition which this critic's prediction was to have. Even as late as 1899, W. S. Scarborough would still cite this *Lippincott's* essay to urge black writers to redeem "the race."[8]

W. H. A. Moore, writing about "A Void in Our Literature" in 1890, called for the appearance of a great black poet whose presence would stand as "an indication of the character of [the Afro-American's] development on those lines which determine the capacity of a people." "The Afro-American," he continues,

> has not given to English literature a great poet. No one of his kind has, up to this day, lent influence to the literature of his time, save Phillis Wheatley. It is not to be expected that he would. And yet every fragment, every whispering of his benighted muse is scanned with eager and curious interest in the hope that here may be found the gathered breathings of a true singer.[9]

"The keynote," Moore concludes, "has not yet been struck." To find a poetic diction which reflects "the inner workings of the subject which it seeks to portray," Moore argues, "is the mission of the race." Moore's essay is merely typical of many others published between 1865 and 1930. For example, in 1893, H. T. Johnson, editor of the *Recorder*, outlined the need for race authors to express racial aspirations. Five years later, H. T. Kealing wrote of the unique contributions that only Negro authors could make. The literature of any people, he said, had an indigenous quality, "the product of the national peculiarities and race idiosyncrasies that no alien could duplicate." He called upon the Negro author not to imitate whites, as had been the case hitherto, but to reach "down to the original and unexplored depths of his own being where lies unused the material that is to provide him a place among the great writers." Similarly, Scarborough, speaking at the Hampton Negro Conference in 1899, called for something higher than the false dialect types depicted by white authors; even Chesnutt's and Dunbar's short stories had not gone far enough in portraying the higher aspirations of the race. Only the Negro author could portray the Negro best—his "loves and hates, his hopes and fears, his ambitions, his whole life, in such a way that the world will weep and laugh . . . forgetting completely that the hero and heroine are God's bronze image, but knowing only that they are men and women with joys and sorrows that belong to the whole human family." In the discussion that followed Scarborough's paper, it was agreed that the types portrayed in "vaudeville" were false. Lucy Laney, principal of the

Haines Norman and Industrial Institute, prefigured a major interest of the 1920s when she spoke of the material for short stories to be found in the rural South and called upon Negro writers to go down to the sea islands of Georgia and South Carolina "where they could study the Negro in his original purity," with a culture and a voice "close to the African."[10]

Into this black milieu wrote Paul Lawrence Dunbar. Perhaps because we tend to read Dunbar backwards, as it were, through the poetry of Sterling A. Brown and the early Langston Hughes, and through the often unfortunate poetic efforts of Dunbar's less talented imitators, we tend to forget how startling was Dunbar's use of black dialect as the basis of a poetic diction. After all, by 1895, dialect had come to connote black innate mental inferiority, the linguistic sign both of human bondage (as origin) and of the continued failure of "improvability" or "progress," two turn-of-the-century keywords. Dialect signified both "black difference" and that the figure of the black in literature existed primarily as object, not subject; and even sympathetic characterizations of the black, such as Uncle Remus by Joel Chandler Harris, were far more related to a racist textual tradition that stemmed from minstrelsy, the plantation novel, and vaudeville than to representations of spoken language. As Scarborough summarized the matter:

> Both northern and southern writers have presented Negro nature, Negro dialect, Negro thought, as they conceived it, too often, alas, as evolved out of their own consciousness. Too often the dialect has been inconsistent, the types presented, mere composite photographs as it were, or uncouth specimens served up so as the humorous side of the literary setting might be properly balanced.[11]

This received literary tradition of plantation and vaudeville art, Scarborough concluded, demanded "realism" to refute the twin gross stereotypes of characterization and the representation of black speech.

For Dunbar to draw upon dialect as the medium through which to posit this mode of realism suggests both a certain boldness as well as a certain opportunism, two qualities that helped to inform Dunbar's mixed results, which we know so well, he lamented to his death. Dunbar, nevertheless, Signified upon the received white racist textual tradition and posited in its stead a black poetic diction which his more gifted literary heirs would, in their turn, Signify upon, with often pathetic results. What Sterling A. Brown would realize in the language of his poetry, Zora Neale Hurston would realize in the language of her fiction. For, after Dunbar, the two separate poles of the debate over black mimetic principles, over the shape of the signifier and the nature of the signified, could no longer be thought of independently. Dunbar's primary rhetorical gesture, as Scarborough concluded in 1899, had been to do just that:

> And here we pause to see what [Dunbar and Chesnutt] have added to our literature, what new artistic value they have discovered. [Both] have followed closely the "suffering side," the portrayal of the old fashioned Negro of "befo'

de wah,"—the Negro that [Thomas Nelson] Page and [Joel Chandler] Harris and others have given a permanent place in literature. But they have done one thing more; they have presented the facts of Negro life with a thread running through both warp and woof that shows not only humour and pathos, humility, self-sacrifice, courtesy and loyalty, but something at times of the higher aims, ambition, desires, hopes, and aspiration of the race—but by no means as fully and to as great an extent as we had hoped they would do.[12]

How the black writer represented, and what he or she represented, were now indissolubly linked in black aesthetic theory.

In the curious manner by which one generation's parenthetical concerns come to form the central questions of a subsequent generation's critical debate, Scarborough's judgment that Dunbar's representations of the folk "befo' de wah" were potentially capable of encompassing more than "humour and pathos" became the lynchpin of James Weldon Johnson's attack on dialect as a poetic diction. I have sketched the debate over dialect elsewhere.[13] Suffice it to say here that that great American realist, William Dean Howells, in 1896, thought that Dunbar's dialect verse was a representation of reality, a "portrait . . . undeniably like." The political import of this artistic achievement, Howells maintained, was unassailable: "A race which has reached this effect in any of its members can no longer be held wholly uncivilized; and intellectually Mr. Dunbar makes a stronger claim for the negro than the negro has yet done."[14] By the 1920s, however, dialect was thought to be a literary trap.

A careful study of the aesthetic theories of the New Negro Renaissance suggests strongly that the issue of dialect as an inappropriate literary language seems to have been raised in order for a second poetic diction to be posited in its place. Indeed, we can with some justification set as boundaries of this literary movement James Weldon Johnson's critiques of dialect, which he published in his separate "Prefaces" to the first and second editions of *The Book of American Negro Poetry*, printed in 1923 and 1931, respectively, but also Johnson's "Introduction" to the first edition of Sterling A. Brown's *Southern Road*, printed in 1932.

In his "Preface," Johnson had defined the urgent task of the new black writer to be the "break away from, not Negro dialect itself, but the limitations of Negro dialect imposed by the fixing effects of long convention." And what were these limitations? Said Johnson, "it is an instrument with but two full stops, humor and pathos," repeating and reversing Scarborough's terms. Nine years later, in his second "Preface," Johnson could assert assuredly that "the passing of traditional dialect as a medium for Negro poets is complete." Just one year later, however, Brown's poetry forced Johnson to admit that, although Brown "began writing just after Negro poets had generally discarded conventionalized dialect, with its minstrel traditions of Negro life," he has "infused his [dialect] poetry with genuine characteristic flavor by adopting as his medium the common, racy living speech of the Negro in certain phases of *real* life." Brown's achievement, Johnson acknowledges, is that he has turned to "folk poetry" as a source of a poetic diction, "deepened its meanings and multiplied its implications. . . . In a word, he has taken this raw material and worked it into original and authentic power." Brown's poetry, then, in a remarkably tangible sense, marks the end of the New Negro Renaissance as well as the resolution, for black poetic diction, of a long debate over its mimetic principles.[15]

Brown's achievement in poetry, however, had no counterpart in fiction. True, Jean Toomer's *Cane* can be thought of as a fictional antecedent of Brown's poetic diction, both of whose works inform the structure of *Their Eyes Were Watching God.* Yet Toomer's use of the privileged oral voice, and especially its poignant silences, is not without its ironies, since Toomer employs the black oral voice in his text both as a counterpoint to that standard English voice of his succession of narrators but also as evidence of the modernist claim that there had existed no privileged, romantic movement of unified consciousness, especially or not even in the cane fields of a rural Georgia echoing its own swan song. Existence, in the world of *Cane,* is bifurcated, fundamentally opposed, as represented by all sorts of binary oppositions, among these standard English and black speech, as well as black and white, male and female, South and North, textual desire and sensual consummation. Even in that fiction's long, final section, called "Kabnis," in which the place of the narrator becomes that of stage directions in a tragedy, the presence of the oral voice retains its primarily antiphonal function, as in the following exchange among Halsey, Layman, and Kabnis:

> Halsey (in a mock religious tone): Amen t that, brother Layman. Amen (turning to Kabnis, half playful, yet somehow dead in earnest). An Mr. Kabnis, kindly remember youre in th land of cotton—hell of a land. Th white folks get the boll; th niggers get th stalk. An dont you dare touch th boll, or even look at it. They'll swing y sho. (Laughs)
> Kabnis: But they wouldn't touch a gentleman—fellows, men like us three here—
> Layman: Nigger's a nigger down this away, Professor. An only two dividins: good an bad. An even they aint permanent categories. They sometimes mixes um up when it comes t lynchin. I've seen um do it.[16]

Toomer's representation of black spoken language, even in this instance, stands essentially as an element of plot and of theme.

Rather than as a self-contained element of literary structure, the oral voice in *Cane* is a motivated sign of duality, of opposition, which Toomer thematizes in each section of his fiction, and specifically in this passage:

> Kabnis: . . . An besides, he aint my past. My ancestors were Southern blue-bloods—
> Lewis: And black.
> Kabnis: Aint much difference between blue an black.
> Lewis: Enough to draw a denial from you. Cant hold them, can you? Master; slave. Soil; and the overarching heavens. Dusk; dawn. They fight and

bastardize you. The sun tint of your cheeks, flame of the great season's multi-colored leaves, tarnished, burned. Split, shredded: easily burned. No use . . .

His gaze shifts to Stella. Stella's face draws back, her breasts come to-wards him.

Stella: I aint got nothin f y, mister. Taint no use t look at me.

It would not be until Zora Neale Hurston began to publish novels that Toomer's rhetorical innovation would be extended in black fiction, although the line between Toomer's lyricism and Brown's regionalism is a direct one. Indeed, although Toomer received enthusiastic praise for *Cane*, this praise remained vague and ill defined. Du Bois, for instance, saw the import of the book as its subject matter, which he defined to be male-female sexual relations, which, he protested, were notably absent from the corpus of black fiction. There is not much truly consummated or untroubled sex in *Cane* either, but at least for Du Bois the text treated its possibility. For Du Bois, this stood as *Cane*'s significant breakthrough.

By 1923, when Toomer published *Cane*, the concern over the nature and function of representation, of what we might profitably think of as the ideology of mimesis, had focused on one aesthetic issue, which Du Bois would call "How Shall the Negro Be Portrayed?" and which we can, boldly I admit, think of as "What to do with the folk?" Despite scores of essays, exchanges, and debates over this problematic of representation, however, by 1929 not only had Toomer's innovations apparently been forgotten, but ironclad "Instructions for Contributors" had been widely circulated among black writers in the "Illustrated Feature Section" of the Negro press. Since these help us to begin to understand the major place of *Their Eyes Were Watching God* in the history of black rhetorical strategies, let me reprint these instructions, written by George S. Schuyler, in full:

> Every manuscript submitted must be written in each-sentence-a-paragraph style.
>
> Stories must be full of human interest. Short, simple words. No attempt to parade erudition to the bewilderment of the reader. No colloquialisms such as "nigger," "darkey," "coon," etc. Plenty of dialogue, and language that is realistic.
>
> We will not accept any stories that are depressing, saddening, or gloomy. Our people have enough troubles without reading about any. We want them to be interested, cheered, and buoyed up; conforted, gladdened, and made to laugh.
>
> Nothing that casts the least reflection on contemporary moral or sex standards will be allowed. Keep away from the erotic! Contributions must be clean and wholesome.
>
> Everything must be written in that intimate manner that wins the reader's confidence at once and makes him or her feel that what is written is being spoken exclusively to that particular reader.
>
> No attempt should be made to be obviously artistic. Be artistic, of course, but "put it over" on the reader so he or she will be unaware of it.
>
> Stories must be swiftly moving, gripping the interest and sweeping on to a climax. The heroine should always be beautiful and desirable, sincere and

virtuous. The hero should be of the he-man type, but not stiff, stereotyped, or vulgar. The villain should obviously be a villain and of the deepest-dyed variety: crafty, unscrupulous, suave, and resourceful. Above all, however, these characters must live and breathe, and be just ordinary folks such as the reader has met. The heroine should be of the brown-skin type.

All matter should deal exclusively with Negro life. Nothing will be permitted that is likely to engender ill feelings between blacks and whites. The color problem is bad enough without adding any fuel to the fire.[17]

It is precisely these strictures, widely circulated in those very journals in which black authors could most readily publish, which, along with the extended controversy over black oral forms, enable us to begin to understand the black milieu against which Hurston would define herself as a writer of fiction. Here we can only recall, with some irony, W. S. Scarborough's 1899 plea for a great black novelist:

We are tired of vaudeville, of minstrelsy and of the Negro's pre-eminence in those lines. We want something higher, something more inspiring than that. We turn to the Negro for it. Shall we have it? The black novelist is like the white novelist, in too many instances swayed by the almighty dollar. . . . Like Esau he is ready to sell his birthright for a mess of pottage.

Let the Negro writer of fiction make of his pen and brain all-compelling forces to treat of that which he well knows, best knows, and give it to the world with all the imaginative power possible, with all the magic touch of an artist. Let him portray the Negro's loves and hates, his hopes and fears, his ambitions, his whole life, in such a way that the world will weep and laugh over the pages, finding the touch that makes all nature kin, forgetting completely that hero and heroine are God's bronze images, but knowing only that they are men and women with joys and sorrows that belong alike to the whole human family. Such is the novelist that the race desires. Who is he that will do it? Who is he that can do it?[18]

He that could do it, it seems, turned out to be a she, Zora Neale Hurston.

II

Zora Neale Hurston is the first writer that our generation of black and feminists critics has brought into the canon, or perhaps I should say the canons. For Hurston is now a cardinal figure in the Afro-American canon, the feminist canon, and the canon of American fiction, especially as our readings of her work become increasingly close readings, which Hurston's texts sustain delightfully. The curious aspect of the widespread critical attention being shown to Hurston's texts is that so many critics embracing such a diversity of theoretic approaches seem to find something new at which to marvel in her texts.

My own method of reading *Their Eyes Were Watching God* stems fundamentally from the debates over modes of representation, over theories of mimesis, which as I have suggested form such a crucial part of the history of Afro-American literature and its theory. Mimetic principles can be both implicitly and explicitly ideological, and the explication of Hurston's rhetorical strategy, which I shall attempt below, is no exception. I wish to read *Their Eyes* in such a way as to move from the broadest notion of *what* it thematizes through an ever-tighter spiral of *how* it thematizes, that is, its rhetorical strategies. I shall attempt to show that Hurston's text not only cleared a rhetorical space for the narrative strategies that Ralph Ellison would render so deftly in *Invisible Man*, but also that Hurston's text is the first example in our tradition of "the speakerly text," by which I mean a text whose rhetorical strategy is designed to represent an oral literary tradition, designed "to emulate the phonetic, grammatical, and lexical patterns of actual speech and produce the 'illusion of oral narration.'"[19] The speakerly text is that text in which all other structural elements seem to be devalued, as important as they remain to the telling of the tale, because the narrative strategy signals attention to its own importance, an importance which would seem to be the privileging of oral speech and its inherent linguistic features. Whereas Toomer's *Cane* draws upon the black oral voice essentially as a different voice from the narrator's, as a repository of socially distinct, contrapuntal meanings and beliefs, a speakerly text would seem primarily to be oriented toward imitating one of the numerous forms of oral narration to be found in classical Afro-American vernacular literature.

Obviously, I am concerned with what we traditionally think of as matters of voice. "Voice" here connotes not only traditional definitions of "point of view," a crucial matter in the reading of *Their Eyes*, but also the linguistic presence of a literary tradition that exists for us as a written text primarily because of the work of sociolinguists and anthropologists such as Hurston. I am concerned in this chapter to discuss the representation of what we might think of as the voice of the black oral tradition—represented here as direct speech—as well as with Hurston's use of free indirect discourse as the rhetorical analogue to the text's metaphors of inside and outside, so fundamental to the depiction of Janie's quest for consciousness, her very quest to become a speaking black subject. Just as we have begun to think of Hurston as an artist whose texts relate to those of Jean Toomer and Sterling A. Brown, let us round out our survey to the tradition by comparing Hurston's concept of voice with that of Richard Wright and Ralph Ellison.

In *American Hunger* (1977), which along with *Black Boy* (1945) comprises the full text of an autobiography he initially called "The Horror and the Glory," Richard Wright succinctly outlines his idea of the ironic relationship between the individual black talent and an Afro-American cultural tradition ravaged and laid waste to by an omnipresent and irresistible white racism:

> What could I dream of that had the barest possibility of coming true? I could think of nothing. And, slowly, it was upon exactly that nothingness that my mind began to dwell, that constant sense of wanting without having, of being

hated without reason. A dim notion of what life meant to a Negro in America was coming to consciousness in me, not in terms of external events, lynchings, Jim Crowism, and the endless brutalities, but in terms of crossed-up feelings, of psyche pain. I sensed that Negro life was a sprawling land of unconscious suffering, and that there were but few Negroes who knew the meaning of their lives, who could tell their [own] story.[20]

Wright, as both of his autobiographies seem intent on claiming, certainly counted himself among those few Negroes who could tell not only their own story but also the woeful tale of their pathetic, voiceless black countrymen. If they were signs of the "horror," then his articulated escape was meant to be our "glory."

In his autobiographies and novels, Wright evolved a curious and complex myth of origins of self and race. Whereas a large part of the black autobiographical tradition, as exemplified by Frederick Douglass's three autobiographies, generally depicts a resplendent self as representative of possibilities denied systematically to one's voiceless fellow blacks, Wright's class of ideal individual black selves seems to have included only Wright. Black Boy, for example, charts how the boy, Dick, through the key texts of naturalism, gave a shape and a purpose to an exceptional inherent nobility of spirit which emerges from within the chaotic depths of the black cultural maelstrom. Wright's humanity is achieved only at the expense of his fellow blacks, pitiable victims of the pathology of slavery and racial segregation who surround and suffocate him. Indeed, Wright wills this especial self into being through the agency of contrast: the sensitive, healthy part is foregrounded against a determined, defeated black whole. He is a noble black savage, in the ironic tradition of Oroonoko and film characters played by Sidney Poitier—the exception, not the rule.

For Ralph Ellison, Wright's notion of the self and its relation to black culture seemed unduly costly. Indeed, it is this dark and brooding fiction of black culture against which both Ellison and James Baldwin railed, drawing upon a rich body of tropes and rhetorical strategies prefigured, among other places, in Hurston's fictions and critical writings. It is this fiction of obliteration that created the great divide in black literature, a fissure first rendered apparent in the late thirties in an extended debate between Hurston and Wright.

The Hurston-Wright debate, staged not only in the lyrical shape of Their Eyes Were Watching God (1937) against the naturalism of Native Son (1940) but also in reviews of each other's books, turns between two poles of a problematic of representation—between what is represented and what represents, between the signifier and the signified. Theirs are diametrically opposed notions of the internal structure of the sign, the very sign of blackness.

Hurston rather self-consciously defined her theory of the novel against that received practice of realism which Wright would attempt to revitalize in *Native Son*. Hurston thought that Wright stood at the center of "the sobbing school of Negrohood who hold that nature somehow has given them a low down dirty deal."[21] Against Wright's idea of psychological destruction and chaos, Hurston framed a counternotion which the repressed and conservative maternal figure of *Their Eyes* articulates: "[It] wasn't for me to fulfill my dreams of whut a woman oughta be and to do. Dat's one of de hold-backs of slavery. But nothing can't stop you from wishin'. You can't beat nobody down so low till you can rob 'em of they will." The sign of this transcendent self would be the shaping of a strong, self-reflective voice: "Ah wanted to preach a great sermon about colored women sittin' on high, but they wasn't no pulpit for me. Freedom found me widh a baby daughter in mah arms, so Ah said Ah'd take a broom and a cook-pot and throw up a highway through de wilderness for her. She would expound what Ah felt. But somehow she got lost offa de highway and next thing Ah knowed here you was in de world. So whilst Ah was tendin' you of nights Ah said Ah'd save de text for you."[22] Hurston revoices this notion of the articulating subject in her autobiography, *Dust Tracks on the Road* (1942), in a curious account of her mother's few moments before death: "Her mouth was slightly open, but her breathing took up so much of her strength that she could not talk. But she looked at me, or so I felt, to speak for her. She depended on me for a voice."[23] We can begin to understand how far apart Hurston and Wright stand in the tradition if we compare Hurston's passage about her mother with the following passage from Wright's *Black Boy*, a deathbed revision of Hurston's passage:

> Once, in the night, my mother called me to her bed and told me that she could not endure the pain, that she wanted to die. I held her hand and begged her to be quiet. That night I ceased to react to my mother; my feelings were frozen.[24]

Wright explains that this event, and his mother's extended suffering, "grew into a symbol in my mind, gathering to itself all the poverty, the ignorance, the helplessness; . . . Her life set the emotional tone of my life, colored the men and women I was to meet in the future, conditioned my relation to events that had not happened, determined my attitude to situations and circumstances I had yet to face." If Hurston figures her final moments with her mother in terms of the search for a voice, then Wright, three years later, figures the significance of a similar scene as responsible for a certain "somberness of spirit that I was never to lose." No two authors in the tradition are more dissimilar than Hurston and Wright.

The narrative voice Hurston created, and her legacy to Afro-American fiction, is a lyrical and disembodied yet individual voice, from which emerges a singular longing and utterance, a transcendent, ultimately racial self, extending far beyond the merely individual. Hurston realized a resonant and authentic narrative voice that echoes and aspires to the status of the impersonality, anonymity, and authority of the black vernacular tradition, a nameless, selfless tradition, at once collective and compelling, true somehow to the unwritten text of a common blackness. For Hurston, the search for a telling form of language, indeed the search for a black literary language itself, defines the search for the self. Similarly, for Ellison, the self can emerge only through the will, as signified by the problematical attempt to write itself into being, a unique black self consolidated and rendered integral within a first-person narrative structure.

For Wright, nature was ruthless, irreducible, and ineffable. Unlike Hurston and Ellison, Wright sees fiction not as a model of reality but as a representative bit of it, a literal report of the real. Art, for Wright, always remains referential. His blackness, therefore, can never be a mere sign; it is rather the text of his great and terrible subject. Accordingly, Wright draws upon the voice of the third-person, past-tense authorial mode and various tools of empirical social science and naturalism to blend public with private experience, inner with outer history. Rarely does he relinquish what Roland Barthes calls the "proprietary consciousness," the constant sign of his presence and of some larger context, which the third-person voice inevitably entails. Rather predictably, Wright found Hurston's great novel to be "counter-revolutionary," while Hurston replied that she wrote novels "and not treatises on sociology."

Hurston, Wright, and Ellison's divergent theories of narrative structure and voice, the cardinal points of a triangle of influence, with their attendant ramifications upon the ideology of form and its relation to knowledge and power, comprise a matrix of issues to which subsequent black fictions, by definition, must respond. The rhetorical question that subsequent texts must answer remained the question which the structure of *Their Eyes* answered for Hurston: "In what voice would the Negro speak for her or himself in the language of fiction?" By discussing *Their Eyes'* topoi and figures, its depiction of the relationship among character, consciousness, and setting, and its engagement of shifting points of view, we can begin to understand how primary Hurston's rhetorical strategies remain in this compelling text.

On the broadest level, *Their Eyes* depicts the search for identity and self-understanding of an Afro-American woman. This quest for self-knowledge, which the text thematizes through an opposition between the inside and the outside of things, directs attention to itself as a central theme of the novel by certain narrative strategies. I am thinking here especially of the use of the narrative frame and of a special form of plot negation. The tale of Janie Crawford-Killicks-Starks-Woods is narrated to her best friend, Phoeby, while the two sit together on Janie's back porch. We, the readers, "overhear" the tale that Janie narrates to her auditor, whose name we recall signifies the poet. Phoeby, as we might suspect, is an ideal listener: to seduce Janie into narrating her story, Phoeby confesses to her friend, 'It's hard for me to understand what you mean, de way you tell it. And then again Ah'm hard of understandin' at times." Phoeby speaks as the true pupil; Janie responds as the true pedagogue:

> "Naw 'tain't nothin' lak you might think. So 'tain't no use in me telling you somethin' unless Ah give you de understandin' to go 'long wid it. Unless you see de fur, a mink skin ain't no different from a coon hide. Looka heah, Phoeby, is Sam waitin' on you for his supper?"

At the end of the telling of Janie's tale, an interruption which the text signifies by ellipses and a broad white space, Phoeby, always the perfect pupil, responds to her teacher as each of us wishes the students to respond:

> "Lawd!" Phoeby breathed out heavily, "Ah done growed ten feet higher from jus' listenin' tuh you, Janie. Ah ain't satisfied wid mahself no mo'. Ah means tuh make Sam take me fishin' wid him after this. Nobody better not criticize yuh in mah hearin."

Such a powerfully transforming tale has effected an enhanced awareness even in Janie's transfixed pupil. And to narrate this tale, Hurston draws upon the framing device, which serves on the order of plot to interrupt the received narrative flow of linear narration of the realistic novel, and which serves on the order of theme to enable Janie to recapitulate, control, and narrate her own story of becoming, the key sign of sophisticated understanding of the self. Indeed, Janie develops from a nameless child, known only as "Alphabet," who cannot even recognize her own likeness as a "colored" person in a photograph, to the implied narrator of her own tale of self-consciousness. This is merely one of Hurston's devices to achieve thematic unity.

Hurston matches the use of the frame with the use of negation as a mode of narrating the separate elements of the plot. The text opens and ends in the third-person omniscient voice, which allows for a maximum of information giving. Its third paragraph commences: "So the beginning of this was a woman and she had come back from burying the dead." By introducing this evidence of the return from burying the dead, Hurston negates her text's themes of discovery, rebirth, and renewal, only to devote the remainder of her text to realizing these same themes. Hurston also draws upon negation to reveal, first, the series of self-images that Janie does not wish to be and, second, to define the matrix of obstacles that frustrate her desire to know herself. The realization of the full text of *Their Eyes* represents the fulfillment of the novel's positive potentialities, by which I mean Janie's discovery of self-knowledge.

How does this negated form of plot development unfold? Hurston rather cleverly develops her plot by depicting a series of intimate relationships in which Janie engages with a fantasy of sexual desire, then with her grandmother, with her first husband (Logan Killicks), her second husband (Joe Starks), and, finally, with her ideal lover, Vergible Woods, "Tea Cake." Her first three relationships are increasingly problematic and self-negating, complex matters which Hurston renders through an inverse relationship between character or consciousness on one hand and setting on the other. If we think about it, Janie comes to occupy progressively larger physical spaces—Nanny's cabin in the backyard of the Washburn's place, Logan Killick's "often-mentioned" sixty acres, and, finally, Joe Starks's big white wooden house, replete with banisters, and his centrally located general store. Indeed, it is fair to say that Mayor Starks owns the town. With each successive move to a larger physical space, however, her housemate seeks to confine Janie's consciousness inversely, seemingly, by just as much. It is only when she eschews what her grandmother had named the "protection" both of material possessions and of rituals of entitlement (i.e., bourgeois marriage) and moves to the swamp, to "the muck," with Vergible "Tea Cake" Woods that she, at last, gains control of her understanding of herself. We can, in fact, conclude that the text opposes bourgeois notions of progress (Killicks owns the only organ "amongst colored folks"; Joe Starks is a man of "positions and possessions") and of the Protestant work ethic, to more creative and lyrical notions of unity. Tea Cake's only possession is a guitar. The relationship between character and setting, then, is ideal for the pedagogical purpose of revealing that character and setting are merely aspects of narrative strategy, and not things in the ordinary sense that we understand a thing to be.

One pleasant way to chart this relationship between consciousness and setting is to examine briefly the metaphor of the tree, which Hurston repeats throughout her text. The use of repetition is fundamental to the process of narration, and Hurston repeats the figure of the tree both to expound her theme of becoming and to render the action of the plot as simultaneous and as unified as possible. In *Dust Tracks on a Road*, Hurston explains that:

> I was only happy in the woods. . . . I made particular friendship with one huge tree and always played about its roots. I named it "the loving pine," and my chums came to know it by that name.

In *Their Eyes*, Janie uses the metaphor of the tree to define her own desires but also to mark the distance of those with whom she lives from these desires. There are well over two dozen repetitions of the figure of the tree in this text. The representation of Janie's narrative to Phoeby commences with the figure of the tree:

> Janie saw her life like a great tree in leaf with the things suffered, things enjoyed, things done and undone. Dawn and doom was in the branches.

"Dawn and doom," we are to learn so poignantly, are the true stuff of Janie's tale. "Dawn and doom *was* in the branches," an example of free indirect discourse, reveals precisely the point at which Janie's voice assumes control over the text's narration, significantly in a metaphor of trees. The text describes her own, rather private dawning sexual awareness through lush and compelling tree imagery. Janie longs for an identity with the tree in imagery the text shall echo when she encounters Tea Cake:

> Oh to be a pear tree—*any* tree in bloom! With kissing bees singing of the beginning of the world! She was sixteen. She had glossy leaves and bursting buds and she wanted to struggle with life but it seemed to elude her. Where were the singing bees for her? Nothing on the place nor in her grandma's house answered her.

To "be a pear tree—*any* tree in bloom," which becomes Janie's master trope on her road to becoming, is first stated as she fantasizes under a tree and experiences her first orgasm. That this metaphor returns when she meets Tea Cake echoes the text's enigmatic statement in its second paragraph that, for women, "The dream is the truth." Thus transformed "through pollinated air," Janie experiences her first kiss with the figure she formerly knew as shiftless Johnny Taylor, now "beglamored" even in his rags in her eyes by the splendors of cross-pollination.

This crucial kiss "across the gatepost" establishes the text's opposition between the dream and the truth, already posited in the text's first two paragraphs which as I said earlier, revise Frederick Douglass's apostrophe to the ships.[25]

The ensuing action, moreover, posits a key opposition for us critics between theory and interpretation. Nanny's discovery of Johnny Taylor's "lacerating her Janie with a kiss" transforms both the event itself and Nanny's physical appearance. For Nanny's reading of the event, her "words," the text tells us, "made Janie's kiss across the gatepost seem like a manure pile after a rain." Nanny's perverse interpretation now transforms her in Janie's eyes into the dreaded figure of Medusa:

> Nanny's head and face looked like the standing roots of some old tree that had been torn away by storm. Foundation of ancient power that no longer mattered. The cooling palma christi leaves that Janie had bound about her grandma's head with a white rag had wilted down and become part and parcel of the woman. Her eyes didn't bore and pierce. They diffused and melted Janie, the room and the world into one comprehension.

When Nanny begins to narrate the story of her oppression in slavery, the narrator informs us that she "thrust back the leaves from her face." "Standing roots from some old tree" is, of course, the negation of the wonderfully lyrical imagery of blossoming pear trees. It is Nanny's "one comprehension" that suffocates, like the stench of the manure pile after a rain. Nanny is truly, as she later says to Janie in her own version of an oral slave narrative delivered just after Janie's sexual experience under the pear tree, a branch without roots, at least the sort of roots that Janie is only just learning to extend.

Afraid that her grandchild will suffer an untimely defoliation, Nanny acts swiftly to gain for her the necessary "protection" to preserve her honor intact. While explaining her dreams for Janie, Nanny tells her that

> when you got big enough to understand things, Ah wanted you to look upon yo'self. Ah don't want yo' feathers always crumpled by folks throwin' up things in yo' face. And Ah can't die easy thinkin' maybe de menfolks white or black is makin' a spit cup outa you: Have some sympathy fuh me. Put me down easy, Janie, Ah'm a cracked plate."

So Nanny, the cracked plate, the Medusa figure, forces Janie to marry Logan Killicks.

As the text states, "The vision of Logan Killicks was desecrating the pear tree." Logan's famed sixty acres strike Janie as "a lonesome place like a stump in the middle of the woods where nobody had ever been," unlike her fecund pear tree. As she complains to Nanny, when after "the new moon had been up and down three times" and love had not yet begun, Janie "wants things sweet wid mah marriage lak when you sit under a pear tree and think. Ah . . .". Love, we learn, never quite finds its way to Logan Killicks's sixty acres. But even in this confined space, Janie comes, by negation, to a measure of knowledge, signified in the language of the trees:

> So Janie waited a bloom time, and a green time and an orange time. But when the pollen again gilded the sun and sifted down on the world she began to stand around the gate and expect things. What things? She didn't know exactly. Her breath was gutsy and short. She knew things that nobody had ever told her. For instance, the words of the trees and the wind.

Ultimately, Janie comes to know that "marriage did not make love." As the text concludes, "Janie's first dream was dead, so she became a woman," an echo of the text's opening paragraphs, which figure the opposition between women and men as that between the identity of dream and truth as a figure for desire (women) and the objectification and personification of desire onto objects over which one has no control (men).

Janie soon is "liberated" from Logan Killicks by the dashing Joe Starks. At their first encounter, at the water pump, Joe tells Janie, twice, that he wishes "to be a big voice" and shares with her his own dreams of dominance "under the tree [where they] talked." Jody is not yet the embodiment of Janie's tree, but he signifies the horizon.

> Every day after that they managed to meet in the scrub oaks across the road and talk about when he would be a big ruler of things with her reaping the benefits. Janie pulled back a long time because he did not represent sun-up and pollen and blooming trees, but he spoke for far horizon.

To accept his proposals, Janie must exchange her own master metaphor for a new master's metaphor: "He spoke for change and chance. Still she hung back. The memory of Nanny was still powerful and strong." The horizon is not only a key figure in *Their Eyes*, serving to unify it by its repetition in the novel's final paragraph, but it has a central place as well in *Dust Tracks*, Hurston's autobiography:

> I had a stifled longing. I used to climb to the top of one of the huge chinaberry trees which guarded our front gate, and look out over the world. The most interesting thing that I saw was the horizon. Everyway I turned, it was there, and the same distance away. Our house then, was in the center of the world. It grew upon me that I ought to walk out to the horizon and see what the end of the world was like.

With Jody, Janie seeks the horizon. In a burst "of sudden newness and change," she heads south to find her freedom.

> From now on until death she was going to have flower dust and springtime sprinkled over everything. A bee for her bloom. Her old thoughts were going to come in handy now, but new words would have to be made and said to fit them.

But Jody, we learn painfully, is a man of words, primarily, a man of "positions and possessions," a man who "talks tuh unlettered folks wid books in his jaws," "uh man dat changes everything, but nothin' don't change him." For him, Janie is merely a possession: the town's people, we are told, "stared at Joe's face, his clothes and his wife." Just before the lamp-lighting ceremony, where Joe, whose favorite parenthetical is "I god," brings light to the town (purchased from Sears and Roebuck), Tony Taylor welcomes "Brother Starks" to town "and all dat you have seen fit tuh bring amongst us—yo' belov-ed wife, yo' store, yo' land—." Joe, all voice and less and less substance, who had seduced Janie in part by telling her, in an echo of Nanny's desire for Janie to "sit on high," that "A pretty doll-baby lak you is made to sit on de front porch and rock and fan yo' self and eat p'taters dat other folks plant just special for you," not only serves to stifle Janie's potentially emerging voice but chops down the town's virgin trees to build his house and store, in which he keeps Janie imprisoned. That which, for Jody, represents the signs of progress, represents for Janie just another muted, fallen tree.

The text figures Janie's denial of a voice by substituting the metaphor of horizon for Janie's tree metaphor. Only with Tea Cake does Janie's lyrical trope of desire return. Metaphors of silence and the death of flora confirm Janie's sadness and oppression. Joe, having just been elected mayor by acclamation, denies Janie Tony Taylor's request that she address the crowd:

> "Thank you fuh yo' compliments, but mah wife don't know nothin' 'bout no speech-makin'. Ah never married her for nothin' lak dat. She's uh woman and her place is in de home."

The text, in Janie's response, conflates the tree imagery with her reactions to Jody's silencing:

> Janie made her face laugh after a short pause, but it wasn't too easy. She had never thought of making a speech, and didn't know if she cared to make one at all. It must have been the way Jody spoke out without giving her a chance to say anything one way or another that took the bloom off of things.

This silencing leads, of course, to a disastrous degeneration; when Janie protests her absence of a voice, Joe responds predictably in a revealing exchange about who is privileged to "tell" what they "see":

> [Joe]: "How come you can't do lak Ah tell yuh?"
> [Janie]: "You sho loves to tell me whut to do, but Ah can't tell you nothin' Ah see!"
> [Joe]: Dat's 'cause you need tellin'," he rejoined hotly. "It would be pitiful if Ah didn't. Somebody got to think for women and chillun and chickens and cows. I god, they sho don't think none theirselves."
> [Janie]: "Ah knows uh few things, and womenfolks thinks sometimes too!"
> [Joe]: "Aw naw they don't. They just think they's thinkin'. When Ah see one thing Ah understands ten. You see ten things and don't understand one."

Their dying relationship soon does. As the narrator tells us, again through the negation of the flowering images:

> The spirit of the marriage left the bedroom and took to living in the parlor. . . . The bed was no longer a daisy-field for her and Joe to play in. It was a place where she went and laid down when she was sleepy and tired.
> She wasn't petal-open anymore with him.

And finally, after Joe slaps her:

> She stood there until something fell off the shelf inside her. Then she went inside there to see what it was. It was her image of Jody tumbled down and shattered. But looking at it she saw that it never was the flesh and blood figure of her dreams. Just something she had grabbed up to drape her dreams over. In a way she turned her back upon the image where it lay and looked further. She had no more blossomy openings dusting pollen over her man, neither any glistening young young fruit where the petals used to be. She found that she had a host of thoughts she had never expressed to him, and numerous emotions she had never let Jody know about. Things packed up and put away in parts of her heart where he could never find them. She was saving up feelings for some man she had never seen. She had an inside and an outside now and suddenly she knew how not to mix them.

With this newly defined sense of her inside and her outside, Janie learns to cross deftly that narrow threshold between her two selves:

> Then one day she sat and watched the shadow of herself going about tending store and prostrating itself before Jody, while all the time she herself sat under a shady tree with the wind blowing through her hair and her clothes. Somebody near about making summertime out of lonesomeness.

Jody finally dies, just after Janie gains her voice on the porch of the story by Signifyin(g) upon Jody. Jody leaves Janie a handsome legacy and frees her to love again. Eventually she meets Tea Cake, and the text's fecund imagery of desire returns:

> He looked like the love thoughts of women. He could be a bee to a blossom—a pear tree blossom in the spring. He seemed to be crushing scent out of the world with his footsteps. Crushing aromatic herbs with every step he took. Spices hung about him. He was a glance from God.

Unlike Jody, who wanted to be seen as the deliverer of light, Tea Cake is the "glance from God" that reflects upon Janie, who in turn reflects her own inner light back upon him. "Nobody else on earth," Tea Cake tells her, "kin hold uh candle tuh you, baby." Tea Cake negates the terms of the material relationship of "marriage" ordained by Nanny and realized by Logan Killicks and Joe Starks. "Dis ain't no business proposition," Janie tells Phoeby, "and no race after property and titles. Dis is uh love game." Tea Cake not only embodies Janie's tree, he is the woods themselves, the delectable veritable woods, as his name connotes ("Vergible" being a vernacular term for "veritable"). Vergible Tea Cake Woods is a sign of verity, one who speaks the truth, one genuine and real, one not counterfeit or spurious, one not false or imaginary but the thing that in fact has been named. "Veritable," we know, also suggests the aptness of metaphor. Hurston now replaces the figure of the tree as the sign of desire with figures of play, rituals of play that cause Janie to "beam with light."

III

Let us "descend" to a more latent level of meaning by examining the figures of play that recur frequently in Janie's narrative of her life with Tea Cake. We can consider these figures of play along with the play of voices that, I wish to argue, make *Their Eyes* an especially rich and complex instance of a multiply vocal text. The mode of narration of *Their Eyes* consists, at either extreme, of narrative commentary (rendered in third-person omniscient and third-person restricted voices) and of characters' discourse (which manifests itself as a direct speech rendered in what Hurston called dialect). Hurston's innovation is to be found in the middle spaces between these two extremes of narration and discourse, in what we might think of as represented discourse, which as I am defining it includes both indirect discourse and free indirect discourse. It was Hurston who introduced free indirect discourse into Afro-American narration. It is this innovation, as I hope to demonstrate, which enables her to represent various traditional modes of Afro-American rhetorical play while simultaneously representing her protagonist's growth in self-consciousness through free indirect discourse. Curiously, Hurston's narrative strategy depends on the blending of the text's two most extreme and seemingly opposed modes of narration—that is, narrative commentary, which begins at least in the diction of standard English, and characters' discourse, which is always foregrounded by quotation marks and by its black diction. As the protagonist approaches self-consciousness, however, not only does the text use free indirect discourse to represent her development, but the diction of the black characters' discourse comes to inform the diction of the voice of narrative commentary such that, in several passages, it is extraordinarily difficult to distinguish the narrator's voice from the protagonist's. In other words, through the use of what Hurston called a highly "adorned" free indirect discourse, which we might think of as a third or mediating term between narrative commentary and direct discourse, *Their Eyes Were Watching God* resolves that implicit tension between standard English and black dialect, the two voices that function as verbal counterpoints in the text's opening paragraphs.

Let us return briefly to the triangle of influence that I have drawn to connect *Invisible Man*, *Native Son*, and *Their Eyes Were Watching God*. As I argued earlier in this chapter, for Hurston the search for a form of narration and discourse, indeed the search for a black formal language itself, both defines the search for the self and is its rhetorical or textual analogue. Not only would Ellison concur, but he would go farther. Ellison's is a literal morality of narration. As he writes in *Invisible Man*, "to remain unaware of one's form is to live death," an idea that Hurston prefigures in *Their Eyes*, from the moment when the child Janie, or "Alphabet," fails to recognize her own image in a group photograph, to the moment in the text when, first, Janie learns to distinguish between her inside and her outside, and when, second, the diction of the black characters' dialect comes to inform heavily the diction of the narrative commentary. We might think of Hurston's formal relation to Wright and Ellison in this way: whereas the narrative strategy of *Native Son* consists primarily of a disembodied, omniscient narrative commentary, similar to the voice that introduces *Their Eyes*, Ellison's first-person narrative strategy in *Invisible Man* revises the possibilities of representing the development of consciousness that Hurston rendered through a dialect-informed free indirect discourse. Wright uses free indirect discourse to some extent in *Native Son*, but its diction is not informed by Bigger's speech. The distinction between figures of speech and figures of thought is one useful way to distinguish between Wright's and Hurston's narrative strategies. The narrative strategies of *Native Son* and *Invisible Man*, then, define the extremes of narrative mode in the tradition, while the narrative strategy of *Their Eyes* partakes of these as well as of a subtle blend of the two. Rhetorically, at least, *Native Son* and *Invisible Man* Signify upon the rhetorical strategies of *Their Eyes Were Watching God*.

Even more curiously, the marvelous potential that *Their Eyes'* mode of narration holds for the representation of black oral forms of storytelling would seem to be remarkably akin to that which Ellison says he is using in his next novel. In an interview with John Hersey, Ellison says that he too has turned away from first-person toward third-person narration "to discover [the text's] most expressive possibilities." As Ellison argues, "I've come to believe that one of the challenges facing a writer who tries to handle the type of materials I'm working with is that of allowing his characters to speak for themselves in whatever artistic way they can." The third person, Ellison concludes, makes it "possible to draw upon broader and deeper resources of American vernacular speech," including multiple narrators and a wide variety of characters.[26] There can be little doubt that this sort of narration, so concerned to represent the sheer multiplicity of American oral narrative forms and voices, is more closely related to the speakerly strategies of *Their Eyes* than it is to most other texts in the Afro-American canon. These are rather large claims to make, but they are firmly supported by the Signifyin(g) strategies of the text itself.

Hurston, whose definition of *signify* in *Mules and Men* is one of the earliest in the linguistic literature, has made *Their Eyes Were Watching God* into a paradigmatic Signifyin(g) text. Its narrative strategies resolve that implicit tension between the literal and the figurative, between the semantic and the rhetorical, contained in standard usages of the term *signifying*. *Their Eyes* draws upon the trope of Signifyin(g) both as thematic matter and as a rhetorical strategy. Janie, as we shall see, gains her voice within her husband's store not only by daring to speak aloud where others might hear, but by engaging in that ritual of Signifyin(g) (which her husband had expressly disallowed) and by openly Signifyin(g) upon the impotency of her husband, Joe, Mayor, "I god," himself. Janie kills her husband, rhetorically, by publicly naming his impotence (with her voice) in a public ritual of Signifyin(g). His image fatally wounded, he soon succumbs to a displaced "kidney" failure.

Their Eyes Signifies upon Toomer's *Cane* in several ways. First, its plot reverses the movement of *Cane*'s plot. Whereas the settings of *Cane* move from broad open fields, through ever-diminishing physical spaces, to a circle of light in a dark and damp cellar (corresponding to the levels of self-consciousness of the central characters), *Their Eyes'* settings within its embedded narrative move from the confines of Nanny's tiny cabin in the Washburn's backyard, through increasingly larger physical structures, finally ending "on the Muck" in the Everglades, where she and her lover, Tea Cake, realize the male-female relationship for which Janie had longed so very urgently. Similarly, whereas *Cane* represents painfully unconsummated relationships, the agony of which seems to intensify in direct proportion to the diminishment of physical setting, true consummation occurs in *Their Eyes* once Janie eschews the values implied by material possessions (such as middle-class houses, especially those on which sit idle women who rock their lives away), learns to play with Tea Cake, and then moves to the swamp. The trope of the swamp, furthermore, in *Their Eyes* signifies exactly the opposite of what it does in Du Bois's *Quest for the Silver Fleece*. Whereas the swamp in Du Bois's text figures an uncontrolled chaos that must be plowed under and controlled, for Hurston the swamp is the trope of the freedom of erotic love, the antithesis of the bourgeois life and order that her protagonist flees but to which Du Bois's protagonists aspire. Whereas Du Bois's characters gain economic security by plowing up and cultivating cotton in the swamp, Janie flees the bourgeois life that Du Bois's characters realize, precisely by abandoning traditional values for the uncertainties and the potential chaos of the uncultivated, untamed swamp, where love and death linger side by side. Du Bois's shadowy figure who seems to dwell in the swamp, we recall, is oddly enough named Zora.

But *Their Eyes* is also a paradigmatic Signifyin(g) text because of its representations, through several subtexts or embedded narratives presented as the characters' discourse, of traditional black rhetorical games or rituals. It is the text's imitation of these examples of traditionally black rhetorical rituals and modes of storytelling that allows us to think of it as a speakerly text. For in a speakerly text certain rhetorical structures seem to exist primarily as representations of oral narration, rather than as integral aspects of plot or character development. These verbal rituals signify the sheer play of black language which *Their Eyes* seems to celebrate. These virtuoso displays of verbal play constitute Hurston's complex response to the New Negro poets' strictures of the use of dialect as a poetic diction. *Their Eyes Were Watching God*'s narrative Signifies upon James Weldon Johnson's arguments against dialect just as surely as Sterling A. Brown's *Southern Road* did. Indeed, we are free to think of these two texts as discursive analogues. Moreover, Hurston's masterful use of free indirect discourse *(style indirect libre)* allows her to Signify upon the tension between the two voices of Toomer's *Cane* by adding to direct and indirect speech a strategy through which she can privilege the black oral tradition, which Toomer found to be problematical and dying.

As I stated earlier, figures of play are the dominant repeated figures in the second half of *Their Eyes* replacing the text's figures of flowering vegetation, which as we have seen repeat at least two dozen times in the first half of the text. After Janie meets Tea Cake, figures of play supplant those floral figures that appeared each time Janie dreamed of consummated love. Moreover, it is the rhetorical play that occurs regularly on the porch of his store that Janie's husband Jody prevents Janie from enjoying. As the text reads:

> Janie loved the conversation and sometimes she thought up good stories
> on the mule, but Joe had forbidden her to indulge. He didn't want her talking

after such trashy people. "You'se Mrs. Mayor Starks, Janie. I god, Ah can't see what uh woman uh yo' sability would want tuh be treasurin' all dat gum-grease from folks dat don't even own de house dey sleep in. 'Tain't no earthly use. Theys jus' some puny humans playin' roun de toes uh Time."

When the Signifyin(g) rituals commence—rituals that the text describes as created by "big picture talkers [who] were using a side of the world for a canvas"—Jody forces Janie to retreat inside the store, much against her will.

Eventually, however, this friction ignites a heated argument between the two, the key terms of which shall be repeated, in reverse, when Janie later falls in love with Tea Cake. Their exchange follows:

"Ah had tuh laugh at de people out dere in de woods dis mornin', Janie. You can't help but laugh at de capers they cuts. But all the same, Ah wish mah people would git mo' business in 'em and not spend so much time on foolishness."

"Everybody can't be lak you, Jody. Somebody is bound tuh want tuh laugh and play."

"Who don't love tuh laugh and play?"

"You make out like you don't, anyhow."

It is this tension between work and play, between maintaining appearances of respectability and control against the seemingly idle, nonquantifiable verbal maneuvers that "produce" nothing, which becomes the central sign of the distance between Janie's unarticulated aspirations and the material aspirations signified by Jody's desire to "be a big voice," a self-designation that Jody repeats with alacrity almost as much as he repeats his favorite parenthetical, "I god."

"Play" is also the text's word for the Signifyin(g) rituals that imitate "courtship," such as the symbolic action executed by Sam Watson, Lige Moss, and Charlie Jones, which the text describes in this way: "They know it's not courtship. It's acting out courtship and everybody is in the play." Play, finally, is the irresistible love potion that Tea Cake administers to Janie. Tea Cake, an apparently unlikely suitor of Joe Starks's widow, since he is a drifter and is generally thought to be "irresponsible," seduces Janie by teaching her to play checkers. Responding to his challenge of a game with "Ah can't play uh lick," Tea Cake proceeds to set up the board and teach Janie the rules. Janie "found herself glowing inside. Somebody wanted her to play. Somebody thought it natural for her to play. That was even nice. She looked him over and got little thrills from every one of his good points." No one had taught her to play in her adulthood. The text repeats Joe's prohibition as Tea Cake's perceptive mode of seduction. As Tea Cake concludes prophetically, "You gointuh be uh good player too, after while." And "after while," Janie and Tea Cake teach each other to become "good players" in what the text depicts as a game of love.

This repeated figure of play is only the thematic analogue to the text's rhetorical play, plays of language that seem to be present essentially to reveal the complexity of black oral forms of narration. For *Their Eyes Were Watching God* is replete with storytellers, or Signifiers as the black tradition has named them. These Signifiers are granted a remarkable amount of space in this text to reveal their talents. These imitations of oral narrations, it is crucial to recall, unfold within what the text represents as Janie's framed tale, the tale of her quests with Tea Cake to the far horizon and her lonely return home. This oral narrative commences in chapter 2, while Janie and her friend, Phoeby, sit on Janie's back porch, and "the kissing, young darkness became a monstropolous old thing while Janie talked." Then follow almost three full pages of Janie's direct speech, "while all around the house, the night time put on flesh and blackness." Two paragraphs of narrative commentary follow Janie's narration; then, curiously, the narrative "fades" into "a spring-time afternoon in West Florida," the springtime of Janie's adolescence.

Without every releasing its proprietary consciousness, the disembodied narrative voice reassumes control over the telling of Janie's story after nine paragraphs of direct discourse. We can characterize this narrative shift as from third person, to "no-person" (that is, the seemingly unmediated representation of Jamie's direct speech), back to the third person of an embedded or framed narrative. This device we encounter most frequently in the storytelling devices of film, in which a first-person narrative yields, as it were, to the form of narration that we associate with the cinema. ("Kabnis," we remember, imitates the drama.) *Their Eyes Were Watching God* would seem to be imitating this mode of narration, with this fundamental difference: the bracketed tale, in the novel, is told by an omniscient, third-person narrator who reports thoughts, feelings, and events that Janie could not possibly have heard or seen. This framed narrative continues for the next eighteen chapters, until in chapter 20 the text indicates the end of Janie's storytelling of Phoeby, which we have overheard by the broad white space and a series of widely spaced ellipses that I mentioned earlier.

This rather unusual form of narration of the tale-within-a-tale has been the subject of some controversy about the success or failure of Janie's depiction as a dynamic character who comes to know herself. Rather than retread that fruitless terrain, I would suggest that the subtleness of this narrative strategy allows for, as would no other mode of narration, the representation of the forms of oral narration that *Their Eyes* imitates so often—so often, in fact, that the very subject of this text would appear to be not primarily Janie's quest but the emulation of the phonetic, grammatical, and lexical structures of actual speech, an emulation designed to produce the illusion of oral narration. Indeed, each of the oral rhetorical structures emulated within Janie's bracketed tale functions to remind the reader that he or she is overhearing Janie's narrative to Phoeby, which unfolds on her porch, that crucial place of storytelling both in this text and in the black community. Each of these playful narratives is, by definition, a tale-within-the-bracketed-tale, and most exist as Significations of rhetorical play rather than events that develop the text's plot. Indeed, these embedded narratives, consisting as they do of long exchanges of direct discourse, often serve as plot impediments but simultaneously enable a multiplicity of narrative voices to assume control of the text, if only for a few paragraphs on a few pages, as Ellison explained his new narrative strategy to John Hersey.

Hurston is one of the few authors of our tradition who both theorized about her narrative process and defended it against the severe critiques of contemporaries such as Wright. Hurston's theory allows us to read *Their Eyes* through her own terms of critical order. It is useful to recount her theory of black oral narration, if only in summary, and then to use this to explicate the various rhetorical stretegies that, collectively, comprise the narrative strategy of *Their Eyes Were Watching God*.

Hurston seems to be not only the first scholar to have defined the trope of Signifyin(g) but also the first to represent the ritual itself. Hurston represents a Signifyin(g) ritual in *Mules and Men*, then glosses the word *signify* as a means of "showing off," rhetorically. The exchange is an appropriate one to repeat, because it demonstrates that women most certainly can, and do, Signify upon men, and because it prefigures the scene of Signification in *Their Eyes* that proves to be a verbal sign of such importance to Janie's quest for consciousness:

> "Talkin' 'bout dogs," put in Gene Oliver, "they got plenty sense. Nobody can't fool dogs much."
>
> "And speakin' 'bout hams," cut in Big Sweet meaningly, "if Joe Willard don't stay out of dat bunk he was in last night, Ah'm gonter springle some salt down his back and sugar-cure *his* hams."
>
> Joe snatched his pole out of the water with a jerk and glared at Big Sweet, who stood sideside looking at him most pointedly.
>
> "Aw, woman, quit tryin' to signify."
>
> "Ah kin signify all Ah please, Mr. Nappy-Chin, so long as Ah know what Ah'm talkin' about."[27]

This is a classic Signification, an exchange of meaning and intention of some urgency between two lovers.

I use the word *exchange* here to echo Hurston's use in her essay, "Characteristics of Negro Expression." In this essay Hurston argues that "language is like money," and its development can be equated metaphorically with the development in the marketplace of the means of exchange from bartered "actual goods," which "evolve into coin" (coins symbolizing wealth). Coins evolve into legal tender, and legal tender evolves into "cheques for certain usages." Hurston's illustrations are especially instructive. People "with highly developed languages," she writes, "have words for detached ideas. That is legal tender." The linguistic equivalent of legal tender consists of words such as "chair," which comes to stand for "that-which-we-squat-on." "Groan-causers" evolves into "spear," and so on. "Cheque words" include those such as "ideation" and "pleonastic." *Paradise Lost* and *Sartor Resartus*, she continues, "are written in cheque words!" But "the primitive man," she argues, eschews legal tender and cheque words; he "exchanges descriptive words," describing "one act . . . in terms of another." More specifically, she concludes, black expression turns upon both the "interpretation of the English language in terms of pictures" and the supplement of what she calls "action words," such as "chop-axe," "sitting-chair," and "cook pot." It is the supplement of action, she maintains, which underscores her use of the word "exchange."

Such an exchange, as we have seen, is that between Big Sweet and Joe Willard. As the exchange continues, not only does the characters' language exemplify Hurston's theory, but the definitions of Signifyin(g) that I have been drawing upon throughout this book are also exemplified:

> "See dat?" Joe appealed to the other men. "We git a day off and figger we kin ketch some fish and enjoy ourselves, but naw, some wimmins got to drag behind us, even to de lake."
>
> "You didn't figger Ah was draggin' behind you when you was bringin' dat Sears and Roebuck catalogue over to my house and beggin' me to choose my ruthers. Lemme tell *you* something, *any* time Ah shack up wid any man Ah gives myself de privilege to go where he might be, night or day. Ah got de law in my mouth."
>
> "Lawd, ain't she specifyin'!" sniggered Wiley.
>
> "Oh, Big Sweet does dat," agreed Richardson. "Ah knewed she had somethin' up her sleeve when she got Lucy and come along."
>
> "Lawd," Willard said bitterly. "'My people, my people,' as de monkey said. You fool with Aunt Hagar's chillun and they'll sho discriminate you and put yo' name in de streets."

Specifying, putting one's name in the streets, and "as de money said" are all figures for Signifyin(g). In *Dust Tracks on a Road*, Hurston even defines specifying as "giving a reading" in the following passage:

> The bookless may have difficulty in reading a paragraph in a newspaper, but when they get down to "playing the dozens" [Signifyin(g)] they have no equal in America, and, I'd risk a sizable bet, in the whole world. Starting off in the first by calling you a seven-sided son-of-a-bitch, and pausing to name the sides, they proceed to "specify" until the tip-top branch of your family tree has been "given a reading."

The sort of close reading that I am attempting here is also an act of specifying.

Let me return briefly to Hurston's theory of "Negro Expression" before turning to explicate rhetorical strategies at work in *Their Eyes Were Watching God*. Her typology of black oral narration, in addition to "picture" and "action" words, consists of what she calls "the will to adorn," by which she means the use of densely figurative language, the presence of "revision," which she defines as "[making] over a great part of the [English] tongue," and the use of "metaphor and simile," "the double-descriptive," and "verbal nouns." It is Hurston's sense of revision, defined as "originality [in] the modification of ideas" and "of language," as well as "reinterpretation," which I have defined in Chapter 2 as the ultimate meaning of the trope of Signifyin(g). By "revision," she also means "imitation" and "mimicry," for which she says "The Negro, the world over, is famous" and which she defines as "an art in itself." The Negro, she claims, imitates and revises, not "from a feeling of inferiority," rather "for the love of it." This notion of imitation, repetition, and revision, she maintains, is fundamental to "all art," indeed is the nature of art itself, even Shakespeare's.

Near the end of her compelling essay, Hurston argues that dialect is "Negro speech," and Negro speech, she contends throughout the essay, is quite capable of expressing the most subtle nuances of meaning, despite "the majority of writers of Negro dialect and the burnt-cork artists." "Fortunately," she concludes, "we don't have to believe them. We may go directly to the Negro and let him speak for himself." Using in large part Hurston's own theory of black oral narration, we can gain some understanding of the modes of narration at work in *Their Eyes* and thereby demonstrate why I have chosen to call it a speakerly text, a phrase that I derive both from Roland Barthes's opposition between the "readerly" and the "writerly" texts—the binarism of which I am here Signifyin(g) upon—as well as from the trope of the Talking Book, which not only is the Afro-American tradition's fundamental repeated trope but also is a phrase used by both Hurston and Ishmael Reed to define their own narrative strategies.

The "white man thinks in a written language," Hurston claims, while "the Negro thinks in hieroglyphics." By hieroglyphics, she means the "wordpictures" or the "thought pictures" as she defines these in *Their Eyes*. It is a fairly straightforward matter to list just a few of what we might think of as Hurston's figures of adornment," the specifically black examples of figurative language that she labels "simile and metaphor," "double-descriptives," and "verbal-nouns." Karla Holloway lists these as expressed in *Their Eyes*:

1. An envious heart makes a treacherous ear.
2. Us colored folks is branches without roots.
3. They's a lost ball in high grass.
4. She . . . left her wintertime wid me.
5. Ah wanted yuh to pick from a higher bush.
6. You got uh willin' mind, but youse too light behind.
7. . . . he's de wind and we'se de grass.
8. He was a man wid salt in him.
9. . . . what dat multiplied cockroach told you.
10. still-bait
11. big-bellies
12. gentlemanfied man

13. cemetary-dead
14. black-dark
15. duskin-down-dark[28]

This list certainly could be extended. Suffice it to say that the diction of both the characters' discourse and the free indirect discourse are replete with the three types of adornment that Hurston argued were fundamental to black oral narration.

In addition to these sorts of figures of adornment, *Their Eyes* is comprised of several long exchanges of direct discourse, which seem to be present in the text more for their own sake than to develop the plot. *Their Eyes* consists of a remarkable percentage of direct speech, rendered in black dialect, as if to display the capacity of black language itself to convey an extraordinarily wide variety of ideas and feelings. Frequently, these exchanges between characters extend for two or three pages, with little or no interruption from the text's narrator. When such narrative commentary does surface, it often serves to function as stage direction rather than as a traditional omniscient voice, as if to underscore Hurston's contention that it is "drama" that "permeates [the Negro's] entire self," and it is the dramatic to which black oral narration aspires. Because, as Hurston writes, "an audience is a necessary part of any drama," these Signifyin(g) rituals tend to occur outdoors, at the communal scene of oral instruction, on the porches of homes and stores.

From the novel's earliest scenes, the porch is both personified and then represented through a series of synecdoches as the undifferentiated "eyes," "mouth," and "ears" of the community. Of these three senses, however, it is the communal speaking voice—"Mouth-Almighty," as the text has it—which emerges early on as the most significant. Indeed, the first time the porch "speaks," the text represents its discourse in one paragraph of "direct quotation" consisting of ten sentences separated only by dashes, as if to emphasize the anonymous if collective voice of the community that the text proceeds to represent in several ways. Against this sort of communal narration the text pits Jody Starks, Janie's second husband, who repeatedly states that he wishes to become "a big voice." This voice, however, is the individual voice of domination. The figure of Jody's big voice comes to stand as a synecdoche of oppression, in opposition to the speech community of whch Janie longs to become an integral part.

The representation of modes of black narration begins, as we have seen, with Janie's narration of her story to Phoeby, the framed tale in which most of the novel's action unfolds. Throughout this narrative, the word *voice* recurs with great frequency. Who speaks, indeed, proves to be of crucial import to Janie's quest for freedom, but who sees and who hears at all points in the text remain fundamental as well. Phoeby's "hungry listening," we recall, "helped Janie to tell her story." Almost as soon as Janie's narrative begins, however, Nanny assumes control of the text and narrates the story of Janie's genealogy, from slavery to the present, as Janie listens painfully. This quasi-slave narrative, rendered as a tale-within-a-tale, is one of the few instances of direct speech that serve as a function of the plot. Subsequent speaking narrators assume control of the narrative primarily to demonstrate forms of traditional oral narration.

These double narratives-within-the-narrative begin as soon as Janie and Jody move to Eatonville. Amos Hicks and Joe Coker engage in a brief and amusing exchange about the nature of storytelling generally and about the nature of figurative language specifically, a discussion to which we shall return. Tony Taylor next demonstrates the ironies of speech-making on the day of dedication of Jody's store, a speech that ends with requests that Janie address the community, only to be thwarted by her husband who says that "mah wife don't know nothin' 'bout no speech-makin.'" Jody's harsh actions, the narrator tell us ominously, "took the bloom off of things" for Janie. Subsequent forms of oral narration include "a traditional prayer-poem," a series of speeches, the sung communal poetry of the spirituals, but especially the front-porch Signifyin(g) rituals that serve to impede the plot. The porch is dominated by three narrators. Sam, Lige, and Walter are known as "the ring-leaders of the mule-talkers," who sit for hours on the storefront porch and Signify upon Matt Bonner's yellow mule. These exchanges about the mule extend for pages and would seem to be present primarily to display the nature of storytelling, allowing a full range of characters' discourse to be heard.

At the end of the second mule Signification, still another tale-within-a-tale-within-a-tale unfolds, which we might think of as the allegory of the buzzards. After the second mule tale concludes with his mock funeral and mock eulogy, the disembodied narrator relates the narrative of "the already impatient buzzards," who proceed in ritual fashion to examine and disembowel the mule's carcass. This allegory, of course, serves to mock the preceding mock eulogy, complete with the speaking characters and a patterned oral ritual. This allegory, more especially, shatters completely any illusion the reader might have had that this was meant to be a realistic fiction, even though the text has naturalized the possibility of such an event occurring, if only by representing storytelling in direct speech as its principal mode of narration. Once the reader encounters the allegory of the buzzards, his or her generic expectations have been severely interrupted.

Two pages later, the text returns to more Signifyin(g) rituals, defined by the narrator as "eternal arguments," which "never ended because there was no end to reach. It was a contest in hyperbole," the narrator concludes, "carried on for no other reason." Sam Watson and Lige Moss then proceed to debate, for six pages, the nature of the subject and whether or not "you got to have a subjick tuh talk from, do yuh can't talk," and whether or not these sorts of "readings" have "points." Just as the two Signifiers are about to commence still another oral narration of High John de Conquer tales, three women come walking down the street and thereby generate three pages of rhetorical courtship rituals. At this point in the narrative, as at the beginning of the first mule tale, the omniscient narrator establishes the context by shifting from the past tense to the present tense, then disappears for pages and pages while the characters narrate, underscoring thereby the illusion of overhearing an event.

The most crucial of these scenes of represented speech is the devastating exchange in which Janie first speaks in public against her husband. This exchange is a Signifyin(g) ritual of the first order because Janie Signifies upon Jody's manhood, thereby ending his dominance over her and over the community, and thereby killing Jody's will to live. The exchange is marvelous. Jody begins the fatal confrontation by insulting Janie for improperly cutting a plug of tobacco:

> "I god almighty! A woman stay round uh store till she get old as Methusalem and still can't cut a little thing like a plug of tobacco! Don't stand dere rollin' yo' pop eyes at me wid yo' rump hangin' nearly to yo' knees!"

After a short, quick "big laugh," the crowd assembled in the store, "got to thinking and stopped. It was like somebody," the narrative continues, "snatched off part of a woman's clothes while she wasn't looking and the streets were crowded." But most remarkably of all, "Janie took the middle of the floor to talk right into Jody's face, and that was something that hadn't been done before."

Janie, as a startled Jody says, is speaking a new language, "Talkin' any such language as dat." "You de one started talkin' under people's clothes," she retorts. "Not me." Then, indeed, Janie proceeds to talk under clothes, after Jody says:

> "'T'ain't no use in gettin' all mad, Janie, 'cause Ah mention you ain't no young gal no mo'. Nobody in heah ain't lookin' for no wife outa yuh. Old as you is."

Janie responds:

> "Naw, Ah ain't no young gal no mo' but den Ah ain't no old woman neither. Ah reckon Ah looks mah age too. But Ah'm uh woman every inch of me, and Ah know it. Dat's uh whole lot more'n *you* kin say. You big-bellies round here and put out a lot of brag, but 'tain't nothin' to it but yo' big voice. Humph! Talkin' 'bout *me* lookin' old! When you pull down yo' britches, you look lak de change uh life."

"Great God from Zion!" Sam Watson gasped. "Y'all really playin' de dozens tuhnight," the text reads, naming the sort of Signifyin(g) ritual that has occurred. "Wha-whut's dat you said?" Joe challenged, hoping that his ears had fooled him, to which lame retort "Walter taunted" in a synesthesia that the text has just naturalized for us: "You heard her, you ain't blind." Jody, we well know, now thoroughly shattered by the force of Janie's voice, soon succumbs to acute humiliation and his displaced kidney disorder. As he lies dying, Janie contemplates "what had happened in the making of a voice out of a man," the devastating synecdoche that names both Jody's deepest aspiration and his subsequent great fall.

It is striking that Janie gains her voice and becomes a speaking subject inside her husband's store. Not only does she, by speaking, defy his expressed prohibition, but the scene itself is a key repetition of the metaphors of inside and outside, which repeat frequently throughout the text and which, as I hope to show, serve as a thematic, if metaphorical, counterpart to the most striking innovation of *Their Eyes'* narrative strategy, the presence of free indirect discourse.

The repeated metaphors of inside and outside begin in the text's first chapter. Janie narrates her tale, as Phoeby listens, outside on her back porch. Janie's metaphorical and densely lyrical "outside observations," the narrator tells us, "buried themselves in her flesh." After she experiences her first orgasm, then kisses Johnny Taylor, she extends "herself outside of her dream" and goes "inside of the house." As we have seen, it is inside houses in which a series of people (first her grandmother, Nanny; then her first husband, Logan Killicks; then her second husband, Joe Starks) attempt to oppress her and prevent her from speaking and aserting herself. Janie dreams outdoors, in metaphors of flowering springtime, often under pear trees. When Logan insults her, the narrator says that "she turned wrongside out just standing there and feeling." Jody seduces her with dreams of "far horizons," "under the tree" and outdoors "in the scrub oaks." What Jody speaks out loud and what Janie thinks inside come to represent an opposition of such dimensions that we are not at all surprised when their final confrontation occurs. Janie, we recall, is forced to retreat inside the store when the storytelling rituals commence.

The text represents Janie's crucial if ironic scene of self-discovery rather subtly in this figurative framework of inside and outside. This coming to consciousness is not represented by a speaking scene, however; rather, it is represented in these inside-outside figures. When she finally does speak, therefore, by Signifyin(g) in the store upon Jody's impotence, the gaining of her own voice is a sign of her authority, but not a sign of a newly found unified identity. Janie's speaking voice, rather, is an outcome of her consciousness of division.[29] Indeed, hers is a rhetoric of division.

The text represents this consciousness of division in two scenes that transpire in the chapter that precedes the chapter in which she Signifies upon Jody. The text reads:

> The spirit of the marriage left the bedroom and took to living in the parlor. It was there to shake hands whenever company came to visit, but it never went back inside the bedroom again. So she put something in there to repre-

sent the spirit like a Virgin Mary image in a church. The bed was no longer
a daisy-field for her and Joe to play in. It was a place where she went and
laid down when she was sleepy and tired.

In this passage, Janie's inner feelings, "the spirit of the marriage," are
projected onto outer contiguous physical spaces (the bedroom and the
parlor). Her inside, in other words, is figured as an outside, in the rooms.
Her bed, moreover, ceases to be a place for lovemaking, as signified by
both the daisy-field metaphor and the metaphor of play (reminding us,
through the repetition, of her central metaphors of dream and aspiration
that repeat so often in the novel's first half). The contiguous relation of
the bedroom and the parlor, both physical spaces, through which the
metaphorical spirit of the marriage now moves, reveals two modes of
figuration overlapping in Janie's indirectly reported throughts for the
first time—that is, one mode dependent upon substitution, the other on
contiguity.[30] Clearly, the rhetorical relation among "sex" and "spirit of
the marriage," and "spirit of the marriage," "bedroom," and "parlor" is
a complex one.

Until this moment in the text, Janie's literacy was represented only
as a metaphorical literacy. Janie's "conscious life," the text tells us, "had
commenced at Nanny's gate," across which she had kissed Johnny Taylor
just after experiencing her first orgasm under her "blossoming pear tree
in the back-yard." In the moving passage that precedes the event but
prepares us for it by describing her increasing awareness of her own
sexuality, rendered in free indirect discourse, Janie names her feelings
in her first metaphor: "The rose of the world was breathing out smell.
It followed her through all her waking moments and caressed her in her
sleep." Janie's first language, the language of her own desire, is regis-
tered in a lyrical and metaphorical diction found in these passages of free
indirect discourse. Janie has mastered, the text tells us early on, "the
words of the trees and the wind." In this metaphorical language, "she
spoke to falling seeds," as they speak to her, in lyrical metaphors, renaming "the world," for example, "a stallion rolling in the blue pasture of
ether." Whereas she speaks, thinks, and dreams in metaphors, the communal voice of the porch describes her in a string of synecdoches, naming
parts of her body—such as her "great rope of black hair," "her pugnacious
breats," her "faded shirt and muddy overalls"—as parts standing for the
whole.

One paragraph later, as a sign that she can name her division, the
direction of her figuration reverses itself. Whereas in the first scene she
projects her inner feelings onto outer physical space, in this scene she
internalizes an outer physical space, her scene of oppression, the store:

Janie stood where he left her for unmeasured time and thought. She stood
there until something fell off the shelf inside her. Then she went inside there
to see what it was. It was her image of Jody tumbled down and shattered.

But looking at it she saw that it never was the flesh and blood figure of her dreams. Just something she had grabbed up to drape her dreams over.

Janie has internalized the store through the synecdoche of the shelf.[31] As Barbara Johnson summarizes the rhetorical import of this scene: "These two figural mini-narratives [represent] a kind of chiasmus, or crossover, in which the first paragraph presents an externalization of the inner, a metaphorically grounded metonymy, while the second paragraph presents an internalization of the outer, or a metonymically grounded metaphor. . . . The reversals operated by the chiasmus map out a reversal of the power relations between Janie and Joe."[32] When she soon speaks aloud in public against Jody and thereby redefines their relationship, it is the awareness of this willed figurative division of which her speaking voice is the sign. As the text reads, Janie "found that she had a host of thoughts she had never expressed to him, and numerous emotions she had never let Jody know about. Things packed up and put away in parts of her heart where he could never find them."

Janie is now truly fluent in the language of the figurative: "She had an inside and an outside now and suddenly knew how not to mix them." Three pages before she Signifies upon Jody, the text represents this fluency as follows:

> Then one day she sat and watched the shadow of herself going about tending the store and prostrating itself before Jody, while all the time she herself sat under a shady tree with the wind blowing through her hair and her clothes. Somebody near about making summertime out of lonesomeness.

Janie's ability to name her own division and move the parts simultaneously through contiguous spaces, her newly found and apparently exhilarating double-consciousness, is that crucial event that enables her to speak and assert herself, after decades of being defined almost exclusively by others.

The text prefigures this event. The sign that this consciousness of her own division liberates her speaking voice is Janie's first instance of voicing her feelings within the store, which occurs in the text midway between the slapping scene in which she first internally names her outside and inside and the scene in which she so tellingly Signifies upon Joe. Janie speaks after listening in a painful silence as Coker and Joe Lindsay discuss the merits of beating women:

> ". . . Tony love her too good," said Coker. "Ah could break her if she wuz mine. Ah'd break her or kill her. Makin' uh fool outa me in front of everybody."
>
> "Tony won't never hit her. He says beatin' women is just like steppin' on baby chickens. He claims 'tain't no place on uh woman tuh hit," Joe Lindsay said with scornful disapproval, "but Ah'd kill uh baby just born dis mawnin' fuh uh thing like dat. 'Taint nothin' but low-down spitefulness 'ginst her husband make her do it."

This exchange, of course, refigures the crucial scene in which Joe slaps Janie because her meal was not well prepared. Joe Lindsay's comparison in this passage of "beatin' women" and "steppin' on baby chickens" echoes Joe's proclamation to Janie that "somebody got to think for women and chillun and chickens and cows," made in their argument about who has the right "to tell." After Joe Lindsay finishes speaking, and after his sexist remarks are affirmed as gospel by Jim Stone, Janie—for the first time—speaks out against the men's opinion about the merits of beatings. As the text states, "Janie did what she had never done before, that is, thrust herself into the conversation":

> "Sometimes God gits familiar wid us womenfolks too and talks His inside business. He told me how surprised He was 'bout y'all turning out so smart after Him makin' yuh different; and how surprised y'all is goin' tuh be if you ever find out you don't know half as much 'bout us as you think you do. It's so easy to make yo'self out God Almighty when you ain't got nothin' tuh strain against but *women and chickens*." (emphasis added)

Janie reveals God's "inside business" to the superficial store-talkers, warning all who can hear her voice that a "surprise" lay in waiting for those who see only appearances and never penetrate to the tenor of things. Joe, we learn just four pages later, is in for the surprise of his life: the killing timbre of Janie's true inner voice. Joe's only response to this first scene of speaking is to tell his wife, "You gettin' too moufy, Janie," a veritable literalizing of the metaphor of mouth, followed by the ultimate sign of ignoring and circumventing Janie's domain, an order to her to "Go fetch me de checker-board *and* de checkers." Joe's turn to the male world of play, at Janie's expense, leads Janie to play the dozens on his sexuality and thus to his death. These metaphorical echoes and exchanges are deadly serious in Hurston's text.

Earlier in the narrative, Hicks defined the metaphorical as "co-talkin'" and says that his is "too deep" for women to understand, which explains, he says, why "Dey love to hear me talk" precisely "because dey can't understand it. . . . Too much co to it," he concludes. As soon as Janie learns to name her inside and outside and to move between them, as we have seen, Jody argues that women "need tellin'" because "somebody got to think for women and chillun and chickens and cows" because a man sees "one thing" and "understands ten," while a woman sees "ten things and don't understand one." Jody ironically accuses Janie of failing to understand how one thing can imply or be substituted for ten, thereby arguing that Janie does not understand metaphor, whereas Janie is a master of metaphor whose self-liberation awaits only the knowledge of how to narrate her figures contiguously. It is Jody who has failed to read the situation properly. As a character in *Mules and Men* argues, most people do not understand the nature of the figurative, which he characterizes as expression that "got a hidden meanin', jus' like de Bible. Everybody can't understand what they mean," he continues. "Most people is thin-brained. They's born wid they feet under the moon. Some folks is born wid they feet on de sun and they kin seek out de inside meanin' of words." Jody, it turns out, is both thin-brained and thin-skinned, and proves to have been born with his feet under the moon. He is all vehicle, no tenor. The "inside meanings of words," of course, we think of as the tenor, or inside meaning of a rhetorical figure, while the outside corresponds to its "vehicle." Janie, as the text repeats again and again in its central metaphor for her character, is a child of the sun.

Hurston's use of free indirect discourse is central to her larger strategy of critiquing what we might think of as a "male writing." Joe Starks, we remember, fondly and unconsciously refers to himself as "I god." During the lamplighting ceremony, as I have suggested earlier, Joe is represented as the creator (or at least the purchaser) of light. Joe is the text's figure of authority and voice, indeed the authority *of* voice:

> "Naw, Jody, it jus' looks lak it keeps us in some way we ain't natural wid one 'nother. You'se always off talkin' and fixin' things, and Ah feels lak Ah'm jus' markin' time. Hope it soon gits over."
> "Over, Janie? I god, Ah ain't even started good. Ah told you in de very first beginnin' dat Ah aimed tuh be uh big voice. You oughta be glad, 'cause dat makes uh big woman outa you."

Joe says that "in de very first beginnin'" he "aimed tuh be uh big voice," an echo of the first verse of the Gospel of John: "In the beginning was the Word, and the Word was with God, and the Word was God." Joe, we know, sees himself, and wishes to be seen as the God-figure of his community. The text tells us that when speakers on formal occasions prefaced their remarks with the phrase "Our beloved Mayor," the phrase was equivalent to "one of those statements that everybody says but nobody believes like 'God is everywhere'." Joe is the figure of the male author, he who has authored both Eatonville and Janie's existences. We remember that when Joe lights the town's newly acquired lamp, Mrs. Bogle's alto voice sings "Jesus, the light of the world":

> We'll walk in de light, de beautiful light
> Come where the dew drops of mercy shine bright
> Shine all around us by day and by night
> Jesus, the light of the world.

So, when Janie Signifies upon Joe, she strips him of his hubristic claim to the godhead and exposes him, through the simile of the "change of life," as impotent and de/masculated. The revelation of the truth kills him. Janie, in effect, has rewritten Joe's text of himself, and liberated herself in the process. Janie writes herself into being by naming, by speaking herself free. As we shall see in Chapter 7, Alice Walker takes this moment in Hurston's text as the moment of revision and creates a character whom we witness literally writing herself into being, but writing herself into being in a language that imitates that idiom spoken by Janie and Hurston's black community generally. This scene, this transformation or reversal of status, is truly the first feminist critique of the fiction of the authority of the male voice, and its sexism, in the Afro-American tradition.

This opposition between metaphor and metonym appears in another form as well, that of strategies of tale-telling. Nanny narrates her slave narrative in a linear, or metonymic, manner, with one event following another in chronological order. Janie, by contrast, narrates her tale in a circular, or framed, narrative replete with vivid, startling metaphors. Janie only liberates herself by selecting alternatives exactly opposed to those advocated by Nanny, eschewing the sort of "protection" afforded by Logan Killicks and so graphically figured for Janie in her grandmother's fantasy of preaching "a great sermon about colored women sittin' on high." Only after Janie satisfies Nancy's desire, "sittin' on high" on Joe Starks's front porch, then rejecting it, will she in turn "preach" her own sermon by narrating her tale to Phoeby in a circular, framed narrative that merges her voice with an omniscient narrator's in free indirect discourse.

IV

If *Their Eyes* makes impressive use of the figures of outside and inside, as well as the metaphor of double-consciousness as the prequisite to becoming a speaking subject, then the text's mode of narration, especially its "speakerliness," serves as the rhetorical analogue to this theme. I use the word double here intentionally, to echo W. E. B. Du Bois's metaphor for the Afro-American's peculiar psychology of citizenship and also to avoid the limited description of free indirect discourse as a "dual voice," in Roy Pascal's term.[33] Rather than a dual voice, free indirect discourse, as manifested in *Their Eyes Were Watching God*, is a dramatic way of expressing a divided self. Janie's self, as we have seen, is a divided self. Long before she becomes aware of her division, of her inside and outside, free indirect discourse communicates this division to the reader. After she becomes aware of her own division, free indirect discourse functions to represent, rhetorically, her interrupted passage from outside to inside. Free indirect discourse in *Their Eyes* reflects both the text's theme of the doubling of Janie's self and that of the problematic relationship between Janie as a speaking subject and spoken language. Free indirect discourse, furthermore, is a central aspect of the rhetoric of the text and serves to disrupt the reader's expectation of the necessity of the shift in point of view from third person to first within Janie's framed narrative. Free indirect discourse is not the voice of both a character and a narrator; rather, it is a bivocal utterance, containing elements of both direct and indirect speech. It is an utterance that no one could have spoken, yet which we recognize because of its characteristic "speakerliness," its paradoxically written manifestation of the aspiration to the oral.

I shall not enter into the terminological controversy over free indirect discourse, except to refer the reader to the controversy itself.[34] My concern with free indirect discourse, for the purposes of this chapter, is limited to its use in *Their Eyes*.[35] I am especially interested in its presence in this text as an implicit critique of that ancient opposition in narrative theory between showing and telling, between mimesis and diegesis. The tension between diegesis, understood here as that which can be represented, and mimesis, that which Hurston repeats in direct quotations, strikes the reader early on as a fundamental opposition in *Their Eyes*. Only actions or events can be represented, in this sense, while discourse here would seem to be overheard or repeated. Hurston's use of this form of repetition creates the illusion of a direct relationship between her text and a black "real world" (which has led some of her most vocal critics to call this an anthropological text), while representation of the sort found in narrative commentary preserves, even insists upon, the difference and the very distance between them.

Free indirect discourse, on the other hand, is a third, mediating term. As Michal Ginsberg argues perceptively, "it is a *mimesis* which tries to pass for a *diegesis*."[36] But it is also, I contend, a diegesis that tries to pass for a mimesis. Indeed, it is precisely this understanding of free indirect discourse that derives from its usages in *Their Eyes Were Watching God*, simply because we are unable to characterize it either as the representation of an action (diegesis) or as the repetition of a character's words (mimesis). When we recall Hurston's insistence that the fundamental indicator of traditional black oral narration is its aspiration to the "dramatic," we can see clearly that her use of free indirect discourse is a profound attempt to remove the distinction between repeated speech and represented events. Here discourse "is not distinct from events." As Ginsberg argues, "Subject and object dissolve into each other. Representation which guaranteed the distance between them is in danger."[37] For Hurston, free indirect discourse is an equation: direct speech equals narrative commentary; representation of an action equals repetition of that action; therefore, narrative commentary aspires to the immediacy of the drama. Janie's quest for consciousness, however, always remains that for the consciousness of her own division, which the dialogical rhetoric of the text—especially as expressed in free indirect discourse—underscores, preserves, and seems to celebrate. It is this theme, and this rhetoric of division, which together comprise the modernism of this text.

A convenient way to think about free indirect discourse is that it appears initially to be indirect discourse (by which I mean that its signals of time and person correspond to a third-person narrator's discourse), "but it is penetrated, in its syntactic and semantic structures, by enunciative properties, thus by the discourse of a character,"[38] and even in Hurston's case by that of characters. In other words, free indirect discourse attempts to represent "consciousness without the apparent intrusion of a narrative voice," thereby "presenting the illusion of a character's acting out his [or her] mental state in an immediate relationship with the reader." Graham Hough defines free indirect discourse as one extreme of "coloured narrative," or narrative-cum-dialogue as in Jane Austen's fictions.[39] Hurston's use of free indirect discourse, we are free to say, is indeed a kind of "coloured narrative"! But Hurston allows us to rename free indirect discourse; near the beginning of her book, the narrator describes the communal, undifferentiated voice of "the porch" as "A mood come alive. Words walking without masters; walking altogether like harmony in a song." Since the narrator attributes these words to "the bander log," or the place where Kipling's monkeys sit, Hurston here gives one more, coded, reference to Signifyin(g): that which the porch (monkeys) has just done is to Signify upon Janie. If Signifyin(g) is "a mood come alive," "words walking without masters," then we can also think of free indirect discourse in this way.

There are numerous indices whereby we identify free indirect discourse in general, among these grammar, intonation, context, idiom, register, and content; it is naturalized in a text by stream of consciousness, irony, empathy, and polyvocality.[40] The principal indices of free indirect discourse in *Their Eyes* include those which "evoke a 'voice' or presence" that supplements the narrator's, especially when one or more sentences of free indirect discourse follow a sentence of indirect discourse. Idiom and register, particularly, Hurston uses as markets of black colloquialism, of the quality of the speakerly informed by the dialect of the direct discourse of the characters. In *Their Eyes*, naturalization would seem to function as part of the theme of the developing but discontinuous self. This function is naturalized primarily by irony, empathy, and polyvocality. When it is used in conjunction with Joe Starks, irony obtains and distancing results; when it is used in conjunction with Janie, empathy obtains and an illusory identification results, as identity we might call lyric fusion between the narrator and Jamie. Bivocalism, finally, or the double-voiced utterance, in which two voices co-occur, is this text's central device of naturalization, again serving to reinforce both Janie's division and paradoxically the narrator's distance from Janie. As Ginsberg concludes so perceptively, "Free indirect discourse is a way of expression of a divided self."[41]

Their Eyes employs three modes of narration to render the words or thoughts of a character. The first is direct discourse:

> "Jody," she smiled up at him, "but s'posin—"
> "Leave de s'posin' and everything else to me."

The next is indirect discourse:

> "The vision of Logan Killicks was desecrating the pear tree, but Janie didn't know how to tell Nanny that."

The third example is free indirect discourse. Significantly, this example occurs when Joe Starks enters the narrative:

> Joe Starks was the name, yeah Joe Starks from in and through Georgy. Been workin' for white folks all his life. Saved up some money—round three hundred dollars, yes indeed, right here in his pocket. Kept hearin' 'bout them buildin' a new state down heah in Floridy and sort of wanted to come. But he was makin' money where he was. But when he heard all about 'em makin' a town all outa colored folks, he knowed dat was de place he wanted to be. He had always wanted to be a big voice, but de white folks had all de sayso where he come from and everywhere else, exceptin' dis place dat colored folks was buildin' theirselves. Dat was right too. De man dat built things oughta boss it. Let colored folks build things too if dey wants to crow over somethin'. He was glad he had his money all saved up. He meant to git dere whilst de town wuz yet a baby. He meant to buy in big.

I selected this example because it includes a number of standard indices of free indirect speech. Although when read aloud it sounds as if entire sections are in, or should be in, direct quotation, none of the sentences in this paragraph is direct discourse. There are no quotation marks here. The character's idiom, interspersed and contrasted colorfully with the narrator's voice, indicates nevertheless that this is an account of the words that Joe spoke to Janie. The sentences imitating dialect clearly are not those of the narrator alone; they are those of Joe Starks and the narrator. Moreover, the presence of the adverb *here* ("yes, indeed, right here in his pocket") as opposed to *there*, which would be required in normal indirect speech because one source would be describing another, informs us that the assertion originates within and reflects the character's sensibilities, not the narrator's. The interspersion of indirect discourse with free indirect discourse, even in the same sentence, serves as another index to its presence, precisely by underscoring Joe's characteristic idiom, whereas the indirect discourse obliterates it. Despite the third person and the past tense, then, of which both indirect and free indirect discourse consist, several sentences in this paragraph appear to report Joe's speech, without the text resorting to either dialogue or direct discourse. The principal indices of free indirect discourse direct the reader to the subjective source of the statement, rendered through a fusion of narrator and a silent but speaking character.

Exclamations and exclamatory questions often introduce free indirect discourse. The text's first few examples occur when Janie experiences the longing for love, and then her first orgasm:

> She saw a dust-bearing bee sink into the sanctum of a bloom; the thousand sister-calyxes arch to meet the love embrace and the ecstatic shiver of the tree from root to tiniest branch creaming in every blossom and frothing with delight. So this was a marriage! . . . Then Janie felt a pain remorseless sweet that left her limp and languid.

Then in the next paragraph:

> She was lying across the bed asleep so Janie tipped on out of the front door.
> Oh to be a pear tree—*any* tree in bloom! With kissing bees singing of the
> beginning of the world! She was sixteen.

Unlike the free indirect discourse that introduces Joe, these three sentences retain the narrator's level of diction, her idiom, as if to emphasize on one hand that Janie represents the potentially lyrical self, but on the other hand that the narrator is interpreting Janie's inarticulate thoughts to the reader on her behalf.

This usage remains fairly consistent until Janie begins to challenge, if only in her thoughts, Joe's authority:

> Janie noted that while he didn't talk the mule himself [Signify], he sat and
> laughed at it. Laughed his big heh, hey laugh too. But then when Lige or
> Sam or Walter or some of the other big picture talkers were using a side of
> the world for a canvas, Joe would hustle her off inside the store to sell something. Look like he took pleasure in doing it. Why couldn't he go himself
> sometimes? She had come to hate the inside of that store anyway.

Here we see Janie's idiom entering, if only in two sentences, the free indirect speech. After she has "slain" Jody, however, her idiom, more and more, informs the free indirect discourse, in sentences such as "Poor Jody! He ought not to have to wrassle in there by himself." Once Janie meets Tea Cake, the reader comes to expect to encounter Janie's doubts and dreams in free indirect discourse, almost always introduced by the narrator explicitly as being Janie's thoughts. Almost never, however, curiously enough, does Janie's free indirect discourse unfold in a strictly black idiom, as does Joe's; rather, it is represented in an idiom informed by the black idiom but translated into what we might think of as a colloquial form of standard English, which always stands in contrast to Janie's direct speech, which is foregrounded in dialect.

This difference between the representations of the level of diction of Janie's direct discourse and the free indirect discourse that the text asks us to accept as the figure of Janie's thoughts reinforces for the reader both Janie's divided consciousness and the double-voiced nature of free indirect discourse, as if the narrative commentary cannot relinquish its proprietary consciousness over Janie as freely as it does for other characters. Nevertheless, after Janie falls in love with Tea Cake, we learn of her feelings through a remarkable amount of free indirect discourse, almost always rendered in what I wish to call idiomatic, but standard, English.

It is this same voice, eventually, which we also come to associate with that of the text's narrator; through empathy and irony, the narrator begins to read Janie's world and everyone in it, through this same rhetorical device, rendered in this identical diction, even when the observation clearly is not Janie's. The effect is as if the lyrical language created by the indeterminate merging of the narrator's voice and Janie's almost totally silences the initial level of diction of the narrator's voice. Let us recall the narrator's voice in the text's opening paragraph:

> Ships at a distance have every man's wish on board. For some they come in with the tide. For others they sail forever on the horizon, never out of sight, never landing until the Watcher turns his eyes away in resignation, his dreams mocked to death by Time. That is the life of men.

Compare that voice with the following:

> So Janie began to think of Death. Death, that strange being with the huge square toes who lived away in the West. The great one who lived in the straight house like a platform without sides to it, and without a roof. What need has Death for a cover, and what winds can blow against him?

Ostensibly, these are Janie's thoughts. But compare this sentence, which is part of the narrator's commentary: "But, don't care how firm your determination is, you can't keep turning round in one place like a horse grinding sugar cane."

This idiomatic voice narrates almost completely the dramatic scene of the hurricane, where "six eyes were questioning *God*." One such passage serves as an excellent example of a communal free indirect discourse, of a narrative voice that is not fused with Janie's but which describes events in the idiom of Janie's free indirect discourse:

> They looked back. Saw people trying to run in raging waters and screaming when they found they couldn't. A huge barrier of the makings of the dike to which the cabins had been added was rolling and tumbling forward. . . . The monstropolous beast had left his bed. . . . The sea was walking the earth with a heavy heel.

At several passages after this narration of the hurricane, the interspersed indirect discourse and free indirect discourse become extraordinarily difficult to isolate because of this similarity in idiom:

> Janie fooled around outside awhile to try and think it wasn't so. . . . Well, she thought, that big old dawg with the hatred in his eyes had killed her after all. She wished she had slipped off that cow-tail and drowned then and there and been done. But to kill her through Tea Cake was too much to bear. Tea Cake, the son of the Evening Sun, had to die for loving her. She looked hard at the sky for a long time. Somewhere up there beyond blue ether's bottom sat He. Was He noticing what was going on around here? . . . Did He *mean* to do this thing to Tea Cake and her? . . . Maybe it was some big tease and when He saw it had gone far enough He'd give her a sign.

Narrative commentary and free indirect discourse, in passage such as this, move toward the indistinguishable. The final instance of free indirect discourse occurs, appropriately enough, in the novel's ultimate paragraph, in which Janie's true figurative synthesis occurs:

> The day of the gun, and the bloody body, and the courthouse came and commenced to sing a sobbing sigh out of every corner in the room; out of each and every chair and thing. Commenced to sing, commenced to sob and sigh,

singing and sobbing. Then Tea Cake came prancing around her where she was and the song of the sigh flew out of the window and lit in the top of the pine trees. Tea Cake, with the sun for a shawl. Of course he wasn't dead. He could never be dead until she herself had finished feeling and thinking. The kiss of his memory made pictures of love and light against the wall. Here was peace. She pulled in her horizon like a great fish-net. Pulled it from around the waist of the world and draped it over her shoulder. So much of life in its meshes! She called in her soul to come and see.

Ephi Paul, in a subtle reading of various tropes in *Their Eyes* (in an unpublished essay, "My Tongue Is in My Friend's Mouth"), argues that this "final moment of transcendence" is also a final moment of control and synthesis of the opposed male and female paradigmatic tropes defined in the novel's first two paragraphs:

> The horizon that she learns about from Joe, that helps her rediscover how to "play" again with Tea Cake, has been transformed from the object of a longing gaze to a figurative "fish-net" which an active subject can pull in. While Joe's desires are, like the men of the first paragraph, "mocked to death by Time," Janie's are still alive and thriving: "The kiss of his memory made pictures of love and light against the wall." Janie finds "peace" in "his memory," just as she has always privileged her inward contemplative self over the outer active one. Yet in its own way, Janie's thriving survival of hard times has been an active process of finding a language to name her desire. The horizon as a fish-net seems to signify the synthesis of "men" and "women's" figuration, because the fish-net's "meshes" seem so like the sifting of women's memories—remembering and forgetting all that they want. So Janie has cast her horizon into a sea of possibilities and sorted out her catch of loves, naming them with an even more accurate figuration of desire. She opens her arms to "the waist of the world" and gathers in her satisfactions, rooted in her power of "feeling and thinking" for herself.

This merging of the opposed modes of figuration in the novel's first two paragraphs stands as an analogue of Janie's transcendent moment because of, as Paul argues,

> the male and female modes of figuration (as established in the "paradigm" of its first two paragraphs)—bringing together the horizon of change and the fish-net of memory. In her search for desire and its naming, Janie shifts back and forth between the alienation of the gazing "Watcher" and the empowerment of women believing that "the dream is the truth." She finds her satisfaction only after using Joe's horizon of "change and chance" to transform the desire she experiences alone under the pear tree; she retains the horizon long after she has dismissed Joe, because she can re-figure it to have meaning for herself.

To this I would only add that both the pulling in of her horizon and the calling in of her soul reveal not a unity of self but a maximum of self-control over the division between self and other. Whereas before Tea Cake Janie was forced to send a mask of herself outward, now, at novel's end, she can invite both her horizon (the figure for her desires after meeting Jody) and her soul inside herself "to come and see." She has internalized her metaphors, and brought them home, across a threshold heretofore impenetrable. This self-willed, active, subjective synthesis is a remarkable trope of self-knowledge. And the numerous sentences of free indirect discourse in this paragraph serve to stress this fact of Janie's self-knowledge and self-control. Her invitation to her soul to come see the horizon that had always before been a figure for external desire, the desire of the other, is the novel's sign of Janie's synthesis.

It is because of these dramatic shifts in the idiom in which the voice of the narrator appears that we might think of *Their Eyes* as a speakerly text. For it is clear that the resonant dialect of the character's discourse has come to color the narrator's idiom such that it resembles rather closely the idiom in which Janie's free indirect discourse is rendered. But *Their Eyes* would seem to be a speakerly text for still another reason. Hurston uses free indirect discourse not only to represent an individual character's speech and thought but also to represent the collective black community's speech and thoughts, as in the hurricane passage. This sort of anonymous, collective, free indirect discourse is not only unusual but quite possibly was Hurston's innovation, as if to emphasize both the immense potential of this literary diction, one dialect-informed as it were, for the tradition, as well as the text's apparent aspiration to imitate oral narration. One example follows:

> Most of the great flame-throwers were there and naturally, handling Big John de Conquer and his works. How he had done everything big on earth, then went up tuh heben without dying atall. Went up there picking a guitar and got all de angels doing the ring-shout round and round de throne . . . that brought them back to Tea Cake. How come he couldn't hit that box a lick or two? Well, all right now, make us know it.

Still another example is even more telling:

> Everybody was talking about it that night. But nobody was worried. The fire dance kept up till nearly dawn. The next day, more Indians moved east, unhurried but steady. Still a blue sky and fair weather. Beans running fine and prices good, so the Indians could be, *must* be, wrong. You couldn't have a hurricane when you're making seven and eight dollars a day picking beans. Indians are dumb anyhow, always were. Another night of Stew Beef making dynamic subtleties with his drum and living, sculptural, grotesques in the dance.

These instances of free indirect discourse are followed in the text by straight diegesis, which retains the dialect-informed echoes of the previous passage:

> Morning came without motion. The winds, to the tiniest, lisping baby breath had left the earth. Even before the sun gave light, dead day was creeping from bush to bush watching man.

There are many other examples of this curious voice. Hurston, in this innovation, is asserting that an entire narration could be rendered, if not in dialect, then in a dialect-informed discourse. This form of collective, impersonal free indirect discourse echoes Hurston's definition of "a mood come alive. Words walking without masters; walking altogether like harmony in a song." The ultimate sign of the dignity and strength of the black voice is this use of a dialect-informed free indirect discourse as narrative commentary beyond that which represents Janie's thoughts and feelings alone.

There are paradoxes and ironies in speakerly texts. The irony of this dialect-informed diction, of course, is that it is not a repetition of a language that anyone speaks; indeed, it can never be spoken. As several other scholars of free indirect discourse have argued, free indirect discourse is speakerless, by which they mean "the presentation of a perspective outside the normal communication paradigm that usually characterizes language."[42] It is literary language, meant to be read in a text. Its paradox is that it comes into use by Hurston so that discourse rendered through direct, indirect, or free indirect means may partake of Hurston's "word-pictures" and "thought-pictures," as we recall she defined the nature of Afro-American spoken language. "The white man thinks in a written language," she argued, "and the Negro thinks in hieroglyphics." The speakerly diction of *Their Eyes* attempts to render these pictures through the imitation of the extensively metaphorical medium of black speech, in an oxymoronic oral hieroglyphic that is meant only for the printed page. Its obvious oral base, nevertheless, suggests that Hurston conceived of it as a third language, as a mediating third term that aspires to resolve the tension between standard English and black vernacular, just as the narrative device of free indirect discourse aspires to define the traditional opposition between mimesis and diegesis as a false opposition. And perhaps this dialogical diction, and this dialogical narrative device, can serve as a metaphor for the critic of black comparative literature whose theoretical endeavor is intentionally double-voiced as well.

If Esu's double voice is figured in *Their Eyes Were Watching God* in the dialogical basis of free indirect discourse, it manifests itself in the fiction of Ishmael Reed in the sustained attempt to critique the strategies of narration central to certain canonical Afro-American texts through parody and pastiche. Like Hurston's text, we may think of Reed's novel as double-voiced, but in an essentially different way. Reed's relation to these authors in the tradition is at all points double-voiced, since he seems to be especially concerned with employing satire to utilize literature in what Frye calls "a special function of analysis, of breaking up the lumber of stereotypes, fossilized beliefs, superstitious terrors, crank theories, pedantic dogmatisms, oppressive fashions, and all other things that impede the free movement . . . of society."[43] Reed, of course, seems to be most concerned with the "free movement" of writing itself. In Reed's work, parody and hidden polemic overlap, in a process Bakhtin describes as follows: "When parody becomes aware of substantial resistance, a certain forcefulness and profundity in the speech act it parodies, it takes on a new dimension of complexity via the tones of the hidden polemic. . . . [A] process of inner dialogization takes place within the parodic speech act."[44] This "internal dialogization" can have curious implications, the most interesting of which perhaps is what Bakhtin describes as "the splitting of double-voice discourse into two speech acts, into two entirely separate and autonomous voices." The clearest evidence that Reed in *Mumbo Jumbo* is Signifyin(g) through parody as hidden polemic is his use of the two autonomous narrative voices in *Mumbo Jumbo*, which Reed employs in the manner of and renders through foregrounding, to parody the two simultaneous stories of detective narration, that of the present and that of the past, in a narrative flow that moves hurriedly from cause to effect. In *Mumbo Jumbo*, however, the second narrative, that of the past, bears an ironic relation to the first narrative, that of the present, because it comments on the other narrative as well as on the nature of its writing itself, in what Frye describes, in another context, as "the constant tendency to self-parody in satiric rhetoric which prevents even the process of writing itself from becoming an oversimplified convention or idea."[45] Reed's rhetorical strategy assumes the form of the relationship between the text and the criticism of that text, which "serves as discourse on that text." If Hurston's novel is a Signifyin(g) structure because it seems to be so concerned to represent Signifyin(g) rituals for their own sake, then Reed's text is a Signifyin(g) structure because he Signifies upon the tradition's convention of representation.

Notes

1. Hurston's revision of Douglass's apostrophe to the sails was suggested to me by Kimberly W. Benston. On chiasmus in *Their Eyes*, see Ephi Paul, "Mah Tongue Is in Mah Friend's Mouf," unpublished essay, pp. 10–12.
2. Thomas Hamilton, "Apology," *The Anglo-African Magazine*, I, no. 1 (January 1859): 1.
3. W. J. Wilson, "The Coming Man," *The Anglo-African Magazine* I, no. 2 (February 1859): 58.
4. Frances E. W. Harper, letter to Thomas Hamilton, dated 1861.
5. A Lady from Philadelphia, "The Coming American Novelist," *Lippincott's Monthly Magazine* xxxvii (April 1886): 440–43.
6. Ibid., p. 441.
7. Ibid., p. 443.
8. Ibid. On Scarborough's citation, see note 12 below.
9. W. H. A. Moore, "A Void in Our Literature," *New York Age* III (July 5, 1890): 3.
10. *Recorder*, August 1, 1893; *A.M.E. Church Review* xv (October 1898): 629–30. On Scarborough, see note 11 below. For an excellent discussion of these

positions, see August Meier, *Negro Thought in America, 1880–1915: Racial Ideologies in the Age of Booker T. Washington* (Ann Arbor: University of Michigan Press, 1969), pp. 265–66.

11. W. S. Scarborough, "The Negro in Fiction as Portrayer and Portrayed," *Hampton Negro Conference* (Hampton, Va.: Hampton Institute, 1899), pp. 65–66.
12. Ibid., p. 67.
13. See "Dis and Dat: Dialect and the Descent," in Henry Louis Gates, Jr., *Figures in Black* (New York: Oxford University Press, 1986), pp. 167–95.
14. Ibid., p. 22.
15. Johnson's 1932 comments are found in his "Preface" to Brown's *Southern Road*, reprinted in *The Collected Poems of Sterling A. Brown* (New York: Harper & Row, 1980), p. 16–17.
16. Jean Toomer, *Cane* (1923; New York: Harper & Row, 1969), pp. 171–72.
17. George Schuyler, "Instructions for Contributors," reprinted in Eugene Gordon, "Negro Fictionist in America," *The Saturday Evening Quill* (April 1929): 20.
18. Scarborough, "The Negro in Fiction," p. 67.
19. I cite a definition of *skaz* deliberately, for this concept of Russian Formalism is similar to what I am calling the speakerly. See Victor Erlich, *Russian Formalism: History-Doctrine* (Mouton: The Hague, 1969), p. 238.
20. Richard Wright, *America Hunger* (New York: Harper & Row, 1979), p. 7.
21. Zora Neale Hurston, "How It Feels to Be Colored Me," *The World Tomorrow* (1928).
22. Zora Neale Hurston, *Their Eyes Were Watching God* (1937; Urbana: University of Illinois, 1978), pp. 31–32.
23. Zora Neale Hurston, *Dust Tracks on a Road: An Autobiography* (Philadelphia: J. D. Lippincott, 1942), pp. 94–95.
24. Richard Wright, *Black Boy* (1945; New York: Harper & Row, 1966), p. 111.
25. See the epigraphs to this chapter.
26. John Hersey, "Interview with Ralph Ellison," in *The Language of Blackness*, ed. by Kimberly W. Benston and Henry Louis Gates, Jr., forthcoming.
27. Zora Neale Hurston, *Mules and Men: Negro Folktales and Voodoo Practices in the South* (1935; New York: Harper & Row, 1970), p. 161.
28. The best discussion of the representation of black speech in Hurston's work is Karla Francesca Holloway, *A Critical Investigation of Literary and Linguistic Structures in the Fiction of Zora Neale Hurston*, Ph.D. dissertation, Michigan State University, 1978. See esp. pp. 93–94, and 101.
29. I wish to thank Barbara Johnson of Harvard University for calling my attention to this ironic mode of self-consciousness.
30. In a brilliant analysis of this scene of the novel, Barbara Johnson writes that "The entire paragraph is an externalization of Janie's feelings onto the outer surroundings in the form of a narrative of movement from private to public space. While the whole figure relates metaphorically, analogically, to the marital situation it is designed to express, it reveals the marriage space to be metonymical, a movement through a series of contiguous rooms. It is a narrative not of union but of separation centered on an image not of conjugality but of virginity." See Barbara Johnson, "Metaphor, Metonymy, and Voice in Zora Neale Hurston's *Their Eyes Were Watching God*," in *Black Literature and Literary Theory*, ed. by H. L. Gates, Jr. (New York: Methuen, 1984), pp. 205–19.
31. Cf. Johnson: "Janie's 'inside' is here represented as a store that she then goes in to inspect. While the former paragraph was an externalization of the

inner, here we find an internalization of the outer; Janie's inner self *resembles* a store. The material for this metaphor is drawn from the narrative world of contiguity; the store is the place where Joe has set himself up as lord, master, and proprietor. But here, Jody's image is broken, and reveals itself never to have been a metaphor, but only a metonymy, of Janie's dream: 'Looking at it she saw that it never was the flesh and blood *figure* of her dreams. Just something to drape her dreams over.'" Ibid.

32. Ibid.
33. See Roy Pascal, *The Dual Voice: Free Indirect Discourse and Its Functioning in the Nineteenth-Century European Novel* (Totowa, N.J.: Rowman and Littlefield, 1977), pp. 1–33.
34. See Brian McHale, "Free Indirect Discourse: A Survey of Recent Accounts," *PTL* 3 (1978): 249–87, for an excellent account of the controversy. I think the most lucid story is Michel Peled Ginsberg, "Free Indirect Discourse: Theme and Narrative Voice in Flaubert, George Eliot, and Verga," Ph.D. dissertation, Yale University, 1977. See also Stephen Ullmann, *Style in the French Novel* (Cambridge: Cambridge University Press, 1957).
35. In a sequel to this book, I would like to compare Hurston's use of free indirect discourse to that of other writers, especially Virginia Woolf.
36. Ginsberg, "Free Indirect Discourse," p. 34.
37. Ibid., p. 35.
38. Oswald Ducrot and Tzvetan Todorov, *Encyclopedic Dictionary of the Sciences of Language*, trans. by Catherine Porter (Baltimore: Johns Hopkins University Press, 1979), p. 303.
39. See Graham Hough, "Narration and Dialogue in Jane Austen," *The Critical Quarterly* xii (1970); and Pascal, *The Dual Voice*, p. 52.
40. McHale, "Free Indirect Discourse," pp. 264–80.
41. Ginsberg, "Free Indirect Discourse," p. 23.
42. Janet Holmgren McKay, *Narration and Discourse in American Realistic Fiction* (Philadelphia: University of Pennsylvania Press, 1982), p. 19.
43. Northrop Frye, *Anatomy of Criticism: Four Essays* (Princeton, N.J., 1957), p. 233.
44. Mikhail Bakhtin, "Discourse Typology in Prose," p. 190.
45. Frye, *Anatomy of Criticism*, p. 234.

◆◆◆◆◆◆◆◆◆◆◆◆◆◆

Language, Speech, and Difference in *Their Eyes Were Watching God*

CYNTHIA BOND

One of the major problems that faces a reader of so-called marginalized texts, reading within the culture that has marginalized the authors of such texts, is the definition and recognition of a literary tradition. What is the nature of a text that presents itself within a language and ideology that necessarily excludes and even represses that text's cultural context? This concern is problematized in different ways for different minority literatures. For Afro-Americans, the literate tradition began as a crime; as we know it was illegal for black slaves to be taught to read and write. Yet throughout the history of blacks in America, this "crime" has been successfully committed over and over again: from the earliest slave narratives, up through the tremendously powerful twentieth century voices of Hughes, Wright, Hurston; Ellison, Bakara and Reed to name a few. It is the textual voice—a concept both irrevocably and richly oxymoronic—which has been problematized by Afro-American literature, situated as it is within complex African and American oral traditions. In describing the significance of this tradition for black textual production, Henry Louis Gates suggests the "Speakerly Text" as a particularly appropriate category in black literary history: "The 'Speakerly Text,' by which I mean a text whose rhetorical strategy is designed to represent an oral literary history."[1] Gates marks Zora Neale Hurston's *Their Eyes Were Watching God* as the beginning in black literature of a self-reflexive understanding of speech and its relationship to written figural language. He argues that it is this linguistic self-reflexivity that is the very basis of the black textual tradition. Gates appropriates the signifier of structuralist poetics and establishes a relational tension with black "signifyin(g)" rituals. Black authors "signify" on texts that precede them and signal this by celebrating and privileging the representation of speech within their own texts.

Their Eyes Were Watching God is a text which addresses the black linguistic tradition, but within the frame of female difference. Janie's grandmother tells her:

> Ah wanted to preach a great sermon about colored women sittin' on high, but they wasn't no pulpit for me. Freedom found me wid a baby daughter in mah arms . . . She would expound what Ah felt. But somehow she got lost offa de highway . . . So whilst Ah was tendin' you of nights Ah said Ah'd save de text for you.[2]

* * *

It is this potential text of women and language which Hurston presents in *Their Eyes*. Janie's ability to narrate her life arises initially from her self-conscious entrance into the performance of figural language. As a child, Hurston had listened to the adults' "signifyin'" rituals on the porch of Eatonville's general store with great interest. These linguistic battles were male dominated, and in *Their Eyes* Hurston makes room on the porch for the female voice's employment of figural language. By the end of the events described in the novel, which is the beginning of Janie's narrative, Janie walks past the voices on the porch, identifying figurative rhetoric as insufficient. She condemns the tropological aspect of language despite the complex understanding of the constitution of figures of speech which she reveals earlier in the novel's narrative. What Janie comes to recognize is the strategic importance of the deployment of figures within the sphere of language spoken "for its own sake," which she distinguishes from, and rejects for, the referential potential of language within the sphere of communicable meaning.

Hurston's expertise at dialect writing is indisputable, and her recognition of the cultural significance of the black oral tradition is central to her work. However, Hurston does not present this tradition without critique. She did, after all, *write;* we are not to hear her as an ethnographic tape recorder. As mentioned above, Gates reads Hurston's representations of dialect and multi-levelled voices as a valorization of the speakerly, and thus an historical recuperation of the oral black linguistic tradition. However, *Their Eyes* encloses a forceful critique of an essentially male signifying tradition, and a pointed critique of figural speech specifically. In *Their Eyes*, Hurston writes herself into, and then back out of, the speakerly tradition.

In beginning an analysis of *Their Eyes*, Hurston's opening is an irresistible starting point; the parable which defines the nature of sexual difference described within the novel:

> Ships at a distance have every man's wish on board. For some they come in with the tide. For others they sail forever on the horizon, never out of sight, never landing until the Watcher turns his eyes away in resignation, his dreams mocked to death by Time. That is the life of men.

Reading this first paragraph, one recognizes a recurrent literary figure; the ship as hope. The "Watcher," the "every man," seems a universal character, a figure of human desire. But the allegorical universality of this parable is collapsed in the next paragraph:

> Now, women forget all those things they don't want to remember, and remember everything they don't want to forget. The dream is the truth. Then they act and do things accordingly.

> So the beginning of this was a woman and she had come back from burying the dead.

These opening paragraphs, in the appositive nature of the bifurcated parable, announce the novel's concern with sexual difference. Men's aspirations are projected out of themselves, often are tied up with commerce and often are frustrated. Women, on the other hand, possess their dreams and will what they desire. The chiasmatic statement preceding "The dream is the truth" leaves a residual negative that suggests the validity of the inverse statement, "The truth is the dream." This suggested equivalence implies a specific female potential for existential and linguistic integration, and the following paragraph justifies this reading: "So the beginning of this was a woman," a statement that follows *necessarily* if we read "so" as a conjunction of necessary consequentiality. That is, women have a distinct opportunity for self-reflective integration and are therefore more reliable subjects for narratives than men. The biblical resonance of this line is important; in the beginning is not the engendering voice of a male deity, but a woman. By the novel's end (which is also its beginning) the figure of woman becomes the figure of textual creation, the voice made material. The prefatory parable suggests a meta-linguistic project. And indeed, what follows is a representation and critique of various figures of speech—figures which, as they are employed by men, involve a play for power. Janie appropriates and subverts the male use of figural language and then rejects it for a notion of linguistic meaning as constituted by truth.

One of the text's most important recurrent images is that of the blossoming pear tree. This figure, as it is created by Janie and as it is used by the text, stands in important opposition to the specifically male rhetorical signifying rituals. It is a more directly mimetic figure, appropriated from the pear tree outside of Janie's girlhood home:

> She had been spending every minute that she could steal from her chores under that tree for the last three days . . . It had called her to come and gaze on a mystery. From barren brown stems to glistening leaf-buds; from the leaf-buds to snowy virginity of bloom. It stirred her tremendously. How? Why? It was like a flute song forgotten in another existence and remembered again . . . This singing she heard that had nothing to do with her ears.

Women remember what they don't want to forget, and the pear tree marks the beginning of Janie's figural memory: a "singing"—a "signing"—that is not received by the ears. It is a figure which is never given vocal status but instead remains a material fact of the text. Janie internalizes the image of the pear tree, using it over and over again to figure her life. "Oh to be a pear tree—*any* tree in bloom" she thinks as a girl; and in her maturity, when she begins the narration of her story, her experience is described as equal to the status of the tree but with the added understanding of figural distance: "Janie saw her life *like* a great tree in leaf with the things suffered, things enjoyed, things done and undone" (emphasis added). The internalization of this metaphor is framed by an awakening self-love, allusively an act of masturbation:

> She saw a dust-bearing bee sink into the sanctum of a bloom; the thousand sister-calyxes arch to meet the love embrace and the ecstatic shiver of the tree from root to tiniest branch creaming in every blossom and frothing with delight. So this was a marriage! . . . Then Janie felt a pain remorseless sweet that left her limp and languid.

It is the "sister-calyxes" which "cream with delight," indicating a self-referentiality that mirrors, and facilitates, the "marriage" of reality and image. This marriage is not only a local metaphor but has linguistic implications for the text as a whole.

Quite distinct from Janie's privatized self-figuration, male tropes occur in "lying," or signifying sessions. As mentioned above, these figurative battles of figuration occur for the most part in social contexts; episodes on the general store porch, the lamp-lighting ceremony, and the burial of the mule are the most notable occasions in the novel. The citizens of Eatonville display a great respect for the importance of figural language in any proper signifying. When Jody and Janie first set up their store in Eatonville, Tony Taylor takes it upon himself to make a welcoming speech, and is subsequently booed down:

> "Brother Starks, we welcomes you and all dat you have seen fit tuh bring amongst us—yo' belov-ed wife, yo' store, yo' land—"
> A big-mouthed burst of laughter cut him short.
> "Dat'll do, Tony," Lige Moss yelled out. "Mist' Starks is uh smart man, we'se all willin' tuh acknowledge tuh dat, but de day he comes waggin' down de road wid two hund'ed acres uf land over his shoulder, Ah wants tuh be dere tuh see it."

Tony then attempts to protect his effort from derision:

> "All yall know whut wuz meant. Ah don't see how come—"
> "'Cause you jump up tuh make speeches and don't know how," Lige said.

Lige proceeds to instruct Tony in the correct method to present a speech, which is to employ analogy:

> ". . . You can't welcome uh man and his wife 'thout you make comparison about Isaac and Rebecca at de well, else it don't show de love between 'em if you don't."
> Everybody agreed that that was right. It was sort of pitiful for Tony not to know he couldn't make a speech without saying that.

Lige understands that communicating what is "meant" is not the object of speeches, figurative rhetoric is the object of speeches. He demonstrates Tony's rhetorical inadequacy by turning his trope back onto him and then suggests the proper trope to be used. The importance of figures is similarly indicated when Janie speaks herself for the first time in the speakerly tradition by delivering an oration on Joe's benevolence in freeing the mule:

> "Freein' dat mule makes uh mighty big man outa you. Something like George Washington and Lincoln. Abraham Lincoln, he had de whole United States tuh rule so he freed de Negroes. You got uh town so you freed uh mule. You have tuh have power tuh free things and dat makes you lak uh king uh something."

Janie's use of the figures of Washington and Lincoln elicit pleasure and appreciation from her audience: "Hambo said, 'Yo' wife is uh born orator, Starks. Us never knowed dat befo'. She put jus' de right words tuh our thoughts." Janie's command of language is described as natural—that is, one that is an *essential* rhetorical facility. Not only does she use analogy effectively, but she puts the "right" ("authentic") words to the thoughts of others. She not only knows how to say, she knows what is "right" to say. The referential importance of language is foregrounded later in the novel when Janie makes a decisive distinction between rhetoric and truth. Janie's articulateness upsets Joe. It is he who had aspired to being a "big voice," a status dependent on the submissive silence of his wife. It is significant that Janie makes reference to the "founding fathers" in her speech, for she is entering into an essentially male tradition of signifying. The fate and fame of men are ships on the horizon, forces that manifest themselves in the outside world. Janie deploys the male symbols of Washington and Lincoln in her speech because she speaks in a male context. Her sexually distinct figure at this point remains the interiorized image of the pear tree.

Male signifying is specifically grounded in competition, and in the mastery of women. After meeting Janie and Joe for the first time, two Eatonville residents discuss the merits of metaphorical facility in the courtship of women:

> ". . . But dat wife uh hisn'! Ah'm uh son of uh combunction if Ah don't go tuh Georgy and git me one just like her."
> "Whut wid?"
> "Wid mah talk, man."
> "It takes money tuh feed pretty women. Dey gits uh lavish uh talk."
> "Not lak mine. Dey loves to hear me talk because dey can't understand it. Mah co-talking is too deep. Too much co to it."

Rhetorical sophistication is here defined as a dazzling deployment of figural language. The very exclusion of women from signifying ensures that they will be taken in by it when it is deployed by men.

In the space of rhetorical rivalry, women are always recognized as the object of such signifying. One evening on Starks' porch the men are engaged in what the narrator calls "acting-out courtship" with three local women when Daisy Blunt, the town beauty, walks by. They proceed to "act out their rivalry":

David said, "Jim don't love Daisy. He don't love yuh lak Ah do."

Jim bellowed indignantly, "Who don't love Daisy? Ah know you ain't talkin' 'bout me."

Dave: "Well all right, less prove dis thing right now who love dis gal de best."

They go on to "prove" their love rhetorically, vying with each other for the most extreme images of devotion:

". . . Ah'd buy Daisy uh passenger train and give it tuh her."

"Humph! Is dat all? Ah'd buy her uh steamship and then Ah'd have some men's tuh run it fur her."

"Daisy, don't let Jim fool you wid his talk. He don't aim tuh do nothin' fur yuh. Uh lil ole steamship! Daisy, Ah'll take uh job cleanin' out de Atlantic Ocean fuh you any time you say you so desire."

The rhetorical logic behind this competition is that the more unactualizable the imagery, the more "truthfully" it represents the speaker's devotion. Dave warns Daisy that Jim's declaration is empty talk but then proceeds to produce the most implausible scenario of wooing yet delivered in the game. That the signifying game takes women as its object and excludes them as speakers is underscored when Jody admonishes Janie to wait on customers, thereby forcing her to miss the rest of the play-acting. Her exclusion is further underscored by Joe's outburst over the empty barrel of pig's feet:

". . . All you got tuh do is mind me. How come you can't do lak Ah tell yuh?"

[Janie:] "You sho loves to tell me whut to do, but Ah can't tell you nothin' Ah see!"

"Dat's cause you need tellin'," he rejoined hotly. "It would be pitiful if Ah didn't. Somebody got to think for women and children and chickens and cows. I god, they sho don't think none theirselves."

Joe's outburst leads Janie to examine the "inside" of her marriage, an examination which reveals important information:

The spirit of the marriage left the bedroom and took to living in the parlor. It was there to shake hands whenever company came to visit, but it never went back inside the bedroom again. So she put something in there to represent the spirit like a Virgin Mary image in a church.

Just as Janie sets up an image to represent her transformed marriage, she similarly recognizes her Joe as an image she once constructed:

She stood there until something fell off the shelf inside her. Then she went inside there to see what it was. It was her image of Jody tumbled down and shattered. But looking at it she saw that it never was the flesh and blood figure of her dreams. Just something she had grabbed up to drape her dreams over. In a way she turned her back upon the image where it lay and looked further. She had no more blossomy openings dusting pollen over her man, neither any glistening your fruit where the petals used to be.

Barbara Johnson marks this point in Janie's understanding as an entrance into the creation of figural language: ". . . she has stepped irrevocably into the necessity of figurative language, where inside and outside are never the same. It is from this point on in the novel that Janie, paradoxically, begins to speak."[3] However, Janie has successfully used figurative language at an earlier point in the novel, in the speech on Jody quoted above. In addition, her self-figuring through the pear tree begins with her adolescence. However, Johnson is correct in marking this revelation as a turning point. It is not that Janie first enters figurative language here, but that she generates a sophisticated conceptualization of representation which is transmuted into the moment of power when she signifies on Jody later in the novel. Essentially what Janie understands here is the displacing power of figures in the external, social world; a power that she herself can deploy for mastery. While Joe's image is "false," she can institute an image to represent her true feelings in its place—the virginal Mary. When she looks further than Joe's fallen image, she looks to her own image, the "blossomy openings." The image of the pear tree bridges the gap between the inside and outside of figures in Janie's life. It is the essentialized figure, the mimetic metaphor internalized yet responsive to external conditions. Janie's installation of images of her marriage is a recognition of *represented* power, a "bow to the outside of things"; while the pear tree remains the privileged image of an inherent yet undeployed power.

While the notion that figurative language empowers its deployer is critiqued later in the novel, the forcefulness of tropes *within signifying sessions* is symbolized in the text as a reification of figures into physical objects. Joe wishes to become a "big voice" in Eatonville; a voice like the voice of God whose word becomes physical in the act of creation. When Joe delivers the mock eulogy for the mule, the narrator says the oration, ". . . made him more solid than building the schoolhouse had done." Rhetoric assumes the integrity of physical objects. The signifying sessions themselves are described as a kind of alchemic process whereby figures are transmuted into objects. The porch talkers pass "nations" through their mouths, they use "a side of the world for a canvas," they "paint" thoughts as "pictures" and pass them around, etc. The mule Joe buys becomes a walking mythological figure which remains present even after its death by virtue of the "lies" told on the porch of Starks' store: "The yaller mule was gone from the town except for the porch talk, and for the children visiting his bleaching bones now and then in the spirit of adventure." While the "content" of the mule is gone, his "form" remains—in bones and figures of speech. It is the "physicalization" of figures that initially marks Janie's rhetorical freedom. She signifies on Joe:

"When you pull down yo' britches, you look lak de change uh life." Joe is stunned and asks Janie to repeat the figure, to which one of the store customers replies, "You heard her, you ain't blind." The verbal figure Janie cuts is so powerful that it is described as an object perceivable by sight. This is the highest achievement of rhetoric in signifying; its figurative reification in space. Janie's "telling" on Joe is her first (and last) entrance into male signifying; that is, signifying which is used explicitly for the purposes of domination. It is significant that she uses as image which in its application simultaneously implies a *de*-sexing, and an androgyny which is essentially sexless for it is by her female passage into male linguistic territory that she is able to free herself from the hierarchical sexual difference prescribed within the roles of her marriage. She figures both the appropriation of male signifying power and the obliteration of sexual difference. Her performance of the image represents a castration, the figurative correlate of male power. And, (as Gates notes) she kills Joe rhetorically."

Their Eyes is indeed a polyphonic text. Hurston weaves among various narrative dictions: the lyrical "standard english" voice of the opening parable; the dialect representation of characters' dialogue; and what Gates identifies as the "free, indirect discourse" of the characters' thoughts. The tension between these modes is similarly manifest in *Tell My Horse*, where Hurston vacillates between the scientific voice of the ethnographer and the passionate voice of the engaged participant. It is this difference that constitutes the text and the very category of text in Hurston's writing. It will be remembered that while Hurston grew up in the middle of the Southern black oral tradition, she was distanced within it by her sexual difference and her literary appetite. Stated reductively, "Hurston was struggling with two concepts of culture . . . She enjoyed Keats, but recognized the poetry in her father's sermons; she read Plato, but told stories of Joe Clarke's wisdom."[4] This struggle is preserved in her work. Hurston's relationship to the speakerly tradition is in essence ambivalent. *Their Eyes* does not wholeheartedly privilege the speakerly as Gates suggests. Hurston's sense of the recuperation of experience potential in texts is suggested in the narrator's statement about Janie at one point: "She didn't read books so she didn't know that she was the world and the heavens boiled down to a drop. Man attempting to climb to painless heights from his dung hill." And in the course of Janie's vocal ascendency, she comes to reject speakerly rhetoric as an insufficient positing of identity.

Janie ends her narrative attempting to distance herself from figurality. Her relationship with Tea Cake plays a large role in this. Gates points out that Tea Cake's first name "Verigible" is a vernacular form of "veritable": "Verigible Tea Cake Woods, is a sign of verity, one who speaks the truth, one genuine and real, one not counterfeit or spurious, one not false or imaginary but the thing that in fact has been named."[5]

Janie moves from her marriage to the "big voice" to a marriage to "verity." The nature of these marriages in relation to Janie's search for identity is perhaps best understood in their negativity—in Janie's "murder" of both Joe and Tea Cake. As mentioned above, the moment of Joe's demise is correlative to Janie's entrance into competitive, figurative speech. She "kills" him rhetorically, by deploying a vicious trope. Joe's death brings Janie the physical and financial freedom of movement which allows her to be with Tea Cake. Her relationship with Tea Cake represents the burgeoning reconciliation of the inside and outside she had so scrupulously separated to live false emotions with Joe. The pear tree symbol drops away in the novel's narrative of Tea Cake's and Janie's life together, precisely because her metaphorical figure of fullfillment has been collapsed into veritable fullfillment. Janie's sense of disjunctive representation is resolved as she experiences with Tea Cake the reconciliation of "inside" and "outside" which is figured by the tree metaphor.

Tea Cake's death initially seems unnecessary to the novel's development; the dynamic of his relationship with Janie does not lose its narrative charm. A cursory biographical note may be of some use here. Hurston had just ended a relationship with a man when she went to Jamaica, where she wrote *Their Eyes*. In her autobiography she wrote, "The plot was far from the circumstances, but I tried to embalm all the tenderness of my passion for him in *Their Eyes Were Watching God*."[6] She left this lover to preserve her work, of which he was jealous. This suggests one reason why Hurston might have "killed off" Tea Cake in the novel. The text must "sacrifice" and subsume its own emblems of lived experience in establishing its material identity outside of that experience.

Obviously, a biographical reading does not explain the structural significance of Tea Cake's death within the novel. Briefly, the events of his demise are as follows: Tea Cake saves Janie from a rabid dog during the flood, but not without being fatally bitten. He catches rabies, detected too late to save him, and is transformed. In his delirium, Tea Cake pulls a pistol on Janie. She recognizes that Tea Cake is no longer Tea Cake at this point; that it is his "suffering brain urging him to kill," that the "fiend in him" fires the gun. Tea Cake is no longer veritable but possessed. She shoots and kills him just as he fires at her. It is not Tea Cake Janie seeks to kill, but the "fiend" inhabiting him.

The trial marks a significant turn in Janie's establishment of a vocal identity. Like the signifying rituals, the courtroom presents a highly social rhetorical occasion. But in the courtroom, Janie seeks to suppress the devices of rhetoric in order to communicate the context of her relationship with Tea Cake. It is precisely her voice that is on trial:

> The court set and Janie saw the judge who had put on a great robe to listen about her and Tea Cake. And twelve more white men had stopped whatever

they were doing to listen and pass on what happened between Janie and Tea Cake Woods.

The emphasis on the activity of listening in this paragraph is crucial, for it is Janie's statement which is her only defense, and she is the only one who can speak it. In the courtroom, the guilty subject's voice is constituted as an identity only as it transcends the "artifice" of speech. Janie is faced with the necessity of clear referentially accurate speech; she is to speak ". . . the truth, the whole truth and nothing but the truth. So help her God." She recognizes the distinct nature of this speakerly occasion:

> First thing she had to remember was she was not at home. She was in the Courthouse fighting something and it wasn't death. It was worse than that. It was lying thoughts. She had to go way back to let them know how she and Tea Cake had been with one another so they could see she could never shoot Tea Cake out of malice.

This passage is a statement of rhetorical strategy. Janie realizes that she must build a narrative rather than deny the facticity of the evidence. She must reply affirmatively rather than negatively. She must create "fictional," narrative, evidence—but fiction that constitutes "truth" rather than the rhetorical facility prized at home. At the trial Janie fears "misunderstanding" more than death and her narrative is an attempt to communicate the true nature of her relationship with Tea Cake. Janie's courtroom speech marks her conscious separation of talk and action, figurality and truth. At the beginning of the novel when she begins telling Pheoby her story, she stresses communicable meaning over formal rhetorical skill. When Pheoby questions her own ability to follow Janie's narrative, Janie reassures her:

> [Pheoby] "It's hard for me to understand what you mean, de way you tell it. And then again, Ah'm hard of understandin' at times."
> [Janie] "Now, 'taint' nothin' lak you might think. So 'taint' no use in telling you somethin' unless Ah give you de understandin' to go 'long wid it."

Janie has moved beyond an admiration of performative language for its own sake—the figurative language of the signifying rituals—to a privileging of language as a means to communicate truth, "de understandin'." As previously suggested, her evolution in thought is figured by her progression from her marriage to Joe (the "big voice" of empty rhetoric) to her marriage to Tea Cake (the veritable language of affirmation).

The trial scene is the only episode in the novel in which whites figure prominently as the source of law. Janie reaches out to them in her testimony, specifically the women, without hostility. It is this type of gesture with its apparent lack of overt racial critique which led Richard Wright and others to condemn Hurston's work as too personal and politically reactionary. The scene is undeniably disturbing. For the first time in the novel, blacks are overtly silenced. This suppression is particularly jarring given the preceding displays of verbal facility. When Sop-de-Bottom speaks up at the trial, he is coldly silenced by the white District Attorney, Mr. Prescott: "We are handling this case. Another word out of *you;* out of any of you niggers back there, and I'll bind you over to the big court." While Hurston is clearly not complicitous with the sentiments of this character, she nevertheless undermines the powerful rhetoric of signifying by pointing up the impotence that contextualizes such rituals:

> They [the black audience] were there with their tongues cocked and loaded, the only real weapon left to weak folks. The only killing tool they are allowed to use in the presence of white folks.

This passage is similar to an earlier description of the porch-sitters watching Janie on her return to Eatonville: "They made burning statements with questions, and killing tools out of laughs. It was mass cruelty. A mood come alive. Words walking without masters. . . ." Here, black verbal skill is denigrated as mean-spirited and ineffectual. The tropes of signifying rituals do not constitute verbal mastery but instead master their speakers. The identification of the racial problem as an essentially black problem is perhaps politically redeemable if we theorize Hurston's development of black identity in terms of the Deleuzian reformation of the Master-Slave dialectic.[7] In *Their Eyes* and in her essays specifically on black identity, Hurston gestures to a politics of human dignity. Empowerment must be distinguished from represented power. Blacks must resist an automatic assumption of weakness in the face of manifested white power; they must resist, in Nietzschean terms, the dialectical slave mentality. At the time, Hurston's critique was seen as callous and racist.[8] This critique also filters into Janie's rejection of the folk of Eatonville:

> "Dem meatskins is *got* tuh rattle tuh make out they's alive. Let 'em consolate theyselves wid talk. 'Course, talkin' don't amount tuh uh hill uh beans when yuh can't do nothin' else . . . It's uh known fact, Pheoby, you got tuh *go* there tuh *know* there."

Speech is described here as a futile attempt to posit existence, a substitution for genuine empowerment. It is action that Janie privileges over speech, or at least the kind of "active" speech represented by her testimony at the trial. Janie's defense speech seeks to suppress the figural aspect of language in favor of a language that posits meaning as truth and ultimately secures salvation.

Hurston's distinction between true and represented mastery is further evidenced by her repeated use of anthropomorphic images. The most striking example of this in *Their Eyes* is the recurrent figure of the mule. In the novel's opening pages, she describes the bestiality of black life: "These sitters had been tongueless, earless, eyeless conveniences all day long. Mules and other brutes had occupied their skins. But now, the sun and the bossman were gone, so the skins felt powerful and human. They became lords of sounds and lesser things." The deprecating irony of this statement is clear. While Hurston references the oppression that brutalizes blacks, she does not posit their refined verbal technique as true empowerment, but merely a self-deluded mastery of "lesser things." It is Janie, ostracized from white and black male culture alike, who walks past the porch rejecting figural, speakerly mastery in favor of a privatized sense of self-determination and action. Mule imagery is used later in the novel to similarly express the impotence of figural language. After Joe frees the mule, the porch voices construct numerous myths about his activities, all of them anthropomorphic in character:

> How he pushed open Lindsay's kitchen door and slept in the place one night and fought until they made coffee for his breakfast . . . he ran Mrs. Tully off of the croquet ground for having such an ugly shape; he ran and caught up with Becky Anderson on the way to Maitland so as to keep his head out of the sun under her umbrella . . .

The men use the mule to figure activities they themselves would like to perform but can only do rhetorically. For Janie, verbal skill—if not constitutive of identity—is only represented mastery, delusively embraced by men as a means to power. Throughout the signifying rituals in the test, the only power accessible to the man with rhetorical skill is a kind of crude domination and subordination of the immediate opponent. As figures of speech are used to dominate, domination will only be figurative.

Janie's progress is cast in the terms of a search for truth, for a horizontal knowledge that can only be obtained through action, defined distinctly from rhetoric. In the novel's opening, Janie passes the opportunity to share feats of oration with the porch sitters, preferring to narrate her tale to one close female friend. While it includes many voices, this narration's unfolding is essentially *textual*—the text of *Their Eyes Were Watching God*. Janie's initial conversation with Pheoby acts as a preface to the textually transmuted experience of Janie's life. The various voices and dictions which constitute the novel's progress are subsumed as a rendering of Janie's life, which is the novel's text. The novel's structure casts linguistic power and identity as a textual recuperation of speakerly rhetoric rather than a valorization of the speakerly as a sufficient, figurally self-reflexive linguistic presence.

At the very end of the novel, Janie defines herself as the material system, the "text" which preserves Tea Cake: "Of course he wasn't dead. He could never be dead until she herself had finished feeling and thinking." This statement echoes Hurston's "embalming" her affection for her lover in the text of *Their Eyes*. Negativity—the death of Tea Cake and the failure of Hurston's love—is ignored and re-figured by the fact of Janie's existence and the material text of the novel. This rejection of negativity is predicated on the reconciliation of interiority and exteriority. Janie reunites her inside and outside in the last paragraph of the novel: "She pulled in her horizon like a great fish-net. Pulled it from around the waist of the world and draped it over her shoulder. So much of life in its meshes! She called in her soul to come and see." Her dreams are no longer draped over the image of Joe, incarnation of the "big voice," but are instead draped over her self, uniting the dream and truth of the opening parable. While existential integration is achieved, the figure that clothes it maintains the ambivalence of representation. For a fishnet both culls vast experience and restrains it. It is both of one piece and riddled with holes. The fishnet as an image of integration figurally maintains the ultimate disjunction of sign and referent. As Johnson suggests, Hurston does indeed recognize disjunction as the irrevocable condition of metaphor. However, the maintenance of a sense of linguistic disjunction is not the enabling force which constitutes the identity of a speaking subject. The priviliging of tropes which mean most "meaningfully" among themselves is identified with the rhetorically would-be power of oppressive male speakers. It is the distinction between verbal and textual representation which Hurston offers as a crucial linguistic disjunction, a fruitful gap which leads to the articulation of identity. Janie achieves a soul by positing a self that masters and transcends its own figuration in constituting identity. In the case of the novel, identity is contingent upon the recognition of linguistic sufficiency as constituted by communicable meaning that is textual rather than by performative rhetorical skill.

I began this essay by suggesting the metaphor of criminality to describe the generation of black literature. This metaphor is rich in potential as a description of the black textual tradition because it illustrates one thematization of absence and presence in marginalized literature. Black authors initially had to appropriate a language which excluded them from textual linguistic production. Through this "theft" the presence of a textual voice, a textual tradition, is posited. The means must be stolen, and is stolen, for a preservation which equals survival. Writers like Hurston were faced with the necessity of fortifying a black *literature*, of creating cultural artifacts that would go beyond the temporality of a human voice, a voice whose very existence was threatened by cultural ephemerality. The means of literate expression was necessarily posited within the context of a rich oral tradition, but sought to establish a more permanent, textual tradition. In the case of black literature, the text may be constituted as a sufficient "presence" above the speakerly since it is the black *textual* existence which is "absented" by the larger cultural milieu. It is the *text* of speech that Janie's grandmother wants to pass on to her, but must be satisfied with an oral narration of the days of slavery. Janie in turn must "orate" her history, but is textually substantiated by Hurston's *Their Eyes Were Watching God*.

Notes

1. Henry Louis Gates, Jr., *The Signifying Monkey.* Quoted from manuscript with the permission of the author.
2. *Their Eyes Were Watching God* (Urbana, Illinois: University of Illinois Press, 1978), p. 32.
3. Barbara Johnson, "Metaphor, Metonymy and Voice in *Their Eyes Were Watching God*," *Black Literature and Literary Theory* (New York: Methuen, 1984), p. 212.
4. Hemenway, p. 99.
5. Gates, p. 427.
6. Hurston, *Dust Tracks on a Road* (Urbana: Univ. of Illinois Press, 1984), p. 260.
7. Gilles Deleuze, *Nietzsche & Philosophy* (New York: Columbia University Press, 1983). See especially "Against the Dialectic," pp. 8–10.
8. Hurston's political beliefs are notoriously contradictory. For more information on her problematic loyalties, see *Dust Tracks on a Road* and Hemenway's *Literary Biography.*

◆◆◆◆◆◆◆◆◆◆◆◆◆◆

Listening and Living: Reading and Experience in *Their Eyes Were Watching God*

MARIA TAI WOLFF

> Yo soy profesor de la vida
> vago estudiante de la muerte
> Y si lo que se no les sirve
> no he dicho nada, sino todo.
> —Pablo Neruda, "Estravagario"[1]

In the opening paragraphs of *Their Eyes Were Watching God*, the narrator presents two models for evaluating life:

> Ships at a distance have every man's wish on board. For some they come in with the tide. For others, they sail forever, on the horizon, never out of sight, never landing until the Watcher turns his eyes away in resignation, his dreams mocked to death by Time. That is the life of men.
> Now, women forget all the things they don't want to remember, and remember all the things they don't want to forget. The dream is the truth. Then they act and do things accordingly.[2]

Men, it seems, stoically watch what reality presents, accepting that which life reveals to them. While they may wish or dream, their inner hopes can be fulfilled only by factors beyond human control; events and circumstances are the "ships at a distance." Men are controlled by Time; if it does not favor their dreams, it will "mock" them, destroy them. "That is the life of men": Life is given, not made. Women, on the other hand, create their own lives from their interpretations of reality. This involves a selective process of willed forgetting and remembering, and it leads to the formulation of a personal image of life, a "dream." On this "truth" of life, women base their actions, living their dreams. Time has less power here; in this process the past is re-shaped and brought into the present, contributing to the acts of the future.

Before introducing the protagonist of the novel, the narrator reveals that this will be a woman's story: "So the beginning of this was a woman . . ." "This" is the narration of life as lived by a woman, the creation of a "dream as truth." It is also the presentation of a model of reading, of understanding an oral or written text.

Ralph Freedman describes the movement of a lyrical novel as evidencing a "qualitative progression" rather than the temporal progression usually found in a novel. In a lyrical novel, the "fictional world" is conceived not as a universe in which men display their actions but as a poet's vision fashioned as a design. The world is reduced to a lyrical point of view." The novel works, then, not as a historical account of narrative of events alone, but as the lyric formulation of a personal vision—or dream. Examining the effects of lyric language on narrative, Freedman writes, "Actions are turned into scenes which embody recognitions."[3]

This transformation of events or actions into elements of a lyrical point of view takes place on several levels in *Their Eyes Were Watching God*. The descriptions of certain crucial scenes, and their repetitions, turn them into emblems or symbols. Yet the transformation of the outside world into a personal vision, of "actions" into self-recognitions, is also the theme of the novel.

A large part of the text is the story of Janie's life; the narrator presents it as Janie tells it to Pheoby. And Janie speaks "full of that oldest human longing—self revelation." It is she who reveals her past to her friend as she speaks, but, in a sense, Janie also narrates the manner in which her identity has been revealed to her. The story is structured around successive scenes of self-recognition which are Janie's repeated attempts to create a clear, satisfying picture of who she is. The events of the narrative, and the other characters, function within this structure. Janie is lead to form her own dream, her own truth, from what she has lived.

Beyond this, though, the text inspires the reader to formulate his or her own personal image of it. The story of Janie is a "revelation" to the reader as well, since the narrative presents a series of perceptions for our evaluation. In hearing, or, indeed, in living, Janie's adventures, the reader is led to re-consider the text within his or her own experience, and to "act and do things accordingly."

The first episode that Janie narrates presents the problem which will structure the series of recognitions in the novel. When she sees herself in a photograph, Janie sees for the first time that she is black. She becomes aware that there are two possible perceptions of her: the intrinsic, natural image she has of herself, and the image held by the rest of the world. In this first experience, the two do not coincide; she says, "'. . . Ah couldn't recognize dat dark chile as me'." The outside world has also attached its perceptions to her as name, although with no consistency: "'Dey all useter call me Alphabet 'cause so many people had named me different names'." She is what she has been called. Until a moment just before the death of Joe Starks, Janie will be unable to separate and evaluate these two perceptions, to understand her own identity.

Janie's "conscious life," and the real beginning of her efforts to know herself, begin when she first becomes aware of her sexuality. On the first occasion of this, the narrator, in a lyric passage, uses several images which will recur whenever Janie meets a new suitor. These symbols are the "blossoming pear tree" and the spreading pollen of spring. The perception of these elements in nature responds to certain forces within Janie:

The rose of the world was breathing out smell. It followed her through all her waking moments and caressed her in her sleep. It connected itself with other vaguely felt matters that had struck her outside observation and buried themselves in her flesh. Now they emerged and quested about her consciousness.

Janie has "been summoned to behold a revelation." These two passages show an essential passivity of her experiences: The world will present itself to her. "She felt an answer seeking her, but where?"

Yet Janie's perception of the world will become an active, transforming one. Of the hero of Rilke's *Malte Laucids Brigge*, Ralph Freedman writes, "He mirrors the world as he sees it and so lends it a specific color or shape, disturbing or displacing it."[4] Janie as well must make a mirror of her consciousness, transforming the "revelation" into part of herself. She must structure her experiences and create or find the answer. In *Their Eyes Were Watching God*, Janie's search for identity is not a temporal, progressive process, but involves the representation and evaluation of a series of experiences or images. These include various "mirrors," or portraits of Janie herself, presented by others or viewed by the heroine. From these, she must choose. In a sense, she learns to make a lyrical formulation of the world—with the text presenting the material for the process of formulation as well.

Janie must select from or reconcile material from two different sources: the information about herself she receives from others, and her own feelings and experiences. In a sense, these are two texts, which often conflict. The first, which comes from the spoken opinions of others and corresponds to the "outside" image of her, is almost forced on Janie. The second is less easily explained: It is something she knows and is always capable of possessing, but it must be brought out and valued.

Janie's grandmother is the first to impose a role on the girl. Noting that Janie is aware of men, she announces to the girl, "'Janie, youse uh 'oman now . . .'." Yet Janie is, supposedly, without knowledge of the world and is deemed incapable of making her own decisions: "'Dat's what makes me skeered. You don't mean no harm. You don't even know where harm is at'." So her grandmother makes it possible for Janie to fulfill the old woman's own "'*dreams of* what a woman *oughta be and to do*'." (emphasis added) She marries Janie to a well-to-do farmer.

The grandmother recounts her history and her dreams in a long sermon. Her deferred plans are to be Janie's: "'. . . Ah said ah'd save the text [of my dreams] for you. Ah been waitin' a long time, Janie, but nothin' Ah been through ain't too much if you just take a stand on high ground lak Ah dreamed'." It is this "text" which Janie is to live out in her first marriage. The grandmother sees it as a suitable mirror for Janie, a means for the girl to protect her own personal identity from the evil tongues and deeds of others: "'Ah wanted you to look upon yo'self'." But the old woman's dream is another of those outside opinions which Janie must evaluate and eventually disregard.

At first, Janie has no experience of love and marriage: "Janie had had no chance to know things, so she had to ask." Common opinion substitutes for and suppresses her own feelings: "Yes, she would love Logan after they were married. She could see no way for it to come about, but Nanny and the old folks had said it, so it must be so." Yet she becomes increasingly disillusioned with Logan Killicks; for her role as a married woman does not correspond to her dreams or images: "'Ah wants things sweet wid mah marriage lak when you sit under a pear tree and think,'" she says.

The narrator uses lyric imagery to present Janie's inner world, including her implicit dissatisfaction with her role or "text":

> . . . when the pollen again gilded the sun and sifted down on the world she began to stand around the gate and expect things. What things? She didn't know exactly. Her breath was gusty and short. She knew things that nobody had ever told her.

The last sentence of this passage presents the dialogue between Janie's thoughts, what she "knows," and what she has been told. Her own experiences must give her something to counter the voices of others. Indeed, this first marriage brings about one development: "She knew now that marriage did not make love. Janie's first dream was dead, so she became a woman." Only experience has made her a "woman"; her grandmother's announcement of the change has been undermined.

There are several episodes in which Janie withdraws into the inner world of her thoughts to evaluate received "texts." Before she leaves Logan Killicks, for instance, Janie isolates herself for a moment: "Janie . . . turned wrongside out just standing there and feeling. When the throbbing calmed a little she gave Logan's speech a hard thought and placed it beside other things she had seen and heard." The received text, Killick's definition of her role as his wife, is reconsidered. It is made part of her system of experiences, what she has "seen and heard." And it is left behind.

Nevertheless, when Janie marries Joe Starks, she has not found a fulfillment of her inner desires, since Joe has his own plan for life:

> Every day after that they managed to meet in the scrub oaks across the road and talk about when he would be a big ruler of things with her reaping the benefits. Janie pulled back a long time because he did not represent sum-up and pollen and blooming trees, but he spoke for far horizon. He spoke for change and chance.

He has also planned her role in his world: "with her reaping the benefits." Although he does not seem to offer what Janie needs, he presents the possibility of new experiences, "speaking" for a new life. She feels, somehow, that her feelings will find a way outside: "Her old thoughts were going to come in handy now, but new words would have to be made and said to fit them."

Yet Joe does not permit Janie's desires to find their words. His aim is to be "a big voice" in the town, and he comes to speak for all of Eatonville. His life, though, becomes nothing more than a series of orders given to others; at his death Janie wonders "what had happened in the making of a voice out of a man." Like Janie's grandmother, Joe imposes a role on Janie, as when he does not permit her to make a speech at the store's opening: "She had never thought of making a speech, and didn't know if she cared to make one at all. It must have been the way Joe spoke out without giving her a chance to say anything one way or another that took the bloom off of things." Considering his wife incapable of good judgment, just as her grandmother had, Joe precludes the possibility of her choosing whether or not to speak. According to them, Janie is to accept others' decisions in place of living through situations herself. In fact, Joe goes so far as to dismiss the validity of her thoughts: "'Somebody got to think for women and chillun and chickens and cows. I god, they sho don't think none theirselves'."

Again, Janie withdraws into herself, experiencing a moment of self-recognition. The passage is introduced in much the same manner as the one previously quoted:

> Janie stood where he left her for unmeasured time and thought. . . . In a way she turned her back upon the image [of Joe] where it lay and looked further. . . . She found that she had a host of thoughts she had never expressed to him, and numerous emotions she had never let Jody know about. Things packed up and put away in parts of her heart where he could never find them. She was saving up feelings for some man she had never seen. She had an inside and an outside now and suddenly she knew how not to mix them.

She looks at her past and re-evaluates it, discovering what had been forgotten and "turning her back" on her illusions. At this point, she makes a clear distinction between her own "feelings"—her "inside"—and the outer self which she presents to the world. The experience needed to fulfill the former—a "man she had never seen"—must be awaited. She resumes her role as Jody's wife, but only by making a conscious "bow to the outside of things." And, especially after she and Jody have moved definitively apart, "new thoughts had to be thought and new words said."

Throughout the marriage, Joe has attempted to force a premature, false aging on her. He tells her repeatedly that she is as "'old as Methusalem'" and creates a story about her age and unattractiveness. Yet, at Joe's death, Janie's self-examination in a mirror produces a visual recognition which undermines the image Joe's text had created: "Years ago, she had told her girl self to wait for her in the looking glass. It had been a long time since she had remembered. Perhaps she'd better look. . . . The young girl was gone, but a handsome woman had taken her place." Here, Janie's own image replaces that which others have made for her. It is a true mirror, and her own eyes, not the verbal mirror of others, show her what she is. Again, the transition in her life from girlhood to womanhood is shown not merely to be an effect of time, but a change in consciousness. Recalling the earlier description of Janie's becoming a woman at the death of her dreams, the reader of this passage observes a more knowledgeable and more secure woman.

After Joe's death, Janie does a series of "re-readings" of her past. She discovers, for example, that "she hated her grandmother and had hidden it from herself all these years under a cloak of pity." She recognizes, as well, her own desires to seek out experiences, to make "a great journey to the horizons," rather than be attached to defined roles, "things." She knows, also, that it is "all according to the way you see things. Some people could look at a mud-puddle and see an ocean with ships." Life may be a "revelation," but it is the acceptance of interpretation of this revelation which is important. Each person must formulate his or her own "way of seeing." Her grandmother had forced on her one perception in the "name of love." Janie, however, recognizes that another's ideas are never adequate. The only truths she will now accept are those derived from her own experience: "This freedom feeling was fine. These men didn't represent a thing she wanted to know about. She had already experienced them through Logan and Joe."

While both of her husbands and her grandmother have imposed a role on Janie, in telling her what she should be, the man she next becomes involved with, Tea Cake, tells her only what she is capable of becoming: "'. . . you got good meat on yo' head. You'll learn'." It seems that Tea Cake is not part of the outside world, but part of her own, personal being: "Seemed as if she had known him all her life." The lyrical language which has heretofore invoked only desire is now used to describe one person: "He could be a bee to a blossom—a pear tree blossom in the spring." Rather than telling her who or what she is, he directs her only to recognize it for herself: "'Ah betcha you don't never go tuh de lookin' glass and enjoy yo' eyes yo'self'." He becomes a mirror for her, but one which refers her back to her own experience.

Tea Cake lets Janie share his experiences; together they define her, and their, roles:

> "Ah'm older than Tea Cake, yes. But he done showed me where it's de thought dat makes de difference in ages. If people thinks de same they can make it all right. So in the beginnin' new thoughts had tuh be thought and new words said. After Ah got used tuh dat, we gits 'long jus' fine. He done taught me de maiden language all over."

For the first time, then, Janie's text and her experience coincide. It is "thoughts," an inner life, that Tea Cake and Janie share; together the two create "new words." Janie learns the "maiden language," the language of possibility. Indeed, Tea Cake seems to share Janie's awareness of the importance of "how one sees things." It is "thought," or evaluation, which makes age important—or unimportant. This is the contrary of Joe's view. Tea Cake offers Janie the role of his wife—a role which is not a role:

"So yuh aims tuh partake wid everything, hunh?"
"Yeah, Tea Cake, don't keer what it is."
"Dat's all Ah wants tuh know."

Theirs is a text as yet unwritten, a text to be created out of "everything." Tea Cake gives Janie the world, from which they will make a "dream" together. He offers her experience.

From her grandmother, Logan Killicks, and Joe Starks, Janie receives a ready-made text, a definition of her role. She is expected to conform to it. From Tea Cake, on the other hand, she receives an invitation to live a text, to formulate a role. In the narrative of Janie's life, knowledge accepted from a prepared text—one that is told—is opposed by knowledge gleaned from experience. And it is the second which is most satisfying, most "true"—although experience includes the hearing and evaluation of others' stories. Janie comes to know herself only after she has carefully examined others' stories, and "put them beside" her own perceptions.

A reader might be led, however, to question the position of *Their Eyes Were Watching God* within this structure. Does it not, after all, present a story told, one which must be accepted completely by the reader, one which limits the reader to passive acceptance? A careful examination of the kinds of "telling" presented in the novel, and a consideration of the modes of narration employed, will answer this question.

Logan Killicks, Joe Starks, and Nanny all claim a certain power of truth for what they say. With their words, they impose opinions on Janie, constrain her actions. Throughout the text, there are scenes in which words are used as weapons. In these, as in Joe's orders to Janie, the teller tries to control or wound another person. This is the case when Janie is on trial for murder near the book's end: The black spectators are there "with their tongues cocked and loaded, the only real weapons left to weak folks." Later, when Janie returns to Eatonville, her neighbors make "burning statements with questions, and killing tools out of laughs. It was mass cruelty. A mood come alive. Words walking without masters. . . ." Talking becomes a kind of performative language, a curse or a constraint. It is not, of course, always done so harshly; Janie's words to Joe, which rob him "of his illusion of irresistable maleness," are also an example of this.

In the first two examples cited above, talking is a substitute—for the "weak," for real experience or action. The porch talkers express the women's "envy they had stored up from other times," their cruel tales reveal the emptiness of the tellers' lives.

There is, though, another kind of telling, which is both more and less related to experience. It is telling for its own sake, for the listener's and teller's enjoyment. Sam and Hicks' conversation about the latter's powers over women is an example. Hicks seems to describe this playful talking when he remarks that women "'loves to hear me talk because dey can't understand it. Mah co-talkin' is too deep'." This kind of talking is a game or a drama, in which all participate: "The girls and everybody else help laugh. They know it's not courtship. It's acting-out courtship and everybody is in the play."

While this narration for narration's sake is less didactic and has less claim to "truth" than do more "serious" passages in the novel, it is more evocative and exciting. We are allowed to hear the "big picture talkers," who use "a side of the world for a canvas." Of Lige and Sam's discussion, the narrator says, "It was a contest in hyperbole and carried on for no other reason." This kind of telling does not necessarily formulate material, but becomes material for formulation by the listener.

After Janie has married Tea Cake, she, too, learns to "tell big stories." Indeed, her entire story to Pheoby could be so classified. It is not an example of the other, forceful telling; Janie does not concern herself with answering the accusing voices of the porch-sitters. Her story has another purpose: It is both a presentation of experience and an encouragement to experience—an experience in itself. Janie tells Pheoby, "'If they wants to see and know, why don't they come kiss and be kissed? Ah could then sit down and tell 'em things.'" Janie does not claim to have found any joy which all can or must achieve in the same way. Love, for example, must be found by each individually: Her neighbors, she says,

> "gointuh make 'miration 'cause mah love didn't work lak they love, if dey ever had any. Then you must tell 'em dat love ain't somethin' lak uh grindstone dat's de same thing everywhere and do de same thing tuh everything it touch. Love is lak de sea. It's uh movin' thing, but still and all, it takes its shape from de shore it meets, and it's different with every shore."

Often talking, or listening to such talk, seems only to be a substitute for experience: "'. . . talkin' don't amount tuh uh hill uh beans,'" remarks Janie, "'when yuh can't do nothin' else. And listenin' tuh dat kind uh talk is jus' lak openin' yo' mouth and lettin' de moon shine down yo' throat. It's uh known fact, Pheoby, you got tuh *go* there tuh *know* there.'" Every text, especially an oral one, directs the listener to go outside or beyond it, to live and to know for oneself. Unless it is done with memory of experience, talking or listening can be only a consolation. Pheoby, Janie's own listener or reader, is moved by Janie's talk to enrich her own life: "'Ah ain't satisfied wid mahself no mo'. Ah means tah make Sam take me fishin' wid him after this'."

Nonetheless, when one can "do something else," there is a certain amount of pleasure to be taken in listening or reading. For the teller and the listener, there comes a kind of participation: We are told, for instance, that, in the Everglades, Janie ". . . could listen and laugh and even talk some herself if she wanted to. She got so she could tell big stories herself from listening to the rest. Because she loved to hear it, and the men loved to hear themselves, they would 'woof' and 'boogeboo' around the games to the limit." Between the teller and the listener there is almost a dialogue, the latter being called in to evaluate the teller's story. Yet the teller must present the story in such a way that the listener can "live through" it. As Janie tells Pheoby: "'. . . 'tain't no use in me telling you somethin' unless Ah give you de understandin' to go 'long wid it. Unless you see de fur, a mink skin ain't no different from a coon hide'." The listener must form an "understanding." Yet telling must become experience in order for this to happen; the listener must "see" the story.

As they discuss women, Sam says to Hicks, "'Ah's much ruther see all dat than to hear 'bout it'." For telling to be successful, it must become a presentation of sights with words. The best talkers are "big picture talkers." In this way, the opposition between listening or reading and experience is broken down—or reading is brought as close to living as possible.

The narrator of *Their Eyes Were Watching God* is, one might say, a "big picture talker" as well, who employs lyrical language in order to allow the reader to make a visual and sensual expression of the text. "*Lyrical Immediacy*," writes Ralph Freedman, "is different from the immediacy of narrative action. . . . It is an immediacy of portraiture, an availability of themes and motifs to the reader's glance without the integration of a narrative world."[5] The narrator presents Janie's story as a series of episodes and pictures. Indeed, nearly all of her story is presented in the third person; in it Janie herself narrates the basic problem she must resolve. The following episodes contain images and experiences which she must organize with reference to her own problem. The reader or listener, on the other hand, is free to form his or her own evaluation from the material presented, to individually "integrate" the world. Pheoby, Janie's listener, is asked only "'for a good thought'"—a sympathetic, active listening.

The narrative is, then, both Janie's story and the reader's, the teller's and the listener's. Wolfgang Iser, in *The Implied Reader*, writes:

> If the reader were given the whole story, and there were nothing left for him to do, then his imagination would never enter the field, the result would be the boredom which inevitably arises when everything is laid out cut and dried before us. A literary text must therefore be conceived in such a way that it will engage the reader's imagination in the task of working things out for himself, for reading is only a pleasure when it is active and creative.[6]

In considering the relationship between Janie and Pheoby, and between Janie and her first two husbands and grandmother, one might substitute "listener" for "reader" here. On the level of the narrative itself, however, the participation of the reader is certainly encouraged. The narrator follows the example of Tea Cake or Janie herself, not of Joe Starks or Nanny.

The narrator uses a variety of narrative stances and techniques to render the text more sensually and visually immediate. I have already noted the sensual language which evokes Janie's inner language. An interior monologue is often introduced to evoke Janie's thoughts and perceptions: "She knew the world was a stallion rolling in the blue pasture of ether. She knew that God tore down the old world every evening and built a new one by sun-up." At times, though, the narration shifts to the direct address of an implied reader: "Daisy is walking a drum tune. You can almost hear it by looking at the way she walks." The narration can also take on the diction of oral language: "Joe Starks was the name, yeah Joe Starks from in and through Georgy. Been workin' for white folks all his life." The book's narration, it seems, is deliberately flexible; it takes on the qualities suitable to the situation it describes. The narrator has many voices. It is not consistent representation which is served, but presentation, or revelation. The text is presented to the "active" and "creative" reader.

The truth of the tale is not at issue so much as its effect on the teller and as its telling. The narrator and Janie are both "tellers"; in fact, one might imagine that they are occasionally as unreliable as Lige or Sam. The situation of their tales is perhaps the same as that of the story Tea Cake tells Janie about his day's absence. Neither she nor the reader have any assurance of its "truth." Yet Janie desires only to share in the adventure—and, ultimately, in the telling: "'Looka heah, Tea Cake, if you ever go off from me and have a good time lak dat and then come back heah tellin' me how nice Ah is, Ah specks tuh kill yuh dead'."

The episode of the buzzards' funeral for the mule, for example, could be interpreted as a challenge to the reader. It is presented in the same way that the other narrated incidents are. Yet it is, obviously, a fantasy. The scene takes place at the end of the mule's funeral, an event which Janie, whom Joe has left at home, does not witness. The funeral itself is a comedy; the people "mocked everything human in death." And the buzzards' funeral is a further parody of this parody, narrated with absolute seriousness. The last sentence of the episode is: "The yaller mule was gone from the town except for the porch talk, and for the children visiting his bleached bones now and then in the spirit of adventure." There is no witness to the scene of the buzzards; one might imagine that this tale is "porch talk," presented for the reader's enjoyment, and his or her rejection or acceptance. Within Janie's tale, told to Pheoby, it might be a story that she has heard and integrated into her own story. And, in the entire text, it points out that the narrator has chosen material to include by following a method other than strict representation, an idea I will return to later.

Near the end of the novel, Janie says, "'Ah done been tuh de horizon and back and now Ah kin sit heah in mah house and live by comparisons'." Having seen the world, she can now evaluate it, perhaps forgetting what she does not wish to remember and remembering what she does not want to forget. Her reading of the past is a selective, personal one. The image of memory is presented almost visually; she sees

> Tea Cake, with the sun for a shawl. Of course he wasn't dead. He could never be dead until she herself had finished feeling and thinking. The kiss of his memory made pictures of love and light against the wall. Here was peace. She pulled in her horizon like a great fish-net. Pulled it from around the waist of the world and draped it over her shoulder. So much of life in its meshes! She called in her soul to come and see.

Her past becomes, at last, something that she can possess. The world is reduced to an image, to be "draped over her shoulder." It is a dream which she has created for herself and in which she can live: "She called in her soul to come and see," This image and her own small room are much larger than Eatonville or Logan Killicks' sixty acres. And her image will allow her to live in the outside world as well, bringing it back to her own thoughts and dreams.

The reader's final experience of this text might be a similar one. In *The Implied Reader*, Iser writes:

> The production of the meaning of literary texts . . . does not merely entail the discovery of the unformulated, which can then be taken over by the active imagination of the reader; it also entails the possibility that we may formulate ourselves and so discover what had previously seemed to elude our consciousness.[7]

While a text presents a reader with a new set of experiences, it can also lead one to re-evaluate his or her own experiences, or "formulate oneself." In a sense, then, every text teaches something. In reading it, one learns how to read, or even how to live. The opening paragraphs of *Their Eyes Were Watching God* certainly have a didactic element, stating flatly two models of reading. They also lend an allegorical tone to the text; Janie is, after all, an example of a "woman." The text, the story, is the narrator's: Through Janie's story, the narrator tells another, a story about reading, and living.

Yet the narrator chooses a model that presents, in a sense, a nonlesson, or a lesson that readers are left to formulate for themselves. The reader's own experiences and dreams will lead him or her to interpret the text in an individual way, to transform it into a personal image. And every image will be the "true" text. Beyond this, though, the text may bring one to re-consider his or her own life, and to live it more fully. If the example of Janie's life teaches anything, it is that nothing can truly be "taught." The truth, the text, comes from, and ends in, the reader's or the liver's own perception. And there are "two things everybody's got tuh do fuh theyselves. They got tuh go tuh God, and they got tuh find out about livin' fuh theyselves.'" What Janie says of "livin'" can be said of reading as well.

Notes

1. I am a professor of life
   A vague student of death
   And if what I know is of no use
   I have not said nothing, but everything.
2. Zora Neale Hurston, *Their Eyes Were Watching God* (1937; rpt. Urbana: Univ. of Illinois Press, 1978), p. 9.
3. Ralph Freedman, *The Lyrical Novel* (Princeton, NJ: Princeton Univ. Press, 1963), p. 8.
4. *The Lyrical Novel*, p. 9.
5. Ibid.
6. (Baltimore, MD: The Johns Hopkins Press, 1964). p. 275.
7. Ibid., p. 294.

◆◆◆◆◆◆◆◆◆◆◆◆◆

Lines of Descent/Dissenting Lines

DEBORAH E. MCDOWELL

If a people's myths are the fullest expression of its spirit and culture, nowhere is this more evident than in African-Americans' appropriation of the story of Moses, the myth of the Israelites' exodus from Egyptian bondage. As Albert Raboteau writes in *Slave Religion*, "the symbols, myths and values of Judeo-Christian tradition helped form the slave community's image of itself." White colonists also identified with this tradition, seeing "the journey across the Atlantic to the New World as the exodus of a new Israel from the bondage of Europe into the promised land of milk and honey." But the colonists' Promised Land was the slaves' Egypt, a reversal made palpable and immortal in such spirituals as "Go Down Moses," "Oh Mary, Don't You Weep," and in the countless refigurations of the Mosaic myth throughout African-American literature, oral and written.

A selective list would include Frances E. W. Harper's "Moses: A Story of the Nile," Paul Laurence Dunbar's "Ante-Bellum Sermon," James Weldon Johnson's "Let My People Go," Robert Hayden's "Runagate, Runagate," Margaret Walker's "Prophets for a New Day" and Martin Luther King's famous last sermon, "I See the Promised Land," delivered on the eve of his assassination. Punctuated with references to Pharaoh and Egypt, the sermon builds to its now famous crescendo: "I've been to the mountaintop," "I've seen the promised land," and the resounding prophecy: "We as a people will get to the promised land."

Thus, when Zora Neale Hurston turned to retelling the Exodus story in *Moses, Man of the Mountain*, she was building on a mountain of a tradition and anticipating its perpetuation. Very early in her literary career, Hurston established her fascination with rewriting the sacred myths of the Judeo-Christian tradition in African-American terms and idioms. She saw and manipulated the possibilities that Old Testament stories held for chronicling the movements in the sluggish odyssey of black Americans toward emancipation in the United States. Her play, *The First One*, submitted to the *Opportunity* magazine contest in 1926, mocked the myth of Ham, seized by pro-slavery advocates as the biblical justification of chattel slavery in the United States. In 1934, she published "The Fire and the Cloud" in the September issue of *Challenge* magazine, edited by Dorothy West. A two-page story in the form of an exchange between a world-weary Moses and an inquisitive lizard, "The Fire and the Cloud" is a synopsis of the trials and triumphs of Moses' leadership, which is at its end. His newly dug grave on Mount Nebo is ready to receive him.

Appearing in that same issue of *Challenge* was a letter to the editor from Arna Bontemps in which he dismissed the doomsayers who had dug an early grave for the Harlem Renaissance "younger writers." The Exodus myth ready at hand, Bontemps denied that the writers were "washed up" and "old before our time. . . . We left Egypt in the late twenties and presently crossed the Red Sea. Naturally the wandering in the wilderness followed. The promised land is ahead." *Moses, Man of the Mountain* might well be seen as Zora Neale Hurston's "promised land," if we take that to mean a realization of her artistic and intellectual powers. It is certainly proof that she was far from "washed up" as a writer.

To claim that this badly flawed novel is a realization of Hurston's artistic power would be, to many, to claim a bit too much. Her contemporaries thought little of it and few scholars now attend to it, choosing, instead, to focus almost all their attention on *Their Eyes Were Watching God*. In his omnibus review in the January 1940 issue of *Opportunity*, Alain Locke offered faint praise for the novel's sustained "characterization and dialogue" but decided that it lacked "vital dramatization," "genuine folk portraiture," substituting "caricature" instead. In the August 5, 1941, issue of *New Masses*, Ralph Ellison surveyed "Recent Negro Fiction," concluding that only Richard Wright and Langston Hughes had taken Negro fiction beyond the narrow confines that bound it in the 1920s. He commended Richard Wright's *Native Son* and *Uncle Tom's Children* for "overcoming the social and cultural isolation of Negro life and moving into a world of unlimited intellectual and imaginative possibilities." He praised Hughes's fiction for its "awareness of the working class and socially dispossessed Negro and his connection with the international scheme of things." Turning to *Moses, Man of the Mountain*, Ellison noted that, although it "possess[ed] technical competence, [it] retain[ed] the blight of calculated burlesque." He offered his ultimate assessment: "For Negro fiction [*Moses, Man of the Mountain*] did nothing."

By this point in Hurston's career, the orthodoxies such as those Locke and Ellison imposed on black writers had come to be expected. Locke tended to reserve especially harsh judgments for the women writers of the Harlem Renaissance. Jessie Fauset was a favorite target. Locke described her novel, *Comedy American Style* (1933) as "too mid-Victorian for moving power today." He also criticized Hurston's *Their Eyes Were Watching God* for "failing to come to grips with the motive and social document fiction." Even if we grant Locke's assumption that "social documentation" constitutes the *sine qua non* of black fiction in the thirties, we would have to conclude that he works with a narrow definition of the "social" in judging Hurston's fiction to be lacking in this regard. That in *Moses* Hurston casts her own social concerns in the terms of antiquity and eschews the urban realism that Wright perfected doesn't mean that she shows no concern for contemporary social issues and how they might be addressed in fiction. She simply offers no easy pieties and tidy solutions. She astutely saw in Wright's work, to which her own was often invidiously compared, pat and unexamined solutions to complex and monumental social ills. For example, in her review of Wright's *Uncle Tom's Children* (1938), she criticized the solution he offered throughout the thirties and forties: "the PARTY—state responsibility for everything and individual responsibility for nothing, not even feeding oneself." In writing this, she doubtless had Wright's novella *Fire and Cloud* in mind. In this piece, Wright tries to reconcile his religious heritage with the teachings of Marxism by fashioning a solution for a community suffering from famine and the grip of Jim Crow. The novella centers on Dan Taylor, the spiritual leader of his community, also described as "Moses, leading his people out of the wilderness and into the Promised Land." Taylor comes to see the futility of old-time religion against the repressive white power structure, and, at the story's end, leads the community in a mass interracial march to City Hall.

Hurston's own story, "The Fire and the Cloud," might be read as a short answer to Wright's version, as well as a preface to *Moses, Man of the Mountain*. The novel goes on to question whether liberation is ever achieved through a single charismatic leader. In *Moses*, Hurston explores and at times critiques the idea of a religious leader who mediates between an oppressed people and God, the state, or any other Presence. She also liberates her pen from what Harold Cruse refers to, in a different context, as the "literary religion of socialist realism." Without doubting that fiction has real power in the world, Hurston seems loath, as Wright does not, to use her fiction to "lead" her readers toward any pat solution to the continuing problem of racism and oppression.

Throughout, Hurston's novel dramatizes and critiques the terms and problematics of liberation. After Moses has led the Israelites to Canaan, he seems to question the wisdom of any people's dependence on a single leader, or deliverer, concluding that "No man may make another free. Freedom was something internal. . . . All you could do was to give the opportunity for freedom and the man himself must make his own emancipation." However, in passing the mantle to Joshua, he explains, "You can't have a state of individuals. Everybody just can't be allowed to do as they please." The chosen people must not "take up too many habits from the nations they come in contact with." Thus, he preserves the idea of one leader even while asking, "How can a nation speak with one voice if they are not one?" Finally, though, it is precisely Moses' "one voice" that does speak for the people.

Hurston transfers her critique of the "Big Voice" from *Their Eyes Were Watching God* to *Moses*. And from her first novel, *Jonah's Gourd Vine*, she transfers her dramatization of the complex relationship between religion and gender. In all three novels, the "Big Voice" is synonymous with the male voice. While the opening of *Moses* is promising in its attempt to establish a triadic parallel between ancient Hebrew slavery, Negro slavery, and female oppression, that parallel is not sustained throughout the novel. In the opening scene, the persecution of the Hebrew male babies is connected (as if through the umbilical cord) to the suffering of their mothers. The one cannot be considered apart from the other, as the public world of male power intrudes into and controls the fruit of women's bodies. And while Moses' mother, Jochebed, fights the law of the state by not permitting her husband to kill her son, in the end that disobedience is not sustained.

The "place" of women in this narrative of patriarchy's origins is to be followers, and the places in which they figure in the novel are perhaps its most troubling. While one is simly tempted to write these passages off, or to read them as throwbacks to "the Gilded Six Bits" and harbingers of *Seraph on the Suwanee* (in both of which works Hurston's feminist bite seems toothless), here, in *Moses*, these passages seem to coincide not so much with any feminist ambivalences on Hurston's part, but rather with the very substance of one of the most sacred and revered narratives Hurston attempts to tell. In retelling the Pentateuch—said to have been written by Moses under divine inspiration—Hurston positions herself in a narrative in which women are marginalized and oppressed. The various feminist critiques of biblical authorship and authority inscribing the law of the father are by now familiar, and it is not simply reading Hurston backward to suggest that she found much about this tradition to decry. We remember Janie's comment to Jodie in *Their Eyes Were Watching God*, "sometimes God gits familiar wid us womenfolks too and talks his inside business," but in *Moses*, it is only the great liberator who talks to God face to face. Implied in that image of talking face to face with God is a logic of equality, of the horizontal, a transgressive logic that runs throughout Hurston's work. However, that same face-to-face conversation is man to man. Although a woman's voice opens the text, speaking the anguish of childbirth, women's voices and desires are hushed and trivialized throughout, subordinated to the greatness of the male.

Moses is advised by a series of men in decreasing hierarchical order. Mentu, the stableman, whom Moses makes his servant, advised him on the strategies of warfare that lead Moses to celebrated success as a conqueror. But it is Jethro, Moses' father-in-law, who is, next to God, the Voice, the man to whose authority Moses most often defers. He advises Moses to "consecrate [himself] for the work" to which God has called him and to remember that "women pull men aside." For almost the duration of his marriage to Jethro's daughter, Zipporah, Moses is away from his family fulfilling his divine mission. Finally, leadership in the novel is reducible to the practice and process of male bonding and filiation. Moses is called by a male God; advised by a revered patriarch; and then passes the mantle of leadership to another man, Joshua.

That leadership is seen as synonymous with an anointed male is made especialy clear in Moses' treatment of his alleged sister, Miriam. He is disturbed to find her among the group of Elders he has summoned on "serious business," but Aaron explains that Miriam is a prophet. Because Moses never speaks to Miriam directly, Aaron must mediate between the two. To Aaron's suggestion that Miriam make a speech before a general meeting, Moses responds, "This is not the time I have appointed for speech making." He does instruct Aaron to "tell her to stay," though, only because "she would be useful in handling the women." Women are thus secondary and peripheral to the strategies and demands of nation-building, forming at best a caste within a nation.

In her long allegorial poem, *Moses: A Story of the Nile*, Frances E. W. Harper tells the story of Moses incorporating the suppressed perspectives of two women (one Hebrew, the other, Egyptian), both represented as Moses' mother. While Hurston does not restore the status of the mother(s) in her telling of the tale, one could say that in putting her mouth on the Mosaic myth, she exposes the structures of gender at its base. In other words, in telling the story of a people's deliverance into a new nation state—a Fatherland, if you will—Hurston says much about the relations between nationalism and masculinity and how, for both, the presence of the feminine is a problem. The place of "race," and the idea of a "people" and its origins are at the heart of that story, which Hurston represents as a war story. The novel identifies concerns with racial origins—and perhaps origins more generally—as the genesis of many of the world's evils. Hurston could not have chosen a more timely year in which to launch these concerns.

1939 was the year in which both Hurston's novel and Freud's *Moses and Monotheism* were published. More uncanny than the fact that both books were published in the same year and reentered this sacred text, was that both ventured boldly to call Moses' racial origins into question. Referring to his book as "The Man Moses; A Historical Novel," Freud sought to establish Moses' Egyptian heritage definitively, arguing on the root of his name, *Mose*—the Egyptian word for child. But, as many biblical scholars have noted, the book rests mainly on hypotheses and conjectures that establish nothing if not Freud's ambivalence toward his own Jewish origins. Conversely, [in] her *Moses*, Hurston is not so much intent on etablishing the patriarch's origins beyond dispute, but rather on casting doubts about Moses' "pure" origins and, by extension, on the very idea of "racial purity."

Hurston's training in anthropology would logically bring her to this place. As a student of Franz Boas, she understood racial divisions as idealized abstractions, albeit with undeniably concrete functions and consequences in the real world. Her concerns with the consequences of racial classification link Hurston with other Harlem Renaissance writers who, through thematizing racial passing, explored race as a cultural construct rather than a biological fact: James Weldon Johnson in *The Autobiography of an Ex-Colored Man* (1912); Walter White in *Flight* (1926); Jessie Fauset in *Plum Bun* (1929); and Nella Larsen in *Passing* (1929). Hurston's *Moses*, like all of these works, can be read as an intervention in the discourses about race raging throughout the 1920s and 1930s, discourses used to justify not only socio-economic stratification of blacks in the United States but also the utter extinction of Jews under Nazi Germany.

That Hurston was concerned with questions of racial purity in a novel published in 1939 gains significance when we consider that this was the year Hitler ordered the attack on Poland and led Germany into a world war, although his borrowed theories of eugenics—based on the idea of racial improvement through selective breeding—were popular long before Hitler came to power and were influential in various countries throughout the twenties and thirties. In the United States the eugenics movement was linked to racist campaigns against blacks and anti-immigration campaigns against European "undesirables." Alfred Wiggam's *The Fruit of the Family Tree* (1924) was just one of a number of works devoted to the proposition that "a mixed population with differing racial inheritances, different minds and blood make for the stability of a nation." Wiggam sought to strengthen his case by posing the question, "Have not all past civilizations gone to pieces when they mixed their breeds?" Eugenics was thus essential to "the production of a great race . . . the sum and meaning of all politics, the one living purpose of the state." Wiggam's propaganda rhymed clearly with Hitler's more belligerent version expounded in but not restricted to his autobiography, *Mein Kampf,* which is by now well known. The Germans were to his mind the "highest species of humanity on earth," chosen by Providence to be the Master Race. But they would remain so only if they guarded and controlled the "purity of their own blood." Hitler's goal was a united Aryan nation, a "folkish state" that "must set race in the center of all life" and "take care to keep it pure." That meant exterminating Jews and Slavs.

The shadow of Nazism is cast from the beginning of *Moses, Man of the Mountain,* which opens on the process of marking Hebrew male babies for extinction. Parents search for places in which to hide their children, "some good cave . . . that the secret police don't know about yet." The Hebrews speculate that there is "Plenty of Hebrew blood [in Pharaoh's] family already. That is why [he] wants to kill us off. He is scared somebody will come along and tell who his real folks are." "The higher-ups who got Hebrew blood in 'em is always the ones to know that the grandmother of Pharaoh was a Hebrew woman." Coincident with the mass annihilation of Hebrew boys, the pharaoh passes laws that condemn Hebrews to slavery and prevent them from becoming citizens of Egypt.

With a double edge on passing as it refers to law and passing as it refers to racial disguise, the slaves interpret the pharaoh's actions: he "figures that it makes a big man out of him to be passing and passing laws and rules."

But the novel spins the greatest mystery around the origins of Moses. From the moment Miriam loses sight of him and then weaves a tale of his disappearance into the Egyptian palace with the pharaoh's daughter, his origins are open to conjecture and dispute. Moses' first wife, a war bride, shrinks from him, because she suspects he is a Hebrew. Jethro's daughters identify him as a "high-born Egyptian." The Hebrews suspect Moses of being an Egyptian, and when Pharaoh and his army come after them soon after their escape, they declare Moses a "pure Egyptian and Pharaoh his brother. He just toled us off so his brother could butcher us in the wilderness."

Most of Moses' problems as the leader of the Hebrews stem from the Hebrews' lack of trust, which is often linked to their doubts about Moses' ancestry. Despite his identification of himself as a Hebrew, the narrative keeps those doubts as to his racial origins alive and unresolved. In sustaining the ambiguities of race throughout the text, Hurston effectively argues against a system of racial classification whose validity she disputes. This tactic squarely positions the novel against the Nazi blood myths and for those Jews who lost their lives to this mythology. But the alliances in the novel are not always so clear-cut.

At first glance, the coordinates of the novel's typology seem clearly drawn: Jewish oppression in Egypt prefigures black oppression in America, which parallels Jewish oppression under Hitler. The fulfillment of democracy equals liberation from oppression, but there the parallel lines of typology crisscross and become as confused and confusing as the lines of genealogy, a confusion perfectly matched to the novel's satiric mode. Satire, which literally means "a dish filled with mixed fruits," envelops and defines *Moses, Man of the Mountain*, a mode perhaps appropriate to a novel which insists that the fruits of everyone's loins are "mixed." The reader is occasionally bewildered and frustrated by this mix in that every attempt to penetrate to some essential, extractable political position or source is concealed behind the mélange of humor, conjure stories, folktales, and braided historical narratives, and is ultimately thwarted. The novel's elusiveness, though, is partly explained by the repressive climate in which it was published.

In writing this political allegory and analogizing Hebrew oppression in biblical antiquity, black oppression in the contemporary United States and Jewish oppression in Nazi Germany, Hurston probably remembered the fact that the U.S. government made aggressive efforts during World War I to stifle any publications that did not lend their full support to the war effort. The black press was the target of heavy surveillance, during that time when the *Messenger* had its second-class mailing permit revoked and *The Crisis* was removed from soldiers' reading rooms abroad because of its "seditious" contents. W. E. B. DuBois answered with his famous "Close Ranks" editorial, encouraging blacks to "forget our special grievances and close our ranks shoulder to shoulder with our own white fellow citizens and the allied nations that are fighting for democracy."

During World War II, surveillance of the black press intensified, though no steps were actually taken against specific publications. According to Patrick Washburn in *A Question of Sedition: The Federal Government's Investigation of the Black Press During World War II*, no less than seven government agencies—the Justice Department, the FBI, the Post Office, the Office of Facts and Figures, the Office of War Information, the Office of Censorship, and the War Production Board—exerted various forms of pressure on the black press to curb its outspoken attacks on the government. The government was obstinate in its beliefs that black publications were "subversive sheets," which were actively pro-Axis. The black press was expected to postpone its agitation for full black citizenship until the end of the war, lest the Axis powers exploit the fact that America preached democracy abroad but practiced Jim Crow at home.

That the events surrounding World Wars I and II have not been seen as logical contexts for reading *Moses, Man of the Mountain* derives partly from a tendency many have to compartmentalize history into neat chronological time segments. While critics have certainly discussed Hurston's World War II journalism, few have looked to *Moses* as the precursor of the later, more controversial writings. That Hurston was concerned with war is evident throughout the novel. In Chapter VIII, which could accurately be titled "Chiefly About War Matters," the war opinions are especially explicit. In fact, drama and dialogue are virtually sacrificed to the narration of Moses' role as commander-in-chief of the Egyptian armies during the period of intensified nationalism and widespread conquest that expanded the Egyptian empire. Whole passages seem to be direct commentaries on aspects and controversies of war, most notably the relations between race and war. One of Moses' first initiatives as commander is to demand that Hebrews be included in the Egyptian army, but he is strenuously opposed by members of the courts and officers of the army.

> They argue that [the Hebrews] were not citizens of Egypt, but enemy-prisoners, and as such, it would be rash to put arms into their hands again. Who knew when they might rise up against their conquerors and turn the tables?

After Egypt has conquered Ethiopia, kept Assyria in fear, and terrorized Babylonia, Moses wants to cease imperialist conquest, "to rest from wars and turn to home problems for a while." But Pharaoh responds that "Egypt has no home problems."

Of course, all of these passages recall arguments about the position of blacks in practically every war in which the United States has fought. More often than not, blacks were excluded from combat because to include them then made it difficult to deny them the rights of full, first-class citizenship. And arming blacks, certainly in the War for Independence, aroused fears that they would retaliate against their true enslavers.

Hurston settles on a clever strategy not only in this chapter but also in the overall design of the novel. She turns the power of historical memory to her advantage, and the U.S. government's sinister hypocrisy against itself. She manipulates the government's expressed concern for preserving democracy and uses it on behalf of blacks persecuted by the forces of Jim Crow in the United States.

Casting contemporary issues of racial oppression in the perspective of antiquity could be seen to represent a distortion of the biblical text and a flagrant disregard for the historical record, however fragmentary and contested they both are. To be sure, in the Old Testament epoch the social category of race had not acquired the meaning it has in modern Western societies, but that does not mean that either racial cateogories or racism are purely latter day constructions. Hurston makes and capitalizes on this very point in *Moses, Man of the Mountain*, without any pretenses toward scholarly authority or discipline. She blurs the distinctions of history just as she blurs the distinctions of race to intriguing effect.

Interestingly, she continued to grapple with the power of the Mosaic myth on her imagination throughout her career. It figures prominently in her efforts to understand the evils of racism. In "Seeing the World as It Is," deleted from the first edition of *Dust Tracks on a Road*, she asserted:

> The Old Testament is devoted to what was right and just from the viewpoint of the Ancient Hebrews. All of their enemies were twenty-two carat evil. They, the Hebrews, were never aggressors. The Lord wanted His Children to have a country full of big grapes and tall corn. Incidentally, while they were getting it, they might as well get rid of some trashy tribes that He never did think much of anyway.

Her editor at Lippincott suggested that she eliminate "international opinions" from the book as they were "irrelevant to autobiography." She complied.

As Robert Hemenway points out in his biography of Hurston, the Japanese attack on Pearl Harbor forced Hurston to delete such commentary and to revise other controversial passages in *Dust Tracks on a Road*. It was only after the war that she unleashed her most direct and venomous attacks on American social institutions, now stripped of the wrap of biblical legend and the American flag. Significantly, these less oblique attacks appeared in black publications such as *Negro Digest*, in which she published "Crazy for This Democracy" (1945). There she referred to Roosevelt's famous phrase "the arsenal of democracy" as the "arse-and-all of democracy," and went on to argue that:

> Jim Crow laws have been put on the books for a purpose and that purpose is . . . to promote in the mind of the smallest white child the conviction of First by Birth, eternal and irrevocable like the place assigned to the Levites by Moses over the other tribes of the Hebrews.

Simply excerpted from their contexts, these passages are disturbing, but when recontextualized they show a writer working back to her cultural origins and all the complications attached to considering them. The complication of race is paramount. The reader cannot stop at the above excerpt from "Seeing the World as It Is," for it is followed by reference to "the kings of Dahomey [who] once marched up and down West Africa, butchering the aged and the helpless of the surrounding tribes and nations and selling the able off into Western slavery" and to Anglo-Saxon greed, rape, and pillaging, all for the "idea . . . that everybody else owes [them] something for being blonde." The entire essay is a diffuse discourse on the history and problematics of "race consciousness," which Hurston had come to see as a "deadly explosive on the tongues of men." No "race" is omitted from her catalogue of "international cannibalism" that implies some disturbing parallels between "nation," "race," "volk" and "folk."

That World War II and Hitler seemed to stimulate these essays that logically follow *Moses* is clear, but here, Hitler might best be seen not simply as a political figure but also as a metaphor for slavery, racism, anti-Semitism, anti-feminism, Jim Crow, and the general repression on which Hurston had declared war. She had left behind the lyricism and pastoralism of *Their Eyes Were Watching God* with its imagery of pear trees and bees dusting pollen, though she retained the justly celebrated language of the "folk."

Hurston's use of folklore has been the convenient "evidence" her detractors have summoned to argue against her fiction's "serious intent." Those critics, like Alain Locke and Richard Wright, mainly saw her work as "folklore fiction" and thus read it as the antithesis of "socially-motivated" fiction. *Moses, Man of the Mountain* annuls that false opposition. Even some of those sympathetic readers of Hurston's work have seen it as only folklore and, hence, to many, it is mere entertainment. For instance, Benjamin Brawley defended Hurston's folklore, noting that she, "like some others who have dealt in folklore . . . [had] not escaped criticism at the hands of those who frowned upon her broad humor and the lowly nature of her material." Ending on a patronizing note, he described Hurston as "taking a bright story wherever it may be found, she passes it on, leaving to others the duty and the pleasure of philosophizing."

Such commentary—by supporters and detractors alike—has overlooked the extent to which the majority of Hurston's writings combine a gift for storytelling with the "pleasure of philosophizing" about "the international scheme of things," Ellison notwithstanding. Judgments like Ellison's are at least partly explained by the prominence of Hurston's hometown of Eatonville in her writing, a prominence which has led scholars to give it supreme explanatory power in estimations of her work. All too often Hurston's readers have cosigned her to Eatonville and left her there on the porch. Adding other dimensions to the characterizations of Hurston's birthplace as an idyllic and sheltered all-black town, and the porch, to quote Blyden Jackson, as "the recurring site of a comedic and animated village forum" is difficult to do, for this characterization is the backbone of Hurston's legendary status. Even when readers stretch her province to New Orleans and the Caribbean, the sites of her fieldwork, they often read these migrations as extensions of Eatonville, seen as the repository of black folk culture on which all Hurston's work is dependent.

But, reducing Eatonville and its symbolic geographic coordinates to the repositories of black "folk" expression that Hurston mined so well "regionalizes" her work and ensures her removal from a more global context of cultural production and exchange. In other words, however important Eatonville is as the site that birthed and nurtured Hurston's creative genius, much is lost in so circumscribing her work and her world. In *Moses, Man of the Mountain* she has clearly traveled far from Eatonville and far from her own earlier "race-conscious" positions. Of course she had lived in America and experienced the humiliations of Jim Crow long enough to know that the discursive problematization of "race" and racialist thinking did not lead to the social elimination of racism. The race wars that she fictionalizes in *Moses, Man of the Mountain* are only one testament to that awareness and sign that she had grown weary of what Marthe Roberts calls the "fatality of filiation," that both enriches and burdens us with origins, with race. The consequences of Hurston's shifting positions on race have yet to alter in any significant way the single most persistent image of her as the folklorist of Eatonville. That is regarded as the single most persistent criterion of her literary value. With this new edition of *Moses* we might begin to enlarge her province, to really see her as one of the characters she described in her fiction— one of the "big picture talkers," who "use[d] a side of the world for a canvas."

◆◆◆◆◆◆◆◆◆◆◆◆◆

Autoethnography: The An-Archic Style of *Dust Tracks on a Road*

FRANCOISE LIONNET-MCCUMBER

One is an artist at the cost of regarding that which all non-artists call 'form' as content, as 'the matter itself.' To be sure, then one belongs in a topsy-turvy world: for henceforth content becomes something merely formal—our life included.

—Nietzsche, 1888

The words do not count. . . . The tune is the unity of the thing.
—Zora Neale Hurston, 1942

The greatness of a man is to be found not in his acts but in his style.
—Frantz Fanon, 1952

One need only glance at the table of contents of Hurston's autobiography to notice that it presents itself as a set of interactive thematic *topoi* superimposed on a loosely chronological framework. The seemingly linear progression from "My Birthplace" to "Looking Things Over" is more deceptive in that regard than truly indicative of a narrator's psychological development, quest for recognition, or journey from innocence to experience as traditionally represented in confessional autobiographies. The chapter entitled "Seeing the World as It Is," which Hurston meant to be the final one in her first draft of the book,[1] is a philosophical essay on power, politics and human relations on a planetary scale: the radical testament of a writer who rejects *ressentiment* and, refusing to align herself with any "party," explains that it is because she does "not have much of a herd instinct." Rather than recounting the events of her life, Hurston is more interested in showing us who she is—or to be more precise, how she has become what she is: an individual who ostensibly values her independence more than any kind of political commitment to a cause, especially the cause of "Race Solidarity" as she puts it. Hers is a very controversial and genealogical[2] enterprise which has been much criticized because it leaves itself open to charges of accommodationism and disappoints the expectations of "frankness" and "truthfulness" which are all too often unproblematically linked to this genre of self-writing. Openly critical of *Dust Tracks* in his introduction to the second edition, her biographer, Robert Hemenway puts it thus: "style . . . becomes a kind of camouflage, an escape from articulating the paradoxes of her personality".[3]

An-archy and Community: 'The stuff of my being is matter, ever changing . . .'

In light of the skepticism with which contemporary literary theory has taught us to view any effort of self-representation in language, I would like to propose a different approach to the issue of Hurston's presumed insincerity and untrustworthiness.[4] It may perhaps be more useful to reconsider *Dust Tracks on a Road* not as "autobiography" but rather as "self-portrait," in the sense redefined by Michel Beaujour in his book *Miroirs D'encre:* "des textes qui se tiennent par eux-mêmes, plutôt que la mimesis d'actions passées"[5] and to try to elaborate a conceptual framework which would not conflict with Hurston's own avowed methodology as essayist and anthropologist. Indeed, what I would like to suggest here is that *Dust Tracks* amounts to "autoethnography," that is, the process of defining one's subjective ethnicity as mediated through language, history and ethnographical analysis; in short, that the book amounts to a kind of "figural anthropology" of the self.[6]

In a recent essay entitled "On Ethnographic Allegory," James Clifford refers to the "allegory of salvage" which generally tended to dominate the representational practice of fieldworkers in the era of Boasian anthropology. For them, the preservation of disappearing cultures and vanishing lore was seen as the vital "redemption" of the "otherness" of primitive cultures from a global process of entropy: "The other is lost, in disintegrating time and place, but saved in the text." This textualization of the object of representation incorporated a move from the oral-discursive field experience of the collector of folklore to his or her written version of that initial intersubjective moment—a transcription which is also a way of speaking *for* the other culture, of adopting a ventriloquist's stance. Having been trained under Boas, Hurston was supposed to be going in the field to do just that: salvage her own "vanishing" Negro culture. Her position of fundamental liminality—being an once a participant in, and an observer of, her culture—would bring home to her the distorting effects of that problematic shift from orality to fixed, rigid textuality, and thus reinforce her skepticism in the anthropological project, in her assigned role as detached, objective interpreter and translator. The fact that she had shared in that rural culture, during her childhood in Eatonville, prevented her from adopting the nostalgic pose so common to those Western ethnographies which implicitly lament the loss of an Edenic and preindustrial past of mankind.[7] This same skepticism about the writing of culture would permeate the writing of the self, the autobiography, turning it into the allegory of an ethnographic project which self-consciously moves from the general (the history of Eatonvile) to the particular (Zora's life, her family and friends) and back to the general (religion, culture, and world politics in the 40s). Unlike spiritual autobiographies which exhibit a similar threefold pattern—death, conversion and rebirth—as well as their author's strong sense of transcendent purpose, *Dust Tracks* does not seek to legitimate itself through appeal to a "powerful source of authorization" such as religion or other organized system of belief.[8] It is in that sense that *Dust Tracks* is a powerfully an-archic work, not anchored in any original and originating story of racial or sexual difference.

The tone of the work and its rhetorical strategy of exaggeration draw attention to its style and away from what it directly denotes. "There were no discrete nuances of life on Joe Clarke's porch. . . . all emotions were naked and nakedly arrived at" is a statement which describes the men's reactions to instances of adultery (a folksy topic), but also carries historical implications about the pioneer spirit in general: "This was the spirit of that whole new part of the state at the time, as it always is where men settle new lands." Similarly, when Zora talks about her unhappy love affair, it is through vivid images which convey, with some irony, the universality of pain rather than deep personal anguish: "I freely admit that everywhere I set my feet down, there were tracks of blood. Blood from the very middle of my heart." Regretting the "halcyon days" of childhood, she bemoans the spirit of gravity which pervades adulthood and makes us unable to "fly with the unseen things that soar." And when discussing race, her affirmation: "instead of Race Pride being a virtue, it is a sapping vice" implicates us directly into that seemingly volatile statement instead of pointing us to the obvious historical context of the moment: fascism, the second world war, colonialism, the hypocrisy and self-satisfaction of "the blond brother," and the preponderance of "instances of human self-bias." Clearly, *Dust Tracks* does not gesture toward a coherent tradition of introspective self-examination with soul baring displays of emotion.

Paradoxically, despite its rich cultural content, the text does not authorize unproblematic recourse to culturally grounded interpretations. It is an orphan-text which attempts to create its own genealogy by simultaneously appealing to, and debunking, the cultural traditions it helps to redefine. Hurston's chosen objects of study, for example, the folktales which come alive during the storytelling or "lying" sessions she observes are indeed never "fixed." Their content is not rigid and unchanging but generally varies according to the tale-telling situation. It is the contextual frame of reference, the situation of the telling, which determines how a tale is reinterpreted by each new tale-teller; hence, for the anthropologist, there is no "essential" quality to be isolated in the content of those tales, but there is a formal structure which can and must be recognized if she is to make sense of, and do justice to, the data gathered. The chapter entitled "Research" puts the matter quite clearly and succinctly:

> I enjoyed collecting folk-tales and I believed the people from whom I collected them enjoyed the telling of them, just as much as I did the hearing. Once they got started, the "lies" just rolled and story-tellers fought for a chance to

talk. It was the same thing with the songs. *The one thing to be guarded against, in the interest of truth, was over-enthusiasm. For instance, if the song was doing good, and the material ran out, the singer was apt to interpolate pieces of other songs into it.* The only way you can know when that happens, is to know your material so well that you can sense the violation. Even if you do not know the song that is being used for padding, you can tell the change in rhythm and tempo. *The words do not count. The subject matter in Negro folk-songs can be anything* and go from love to work, to travel, to food, to weather, to fight, to demanding the return of a wig by a woman who has turned unfaithful. *The tune is the unity of the thing.* And you have to know what you are doing when you begin to pass on that, because Negroes can fit in more words and leave out more and still keep the tune better than anyone I can think of (my italics).

The whole issue of form and content, style and message is very astutely condemned here: "truth" is clearly a matter of degree, and can easily be distorted by the "over-enthusiasm" of the performer. If "over-enthusiasm" can be seen as another word for hyperbole, then Hurston the writer is hereby cautioning her own reader to defer judgment about the explicit referentiality of her text. Why come to it with preconceived notions of autobiographical truths when the tendency to make hyperbolic and over-enthusiastic statements about her subject matter is part of her "style" as a writer? Hurston is fully aware of the gaps and discrepancies which can exist between intention and execution, reality and representation, reason and imagination, in short between the "words" (or "subject matter") and the "tune" which is the source of "unity" for the singers on the porch. For her too, the flow of creative energy is a process of imaginative transfiguration of literal truth/content through rhetorical procedures. The resulting text/performance thus transcends pedestrian notions of referentiality, for the staging of the event is part of the process of "passing on," of elaborating cultural forms which are not static and inviolable but dynamically involved in the creation of culture itself. It is thus not surprising that Hurston should view the self, and especially the "racial self," as a fluid and changing concept, as an arbitrary signifier with which she had better dispense if it inhibited (as any kind of reductive labeling might) the inherent plasticity of individuals.[9] Viewed from such an angle, we might say that far from being a "camouflage" and an "escape," *Dust Tracks* does indeed *exemplify* the "paradoxes of her personality" by revealing a fluid and multidimensional self which refuses to allow itself to be framed and packaged for the benefit of those human, all too human mortals, "both black and white who [claim] special blessings on the basis of race."

Indeed, in the case of the folkloric forms she studies, the plasticity of the "subject matter" of songs and tales is corroborated by her research experience in the field; if we can be justified in seeing the "subject" of the autobiography and the "subject matter" of folklore as homologous structures or *topoi* reflecting and mirroring each other, then it is the dialogue between these homologies which shapes the autobiographical text while revealing the paradoxes of the genre. This dialogue serves to illuminate Hurston's combined identities as anthropologist and writer, as these simultaneously begin to emerge and to converge in *Dust Tracks:* in the process of articulating their differences, she actually establishes their inescapable similarities, prefiguring the practice of such theorists as Clifford Geertz or Victor Turner. As Hemenway rightly points out, "Zora never became a professional academic folklorist because such vocation was alien to her exuberant sense of self, to her admittedly artistic, sometimes erratic temperament, and to her awareness of the esthetic content of black folklore." But such a psychologizing approach does not suffice to clarify the work and explain Hurston's liminal position, her confident straddling of "high" (academic) and "low" (folk) cultures, the ease with which she brings to the theoretical enterprise of the academic collector of lore the insights and perceptivity of the teller of tales. What makes the autobiography interesting is that it unfolds the structures of meaning—the cultural "topics"; history, geography, mythology, kinship, education, work, travels, friendship, love, religion, politics, philosophy, etc.—through which the creative artist gives shape to her personal experiences as seen through the "spy-glass" of anthropology.[10]

Moving away from what might be the sterile analyses of a field worker to the inspirational language of an artist, Hurston involves herself and her reader in a transformative process: to look at life from an esthetic point of view and to celebrate her ethnic heritage are thus two complementary projects for her. Life is an esthetic experience, a staged performance, reflected in the autobiography as well as the fictional writings, and literature is a means of recording with "a studied antiscientific approach" the lives and subjective realities of a particular people, in a specific time and place: it is this apparently antagonistic movement between life and literature, reality and its representation, orality and literacy which informs the structural coherence of *Dust Tracks*, rather than the simply linear progression through the lived life. What the text puts in motion is a strategy of displacement regarding the expectations governing two modes of discourse; the "objective" exteriority is that of the autobiographer whose "inside search" does not bear out its promise of introspection and the "intimate" tone is that of the anthropologist who implicates herself in her "research" by delving into Hoodoo, by performing initiation rites and, in an ironic and clever reversal of the ventriloquism of ethnography, by letting her informants inform *us* about Zora's persona in the field: as Big Sweet puts it, "You ain't like me. You don't even sleep with no men. . . . I think it's nice for you to be like that. You just keep on writing down them lies."

So, if Hurston sometimes seems to be aspiring toward some kind of "raceless ideal," it is not because she is interested in the "universality" of human experiences; quite the contrary, she wants to expose, as Hemenway explains, "the inadequacy of sterile reason to deal with the phenomena of living," and "race" in that context is but a reasonable, pseudoscientific category for dealing with a basically fluid, diverse and multifarious reality: "The stuff of my being is matter, ever changing, ever moving, but never lost." Her philosophical position in *Dust Tracks* is in fact echoed more than twenty years later by Frantz Fanon in *Les Damnés de la terre:* "Cette obligation historique dans laquelle se sont trouvés les hommes de culture africains de racialiser leurs revendications, de parler devantage de culture africaine que de culture nationale va les conduire à un cul-de-sac." Fanon's warning that the undefined and vague entity "African culture" was a creation of European colonialism led him to emphasize local, historically and geographically specific contingencies, rather than "race" as a general and abstract concept: "Et il est bien vrai que les grands responsables de cette racialisation de la pensée, ou du moins des démarches de la pensée, sont et demeurent les Européens qui n'ont pas cessé d'opposer la culture blanche aux autres incultures." Similarly, Hurston's interest in the folk communities of Eatonville, Polk County, Mobile, New Orleans, Nassau, Jamaica and Haiti stemmed from the belief that the universal can only be known through the specific, and that knowledge grounded in first-hand experience can yield more insights into the human condition, and into the processes of acculturation, differentiation, and historicization to which human beings are subjected. I would thus argue that her unstated aim is identical to Fanon's later formulation: to destroy the white stereotype of black *"inculture"* not by privileging "blackness" as an oppositional category to "whiteness" in culture, but by unequivocally showing the vitality and diversity of nonwhite cultures around the Caribbean and the coastal areas of the South, thereby dispensing completely with "white" as a concept and as a point of reference. Unlike the proponents of the négritude movement whose initial thrust was to fight against white racism and prejudice, Hurston assumes the supremely confident posture of the anthropologist who need not *justify* the validity of her enterprise, but can simply *affirm* by her study the existence of richly varied black cultures, thus delineating the semiotics of spaces where "white culture's representations are squeezed to zero volume, producing a new expressive order."[11]

What must not be overlooked, therefore, in the above passage from "Research" is the emphasis Hurston puts on contextual considerations and the implicit distinctions which she then draws between her own position as anthropologist observing the event and the role of the singers who are directly involved in the performance. For example, it is important for the anthropologist—and for the literary critic attempting to model her approach on Hurston's—to know the "material," that is, to be steeped in the historical, geographical and vernacular contexts of the "songs" in order to be able to determine where "pieces of other songs" are "interpolated" and used as "padding" when the original material "ran out." Does this imply that for Hurston there is a certain autonomy of the original text which is "violated" by the "interpolation" of fragments of other songs? It would seem rather that as an anthropologist she feels that it is important to make those kinds of distinctions, yet recognizes that for the singers this is a very unimportant question: the song goes on, the participants collectively "keep the tune" and do not worry about the singularity or inviolability of a given text or song. In other words, the question of intertextuality or of hybridization of content is not a significant one for the artists (they do not see it as a transgression of rules of identity), however important it may be for the observer who wants to be able to determine where one particular song ends and where the next one starts. The question of establishing boundaries is thus raised and examined by the anthropologist while the artist in her recognizes both the futility of making such conceptual distinctions and the severely limiting project of establishing the "true" identity and originality of the subject matter—or of authorial subjectivity, permeated as it is by the polyphonic voices of the community which resonate throughout the text and thereby reflect different narrative stances, different points of view on life and on Zora herself.[12] Indeed, since "no two moments are any more alike than two snowflakes" there is no inconsistency in presenting a multitude of personae and being nonetheless sincere. As a well-known folk aphorism puts it, "Li'l flakes make de deepest snow," or what appears to be homogeneous is in fact a complicated layering of vastly disparate elements.

The chapter "Seeing the World as It Is" emphasizes her intentions and method: "I do not wish to close the frontiers of life upon my own self. I do not wish to deny myself the expansion of seeking into individual capabilities and depths by living in a space whose boundaries are race and nation. Clearly here, race and nation are singled out as colonizing signs produced by an essentializing and controlling power external to the inner self and bent on denying her access to "spaces" other than the ones to which she ostensibly belongs by virtue of her concrete situation. Her free-spirit call for "less race consciousness" is to be understood in the context of her unabashed denunciation of "democracy" as just another name for selfish profiteering by the West at the expense of those "others" who live far away from the so-called democratic nations of Europe and America. These subversive and politically anarchic statements—which provoked the Procrustean editing of the autobiography—are the logical consequence of the ethnographer's skepticism. Because she remains radically *critical* without proposing positive and totalizing alternatives, she exemplifies a truly philosophical sensibility:[13] her urge to ask questions rather than propose solutions is a hallmark of the kind of attentiveness which alone will invite and provoke her readers to think beyond the commonplaces and received ideas of our cultures, beyond those proverbial voices of the community, *vax populi, oui-dire*, Heideggerian *Gerade* or Barthesian *bêtise*—always rendered in free indirect speech—which enunciate the webs of beliefs that structure local consciousness of self.[14] Reporting those quotidian voices, she establishes cultural context, but by her skeptical detachment, she proceeds to undermine the gregarious values of the group, be it those of the folk community (involved in "specifying", in "adult double talk," and whose verbal creativity is nonetheless celebrated) or the social consensus which articulates interdictions and contradictions of all sorts ("This book-reading business was a hold-back and an unrelieved evil"; "Not only is the scholastic rating at Howard high, but tea is poured in the manner!"; "If it was so honorable and glorious to be black, why was it the yellow-skinned people among us had so much prestige?"). These "common" values are now made available for parody. She thus opens up a space of resistance between the individual *(auto-)* and the collective *(-ethno-)* where the writing *(-graphy)* of singularity cannot be foreclosed.

Yet, a nagging question remains: how can Hurston's historical, embodied self, subject to the determinants of time and place—a Black American woman confronting racism and a world war—represent the site of a privileged resistance to those webs of belief which might encourage resentment and fixation on an unjust and painful past? As she puts it: "To me, bitterness is the under-arm odor of wishful weakness. It is the graceless acknowledgment of defeat." Since both the perpetrators and the immediate victims of slavery are long dead, and since she has "no personal memory of those times, and no responsibility for them," she affirms that she would rather "turn all [her] thoughts and energies on the present." This affirmation of life against "the clutching hand of Time" is a creative release from the imposition of origin and the prison of history. Zora becomes a joyful Zarathustra whose world is no longer limited and bound by the reality principle and who advocates deliverance from the spirit of revenge. But can this visionary posture of the self-portraitist allow for a positive involvement in the shaping of reality, present and future? How can it be reconciled with the anthropological claim to locally-specific knowledge and with the historical novelist's success in drawing the suggestive allegorical fresco of a mythic Afro-Mediterranean past in *Moses, Man of the Mountain*?

Since Fanon too denounced revenge and fixation on the past as "a crystallization of guilt," perhaps he can provide the answer to the question we ask of Hurston. If resentment is the essence of negative potentiality for the self, it is clear why Hurston rejects it outright: she wants the utmost freedom in "seeking into individual capabilities." Her refusal to adopt the "herd" mentality for the sake of solidarity actually places her in a long tradition of thinkers, all essayists or masters of hyperbolic aphorisms: Heraclitus, Montaigne, Nietzsche, Walter Benjamin, Frantz Fanon and Roland Barthes. Fanon, in particular, was well aware of the peculiarly *racial* dilemma facing the children of the colonialist diaspora; their marginality could not simply be articulated in terms of binary categories of black versus white. Fanon's plea against racialist attitudes thus echoes Hurston's reformulation of freedom and responsibility on a planetary scale:

> I as a man of color do not have the right to hope that in the white man there will be a crystallization of guilt toward the past of my race. [. . .]
> I find myself—I, a man—in a world where words wrap themselves in silence; in a world where the other endlessly hardens himself. [. . .]
> I am not a prisoner of history. I should not seek there for the meaning of my destiny.
> I should constantly remind myself that the real *leap* consists in introducing invention into existence.
> It is through the effort *to recapture the self and to scrutinize the self,* it is through the lasting tension of their freedom that men will be able to create the ideal conditions of existence for a human world (my italics).

The wish to "create . . . ideal conditions of existence" is synonymous here with the fight against all petit bourgeois mental habits which tend to favor manifestations of closure. Fanon wants to demythologize history and prevent it from being used as the source of "reactional" behavior because, as "Nietzsche had already pointed out," and as he himself elaborates, "there is always resentment in a *reaction.*" While severely criticizing his fellow colonized intellectuals for simply reproducing the values of the colonizer and adopting racialist thinking, Fanon did not hesitate to state that the quest for disalienation must be mediated by the refusal to accept the "Tower of the Past" and the problems of the present as definitive, in other words, by the belief that only the poetry of the future can move and inspire humans to action and to revolution. Unlike Fanon, Hurston did not develop the visionary perspective into a revolutionary one, but her mystical desire to be one with the universe stems from a similar utopian need for a "waking dream"[15] of the possible which might inspire us to see beyond the constraints of the here and now to the idealized vision of a perfect future—albeit, in *Dust Tracks*, a life after death in which the substance of her being is again "part and parcel of the world" and "one with the infinite." Both Fanon and Hurston suggest that we urgently need to retrieve those past traditions which can become the source of reconciliation and wholeness: it is more important to learn from those traditions than to dwell on pain and injustice.

For Hurston, the tensions involved in "the effort to recapture . . . and to scrutinize the self" is a project grounded in the quicksand of linguistic performance and thus inseparable from what Beaujour has called "a type of memory, both very archaic and very modern, by which the events of an individual life are eclipsed by the recollection of an entire culture." As M. M. J. Fischer has stressed, ethnic memory is not only past-, but future-, oriented.[16] The dynamics of interpersonal knowledge within the intercultural strands of memory define the project of self-portraiture for Hurston, since to recapture the past is literally to create a new field of knowledge within her academic discipline: ". . . if science ever gets to the bottom of Voodoo in Haiti and Africa, it will be found that some important medical secrets, still unknown to medical science, give it its power, rather than the gestures of ceremony."[16] By suggesting historically valid mythological connections between ancient deities and prophets such as Isis and Persephone on the one hand, and Damballah, Thoth and Moses on the other, and between those figures and the "two-headed" magicians of Hoodoo who know the creative power of words, Hurston leaves the door open for a historical re-vision, both of Hoodoo religion and of Antiquity, implying "two-headed" origins in Egyptian and Greek contexts for both Euro- and Afro-Americans. Because such a thesis would have been rejected by contemporary scholars who then followed the "Aryan model" of Antiquity, Hurston can only allude to it through literature.[17]

A comparison of the thematic similarities in her work does show that she was quite consciously using those ancient "personae" as multiple facets of her own self and of her own Afro-Mediterranean genealogy. One of her first published stories, "Drenched in Light," is the story of "Isis Watts," a protagonist who is clearly autobiographical, as is "Isis Potts" of *Jonah's Gourd Vine*. This same persona is reintroduced in *Dust Tracks* under the name of "Persephone." The similarity of the protagonists suggests that the three narratives form a triptych: it is only when taking into consideration the mythological background of the protagonists' names that we can accurately understand the process of self-discovery through self-invention which characterizes Hurston's method. Tellingly, this process is a search for familial and maternal connections, for "mirrors" which can reflect positive aspects of the past instead of being the alienating images of subaltern faces.

The Shuttle of Persephone: Self-portraiture and Death

It is thus significant that the only events of her "private" life on which Hurston dwells in *Dust Tracks* are those which acquire deep symbolic and cultural value: the death of the mother and subsequent dispersion of the siblings echo the collective memory of her people's separation from Africa-as-mother and their ineluctable diaspora. That is why Kossola/ Cudjo Lewis' story emblematizes her own sense of bereavement and deprivation: "After seventy-five years, he still had that tragic sense of loss. That yearning for blood and cultural ties. That sense of mutilation. It gave me something to think about." Narrated at the end of the "Research" chapter, the embedded narrative of Kossola's life serves as a powerful counterpoint to Zora's own story of strife and reconciliation with her brothers. It is thanks to her research and professional travels that she becomes, like the legendary isis of Egyptian mythology, the link which reunites, reconnects the dispersed siblings who can now "touch each other in the spirit if not in the flesh." The imagery which describes the disintegration of the family unit is a clear reminder of the historic conditions of the Middle Passage:

> I felt the warm embrace of kin and kind for the first time since the night after my mother's funeral, when we had huddled about the organ all sodden and bewildered, with the walls of our home suddenly blown down. On September 18th, that house had been a hovering home. September 19th, it had turned into a bleak place of desolation with unknown dangers creeping upon us from unseen quarters that made of us a whimpering huddle, though then we could not see why. But now that was all over.

As private experiences echo collective ones and punctuate the deployment of the self-portrait, a picture of the field worker as keeper of important knowledge, as go-between whose role is to faciliate the articulation of collective memory, emerges. By foregrounding the fact that the field research is the causal link to an empowering reunion with her scattered siblings, Hurston makes a narrative move which has much broader implications for the social lives of Afro-Americans. She implies that connections to the past must not be severed if we are to regain a sense of what "touch[ing] each other in the spirit" can be like, but also that a sense of history must not simply be allowed to degenerate into the remembrance of paralyzing images. That is why she also remarks that "any religion that satisfies the individual urge is valid for that person," since ancient traditions such as Hoodoo contain "the old, old mysticism of the world in African terms," are useful to a "thick description"[18] of cultural nuances, and help demarcate the historical context relevant to the study of folklore.

Hurston's aim is to maintain the integrity of black culture without diluting it and to celebrate its values, while remaining critical of those pressures from within the "family" which can mutilate individual aspirations—as her oldest brother Bob had been guilty of doing to her when she went to live with him hoping that he would help put her through school, only to find herself playing the role of maid to his wife. It is this *de facto* lack of solidarity among "brothers" which Hurston observes and which forms the basis for her critique of a blanket endorsement of simpleminded, universal "Race Solidarity." The text of *Dust Tracks* thus shuttles between appreciation and opprobrium, finding its impetus in the joyful affirmation of its contradictions. To recall the past in order to transcend it, Fanon will also point out, is the only emancipatory stance we can confidently adopt without risk of falling prey to reactionary forces.

Thus, the chapter entitled "Religion," reveals Hurston's total indifference to the "consolation" traditional religion affords: "I am one with the infite and need no other assurance." Her style subverts the need for such "organized creeds" which are but "collections of words around a wish," and which Fanon will denounce as the motor of a "closed society . . . in which ideas and people are in a state of decay" (my translation here).[19] Comfortable in the knowledge that the whole world is in a Heraclitean flux of becoming, Hurston affirms a principle of eternal change based in her observation of the radical fluidity of inorganic, organic, social and cultural forces:

> I have achieved a certain peace within myself, but perhaps the seeking after the inner heart of truth will never cease in me. [. . .] So, having looked at the subject from many sides, studied beliefs by word of mouth and then *as they fit into great rigid forms, I find I know a great deal about form, but little or nothing about the mysteries I sought as a child* [. . .] But certain things have seemed to me to be true as I heard the tongues of those who had speech, and listened at the lips of books. [. . .] The springing of the yellow line of morning out of the misty deep of dawn, is glory enough for me. I know that nothing is destructible; things merely change forms (my italics).[20]

Poetic speech has now replaced the folk idiom, the artist, the anthropologist. The distinction between form and content ("mysteries") is again made, but then put under erasure: "things merely change forms" and content is never lost; yet knowledge of content is determined by the "great rigid forms" which structure the universe while veiling the motley appearance of "matter." These allegories of death and rebirth, change and permanence, temporality and eternity map retroactively the territory of the autobiographical text and the life it attempts to represent. By retracing those ephemeral "dust tracks" which the trajectory of the table of contents surveys, Hurston seems to spiral out into infinity and the cosmos: "The cosmic Zora emerges" (How it feels . . .). Her journey, like that of the storytellers who never leave the porch, is an itinerary through language, "a journeying by way of narrating."[21] That is why it is impossible to make, on a theoretical level, "any clear-cut division between theme and form, between journey as geography and journey as narrative." The "curve in the road" at which Hurston sees her first "vision" is a mythical point of departure for the global adventure during which she will learn to take distance from the "tight chemise" and the "crib of negroism" which have shaped her. Distance alone can enable her to recognize and assemble the fragments of her changing folk culture in the New World, and because she is dealing with familiar territory, she does not run the risk of subjugating the "other" to her self, of making them into marionettes for the benefit of those patrons who are only interested in the static "primitive" aspects of her research. Being engaged in a truly dialogical enterprise, and not in the delusions of Boasian "pure objectivity" to which she alludes ironically, she can negotiate the terms of her insertion within and without the ethnographic field, and even parody popular beliefs with impunity: the jokes comes naturally with the territory of storytelling.

Similarly, the discursive enterprise of self-portraiture is a process of collecting and gathering, of assembling images and metaphors to portray a figural self, always already caught in entropy and in permanent danger of returning to "dust," of becoming again "part and parcel" of the universe. In what follows, then, I would like to examine briefly the textual mechanism which generates the journey of ethnic self-scrutiny, the slippage between particular and universal, individual and collective, daughter and mother(s), the self and its mythologies. In describing these displacements, I want to show how the collective functions as a silverless mirror, capable of absorbing the self into a duplicitous game where one code—singularity—is set aslant by another—syncretic unity with the universe, thus preventing narrative closure.[22] The tensions which are at work in *Dust Tracks* between these two sets of expectations are not simply resolvable through (ethnographic) narrative moves: they constitute what Stephen Tyler has called the proper domain of "post-modern ethnography," "neither the upward spiral into the Platonic . . . realm of conscious thought and faceless abstraction . . . nor the descent 'beneath the surface' into the Plutonic 'other of separation'."[23] Hurston's approach to the study of culture indeed prefigures the future trend of the discipline as outlined by Tyler:

> The ethnographic text will . . . achieve its purposes not by revealing them, but by making purposes possible. It will be a text of the physical, the spoken, and the performed, an evocation of quotidian experience, a palpable reality that uses everyday speech to suggest what is ineffable, not through abstraction, but by means of the concrete. It will be a text to read not with the eyes alone, but with the ears in order to hear 'the voices of the pages'."

Hurston too captures the voices of the people and relays them through the "lips of books" which do not "announce" their purpose but braid "palpable reality" with the incommensurable, the quotidian with the ineffable. She makes it possible to envisage purposive, enabling and empowering structures of meaning that do not coerce the subject into historically and Eurocentrically determined racial metaphors of the self. She succeeds in tracing a map of her territory—a symbolic geography—by using the same accomodating principles which governed the expedient building of roads over the winding path of the foot trail between Orlando and Maitland: the metaphor of the road which curves effortlessly around "the numerous big pine trees and oaks" reinforces a principle of flexibility, a respect for nature rather than the need to dominate it, a pliability which connotes the plasticity of human forms, the capacity to undergo mutations, to endure and survive hardships in that middle passage from birth to death, from mud to dust.

The allegory of the voyage which is only a return to one's point of departure is already present in the first chapter, "My Birthplace." The "three frontier-seekers" who embark for Brazil only to return to the US prefigure Hurston's journeying through Black folklore in order to rediscover the "geography . . . within," the lost community of her child-hood in "a pure Negro town!." Her search for an originary plenitude is the universal biblical "return to dust" at the end of the road of life—not the romantic nostalgia for a prelapsarian time of innocence. In that respect, the death of her mother represents the first moment in a chain of destablizing experiences which undermine forever her sense of belonging to a specific place:

> That hour began my wanderings. Not so much in geography, but in time. Then not so much in time as in spirit.
> Mama died at sundown and changed a world. That is, the world which had been built out of her body and her heart. Even the physical aspects fell apart with a suddenness that was startling.

The death scene of the speechless mother becomes the motivating factor for writing, for the effort of self-fashioning which is also an effort to stave off death: Hurston's wandering phase will be the result of this experience of absence and loss which is repeated on different levels throughout the next chapters. The narrator attempts to fill the void of death by journeying *and* by narrating.

That is why it is interesting to note that the description of the mother's death in *Dust Tracks* closely parallels the fictional rendering of that scene in *Jonah's Gourd Vine*. Telling details are repeated almost word for word: "I could see the huge drop of sweat collected in the hollow at Mama's elbow and it hurt me so" and "Isis saw a pool of sweat standing in a hollow at the elbow"; "I thought that she looked to me. [. . .] I think she was trying to say something, and I think she was trying to speak to me" and "Isis thought her mother's eyes followed her and she strained her ears to catch her words." "Isis" is indeed the fictional alter ego that Hurston chooses for herself, the name of an ancient Egyptian goddess who wandered the world in search of her dismembered brother, a mythical representation of interiority as experience of death. In Egyptian mythology, Isis's brother Osiris is both the god of fertility (like Demeter/ Ceres in the Greco-Roman myth) and the king and judge of the dead. He is also the companion of Thoth, god of death and of writing, who helps him preside in the underworld. Hurston thus makes an implicit connection between the Osirian mysteries which were tied to the cult of the dead and of which Isis was the high priestess, and the occult practices of Hoodoo of which Hurston herself became an initiate. Having flippantly named herself the "queen of the niggerati"[24] in one of her histrionic moments among her New York friends, Hurston then proceeded to develop (in the autobiographical triptych) in a mythically accurate and artistically sensible manner the theme of a life lived in the shadow of Isis/ Persephone, queens of the underworld, of the "dark realm" of otherness. The persona "Isis"—both the goddess and the fictional daughter of Lucy Potts—is like the mirror which figures prominently in the mother's death scene. She is an image of memory and interiority, an "other" who focuses, cristallizes and gives sharp contours to the project of self-invention. She is an important thread in the process of re-membering one's past and one's own mortality as one pays hommage to the dead and departed. Here, the folk custom of veiling the mirror (so that the dead may rest in peace and not trouble the living) is implicitly criticized: the dying mother suggests that the mirror should not be veiled if the past, and the faces of our mothers in it, are to leave their imprint on the memory of the living so that *we* may live in peace with history, and be thus able to "think back through our mothers," as Virginia Woolf believed it was important for women to be able to do.[25]

What the death scene allegorizes then is Hurston's subtle and complex view of the relationship of individuals to culture and history: some elements of culture, because they are unexamined traditions, "village customs," "mores," upheld by the voices of patriarchy (the "village demes" or phallic women, and the father, who together prevent her from fulfilling her mother's wishes), are destructive and stultifying. The child's (Isis' and Zora's) experience of anxiety and guilt is the result of those unexamined cultural myths who thwart the mother's desire to remain imprinted on the daughter's memory. As Adrienne Rich has put it: "the loss of the daughter to the mother, the mother to the daughter, is the essential female tragedy."[26] The loss entailed because of the patriarchal customs of the "village" is a painful enactment of separation and fragmentation, of lost connections to the mother as symbols for a veiled and occulted historical past. As both Albert Memmi and Frantz Fanon will point out, our problem as colonized people is that we all suffer from collective amnesia. The self-portrait which Hurston draws in *Dust Tracks* is the performance of an anamnesis: not self-contemplation but a painstaking effort to be the voice of that occluded past, to fill the void of collective memory.

Indeed, Zora feels that her mother "depended on [her] for a voice," and in *Dust Tracks* she chooses the mythical Persephone as alter ego: the Greek word for voice is *phone* and the scene of the mother's death is symbolic of the daughter's responsibility to articulate her story, to exhume it from the rubble of patriarchal obfuscation. Martin Bernal has pointed out that the Eleusinian story of Demeter searching for Persephone has its roots in the Egyptian myth of Isis and Osiris.[27] By identifying with Persephone in *Dust Tracks*, Hurston makes a brilliant and sophisticated rapprochement between the two myths—a connection, says Bernal, that classicists who follow the "Aryan model" of antiquity have studiously avoided to make. Hurston approaches Afro-Mediterranean Antiquity with the intuitions of the anthropologist who sees connections where traditional classical scholarship had not.

The displacement from Isis to Persephone as choice of objective persona is significant in helping us understand Hurston's feeling of being an orphan, of being cut off from her origins or *arche*. "Isis" is the wanderer who conducts her research, establishes spatio-temporal connections among the children of the diaspora, and re-members the scattered body of folk material so that siblings can again "touch each other." "Persephone," on the other hand, is not a rescuer, but rather a lost daughter whose mother searches for her with passion: an ambiguous figure "with her loving and hellish aspects."[28] Ironically, it is Zora's reading of the Greco-Roman myth ("one of [her] favorites") during the visit of two white women at her school that attracts attention to her brilliance and configures her later "rescue" by other white mentors, friends who become surrogate mothers (as is Helen in "Drenched in Light"). If, as Ronnie Scharfman has noted,[29] "mirroring" and "mothering" are twin terms for defining the reciprocal nurturing bonds which a female subject needs in order to feel anchored in the tradition linking her to her mother(s), then Zora's vain efforts to prevent the veiling of the mirror in the mother's room must be understood as an allegorical attempt to look into the mirror of her mother's soul, to retain severed connections, to recapture and to "read" the dark face of the mother in the silverless mirror of the past, and to become the voice that bridges generations. Those efforts also prefigure her professional predicament as an adult: Persephone was the queen of Pluto's dark realm of the dead, but she also travelled back and forth between the underworld and "the sunlit earth," like Hurston who retrieves the voices of her black culture in order to call her readers "back to primal ground." Caught between the upper and the lower realms, the black and the white world, life and death, she bridges the tragic gap of separation by writing: "l'autoportrait tente de réunir les deux mondes séparés de la vie et de la mort."

Her description of a ceremony in which she participates in New Orleans draws the obvious parallels: "I had to sit at the crossroads at midnight in complete darkness and meet the devil, and make a compact. There was a long, long hour as I sat flat on the ground there alone and invited the King of Hell." Since we also know that fasting was an essential part of her initiation, the parallel with Persephone is even more convincing, as Persephone's fate was to be Pluto's queen for three months of each year because "she had bitten the pomegranate." Cleansing by fasting is of course a common part of initiatory practices in numerous religions and underscores Hurston's philosophy of the universal oneness of religious symbolisms.

When the child's experience of absence, in *Dust Tracks*, becomes specifically racial, we have a new and negative dimension to the metaphor of the mirror. As she puts it, "Jacksonville made me know that I was a little colored girl." This discovery of the ethnic self as mirrored by the other, the white culture of Jacksonville, functions in the text as another moment of anarchic self-discovery. The image reflected in the mirror of white culture is like the photograph on which Janie, in *Their Eyes Were Watching God*, cannot recognize herself because she does not yet know that she is colored, that for the white family who calls her "Alphabet," she is different because she symbolizes namelessness, darkness, absence and lack. This is Janie's first experience of difference: that of her face as a bad photograph, as a "negative" and a flaw in the developed picture she holds in her hand. This scene of non-recognition, like the deathbed scene, is the primal motivation for the journey of self-discovery through language. Isis, Persephone, Thoth and Osiris are thus the four poles which mark the perimeter of Hurston's cultural mythology of the self. Thoth's gift links writing to death and to immortality; here the threads of memory and narrative allow Janie/Zora to "[pull] in her horizon like a great fish-net" in which the fragments of a faceless past are reassembled and given new names, new origins.

When we look at the allegory of the veiling of the mirror in *Dust Tracks* in the context of those similar scenes in the novels, a very strong statement about the self and its enabling and distorting mirrors emerges. The idea that a mirror can be the vehicle of a negative self-image (depersonalization and loss) seems to be tied to two cultural myths, perceived as destructive and debilitating by the child: the patriarchal folk belief about mirrors and death; and the white culture's myths about blackness as radical otherness and absence. In both cases, reflections are void, absent or distorted because they emanate from a reductionist context: the realities of a culture's myths about death and otherness become a burden and a distortion of the historical metaphors by which women must learn to live if we are to recapture the faces of our mothers in the mirrors of the past. It is by uncovering those mirrors that we can begin to articulate connections to ancient and empowering symbols of femaleness. Hence the anguish of the child at not being able to fend off the voices of white and black patriarchy which rob her forever of the peace which comes from seeing the face(s)—and knowing the mythical name(s)—that connect her to a cultural tradition not grounded only in darkness and silence. As Beaujour says, "l'autoportrait se construi[t] autour d'une structure absente: lieux évanouis, harmonies défaites." The experience of death generates the writing of a self-portrait through which appears, pentimento, the mother's lost face.

The child who leaves Eatonville after her mother's death experiences alterity and dislocation, distances herself forever from the illusory possibility of an unexamined and unmediated participation in the network of relations which constitute culture. In effect, her avocation as anthropologist starts right then and there: her exile from Eatonville is the first step on the nomadic road of lore collecting, a road where "le sujet se cherche des semblables tout en affirmant sa différence absolue." That is why the collective voice is so often relayed with irony and pathos: the self-portrait is the medium of subversion par excellence which relativizes the fetishistic recourse to a foundational world beyond its discourse. It evokes the ethnic reality of which it partakes, but in so doing puts into question the mimetic principles of description and classification which inform its writing. It thus simultaneously demystifies the writing of both the life (auto) and the culture (ethno) because it involves the self and its cultural contexts in a dialogue which transcends all possibility of reducing one to the other:

> Miroir du sujet et miroir du monde, miroir du JE se cherchant à travers celui de l'univers: ce qui pouvait d'abord passer pour un simple rapprochement, ou pour une analogie commode, se révèle à l'examen comme une isotopie sanctionnée par la tradition rhétorique et par l'histoire des lettres.

Beaujour's formulation can be applied with an important modification: it is not the medieval rhetorical tradition which furnishes the topics of mimesis, but the anthropological essay with its system of categories which locate culture at the nexus of history and geography, religion and myth, as mentioned above. What this means for the "self-portrait" according to Beaujour is that writing is engendered primarily by the *impossibility* of self-presence, by the realization that realist narratives are functionally distorting and that myths are more appropriately evocative and suggestive of a subject's liminal position in the world of discursive representation.

Here, a myth of ancient Afro-Mediterranean folklore establishes the parameters according to which Hurston will go on performing the role of daughter after her mother's death and until they can both be syncretically reunited. The faceless woman encountered on a porch in Jacksonville during a school walk, and "who looked at a distance like Mama" prefigures the last of her twelve "visions": the two women, one young (herself?), one old (the mother?), whose faces are averted as they are "arranging some queer-shaped flowers such as [she] had never seen." This indirect allusion to the funeral flower—the narcissus—is also the figure of the self reflected in the pool of language, the dark ("miroirs d'encre") medium of self-knowledge, the white (the narcissus) symbol of death's attraction. It is an unformulated, unnamed, but richly suggestive allusion to the desire for the absent mother which will be reenacted both in the bonds of female friendships (the visitors at the school, Big Sweet, Fannie Hurst, Ethel Waters, the Dahoman Amazons, etc.) and in those of hatred or rivalry with other women (her stepmother and knife-toting "Lucy").[30] At once Persephone and Narcissus, the autobiographical narrator attempts to recapture the (m)other in the self and the self through the (m)other:[31]

> Once or twice I saw the old faceless woman standing outdoors beside a tall plant with that same off-shape white flower. She turned suddenly from it to

welcome me. I knew what was going on in the house without going in, it was all so familiar to me.

I never told anyone around me about these strange things. It was to different. They would laugh me off as a story-teller. Besides, I had a feeling of difference from my fellow men, and I did not want it to be found out.

Her experiences of singularity and difference are intimately connected to her visions of death. Not surprisingly, the reference to "Pluto's dark realm" and to the temporary reunification of Persephone with her mother turns upside down the circumstances of her life and transforms the past by reorienting it toward an unlived future where the lost potentialities of love and daughterhood are given a second chance and an elusive possibility of peace and transfiguration:

I stood in a world of vanished communion with my kind, which is worse than if it had never been. Nothing is so desolate as a place where life has been and gone. I stood on a soundless island in a tideless sea.

Time was to prove the truth of my visions . . . bringing me nearer to the big house, with the kind women and the strange white flowers."

If the mother is a figure for the "lost" potentialities of history and for the "dark" continent of Africa, it is not surprising that images of death and decay begin to pervade her self-recollection during those years of loneliness and wandering in which she feels "haunted." Just like "Lazarus after his resurrection," she cannot experience her own self in a unified way, since past and present, mind and body can never coincide completely: "I walked by my corpse. I smelt it and felt it. I smelt the corpses of those among whom I must live, though they did not. They were as much at home with theirs as death in a tomb." Like the Zombies she will later study, she is a living-dead whose childhood memories of that time—between ten and fourteen years of age—is the undeveloped photographic negative of the singular images of blankness which keep recurring in later chapters: for instance, her first love affair, although it provides the closeness and warmth she had sorely missed ever since her mother's death, turns into an oppressive relationship which imprisons her inside feelings of doubt and unreality that cannot be shared with the husband: "Somebody had turned a hose on the sun. What I had taken for eternity turned out to be a monument walking in its sleep. [. . .] A wind full of memories blew out of the past and brought a chilling fog."

Numbed by the impossibility to communicate, life is drained out of her, and she buries herself in her work. The next time she falls in love, the pattern seems to repeat itself. She is thwarted by the conflicts caused by her career, the man's possessiveness and his complaints that her "real self had escaped him": she is not permitted to have a life of her own, is retrained by limiting circumstances, "[c]aught in a fiendish trap." Love is never experienced as an empowering force—unlike friendship, this "mysterious and ocean-bottom thing" without which life is not worth much: "to live without friends is like milking a bear to get cream for your morning coffee." In contrast to the flatness of her lovelife, her affective landscape is peopled with many picturesque and vivid portrayals of friends. The topic of "friendship" is a much richer and more satisfying one than "love," and the treatment it receives in *Dust Tracks* bears testimony to the importance that self-portraitists have accorded to the interface with an "other" whose ambivalent companionship may be the spur which compells a writer to articulate the potentialities of his or her vision.[32] "Conversation is the ceremony of companionship," Ethel Waters says: the self-portrait is a conversation with the past, a ceremony for the dead mother(s), but one which simultaneously empowers the living.

The narrator also experiences singularity as separation from the realm of nature. After her departure to Jacksonville, her introduction to formal education goes together with another deprivation which adds to her grief and mourning: "the loving pine, the lakes, the wild violets in the woods and the animals [she] used to know" are no longer part of her daily life. Orphaned for a second time when her father asks the school to "adopt" her, and she is nonetheless sent home on the riverboat, and experiences a thrilling form of rebirth because she is again part and parcel of nature:

> The water life, the smothering foliage that draped the river banks, the miles of purple hyacinths, all thrilled me anew. The wild thing was back in the jungle.
> The curtain of trees along the river shut out the world so that it seemed that the river and the chugging boat was all that there was, and that pleased me a lot.

The floating boat and the trees which "shut out the world" are like the protective layers of a womb; the boat's chugging motor connotes a maternal heartbeat, a reassuring companion which spells the return to an earlier form of peace and harmony. These layered allusions to the archaic times of a prenatal life and the historical moments of preslavery days in Africa again form the mother as the sheltering presence. Her disappearance generates the nomadic search for collective meanings that will establish a system of resonance between seemingly heterogeneous entities or "topics," such as daughterhood, friendship, nature and antiquity. All of these topics can be seen as so many inaugurating moments of similarity within difference, of self-absorption in an enigmatic mirror: the Augustinian "per speculum in aenigmate," which is contrasted and paralleled with death itself, the "face that reflects the face of all things, but neither changes itself, nor is mirrored anywhere."

Later on, when working as a maid for the soprano of the travelling opera company, Zora becomes a kind of mascot for the whole company and her writing career gets started: "I got a scrapbook . . . and wrote comments under each picture. . . . Then I got another idea. I would comment on daily doings and post the sheets on the call-board. . . . The results stayed strictly mine less than a week because members of the cast began to call me aside and tell me things to put in about others . . . It was just my handwriting, mostly." She becomes the repository of other people's words, a kind of transparent mind or ghost writer: another form of Zombiehood, mediated by the acquisition of language, by the absorption of other voices, just like all that "early reading" which had given her "great anguish through all [her] childhood and adolescence" because as she puts it, "My soul was with the gods and my body in the village. People just would not act like gods." Her experiences at school, in Baltimore, follow the same pattern: "And here I was, with my face looking like it had been chopped out of a knot of pine wood with a hatchet on somebody's off day, sitting up in the middle of all this pretty." Unde-fined features, "a woman half in shadow": the self-portraitist draws a picture of herself which remains "a figure in bas relief,"[33] an intaglio, "l'entrelacement d'une anthropologie et d'une thanatographie"

These echoing patterns of disfiguration and death provide an improvi-sational rhythm to the text, giving it the ebb and flow of musical counter-point, and suspending meaning between suggestive similarities which the reader is free to associate or not. One subtle parallel which the text thus draws is between two gruesome events: the decapitation of Cousin Jimmie, "mother's favorite nephew" who had been assassinated before Zora's birth and whose unintentional shooting by a white man had been covered up to look as though a train had killed him and the similar fate which had befallen the son of Kossola/Cudjo, David, who was actually beheaded in a train accident. In both cases, it is the grief of the parental figures which resonates in the text, rather than a hypothetical repetition of real-life events. Indeed, framing as they do Hurston's vision of the two faceless women and Kossola's stories of famed Dahoman Amazons who sack cities and carry "clusters of human heads at their belts," the stories underscore a pattern of singular repetition which would seem to point not to referents beyond the text, but to the allegorical disfiguring of generation upon generation of black individuals whose plight is ignored or covered up, except in the memory of those who grieve for them (as Cudjo's Takkoi King, beheaded by the Amazons, is mourned by his people).

The ephemeral quality of collective memory itself is reflected in the transient nature of Hurston's "first publication": "on the blackboard . . . I decided to write an allegory using the faculty members as characters." The "allegory" is the source of much entertainment and laughter for her schoolmates, a successful rehearsal for her future tale-telling and an important metaphoric hyphen between the immediacy of oral perfor-mance and the permanence of the written words. Like these allegorical portraits which will be erased once they have served their purpose, her twelve visions which were initially meant to structure the deployment of the autobiography are soon forgotten because they do not need to be used. The tale-teller dynamically reshapes her material as she goes along, the content of the visions becoming irrelevant since the essayistic form of the latter chapters ("My People! My People!" "Looking Things Over," "The Inside Light,") spontaneously generate a framework through which to communicate her philosophy.

As she ironically suggests when referring to the religious congregation's telling of their experiences:

> These visions are traditional. I knew them by heart as did the rest of the congregation, but still it was exciting to see *how the converts would handle them. Some of them made up new details. Some of them would forget a part and improvise clumsily or fill up the gap with shouting.* The audience knew, but everybody acted as if every word of it was new" (my italics).

Inconsistencies are inherent to the performance of traditional cultural forms: it is precisely in the way they individually diverge from the set norms that the "converts" excite interest in the "audience." The "origin" of the tradition must be acknowledged but this does not give sanction to simple repetition of form: each new performer signifies upon that origin by transforming it and by allowing for infinite possibilities of permutations. To approach a form genealogically, then, is to attempt to retrace its transformations back to an origin—*arche*—which will always prove elusive since every discrete manifestation is the interpellation of a previous one which sets the stage for the next one, and so on ad infinitum. Whether Hurston's twelve visions signify upon the religious tradition or the vernacular ritual of the "dozens" or both is of no importance since in either case, she can make vicarious use of the clichés, parody some of them, ignore the rest and "tell a story the way [she] wanted, or rather the way the story told itself to [her]." Since "playing the dozens" or "specifying" is a form of invective and name-calling which points genealogically to a fictitious origin—"they proceed to "specify" until the tip-top branch of your family tree has been given a reading"—we can readily infer that this "self-affirming form of discourse"[34] does not require foundational support in reality. It is by virtue of its style of speaking function that it affirms the underlying gutsiness and creativity of the agent of discourse, drawing a portrait of the self as capable of enduring, diverging and surviving because of adhesion to the formal aspects of a cultural tradition which is dynamic and improvisational and allows the storyteller to "keep the tune" for the benefit of the collectivity, to lift the veil on the mirror of a different history, to be a "keeper of memories."

In *Dust Tracks*, we have a clear example of the braiding or *métissage* of cultural forms, since Persephone figures both as the voice of the dead mother and as the boundary crosser who links up two different worlds. Turning upside down the mythical relation between Ceras and her daughter, Hurston invents her own reading of the tradition, "signifying" upon that tradition in a specifically "black" way, diverging from the Greco-Roman text in the only possible way for the Afro-American self-portraitist; to rejoin her mother, Zora/Persephone must travel back to the underworld, to the "dark realm" of her own people, to the friendship with Big Sweet, in order to learn to say what her dying mother could not, in order to name the chain of legendary female figures who can teach her to re-member and to speak the past.

Notes

1. See Hemenway in "Appendix" to *Dust Tracks on a Road*, p. 288.
2. By *genealogical* I mean the reconstruction of the self through interpretations which integrate as many aspects of the past as deemed *significant* by the agent of the narrative discourse. It is clear that Hurston deems cultural forms more significant than specific events. The self which she thus fashions through language is not a fixed essence, partaking of an immutable and originary racial substance. Rather it is a *process* of active self-discovery through self-invention via the folk narratives of ethnic interest. For a recent, thorough and definitive analysis of these Nietzschean questions, see Alexander Nehamas, *Nietzsche: Life as Literature* (Cambridge: Harvard University Press, 1986). David Hoy has done an excellent and very useful review of this book: see "Different Stories" in *The London Review of Books*, 8 January 1987, pp. 15–17. In the Afro-American context, genealogical revisionism is of course a common theme of literature. See Kimberley W. Benston, "'I Yam What I Yam': Naming and Unnaming in Afro-American Literature," *Black American Literature Forum* 16 (Spring 1982) as well as Jahnheinz Jahn, *Muntu: An Outline of the New African Culture* (New York: Grove Press, 1961), p. 125.
3. See also Hemenway's "Introduction," e.g., pp. xxxiv.
4. For an overview of contemporary theories of autobiography, see P. J. Eakin, *Fictions in Autobiography* (Princeton: Princeton University Press, 1985), Chapter 4 in particular.
5. (Paris: Seuil, 1980), p. 348: "texts which are self-contained rather than being representation of past actions."
6. Serres, *The Parasite*, pp. 6–13, "anthro. figurée."
7. in *Writing Culture*, Clifford and Marcus, eds. (Berkeley: University of California Press, 1986), pp. 113–115.
8. See W. L. Andrews, ed., *Sisters of the Spirit*, p. 13. Hurston is not interested in *organized* resistance to patterns of social injustice, which does not imply that she is not strongly critical of injustice: see *Dust Tracks*, pp. 336 ff.
9. This is not the place to engage in a detailed analysis of the methods and assumptions of Hurston's great teacher and mentor, "Papa" Franz Boas. Suffice it to say that as an anthropologist he was a firm believer in "the plasticity of human types": his research on *Changes in Bodily Forms of Descendants of Immigrants*, published in 1911, served to convince him that physical and mental characteristics were not simply inherited but did undergo profound modifications over time and in new sourroundings. Fur-

thermore, his views on "The Race Problem in Modern Society," published in a work which was to be widely influential and of fundamental importance to the field of anthropology, *The Mind of Primitive Man*, could not fail to influence Zora Neale Hurston's own attitudes about the race problem in America, to reinforce her personal tendency toward individualism and to strengthen her belief that humans are infinitely variable and not classifiable into distinctive national or racial categories. As Boas put it, "Our tendency to evaluate an individual according to the picture that we form of the class to which we assign him, although he may not feel any inner connection with that class, is a survival of primitive forms of thought. The characteristics of the members of the class are highly variable and the type that we construct from the most frequent characteristics supposed to belong to the class is never more than an abstraction hardly ever realized in a single individual, often not even a result of observation, but an often heard tradition that determines our judgement" [from *The Mind of Primitive Man*, 1911, cited in Ashley Montagu, *Frontiers of Anthropology* (New York: G. P. Putnam's and Sons, 1974), pp. 320–332]. Boas recognizes the role played by "tradition" and ideology in our construction of the world and his work paves the way for what I would call Hurston's dynamic and contextual approach to culture and to private forms of behavior.

10. See *Mules and Men*, p. 3 and Barbara Johnson, "Thresholds of Difference: Structures of Address in Zora Neale Hurston," in *"Race," Writing, and Difference*, H. L. Gates, Jr., ed. (Chicago: University of Chicago Press, 1985), pp. 317–328.

11. See Houston A. Baker, Jr., *Blues, Ideology, and Afro-American Literature: A Vernacular Theory* (Chicago: University of Chicago Press, 1984), p. 152.

12. See Claudine Raynaud, *"Dust Tracks on A Road:* Autobiography as a 'Lying' Session," forthcoming in *Studies in Black American Literature*. Whereas Raynaud would tend to see the autobiography as founding the self in a gesture of appropriation of the perennial proverbs and sayings of the community, I prefer to see in the text a continuing tension between philosophical skepticism about communal values and visionary creation.

13. It might perhaps be appropriate to add here that Hurston shows a truly "metaphysical" turn of mind on top of her properly "exegetical" talents! See a reference to the Robert Penn Warren and Sterling Brown debate in H. L. Gates, Jr., *Figures in Black* (New York: Oxford University Press, 1987), p. xix. And indeed, Fanon takes up the same relay: the last words of *Black Skin, White Masks* are "O my body, make me always a man who questions!" It is not likely that Fanon either knew or read Hurston, although he was familiar with the work of Langston Hughes, but their accomplishments in *Dust Tracks on a Road* and *Black Skin, White Masks* derive from a parallel need to shake off the totalizing traps of historical determinism, and to do so in a style which is its own message: narrative and aphoristic in order to subvert the cultural commonplaces they both abhor. See also Chester J. Fontenot's study of Fanon and his useful discussion of form and content in *Black Skin, White Masks:* "Visionaries, Mystics and Revolutionaries: Narrative Postures in Black Fiction" in *Studies in Black American Literature*, vol. 1, Joe Weixlmann and Chester J. Fontenot, eds. (Greenwood: Penkevill Annuals, 1983), pp. 63–87.

14. For a detailed discussion of the philosophical and linguistic implications of the "discours indirect libre," see Gilles Deleuze & Félix Guattari, *Mille Plateaux* (Paris: Editions de Minuit, 1980), pp. 95–109.

15. The phrase is Ernst Bloch's. See Anson Rabinbach, "Unclaimed Heritage: Ernst Bloch's *Heritage of Our Times* and the Theory of Fascism," *New*

German Critique 11 (Spring 1977), pp. 5–21. Hurston was familiar with the German philosophical tradition of utopian thinking. She mentions Spinoza for example in *Dust Tracks*, p. 285. See also my comments in note 20 below.

16. See his "Ethnicity and The Post-Modern Arts of Memory" in *Writing Culture*, pp. 194–233.
17. See Martin Bernal's revision of that model in *Black Athena* (London: Free Association Books, 1987).
18. In Clifford Geertz's sense. See *The Interpretation of Cultures*.
19. See Fontenot, art. cit., p. 84 for a discussion of "open" and "closed" society as defined by Fanon.
20. Hurston's Spinozist philosophy is evident here. See B. Spinoza, *Ethics* (n.c.: Joseph Simon, 1981), Part 1, Proposition VIII: "Every subtance is necessarily infinite." As SPR Charter puts it in the Introduction to the above edition, "Spinoza attempted to unite the mind/body complexity and the realities of existence with the all-embracing actuality of Nature, and to do so organically—that is, without the imposition of man-made religious structures."
21. See Alexander Gelley, *Narrative Crossings* (Baltimore: The Johns Hopkins University Press, 1987), p. 31.
22. What I call the silverless mirror here is to some extent assimilable to what Houston A. Baker, Jr. associates with the term "black (w)hole": "a *singularly* black route of escape." See *Op. cit* p. 155. By analogy, it refers also to the covered looking glass in the room of the dying mother: I return to this below.
23. See "Post-Modern Ethnography: From Document of the Occult to Occult Document," in *Writing Culture*, pp. 122–140.
24. See Karla Holloway, *The Character of the Word* (Westport: Greenwood Press, 1987), p. 24.
25. See Jane Marcus, "Thinking Back Through Our Mothers" in *New Feminist Essays on Virginia Woolf* (Lincoln: University of Nebraska Press, 1981), pp. 1–30.
26. *Of Woman Born* (New York: W.W. Norton, 1976) p. 237. Gilbert and Guber's concept of an "anxiety of authorship" due to the lack of a female tradition is highly relevant here.
27. Bernal, pp. 69–73.
28. Bernal, p. 70.
29. See "Mirroring and Mothering in Simone Schwarz-Bart's *Pluie et vent sur Télumée Miracle* and Jean Rhys' *Wide Sargasso Sea*," *Yale French Studies* 62 (1981), 88–106.
30. For an analysis of the "thematic consistency . . . found in these echoing episodes of female strength," see Raynaud, art. cit. On this aspect of the text, I am in complete agreement with Raynaud.
31. See Beaujour's fascinating discussion of the associations between Demeter, Persephone and Narcissus in Greek mythology, and the connections between these divinities and death. His argument is that narcissism as commonly understood in psychoanalytic terminology is a distorted and reductive interpretation of the myth and that far from being "narcissistic" in that sense, "l'autoportrait tente de réunir les deux mondes séparés de la vie et de la mort. [. . .] Narcisse accède par l'anamnèse à . . . l'invention poétique des "souvenirs d'enfance," qui restitue un paradis intemporel: à la fois trésor individuel et topique culturelle." *Op. cit.*, pp. 156–162.
32. Augustine, Montaigne (O un amy!), Gertrude Stein, Christopher Isherwood, Roland Barthes, to name but a few. See Réda Benøsmaïa, *The Barthes Effect: The Essay as Reflective Text* (Minneapolis: University of Minnesota Press, 1987), pp. 62–89 especially.
33. I am using here two phrases of Fannie Hurst's in her "A Personality Sketch"

reprinted in *Zora Neale Hurston*, edited by Harold Bloom (New York: Chelsea House Publishers, 1986), pp. 23, 24. The first one is also the title of Mary Helen Washington's introduction to *I Love Myself When I am Laughing: A Zora Neale Hurston Reader* (New York: The Feminist Press, 1979).

34. See Susan Willis, *Specifying* (Madison: The University of Wisconsin Press, 1987), p. 31.

◆◆◆◆◆◆◆◆◆◆◆◆◆

Seraph on the Suwanee

LILLIE HOWARD

Appearing on October 11, 1948, *Seraph on the Suwanee*[1] was Hurston's last published novel. It was variously called *Angel in the Bed, Sang the Suwanee in the Spring, The Seraph's Man, Good Morning Sun,* and *Sign of the Sun* before Zora settled on *Seraph on the Suwanee.* Because this novel deals with whites instead of the usual black folks, it has led to charges of assimilationism against Hurston. Perhaps, as some critics have suggested, she was following a new trend among black writers like Willard Motley, Chester Himes, and Ann Petry, who avoided concentrating on black characters. She had written to her editor at Scribner's that "it was 'very much by design' that the book had primarily white characters,"[2] and to Carl Van Vechten on November 2, 1942, that "I have hopes of breaking that old silly rule about Negroes not writing about white people. . . . I am working on the story now."[3] That "story" was *Seraph on the Suwanee.* As Hemenway has noted, however, "The peril in deliberately choosing a white subject is considerable. There is nothing which prohibits a black writer from creating successful white characters, and black literature is full of brilliant white portraits. But if the novelist consciously seeks to portray whites in order to validate his talent, to prove to the world there are no limits to his genius, the very assumptions of the decision become self-defeating."[4] Whether *Seraph on the Suwanee* is self-defeating is debatable, but whatever Hurston's reasons for writing *Seraph on the Suwanee,* to her readers she seemed to be turning traitor, deserting the colorful black folks with whom she had hitherto aligned herself.

Robert Bone dismissed the novel as an assimilationist work which was "written less forcibly than *Their Eyes Were Watching God*"[5] while Darwin Turner explained it as "a conscious adjustment to the tastes of a new generation of readers"[6]—readers, presumably, who would no longer tolerate blacks as fictional characters. What these critics have ignored, however, is the fact that Hurston never leaves the folk milieu in *Seraph on the Suwanee.* She does change the color of her characters but she does not change her themes or environment in any significant way. Although Arvay Henson, the novel's heroine, is white, she, like all Hurston protagonists, searches for self-actualization and love, for life-affirming rather than life-denying experiences. White folks, Hurston perceptively realized, must want those things, too.

As early as *Jonah's Gourd Vine* (1934) Hurston had paved the way for such a novel as *Seraph on the Suwanee.* By insisting upon writing her story about "a man" instead of one about the "traditional lay figures" found in protest fiction about the "Negro Problem," Hurston was practicing her philosophy that "Human beings react pretty much the same to the same stimuli. Different idioms, yes, circumstances and conditions having power to influence, yes. Inherent differences, no." She was interested in causal analysis, in "what makes a man or a woman do such-and-so, regardless of his color." In *Seraph on the Suwanee* we have an individual whose reasons for doing "such-and-so" have little to do with the color of her skin and everything to do with the state of her mind, a poor image of self, and a chauvinistic, though extremely loving, husband. In fact, Hurston had written to Burroughs Mitchell, at Scribner's, that she had endowed Arvay with feelings that she herself had once felt: "Though brash enough otherwise, I got an overwhelming complex about my looks before I was grown, and it was very hard for a long time for me to believe that any man really cared for me. I set out to win my fight against this feeling, and I did."[7]

Although the main characters are white and the style not as lively or humorous as is typical in Hurston, *Seraph on the Suwanee*'s subject matter differs little from that of Hurston's other novels. As in most of the other works, including the short stories, the marriage relationship, the search for true love, and the growth of the individual are the main focus. Like Hurston's best novel, *Their Eyes Were Watching God, Seraph on the Suwanee* explores at some length the feminine psyche. Whereas Janie Crawford is in conflict with the traditions and mores of the society in which she lives, however, Arvay Henson is in conflict with herself. Though she genuinely desires love and happiness, like Emmaline of the play *Color Struck*, she does everything in her power to make that love and happiness impossible. She must end this life-denying battle by learning to appreciate and respect her worth as a human being. By the time the novel ends, she has emerged the victor. Having found a comfortable, nurturing spot for herself, she lives.

Other similarities between the two novels are also apparent. The relationship between Arvay and Jim Meserve, her husband, as between Janie and Tea Cake, is tender and strong, sexual and alive. Like Janie, Arvay, who is also a member of the lower class of southern society, seeks love. And, again like Janie, she almost misses true love by adhering to the old, traditional way of life. In this case, Arvay feels bound to her folks who are, in a sense, tradition. Like Tea Cake, Jim courts boldly and charmingly, offering a vitally different life from that to which Arvay had been accustomed. Like both Jody Starks (Janie's second husband) and Tea Cake, Jim devotes himself to providing comfort for his mate, though his philosophy is not always the *carpe diem* one of Tea Cake. Like Jody Starks, Jim continuously seeks bigger and better business ventures.

Seraph on the Suwanee takes place near the turn of this century in various parts of Florida, and unfolds the complex story of Arvay Henson Meserve, a poor white woman of Sawley. At sixteen Arvay renounces the world to become a missionary because her sister Larraine marries the man with whom Arvay imagines herself to be in love. Arvay sees the marriage as an omen that nothing good will ever happen to her. To compound her unhappiness she fantasizes about an adulterous relationship with her sister's husband, and experiences guilt that manifests itself in the form of body spasms. These fits, sometimes real, sometimes simulated, keep all potential suitors at a distance until the manly Jim Meserve arrives in town. By that time, Arvay is twenty-one.

Jim Meserve is a high-class, rakish Irishman who subdues, seduces, and marries Arvay, and takes her away from Sawley to Citrabelle. Though their marriage is occasionally happy, Arvay's feelings of inferiority and self-pity constantly gnaw at the relationship until Jim leaves her to find herself and seek him out. Arvay does so but only after shaking off the shackles of the past and embracing what she considers to be her true role—mothering and serving. The bulk of the book is about Arvay's grail-like quest for self-actualization. Her task is the more difficult because for over twenty years she belittles herself while simultaneously extolling her folks and the backwoods; she lacks the basic understanding and communicative ability necessary to a good marriage, and seeks shelter from the world rather than active involvement in it.

I   "A Cracker Bred, a Cracker Born"

Arvay Henson Meserve is a woman who does not think much of herself. This point is brought painfully home so often in the book that the reader gets as sick of the whining heroine as Hurston got when she wrote the novel.[8] At sixteen she believes that "happiness, love and normal relationships were not meant for her. Somehow, God had denied her the fate of sharing in the common happiness and joys of the world." Even when the manly and highly sought-after Jim Meserve expresses an interest in her, Arvay believes herself undeserving: "Ah, no, this pretty laughing fellow was too far out of her reach. Things as wonderful as this were never meant for nobody like her. This was first-class, and she was born to take other people's leavings." She idolizes Jim in direct proportion to her beratement of self. When Jim mentions marriage, "Arvay began to believe a little in Jim's sincerity. . . . Then a terrible feeling of guilt came over her. Even if Jim meant it, she was not fitten. Here was the most wonderful man in all the world pomping her all up, and she had been living in mental adultery with her sister's husband for all of those wasted years. She was not fitten for a fine man like Jim. He was worth more than she was able to give him." Several years into the marriage she still hopes that she might "come to win this great and perfect man some day."

Arvay is so preoccupied with her "adultery of the mind" that she sees the deformity of Earl, her first child, as "punishment for the way I used to be. I thought that I had done paid off, but I reckon not. I never thought it would come like this, but it must be the chastisement I been looking for." She completely ignores the fact that Earl's condition is hereditary—from her father's side of the family. She must heap the blame for everything upon herself.

Because she thinks so little of herself, Arvay thinks extraordinarily high of Jim Meserve. Not only is he a "perfect man" to her, but often she attributes God-like qualities to him. When Jim first expresses his intentions to marry Arvay, for instance, she thinks:

> But this was like coming through religion. . . . Like your thoughts while you were out at the praying-ground in the depths of the woods, or being down at the mourners'-bench during protracted meetings with the preacher, deacons and all the folks from the Amen corner standing around and over you begging and pleading with you to turn loose your doubting and only believe. Put your whole faith in the mercy of God and believe. Eternal life, Heaven and its immortal glory were yours if you only would believe.

Later, when a posse seeks to destroy Earl, who has gone berserk, the narrator explains Arvay's opinion of Jim:

> But for too many years Arvay had thought of her husband as a being stronger than all others on the earth. What God neglected, Jim Meserve took care of. Between the two, God and Jim, all things came to pass. They had charge of things. She had been praying ever since she had found out that Earl was surrounded in that swamp. So far God had not made a move so it was up to Jim. So now, Arvay went to her husband and hung by her arms around his neck as she sank to her knees beside his chair.

Clearly she is about to offer a prayer to this, her second and perhaps greater, god. Even Jim's kiss on her lips "came as a great mercy and a blessing, and Arvay departed from herself and knew nothing until she came to earth again and found herself in the familiar bed." When she reminisces about the twenty years of marriage with Jim, she recalls that "she had stood for moments on the right hand side of God" and that "the most ordinary minute of peace with Jim in the past appeared like time spent in Paradise."

After realizing that most of the people whom she had envied and looked up to actually envied and looked up to her, Arvay comes to accept that though she was a "Cracker bred and a Cracker born," when she died, there did not have to be merely a "Cracker gone." She had the potential for infinitely more than that.

II *"See Ten Things and Understand None"*

At one point in the novel, Jim excuses Arvay's shortcomings by re-peating what Jody Starks says of women in *Their Eyes Were Watching God*—that men see one thing and understand ten while women "see ten things and can't even understand one." Such an opinion is chauvinistic and unflattering to women everywhere, but Arvay's consistent actions are a poor defense against the charge. Not only must most things be explained to her, but they often must be explained without her seeking an explanation or even knowing that she should. Jim compares her to "an unthankful and unknowing hog under a [*sic*] acorn tree. Eating and grunting with your ears hanging over your eyes, and never even looking up to see where the acorns are coming from." The evidence in favor of Jim's simile is overwhelming and begins to blatantly accumulate when Jim moves his family to Citrabelle, Florida.

In Citrabelle, Arvay only looks at the surface of things and concludes accordingly. She sees the fruit-pickers as "sinfully" living on a flowery bed of ease:

> Things had a picnicky, pleasury look that, while it was pretty, made Arvay wonder if folks were not taking things too easy down in here. Heaven wasn't going to be any refreshment to folks if they got along with no more trouble than this. . . . It was the duty of man to suffer in this world, and these people round down here in south Florida were plainly shirking their duty. They were living entirely too easy.

While Arvay is looking at and judging by appearances, the narrator points out the realities: "She did not know that fruit-cutters seldom worked at all from the end of the season early in June until it opened around the middle of September when they began to cut grapefruit, however short of money they might be." Nor did she know about "the desperate struggle Jim was going through for their very existence." When Jim learns something about citrus-fruit production, acquires a crew, augments the number of boxes the crew cuts by encouraging com-petition among them, and receives a Christmas turkey as a token of appreciation from the packinghouse manager, "Arvay baked it, and they ate it, but she never asked for the story behind it." That the Meserve couple is at odds is made apparent by the narrator's observations:

> Who shall ascend into the hill of the Lord? And who shall stand in His holy place? Arvay thought that it would be herself when and if she could birth Jim a perfect child and by this means tie him forever to her. Jim felt that he would stand on the mount of transfiguration when Arvay showed some appreciation of his love as expressed by what he was striving to do for her. Thus they fumbled and searched for each other in silent darkness. . . . Arvay just had no idea. She had no understanding to what extent she was benefiting from the good will that Jim had been building up ever since he had come to town. She knew nothing of his twisting and turning and conniving to make life

pleasant for her sake. . . . She never asked anything, and so Jim never volunteered to tell her.

Perhaps what best epitomizes Arvay's "deficiencies" is what happens when she is in her third pregnancy. When Jim learns of the pregnancy he playfully tells Arvay, "You can have that baby, providing that you swear and promise me to bring it here a boy." Though Jim believes that "anybody atall would see through a joke like that. Anybody with even a teaspoonful of sense knows that you can't tell what a child'll turn out to be until it gets born," Arvay spends several painful months "muttering prayers for deliverance from her fancied danger" and caressing her stomach in a plea with the unborn child to "be nice, now, and come here a boy-child for your mama. You see the fix I'm in. Jim is liable to leave me if you ain't a boy." Jim is understating when he says, "There was not sufficient understanding in his marriage."

The climax comes when Jim, ever trying to please and solicit praise and appreciation from Arvay, foolishly pits his strength against that of a rattlesnake. He loses the battle and almost loses his life. Because Arvay can only stand and gawk when action is required, Jim decides to leave her. As he explains it,

> "I feel and believe that you do love me, Arvay, but I don't want that standstill, haphazard kind of love. I'm just as hungry as a dog for a knowing and a doing love. You love like a coward. Don't take no steps at all. Just stand around and hope for things to happen out right.
> "Your kind of love, Arvay, don't seem to be the right thing for me. . . . I'm sick and tired of hauling and dragging you along. I'm tired of excusing you because you don't understand. I'm tired of waiting for you to meet me on some high place and locking arms with me and going my way. I'm tired of hunting you, and trying to free your soul. I'm tired. . . . I'm pushing fifty now, Arvay, and no use in me hoping no more. I ever loved married life, but since I've missed it so far, no use in me hoping no further. . . . Oh, we got the proper papers all right, and without a doubt, the folks around the courthouse are more than satisfied. But to come right down to the fact of the matter, you and me have never been really married. Our bonds have never been consecrated. Two people ain't never married until they come to the same point of view. That we don't seem to be able to do, so I'm moving over to the coast tomorrow for good."

Arvay must take the first step toward reconciliation. Before she can do that, however, she must become more communicative, more understanding. The key is back in Sawley.

III Tradition

The town of Sawley, its traditions, and Arvay's perception of them are the trouble with Arvay and her marriage. Though Arvay has always seen herself as a "Cracker," she is secretly proud of her heritage and considers it a vantage point from which to look down upon others, mainly blacks, foreigners, and Northerners. She stubbornly clings to the old ways and allows them to wreak havoc with her life. She often retreats to the Bible for answers—a carryover from her teenage days, since the narrator records no instance of Arvay even attending church after she marries Jim—and dismisses problems as merely in God's plans for her. She must break with her past before she can live her life.

Arvay returns to Sawley when she learns that her mother is terminally ill. The telegram which brings the message seems like a Godsend to her:

> God worked in mysterious ways His wonders to perform. . . . God was taking a hand in her troubles. He was directing her ways. The answer was plain. He meant for her to go back home. This was His way of showing her what to do. The Bible said, "Everything after its own kind," and her kind was up there in the piney woods around Sawley. Her family, and the folks she used to know before she fooled herself and linked up with a man who was not her kind. Arvay tossed her head defiantly and rhymed out that she was a Cracker bred and a Cracker born, and when she was dead there'd be a Cracker gone.

As the narrator indicates, however, Arvay is misinterpreting things again:

> Arvay was conscious at that moment that she had not really been trying to find the answer that Jim expected of her. As always, she had been trying to defend her background and justify it so that Jim could accept it and her along with it. She had been on the defensive ever since her marriage. The corroding poverty of her childhood became a growing virtue, and a state to be desired. Arvay scorned off learning as a source of evil knowledge and thought fondly of ignorance as the foundation of good-heartedness and honesty. Peace, contentment and virtue hung like a rainbow over turpentine shacks and shanties. . . . Arvay felt eager to get back in the atmosphere of her humble beginnings.

When she reaches Sawley, Arvay at first stubbornly clings to the old ways of seeing things. She is distraught to learn that even Sawley has changed: turpentining has been replaced by peanut crops; there are new paved highways, hotels, restaurants, and taxis, none of which, one taxi driver tells Arvay, "the old fogies and dumb peckerwoods" like. Arvay, however, "took sides with the peckerwoods in a timid way." When she expresses her opinion that "in the good old days, the folks in Sawley was good and kind and neighborly," the cab driver belligerently differs:

> "Lady! You must not know this town too good. I moved in here fifteen years ago and I done summered and wintered with these folks. I hauled the mud to make some of 'em, and know 'em inside and out. I ain't seen no more goodness and kind-heartedness here than nowhere else. Such another back-biting and carrying on you never seen. They hate like sin to take a forward step. Just like they was took out their cradles, they'll be screwed down in their coffins."

* * *

When the taxi drops Arvay at the old Henson place she finds appalling corroborative evidence of the driver's statements. The house is dilapidated; her sister Larraine, whom she had envied years before, is "in a ton of coarse-looking flesh, a cheap cotton dress and dirty white cotton stockings"; her brother-in-law Carl, for whom she had renounced the world when she was sixteen, is now clearly "soiled", "heavy-set," "drab," "marred," "chuckle-headed"—"But for 'Raines intervention, she might have been married to Carl. Been the mother of those awful-looking young men and women that he had fathered. Had to get in bed with something like that! Do Jesus!" Arvay begins to renounce the house, the people, their lives.

Larraine and Carl behave so niggardly that it is easy for Arvay to turn her back on them. The house, however, must be burned because it stands between her mulberry tree, beneath which "her real life had begun," and the world. It epitomizes and symbolizes her stifled life:

> Seeing it from the meaning of the tree it was no house at all. It was an evil, ill-deformed monstropolous accumulation of time and scum. It had soaked in so much of doing-without, of soul-starvation, of brutish vacancy of aim, of absent dreams, envy of trifles, ambitions for littleness, smothered cries and trampled love, that it was a sanctuary of tiny and sanctioned vices. Its walls were smoked over with the vapors from dead souls like smokey kerosene lamps. . . . The house had caught a distemper from the people who had lived in it, and had then diseased up people. No, it was no longer just a building. It had caught a soul of its own now. It caught people and twisted the limbs of their minds. . . . How much had it blinded her from seeing and feeling through the years!

After burning the house, Arvay "had made a peace and was in harmony with her life." She has come to the same viewpoint as her husband. Nothing remains but to seek him out and belatedly begin her marriage.

IV   "The Morning" of Arvay's Life

After the timely revelations back in Sawley, Arvay concludes that "Certainly the afternoon of her life was more pleasant than the morning had been." The "morning" had been so unpleasant because it had been full of shelters and havens, all escapes from the realities of life. Even her decision to become a missionary was an attempt to retire from the world.

When Jim first meets Arvay he responds to her pleas to leave her alone with "You need my help and my protection too bad for that. . . . I have to stay with you and stand by you and give my protection to keep you from hurting your ownself too much." Arvay comes to believe him and has "a tremulous desire to take refuge in this man. To be forever warm and included in the atmosphere that he stirred up around him."

Jim throws his "strong arm of protection" around her, all to no avail. He cannot free her soul. Only Arvay can do that. As Moses learns in *Moses, Man of the Mountain*, one individual may not make another free. One must do that for himself. By destroying her shackling past, Arvay breaks free and is finally ready to embrace life. Significantly, this is only made possible when Jim removes his "strong arm of protection." Unsheltered, unprotected, Arvay tackles her past and wins. She is self-sufficient, an individual in her own right. She can now protect Jim, "prop him up on every leaning side." By the end of the novel, the trend has been ironically reversed. Arvay is now hovering Jim: "Inside he was nothing but a little boy to take care of, and he hungered for her hovering. Look at him now! Snuggled down and clutching onto her like Kenny when he wore diapers. Arvay felt such a swelling to protect and comfort Jim that tears came up in her eyes. So helpess sleeping there in her arms and trusting himself to her."

V *Chauvinism*

Unflattering attitudes about women occupy a more prominent position in this novel than in any of the other Hurston works. The view that Hurston has her characters present is the traditional male one, and shows that women have been regarded as brainless, thoughtless, inferior, helpless wretches for many, many years. Early in the novel, Jim rather authoritatively declares that

> women folks don't have no mind to make up nohow. They wasn't made for that. Lady folks were just made to laugh and act loving and kind and have a good man to do for them all he's able, and have him as many boy-children as he figgers he'd like to have, and make him so happy that he's willing to work and fetch in every dad-blamed thing that his wife thinks she would like to have. That's what women are made for.

Believing that "a woman knows who her master is," Jim continues to verbalize his opinions throughout the novel. Before her marriage, Arvay correctly interprets his meaning:

> He had just as good as excused the woman he married from all worry and bother. In so many words he had said, "Love and marry me and sleep with me. That is all I need you for. Your brains are not sufficient to help me with my work; you can't think with me. Putting your head on the same pillow with mine is not the same thing as mingling your brains with mine anymore than crying when I cry is giving you the power to feel my sorrow. You can feel my sympathy but not my sorrow." All in all, that meant that if she married Jim Meserve, her whole duty as a wife was to just love him good, be nice and kind around the house and have children for him.

Jim obviously feels that women are to be subjugated to the will and whim of men. Once when Arvay is particularly irritating, for instance, he orders her to strip. When she tries to cover herself, Jim responds with:

"Don't you move! You're my damn property, and I want you right where you are, and I want you naked. Stand right there in your tracks until I tell you that you can move." When Jim finally "allows" Arvay to get in bed, he "stretched himself full length upon her, but in the same way that he might have laid himself down on a couch."

Even Joe Kelsey, an oppressed minority himself, believes women to be property. When Jim tells of his difficulty understanding Arvay, Joe advises: "Make 'em knuckle under. From the very first jump, get the bridle in they mouth and ride 'em hard and stop 'em short. Theys all alike, boss. Take 'em and break 'em." Joe's advice is very much like Killicks's practice with Janie in *Their Eyes Were Watching God:* Janie's grandmother is right, then, in believing that some men will treat a woman like a spit cup.

When Arvay worries herself sick in fear of giving birth to a girl when Jim has expressed a firm desire to have a boy, Jim excuses her and blames it on her sex:

> Arvay had acted dumb, but what more could you expect? She was a woman and women folks were not given to thinking nohow. It was not in their make-up to do much thinking. That was what men were made for. Women were made to hover and to feel.

Jim Meserve, then, is a chauvinist who believes that a woman's role is to mother and to serve. Even his name—"Me-serve"—emphasizes his attitude. On the other hand, however, Jim's name can mean "Me serve you." Certainly he does serve Arvay, and it soon becomes apparent to everyone but Arvay that he wants more from her than just "loving him good, being nice and kind around the house and having children for him." His name, then, like his attitude, is often ambivalent. Too, Jim seems to need a mother and looks to Arvay to fulfill that need:

> There was something about Arvay that put him in mind of his mother. They didn't favor each other in the face, but there was something there that was the same. Maybe that was what had caught his attention the first time that he had laid eyes on Arvay. Maybe that was why he had never missed his family since he married her. All the agony of his lost mother was gone when he could rest his head on Arvay's bosom and go to sleep at nights.

As far as Jim is concerned, his marriage to Avray will never be a real one until she sees things as he does. By the end of the novel, their views are the same because Avray has come to accept her role as mother. When Jim snuggles up to her in the last scene in the novel, she realizes that

> her job was mothering. What more could any woman want and need?. . . . Jim was hers and it was her privilege to serve him. To keep on like that in happiness and peace until they died together giving Jim the hovering that he needed.

Whether Arvay makes the right decision here is questionable. She has, after all, consciously chosen to mother and serve. And as Robert

Hemenway laments, "Just as Arvay begins to become interesting, she is lost again to domestic service."[9] Perhaps the important thing here, however, is that, for the first time in her life, Arvay has found a place for herself and is totally happy. Jim is happy and their relationship seems complete. Perhaps, then, whatever makes both of them happy and content is the right decision. Too, because Arvay now appreciates her own worth, and has elected a spot that will be nurturing and fulfilling, her potential for growth is greatly increased.

Where Hurston stands on all this is unclear. At times she does seem distantly ironic when she has Arvay ask, "What more could a woman want?" Too, when this novel is compared with *Their Eyes Were Watching God*, contradictions are noticeable. Janie Starks, for instance, chooses not to serve Killicks and Starks, not to conform to their ideas of the subservient role of woman. Perhaps Arvay's decision to serve in *Seraph on the Suwanee* illustrates Hurston's belief that people are individuals— that is, what is right for one is not necessarily right for another. To Hurston, the happiness of the individual is paramount. And, undeniably, Arvay Henson is happy. By contrast, Zora Hurston was never able to put love, mothering or serving before her own career. Though she was married at least twice and involved in a number of love affairs, she always returned, sometimes even escaped, to her career.

The omission of folktales (though some familiar—familiar mostly because of other Hurston works—folk sayings and metaphors are included) makes *Seraph on the Suwanee* an anomaly among Hurston's works. She was obviously moving in a more somber and complex direction in this novel. The language and style are controlled as the reader is given an unrelieved, in-depth view into the mind of a sick woman. No comic relief is forthcoming in this novel; no deceptively simple, engaging style is apparent. The language no longer flows along smoothly and naturally. Rather, it moves slowly and must be read slowly. It is not poetic, as Hurston's language generally is, but is, instead, what Robert Bone would call prosaic and "causes many readers to yearn for the alleviating farce and carefree gaiety of the earlier works."[10]

Perhaps Hurston was consciously aligning her style with the kind of story she was relating. Arvay Henson, after all, is a character completely without a sense of humor. And, although narrated in the third person, almost everything in the story is filtered through her consciousness. What style is more appropriate, then, than one which is as somber as the heroine whose story it relates? Too, the style seems appropriate because Hurston seemed to see whites as being more somber, more materialistic, more prosaic, and thus less unrelieved (see the chapter on *Their Eyes Were Watching God*) than blacks. Whereas Janie Starks can laugh and play as well as cry and work, Arvay Henson seems incapable of such a gamut of emotions. And whereas Janie and Tea Cake form a real team,

Arvay constantly fights Jim because she believes that his playing is sinful.

VI Hurston: An Assimilationist?

Seraph on the Suwanee, then, is a complex and different novel, but it is not necessarily an assimilationist one. It is true that all of the major characters are white, but, as in her other novels, Hurston simply seems to be writing about people, about individuals coming to terms with themselves, regardless of their color. Since Hurston only published one novel about white characters, it is difficult to determine whether she was becoming an assimilationist or whether she was simply writing a novel to exemplify her personal beliefs about people. Had other novels followed the publication of *Seraph on the Suwanee*, it would been easier to determine the direction in which Hurston was moving. When she died in 1960, however, she was working on a history of Herod the Great, hardly an assimilationist piece.

In her works, Hurston seems to be writing about people who have been hurt, sometimes by themselves, sometimes by others, but who must heal themselves, who must realize that the individual has the means to pull himself up. In *Their Eyes Were Watching God*, it takes Janie almost thirty years; in *Seraph on the Suwanee*, it takes Arvay at least twenty. But both, one black, the other white, succeed and are happy. In *Seraph on the Suwanee*, Hurston appears confident in her medium and in her ability, though as she told Marjorie Kinnan Rawlings, she was not particularly pleased with the novel: "I am not so sure that I have done my best, but I tried. I need not tell you that my goal eludes me. I am in despair because it keeps ever ahead of me."[11] Hurston died before she could reach her goal. Her mother had encouraged her to jump at the stars. She had jumped but had apparently fallen short of the mark. In her autobiography she wrote:

> I regret all of my books. It is one of the tragedies of life that one cannot have all the wisdom one is ever to possess in the beginning. Perhaps, it is just as well to be rash and foolish for a while. If writers were too wise, perhaps no books would be written at all. It might be better to ask yourself "Why?" afterwards than before. Anyway, the force from somewhere in Space, which commands you to write in the first place, gives you no choice. You take up the pen when you are told, and write what is commanded. There is no agony like bearing an untold story inside you.[12]

Hurston wrote this at least six years before *Seraph on the Suwanee* was published. She never gave up the battle, then. Those stories had to be told. Though her goal might have eluded her, at least her agony was significantly decreased.

Notes

1. (New York, 1948).
2. Quoted in Hemenway, p. 308.
3. Hurston to Van Vechten, November 2, 1942, Johnson Collection, Yale University Library.
4. Hemenway, p. 307.
5. Bone, *The Negro Novel in America*, p. 169.
6. Turner, *In a Minor Chord*, p. 111.
7. Hurston to Burroughs Mitchell, October 1947; quoted in Hemenway, p. 310.
8. Hurston to Mitchell, as quoted in Hemenway, p. 312. Hemenway obtained his information from the Hurston files at Scribner's.
9. Hemenway, p. 314.
10. Turner, p. 111.
11. Hemenway, p. 315.
12. *Dust Tracks on a Road*, pp. 220–21.

♦♦♦♦♦♦♦♦♦♦♦♦♦♦♦

Workings of the Spirit: Conjure and the Space of Black Women's Creativity

HOUSTON A. BAKER, JR.

[N]o one may approach the Altar without the crown, and none may wear the crown of power without preparation. *It must be earned.* And what is this crown of power? Nothing definite in material. Turner crowned me with a consecrated snake skin. I have been crowned in other places with flowers, with ornamental paper, with cloth, with sycamore bark, with egg-shells. It is the meaning, not the material that counts.

Mules and Men

Conjure: conspiracy, c1540 Surrey *Ecclesiastes* iv.41 And by conjures the seed of kings is thrust from state.
Conjurement: The exercise of magical or occult influence.
Conjurer: One who performs tricks with words.

Oxford English Dictionary

The word "context" carries a certain intimacy, bearing always nuances of enclosure and stability. "Meaning," by contrast—especially in critical and theoretical arenas marked by a poststructuralist sensibility—carries visions of openness, uncertainty, indeterminancy. The human metaphysical and analytical inclination is to conceive "context" as a determinable place that stands in causal relationship to an always elusive "meaning." Context, thus, becomes, out of a bent for certainty, the meaning of meaning.

Attempting to discover why these somewhat comforting speculations on matters left me irreducibly uncomfortable, I realized that at the root of such thinking was what Bachelard calls the "lazy certainties of the geometrical intuitions."[1] Geometrism, according to Bachelard, seeks always a symmetry of oppositions. For example, if one cannot control or apprehend the meaning of an expression, one can, at least (and some would argue more importantly), determine the context (often labeled "historical") that generates, gives birth to, or produces the expression. An "outside" uncertainty is, thus, geometrically balanced by comforting images of contextual containment. Analytic and historicized interiors protect one, as it were, from immense reaches and troubling figurative exteriors.

What I find helpful about Bachelard's formulations, however, is not a facile or tendentious condemnation of geometrism, but rather, their promotion and investigation of the poetic image. The poetic image for Bachelard is a means of liberation from a reductive dialectics of order.

The poetic image disrupts, exaggerates, transgresses, transforms. Its unpredictability makes us aware of possibilities of freedom.

The phenomenological arguments adduced by Bachelard, as I have already suggested, are not without their contradictions and valorizations of the "speaking subject." Nonetheless, his stance enables him to localize the dialectics of inside and outside, open and closed, in language. They permit the image to stand in contrast to meaning. "And language," he asserts, "bears within itself the dialectics of open and closed. Through meaning it encloses, while through poetic expression it opens up." Confirming consciousness to language, he sees, nonetheless, imagistic means for consciousness to escape oppositions that accompany language as a sign of closed self-sameness. The image is contrastive to an oppositional order that pits a masterful "I" against a subjugated "other," a civilized "inside" against a wild "exterior." The poetic image, rather than creating or fostering division, relies on and promotes transubjectivity:

> When I receive a new poetic image, I experience its quality of inter-subjectivity. I know that I am going to repeat it in order to communicate my enthusiasm. When considered in transmission from one soul to another, it becomes evident that a poetic image eludes causality. Doctrines that are timidly causal, such as psychology, or strongly causal, such as psychoanalysis, can hardly determine the ontology of what is poetic. For nothing prepares a poetic image, especially not culture, in the literary sense, and especially not perception, in the psychological sense. I always come to the same conclusion: The essential newness of the poetic image poses the problem of the speaking being's creativeness.

Extrapolating from Bachelard, one might claim that the poetic image is coextensive with the poetic trope.[2] It is a pivotal and reflexive surface that defies a rigorous opposition of subject and object. It absorbs energies of its creator as subject, but is effectively sonorous only through the matching subjectivity of its recipient. Its force is felt in its disruptive effects, in its liberation of creator and recipient alike from boundaries of conceptual overdeterminations.

One can suggest, in fact, that the poetic image is a reverberant space of habitation. One may also suggest that it is a locus of value characterized by the function of inhabiting. Writing of the poetics of corners, Bachelard says:

> For to great dreamers of corners and holes nothing is ever empty, the dialectics of full and empty only correspond to two geometrical non-realities. The function of inhabiting constitutes the link between full and empty. A living creature fills an empty refuge, images inhabit, and all corners are haunted, if not "inhabited."

Creation, apprehension, re-creation comprise the process that makes the image habitable space. The process involves passage, for creativity is not an individualistic and radically material endeavor, but a passage of the liberating spirit summoned by the image through the image's inhabitant.

One problem with this statement as a possible model for the study of expressive culture is that it requires a definition of *space*. For what, after all, does it mean to designate an image as a space or to invoke the vocabulary of inhibiting? In *Space and Place*,[3] the writer Yi-Fu Tuan offers the following definition:

> In experience the meaning of space often merges with that of place. 'Space' is more abstract than 'place.' What begins as undifferentiated space becomes place as we get to know it better and endow it with value. Architects talk about the spatial qualities of place; they can equally well speak of the locational (place) qualities of space. The ideas 'space" and 'place" require each other for definition. From the security and stability of place we are aware of the openness, freedom, and threat of space, and vice versa. Furthermore, if we think of space as that which allows movement, then place is pause; each pause in movement makes it possible for location to be transformed into place.

On the basis of Tuan's observations, we might say that *space* is the condition of possibility of movement, a possibility that can be affirmed by sight or vision and confirmed by touch. Place, as a complement, is a locational pause contoured by distinguishable interests. Hence, place, insofar as interests mark its boundaries, may be thought of as "a focus of value, of nurture, and support."

The relational semantics of Tuan's formulation enable us to define the poetic image as a space offering conditions of possibility for movement. Those who take up and perpetuate the image and leave behind records of their encounters provide pauses, locational moments, that enable us to define the image as what Bachelard terms "eulogized space."

> Space that has been seized upon by the imagination cannot remain indifferent space subject to the measures and estimates of the surveyor. It has been lived in, not in its positivity, but with all the partiality of the imagination. Particularly, it nearly always exercises an attraction. For it concentrates being within limits that protect. In the realm of images, the play between the exterior and intimacy is not a balanced one.

Eulogized, imagistic space "exercises an attraction" through its potential to liberate us. Our freedom is a function of our ability to mine locational pauses—*places* of record within space—that comprise instances of passage or moments on a space-place continuum that are sites of interest.

What I want to claim within the spatially imagistic frame sketched is that Zora Neale Hurston's *Mules and Men* (1935)[4] is a *locus classicus* for black women's creativity. The work assumes this status through its *instantiation* (a word that marks time and suggests place) of the conjure woman as a peculiar, imagistic, Afro-American space. Hurston's collection constitutes a locational moment of perception and half-creation within the space comprised by the voodoo doctor, the hoodoo fixer, the two-headed bearer of wisdom in Afro-America. To make clear the type of classical/spatial relationship I have in mind I want to invoke two universes of discourse—architecture and literary criticism.

Space is perhaps the architect's primary consideration. Architecture is an abstract art risking dreadful banality when it resorts to representational designs like ice-cream cones, hot dogs, brown derbies, and golden arches. Abstraction demands not concretization or reification but relation and relationship. The idea must be translated through appropriate communicative channels and set in just relationship to features comprising the space into which it is to move. Material is important in translation or communication, but the "material" can be virtually immaterial. Air, light, and space, for example, are all elements of architectural design. The dissolving of boundaries between traditionally material and immaterial phenomena that marks the architectural enterprise is similar to the transformation of space that constitutes architectural relationship. Any building project must decide to seek harmony with the extant landscape, or to disrupt that harmony through counter-spatial design, or to combine these strategies, adding new dimensions while, at the same instant, preserving fidelity to the existing landscape. We can think of successful architectural projects in terms mapped for literary classics by T. S. Eliot's justly famous essay "Tradition and the Individual Talent."[5] Speaking of a literary succession from Homer to his own century, Eliot writes:

> The existing monuments form an ideal order among themselves, which is modified by the introduction of the new (the really new) work of art among them. The existing order is complete before the new work arrives; for order to persist after the supervention of novelty, the *whole* existing order must be, if ever so slightly, altered; and so the relations, proportions, values of each work of art toward the whole are readjusted; and this is conformity between the old and the new. Whoever has approved this idea of order, of the form of European, of English literature will not find it preposterous that the past should be altered by the present as much as the present is directed by the past. And the poet who is aware of this will be aware of great difficulties and responsibilities.

The terms of Eliot's description are spatial and abstract. He invokes "relations," "proportions," and "values" in his effort to suggest how classics are created and sustained.

I want to suggest that a relationship of identity exists between the successful architectural project and a classic work of verbal expressiveness because both are spatially constituted. Their material inscriptions are less important than the cultural dynamics they encompass and facilitate. Rather than simple reifications of ideas of their individualistic creators, they are transmitters of cultural dynamics. And they must accomplish their transmission in historically harmonious, yet contemporaneously efficacious, ways. A *classic* in any culture, one might say, is a space in which the spirit works. The very sign "classic" denotes an absence of temporal and material boundaries and suggests the accomplishment of effects through means outstripping the tangible and immediate.

If one seeks the classical in Afro-American expressive culture, one discovers without great difficulty a mode of discourse or performance that I call "mythomania.."[6] Mythomania is the classical spirit work of Afro-America. Zora Neale Hurston's *Mules and Men* is simply one instance within this world of production. Mythomania is most aptly defined as: "a compulsion to embroider the truth, to exaggerate, or to tell lies." The French scholar Ernest Pierre Dupré in his attempt to describe psychic states achieved in voodoo rituals labels such a compulsion a *"pathologie de l'imagination,"* a sickness of the imagination and feelings.[7] Louis Mars, by contrast, in describing the authentic crisis of possession accompanying seizure by a *loa* in voodoo ritual (and paying close attention to the work of Dupré) distinguishes between the affectivity of possession and the compulsions of mythomania.[8] According to Mars, a person possessed by a *loa* (a spiritual intermediary between human and supernatural) loses all control of a first person and personality to the possessing spirit. The mythomaniac, by contrast, is, in Mars's account, akin to the hysteric.

In one definition, "the hysteric lies mostly with his body."[9] The distinction that interests Mars is between an emotive-kinetic mysticism and an objectivized fiction in which a mythomaniac tells, mimes, and performs with his or her own physical and mental personality. The distinction resides in the degree of conscious control separating the possessed from the performer. Hence, mythomania can be taken out of a strictly mythic domain and employed as a sign for any Afro-American "fabricating" performance designed for encounters with and manipulations of the Afro-American cultural anima, or spirit. And it might, possibly, be renamed as "mythophilia" in the estimate of the Nigerian poet Niyi Osundare, who recently made the suggestion to me in Ibadan. Such a renaming would accord very well with the process I have in mind, lending to it a fully affirmative cast. For the present, however, it seems wise to maintain "mythomania" as a marker of the tradition of commentary on "voodoo" or "conjure" in which this discussion is situated.

A primary component of what might be termed "classical" Afro-American discourse is "soul." In more sacral dimensions, this component is labeled "spirit." Soul motivates; spirit moves. The generative source of style in Afro-America is soul; the impetus for salvation is spirit. *The spirit* is the origin of species, one might say, for countless black generations who did not choose material deprivation, but who were brutally denied, as I have suggested earlier, ownership or control of *material* means of production. If these generations had not possessed nonmaterial modes of production, there would have been no production at all. Their situation would have been equivalent to the possession of "luck" in the blues: "If I didn't have hard luck, I wouldn't have *no* luck at all."

The preeminent question vis-à-vis Afro-America's classical performances designed to move the spirit is: How is spirit work accomplished? The answer is that spirit creativity, like *spirit* itself, is an ever innovative production. In psychoanalytical definition, spirit is an active projection. It is desire's objectification of a something other, a secondary inhabitant of a cosmos that it both constitutes as primary material and infuses. A topos bringing together both psychoanalytical and literary expressive deployment of the spirit appears in a quatrain from James Weldon Johnson's "The Creation."[10]

> And God stepped out on space,
> And he looked around and said:
> I'm lonely——I'll make me a world.

God's smile rolls up darkness; light stands shining on the far side. The topos reveals not only the production of a "secondary inhabitant," but also the deployment of the spirited word to move from singularity and aloneness to the birth of light. And this topos is as variable as the spirit creation—the fabricating performance—that sets it in motion. The words of Professor Eleanor Traylor encoding Robert Hayden's magnificent poem "Runagate Runagate" come to mind as a variation on Johnson's topos.[11] That which "Runs falls rises stumbles on from darkness into darkness"[12] in Hayden's poem, according to Traylor, is Afro-American cultural anima. It is unbounded spirit moving "over trestles of dew, through caves of the wish" to light.

In classical Afro-American discourse, the spirit may assume various guises. For the classically successful performance is contingent upon the ability to fabricate outrageously, to improvise and embroider in outlandish fashion. The "power" of classical strategies in black America resides in one's ability to provide the nonce lie. For example, the arch impostor of Ralph Ellison's college scene in *Invisible Man* is President Bledsoe.[13] When the protagonist of the novel insists that he is in trouble because he followed a white trustee's orders, Bledsoe responds, "He *ordered* you. Dammit, white folk are always giving orders, it's a habit with them. . . . My God, Boy! You're black and living in the South—did you forget how to lie?" If being "in the South" is taken as a metaphor for a traditionally oppressed or bounded situation, if it is a sign that gestures, for example, toward the closures of over-determined *meanings* in language, then one understands "the lie" as a performance designed to forward the cultural anima's always already impulse toward freedom or liberation. And in such culturally grounded and always poetic performances, distinctions between matter and spirit, form and content, written and spoken are dissolved.

Spirit work, mythomanic (or, *pace* Osundare, "mythophilic") fabrication, is kaleidoscopic, and its variations reflect a limitless cultural repertoire. A trickster rabbit, for example, like a funky blues singer, makes impossible a clear distinction between the singer and the song, the artful dodger and the dodge. Furthermore, genre in classical Afro-American spirit work is noncategorical; spaces that might be deemed "separate" are dissolved in the general medium of the spirit. Rather than rigid formal categories and a restricted economy of content, Afro-American spirit work is as boundless in its efficacy as the gift in Marcel Mauss's classic formulation.[14] For in Afro-America what are traditionally defined as *gifts of the spirit*—discernment, prophecy, and healing—are frequently functions of work that transmits *spirit* in an efficacious manner. Such transmission preserves the spirit's gifts alive through continual circulation. (Bob Nesta Marley singing "pass it on, pass it on" comes to mind.) Mauss insists that gifts remain [powerful] gifts only as long as they are kept in passage, for passage forestalls the promotion of any single "possessor" (One might say any "individualistic creator") to a hierarchical inequality. Gift passage, like Afro-American spirit work, assures the benefits of spirit only to a *community*.

A concern that poses itself here is the relationship between considerations of space as habitable poetic territory and mythomania as performance. While I have used the general term "mythomania" to denote the performance that defines the classical in Afro-American culture, I have also suggested that in mythomania, strategies are multiple, guises of the spirit manifold, and genre, paradoxically, an almost noncategorical denominator. Such flexibleness and permeability are functions of the nonmateriality of classical space, which is always a *medium* rather than a signally distinctive substance. The classical space, one might insist, is a channel of passage and code of transmission rather than a temporally bounded *message*. The most intriguing way that Afro-American spirit has moved us toward liberation has been through what we can term the *medium's* transmission through the *medium* of fabrication, innovation, and improvisation. And definitions of "medium" bring us appropriately to the principal poetic image—that of the Afro-American hoodoo person or conjurer—which emerges in a discussion of *Mules and Men*.

A "medium" is: "an agency, such as a person, object, or quality, by means of which something is accomplished, conveyed, or transferred." A medium is also: "an intervening channel through which something is transmitted or carried on, such as an agency for transmitting energy." And, as we know from what is frequently labeled "popular culture," a medium is: "a person thought to have powers of communicating with the spirits of the dead." I believe the Afro-American cultural sign that appropriately unites mythomania as classical cultural performance, notions of the classical medium's space, and useful notions of the poetic image is the sign "conjure."

The conjurer in Afro-American culture is frequently referred to as a "two-headed doctor," a person of double wisdom who "carries power" as a result of his or her initiation into the mysteries of the spirit. Such a person is a medium; she works within the medium of a tradition called voodoo, or hoodoo.

In Hurston's work we find the genealogy of the founders of hoodoo, beginning with God and Jethro and moving on to Moses, who in hoodoo's genesis story was the first to know God's names, to learn the making words, to acquire the art of writing, and to carry the signifying rod of power. God, in hoodoo lineage,

> took Moses and crowned him and taught him. So Moses passed on beyond Jethro with his rod. He lifted it up and tore a nation out of Pharaoh's side, and Pharaoh couldn't help himself. Moses talked with the snake that lives in a hole right under God's foot-rest. Moses had fire in his head and a cloud in his mouth. The snake had told him God's making words. The words of doing and the words of obedience. Many a man thinks he is making something when he's only changing things around. But God let Moses make. And then Moses had so much power he made the eight winged angels split open a mountain to bury him in, and shut up the hole behind him.

But the (w)hole opens to allow the passage of the aboriginal powers of hoodoo to the descendant and founder of the "modern" line—Maria Leveau, quadroon child of a grandmother and mother who were hoodoo doctors.

Describing Marie Leveau's interactions with the spirit, one of Hurston's informants, Luke Turner, tells how the greatest of the two-headed healers (student of the powerful Alexander) did her *work:*

> She go to her great Altar and seek until she become the same as the spirit, then she come into the room where she listens to them that come to ask. When they finish she answer them as a god. If a lady have a bad enemy and come to her she go into her altar room and when she come out and take her seat . . . Marie Leveau is not a woman. . . . No. She is a god, yes. Whatever she say, it will come so.

The merger of Leveau with the spirit at the great altar, her ability to put to confusion enemies of those who seek her aid, combined with her prophetic gift of articulating events that *must* come to pass, provide a striking image of the Afro-American cultural imagination. In Hurston's hands this poetic image of the conjurer becomes more excitingly resonant than the one in the work of the Afro-American writer Charles Chesnutt, whose collected stories entitled *The Conjure Woman* (1899) project the veritable control of a plantation by the conjure woman's ministrations.[15] Chesnutt, unlike Hurston, never puts forward a truly scintillating image of the woman prophet, magician, or healer herself as a figure irradiant in the magnificence of her specific powers. In fact, the turn-of-the-century black writer's Aunt Peggy is a function of a specifically male appropriation of the conjure woman's work. For Uncle Julius McAdoo's telling of the "work" of Aunt Peggy is, like the conjure woman's work itself, designed to influence the economy of *his* situation. His telling of the work is meant to gain, as it were, clearly male material benefits. His ultimate aim is to alter the controlling interests of the white entrepreneur who has purchased the former plantation that Julius calls home. Julius, however, does not "carry power" in the form signified by either Aunt Peggy or Marie Leveau.

In effect, the virtue of *Mules and Men* is that it amply defines the type of the conjure woman not only through stirring images like that of Marie Leveau but also (and with magnificent cleverness) through the writer's own initiation into the spiritual world of hoodoo. The last quarter of Hurston's collection chronicles her own initiations into the mysteries, first by Eulalia and then by a succession of male "doctors," culminating, at last, in her apprenticeship to Kitty Brown.

It seems to me that much of the positive cultural resonance accompanying Hurston's concluding relationship to *conjure* is a function of the importance conjure has historically possessed for an African diasporic community. Writing in opposition to one traditional, white historical thesis that claims enslaved blacks had no significant others to look to but members of the master class, the historian John Blassingame asserts:

> In addition to these activities [religious and recreational], several other customs prevented the slaves from identifying with the ideals of their masters. Because of their superstitions and beliefs in fortune tellers, witches, magic and conjurers, many of the slaves constructed a psychological defense against total dependence on and submission to their masters. Whatever his power, the master was a puny man compared to the supernatural. Often the most powerful and significant individual on the plantation was the conjurer.[16]

One reason the conjurer held such a powerful position in diasporic African communities was her direct descent from the African medicine man and her place in a religion that had definable African antecedents. There are various perspectives on the origin of conjure as an established practice in the United States, and some are far more gratifying to Afro-Americans than others. Less positive explanations tend to read like a 1951 *Encyclopaedia Britannica* entry that concludes: "Serpent-worship and obscene rites involving the use of human blood, preferably that of a white child, were considered features of this religion."[17] One suspects that it was the high theatrics of those who sought to turn white credulity to profit that resulted in such a stupidly condescending description. These theatrics are captured in a report from the New Orleans *Times-Democrat* of 24 June 1896.[18] Describing a voodoo festival it reads as follows; "The rites consisted in building a large fire, in a dance on the part of the central personage, the destruction of a black cat and its devouring raw. The scene concluded with an orgie, in which the savage actors ended by tearing off their garments." The participants in the festival were doubtless "actors" who must have been delighted with the newspaper's "savage" accounting since it probably increased the white patronage of future occasions. Chroniclers of voodoo, or conjure, who view it as a scene of primitivism usually define it as derivative—an aberration of certain orthodox and heretical practices of European Catholicism. For example, there is an etymology that considers the word *voodoo* an extension of the French *vaudois* meaning "witch." The next step in this etymology is to trace voodoo to the heretical Christian sect of the Waldenses which arose in the south of France in the Middle Ages. The reason for such a spurious French lineage, presumably, is the strength and the syncretic (combining Catholic and African elements) nature of voodoo in Haiti.

If there is a kind of "colonialist" history of conjure, however, there is also a more accurate and gratifying one. Michel Laguerre, in his 1980 study *Voodoo Heritage*, traces the origins of conjure to a set of religious practices of the Yoruba people of the West Coast of Africa.[19] The name *voodoo* derives from Vodun, the name of the principal deity of these Yoruba rites. Vodun rituals feature both a priest and a priestess, with the priestess (called the *Mambo* in Haiti) as the central figure—the person who is oracle to the spirit of Vodun carried in the sacred serpent. Combining with colonial French Catholicism, voodoo became the dominant religion of the masses in Haiti and a powerful and pervasive force among the African population of New Orleans (especially in Algiers, the city called "hoodoo town," across the river from New Orleans) and the southern Black Belt. The influence and effects of voodoo as a diasporic African religious practice can be traced to the early eighteenth century. And voodoo, or conjure, has been an affective presence among blacks from that time until the present.

Newell Niles Puckett, writing of *Folk Beliefs of the Southern Negro*[20] in 1926, not only asserts that "perhaps a hundred old men and women" practiced voodooism as a profession in 1885, but also cites instances of the effects and influences of conjure in places like Philadelphia and the Black Belt of his own day. The historian Charles Blockson calls attention to the twentieth-century conjure and healing work of Hannah Prosser of Lancaster County, Pennsylvania.[21] And Ralph Ellison's *Invisible Man* includes among its significant details of the Harlem environment the following shopwindow scene: "A flash of red and gold from a window filled with religious articles caught my eye. And behind the film of frost etching the glass I saw two brashly painted plaster images of Mary and Jesus surrounded by dream books, love powders, God-Is-Love signs, money drawing oil and plastic dice." The Afro-American comedian Richard Pryor has grafted the conjure woman onto the popular imagination with his magnificent rendition of the story of Miss Rudolph, who has a three-legged monkey and wears a monkey foot around her neck. The African American type of the hoodoo or conjure woman, thus, has not only discernible African religious origins, but also perduring resonance.

While it is true that one receives less sense of conjure as a mass religion from accounts of United States practices than from accounts of

Haitian voodoo, it is also true that mass belief in conjure among Afro-Americans is amply attested by the gigantic collecting work done by Harry M. Hyatt in his five-volume compendium of *Hoodoo, Conjuration, Witchcraft, Rootwork*.[22] Zora Hurston, as a scholarly compeer to Hyatt, offers one of the most profound pictures of Haitian voodoo in her 1938 book, *Tell My Horse*.[23] Voodoo, according to Hurston, "is the old, old mysticism of the world in African terms." The strikingly womanist power of this African practice is captured in the opening anecdote to the voodoo section of *Tell My Horse*. Hurston reports:

> "What is the truth?" Dr. Holly asked me, and knowing that I could not answer him he answered himself through a Voodoo ceremony in which the Mambo, that is the priestess, richly dressed, is asked this question ritualistically. She replies by throwing back her veil and revealing her sex organs. The ceremony means that this is the infinite, the ultimate truth. There is no mystery beyond the mysterious sources of life.

What draws together the voodoo of Haiti and the conjure of the United States—in addition to their common African origin and enduring mass appeal—is their relationship to what I have earlier called workings of the spirit, mythomania, or nonce fabrication. One informant from Mary A. Owen's 1881 account called *Among the Voodoos* asserted: "To be 'strong in de haid'—that is, of great strength of will—is the most important characteristic of a 'conjurer' or 'voodoo.' Never mind what you mix—blood, bones, feathers, grave-dust, herbs, saliva, or hair—it will be powerful or feeble in proportion to the dauntless spirit infused by you, the priest or priestess, at the time you represent the god."[24] Puckett reports: "It is difficult to generalize upon the matter of hoodooing, since the charms are seldom made twice in the same manner; the materials used and the way of putting them together depending almost entirely upon the momentary whim of the individual conjurer." In *Tell My Horse*, the *houngan*, or priest of voodoo, is the carrier of the powerful Ascon (a version of Moses's scared staff). He speaks the secret "language" dictated by the *loas*, abolishes evil spirits, initiates believers into the mysteries, commands the *ververs* (or signatures) of the gods, and may even have the transformative power to convert himself into a Bocor, or dealer in zombies. He is, in short, a powerful spirit worker who gives credence to the general character of voodoo or conjure as it has functioned in diasporic African history. That character is best stated in a phrase drawn from Hyatt's monumental collection: "To catch a spirit, or to protect your spirit against the catching, or to release your caught spirit—this is the complete theory and practice of hoodoo."[25]

The fullest resonance of Hurston's habitation of conjure can be seen in the role it plays in her corpus. Three of her seven well-known volumes are directly dependent upon the type of the *houngan*, hoodoo doctor, or conjurer. *Moses, Man of the Mountain, Tell My Horse*, and of course, *Mules and Men* are all conjure books of the first magnitude. And the

1935 *Mules and Men*, as I have suggested earlier, demonstrates the efficacies of conjure as a cultural image in what might be conceived as a self-contained manner—that is to say, through the writer's own self-recorded journey home, her theoretical return. The power of the narrative's final sections—the implications and resonances of their *conjure*—is contingent upon a textual orchestration that commences with the first words of the narrative. We understand the force of Hurston's specific habitation of the image only by following the narrative's riffs and improvisations, subtleties and significations from the outset.

The first voice encountered in *Mules and Men* is that of the anthropologist Franz Boas, a German Jewish scholar referred to by Hurston in her autobiography *Dust Tracks on a Road* as "the king of kings." Boas's preface to the narrative begins as follows: "Ever since the time of Uncle Remus, Negro folk-lore has exerted a strong attraction upon the imagination of the American public." The second voice presented is Hurston's, in the introduction to the narrative. She describes first her gratitude when Boas told her "You may go and collect Negro folk-lore." She continues by telling how anthropology as a discipline provided a uniquely objective perspective on a folklore that she had known since birth.

While Boas praises Hurston's access to the subjective "inner life of the Negro," Hurston pays tribute to the objective perspective of Boas's anthropology. She enhances her introduction with a story about a Jewish man who steals the inner "soul-piece"—who appropriates to himself the inner essence of humanity—that God meant to distribute to all people in equal measure. Unable to contain or carry the power of the "soul-piece," the thief scatters bits over the ground as he is lifted violently across the mountains. People are only able to obtain "chips and pieces" of soul. In time, says the narrator, God is going to "ketch dat Jew. . . . [and] He's going to 'vide things up more ekal.'"

The concluding paragraph of the introduction offers gratitude to Mrs. R. Osgood Mason of New York City, who is described as a "Great Soul" and the "world's most gallant woman." Mrs. Mason not only possesses more than her fair share of soul but also has the financial resources that allowed her to support and contour Hurston's collecting enterprise at the rate of two hundred dollars a month for two years. Mrs. Mason is, in Hurston's phrase from *Dust Tracks*, a queenly "Godmother." Hurston's introductory discursive gestures combine with the narrative action of *Mules and Men*'s chapters 6 through 10 of part 1 to give point to the narrative's scenes of initiation and hoodoo work.

In the five chapters mentioned, we are introduced to a lively cast of characters who enact a drama of spiraling violence and intracultural conflict that implicitly seeks the ameliorating mythomanic healer found in *Mules and Men*'s concluding part. First, we meet Jim Allen, husband of Mrs. Allen, who runs the boardinghouse for the Everglades Cypress

Lumber Company in Loughman, Florida—the sawmill camp in Polk County where Hurston collected the bulk of her tales for *Mules and Men*. A *lying* session (continuously, the tales in the narrative are designated "lies") has been in furious and prolific progress when Mr. Allen intones:

> "Y'all sho must not b'long to no church de way y'all tells lies. Y'all done quit tellin' em. Y'all done gone to moldin' em. But y'all want to know how come snakes got poison in they mouth and nothin' else ain't got it?"

One of the young men participating in the session responds: "Yeah, tell it, Jim." Mr. Allen angrily retorts:

> "Don't you be callin' me by my first name. Ah'm old enough for yo' grand paw! You respect my gray hairs. Ah don't play wid chillun. Play wid a puppy and he'll lick yo' mouf."

The young man apologizes, then uses proper address, saying, "Mr. Jim, please tell how come de snake got poison."

In this exchange between Mr. Allen and Arthur Hopkins, cultural hierarchies and narrational proprieties are threatened for a moment, but are quickly—and deferentially—restored. Cultural discourse continues in harmonious fashion. But conditions of possibility for greater disruption have been foreshadowed by circumstances leading up to the lying session itself. The reason a moment exists for leisurely fishing by the Everglade Cypress loggers is a personnel shortage. Two weeks before their excursion, the camp's "watchman who sleeps out in the swamp and gets up steam in the skitter every morning before the men get to the cypress swamp, had been killed by a panther." Moreover, on the day of the fishing trip, the swamp boss fails to appear and the logging train must be deployed elsewhere.

An unusual series of events, thus, leads to leisure, and an unusual party is formed for the exercise of leisure. A traditionally all-male fishing party is replaced by a group containing Lucy and Big Sweet—women more than capable of holding their own on "the job." (Zora is also present and by narrative implication takes on the character of the other women by association.) These unusual circumstances come to a disruptive head shortly after Mr. Allen's injunction to Arthur Hopkins on age and respect.

The men have been telling stories of cats when Gene Oliver changes topics. "Talking 'bout dogs," he says, "they got plenty sense. Nobody can't fool dogs much." But what might be a transition within subject categories becomes a disruption when Big Sweet says, "And speakin' 'bout hams, if Joe Willard don't stay out of dat bunk he was in last night, Ah'm gointer sprinkle some salt down his back and sugarcure *his* hams." The low-grade (but always threatening) competition for narrative authority between men and women seen in *Mules and Men*'s encounters between Gold and Gene, Mathilda and B. Moseley, and Shug and Bennie

Lee in chapter 2 breaks forth into a palpable animosity with Big Sweet's remark.

Joe responds by telling Sweet to "quit tryin' to signify," and he bemoans the impropriety that has allowed her to be present. But Sweet is implacable. Jim Allen tries to smooth things over with a quip. "Well, you know what they say—a man can cackerlate his life till he get mixed up wid a woman or get straddle of a cow." Big Sweet turns on him viciously and says, "Who you callin' a cow, fool? Ah know you ain't namin' *my* mama's daughter no cow." Her challenge, unlike the earlier and unintentional slight of Arthur Hopkins, cannot be simply answered or transformed. Instead, it demands a detailing of the hermeneutics of Afro-American narration itself.

Mr. Allen defensively responds: "Now all y'all heard what Ah said. Ah ain't called nobody no cow. Dat's just an old time by-word 'bout no man kin tell what's gointer happen when he gits mixed up wid a woman or set straddle of a cow." Larkins White, one of the younger men, verifies the ontology of "by-words": "There's a whole heap of them kinda by-words. They all got a hidden meanin', jus' like de Bible." The distinction that Larkins makes is between a primary or visible scripture and a condensed, poetic distillate that constitutes earned, improvisational cultural wisdom.

Interpretive ability is of the essence of poetic faith. Larkins explains such abilities through a fitting invocation from his own stock of bywords. He says, "Most people is thin-brained. They's born wid they feet under de moon. Some folks is born wid they feet on de sun and they can seek out de inside meanin' of words." After Larkins speaks, the ground is once more clear—the conversational floor reestablished, as it were—for Mr. Allen to step forth as a speaker. He tells the story of a recent college graduate who recommends that his father be tied astraddle a cow to keep the cow from bucking and kicking over the pail during milking. The father, who trades his intuitive sense for a bookish recommendation, comes to distress.

The full text of the tale from which Mr. Allen's aphorism (byword) has come does more than provide an example of the elder man's restored, communally sanctioned narrative authority. It also focuses on cows and preposterous college boys, displacing one term of the byword's unflattering comparison. Woman as a source and cause of unpredictability is, in fact, altogether absent from the full *ur*-text as recounted by Mr. Allen. The center of the story as he tells it is a "thin-brained" interpretation and solution that lead to a father's incalculable fate. Tied to the runaway cow, his answer to an inquirer who seeks to know where he is headed is: "Only God and dis cow knows." Big Sweet's interruption and threat to the continuance of cultural discourse is, thus, only momentarily displaced. The breach is cleverly, but only momentarily, bridged by the suppression of an unflattering comparison.

The latent violence and threatened disharmony between men and women that surface most patently in the Big Sweet/Joe Willard exchange seem to receive ominous reinforcement through a shift in folktale content that appears at the beginging of chapter 8. In this chapter, the Afro-American folk figure John, who serves as the humorous trickster of a well-known postbellum cycle, is transformed. Generally pictured as a clownish fellow who outwits Ole Massa with luck and cunning, he is the entertaining and roguish hero of stories the loggers tell as they wait for the swamp boss. In chapter 8, however, he appears uncharacteristically as a Bad Man hero. With razor and gun, he convinces the bear and the lion that he properly owns the title "King of the World." "Yeah", says the transfigured John, "Ah'm de king. Don't you like it, don't you take it. Here's mah coller, come and shake it." Big Sweet assumes a character similar to John's before the chapter concludes. "Well," she says, "if Joe Willard try to take these few fishes he done caught where he shackup last night, Ah'm gointer take my Tampa switch-blade knife, and Ah'm goin' round de hambone lookin' for meat." Joe Willard, the wandering philanderer who needs to be cured of his roving ways, is under threat, and there is an absence of heterosexual bonding that seems to point to a more general cultural instability and absence of communal integrity. Lucy, for example, who is supposed to be Big Sweet's friend and ally is, in fact, in league with Ella Wall, the rival from Mulberry who has attracted Joe's attention. No general and trustworthy female alliance seems extant.

In chapters 9 and 10—the last sections of part 1—threatened violence forcefully erupts. Big Sweet and Ella Wall, who are bent on deadly confrontation, are only prevented from bloodshed by the intervention of the quarter boss. Lucy tries to stab Zora because she believes the folklorist has alienated the affections of her man, Slim. (As, indeed, Hurston has.) Hurston decides that it is time for her to depart the sawmill camp.

Only a momentary focus on her new collecting site "in the phosphate country around Mulberry" forestalls part 1's concluding scene of disorder and chaos. The setting in Ella Wall's territory heightens rather than diminishes the threats of violence. The moment of delay is filled with hints of disharmony, conflict, and murder. The world evoked by Mulberry storytellers is populated by Raw Head, Big Sixteen, High Walker, and the Devil. We witness a man and wife parted by a devil's accomplice, see an expectant woman hoping for marriage frozen to death, and learn of High Walker's decapitation.

When Zora returns to the Everglades Cypress camp (ironically, to attend a wedding that projects a sense of harmony), it is only a matter of when and not whether a scene of disorder will occur. Bringing early narrative foreshadowings to fullness is the appearance of Crip. He is the new skitter man who replaces the watchman killed by a panther. Lucy has become his lover in return for his promise to aid her in killing Zora.

A fight breaks out at the Pine Mill jook joint in which Joe Willard and Big Sweet are pitted against Crip and Lucy. The description of a community in disorder—a world undone by philandering males and women in competition—reads as follows:

> Lucy was screaming. Crip had hold of Big Sweet's clothes in the back and Joe was slugging him loose. Curses, oaths, cries and the whole place was in motion. Blood was on the floor. I fell out of the door over a man lying on the steps, who either fell himself trying to run or got knocked down.

No restorative is immediately available. Narrative, fabricating, or poetic authority—like all other ordering principles—is absent. Flight from, rather than a cure for, disharmony is the narrator's response: "I was in the car in a second and in high just too quick."

What she leaves behind are men and women who claim to carry "the law" in their mouths, who are of titanic proportions and energies. It would seem that only a set of cultural doctrines that go deeper than the lore of everyday life issuing from culture bearers such as Mr. Allen can compel and regulate this gigantic, vernacular cultural force. Big Sweet, for example, not only backs down a two-gun bearing quarter boss, but also stands as the recipient of Joe Willard's high praise: "You wuz noble! You wuz uh whole women and half a man. You made dat cracker stand offa you." Ella Wall, too, is full of robust energy that sounds much like John's when she intones: "I'm raggedy, but right; patchey but tight; stringy but I *will* hang on." A portrait of energetic men who require a strong cultural brew is presented when Hurston confides that many of the sawmill hands were fugitives from justice—outlaws on the job who

> not only . . . chop rhythmically, but . . . do a beautiful twirl above their heads with the ascending axe before it begins that accurate and bird-like descent. They can hurl their axes great distances and behead moccasins or sink the blade into an alligator's skull. In fact, they seem to be able to do everything with their instrument that a blade can do. It is a magnificent sight to watch the marvelous co-ordination between the handsome black torsos and the twirling axes.

Though *Mules and Men*'s narrator, fearing her own death, refers to the sawmill camp as *sordid*, one can infer from scenes in chapters 6 through 10 that she is thoroughly absorbed by the rhythms of a full-muscled heroically womaned, fiercely articulate vernacular community represented by the Everglades camp. One also infers that she understands that only a powerful, indigenously constructed set of guidelines and procedures will suffice to order such a community. Perhaps only an "outlaw religion."

Part 2 of *Mules and Men* virtually begins with the statement "The city of New Orleans has a law against fotune tellers, hoodoo doctors and the like." *Conjure*, the poetic image of primary concern, is a sign for "a suppressed religion. . . . [that has] thousands of secret adherents . . .

[and] adapts itself . . . to its locale." "New Orleans is now and ever has been the hoodoo capital of America." In the capital city of conjure Hurston takes up the mysterious and magical work that can harmonize and renew a disrupted community. Her journey begins in spring and has the flamelike intensity of the very conjure she strives to inhabit. When Mrs. Viney asks, "But looka here, Zora, whut you want wid a two-headed doctor? Is somebody done throwed a old shoe at *you*?" the folklorist responds, "Not exactly neither one, Mrs. Viney. Just want to learn how to do things myself."

We come, therefore, to the successive initiations that Hurston undergoes before becoming a friend, apprentice, and coworker to Kitty Brown. Behind her and behind the reader of *Mules and Men* is a vision of a ruptured, but productive, vernacular community, a world whose undoing seems the result of competition for narrative authority, an absence of female bonding, and a philandering propensity of axe-twirling, prolifically articulate males. What type of initiation into what manner of poetic or spiritual space enables Zora to occupy a role in *conjure*?

Her initiations, like those of all doctors in the founding line of conjure, occur at the hands of those who have been assured of their ability to carry power and to engage in activities akin to God's. For the initiation rites are designed to teach, to pass on making words, and to ready initiates for the crown of power. The Africanness of conjure's genealogy in Hurston's account begins with Jethro the Ethiopian, whose daughter married Moses. It is strengthened by the Ethiopian wisdom transported by Sheba to Solomon by means of her talking ring.

The poetry of *conjure* as an image resides in the secrecy and mysteriousness of its sources of power, in its connection to ancient African sources syncretized by a community of diasporic believers with Christian scriptures, and in the masterful improvisational skills of its most dramatic practitioners. The notion of Marie Leveau captured by Luke Turner's description of her first appearance to him gives a sense of the majesty of a poetic conjure in the folk imagination. Speaking of the annual feast conducted by Leveau on the Eve of St. John, Turner says:

> "But Nobody see Marie Leveau for nine days before the feast. But when the great crowd of people at the feast call upon her, she would rise out of the waters of the lake with a great communion candle burning upon her head and another in each one of her hands. She walked upon the waters to the shore. As a little boy I saw her myself. When the feast was over, she went back into the lake, and nobody saw her for nine days again."

The description provides some idea why Leveau is called the "Queen of Conjure" and why she represents one instance of a general poetics associated with carrying power. She is the grand worker, the closest *modern* (born 2 February 1827) figuration of a line of spirit workers that begins with the world's creation.

In order to obtain even a modicum of the conjure resources possessed by Leveau, Hurston must apprentice herself to those who carry power in New Orleans. She describes her initiations in both mystical and educational terms. Learning conjure requires one to pay "tuition," to assume the status of "pupil," and to look upon conjures practitioners as members of the "college of hoodoo doctors." Of the initiation's mystical character, she writes:

> [The] preparation period is akin to that of all mystics. Clean living, even to clean thoughts. A sort of going to the wilderness in the spirit. The details do not matter.

Elsewhere, she compares her initiation to a movement from a novitiate to a sacred wedding with The Spirit.

I take her phrase "the details do not matter" as a caution not to view any single set of procedures as the only access or fit initiation to The Spirit. Union with what is variously called "The Great One," "The Power-Giver," "The Man God," and "The Spirit" can only be effected in the first instance by those capable of "carrying power"—presumably a genetic *and* culturally specific capability. Furthermore, even those who seem gifted to carry power must await the Spirit's voice and accept the Spirit's dictates before approaching the altar. "Spirit!" intones Luke Turner after Zora's hours of fasting and accompanying psychic experiences, "I ask you to take her. Do you hear me, Spirit? Will you take her? Spirit, I want you to take her, she is worthy." Bestowing the sobriquet "Rain Bringer," the Spirit does indeed accept Zora as a conjurer.

The conjure work in which she engages can be classified as retribution, redress, reward, and renewal. Enemies are repaid with punishment; grievances are remedied; faith yields dividends of good luck and found love; the ailing are renewed. Successful work is contingent upon the doctor's skill, the client's faith, and an adequate sum of money invested toward change. While Zora does aid in rituals designed to bring death to an enemy, to prevent the rise of a rival professional, and to gain a favorable court decision for an accused felon, the primary petitioners for retribution and redress are women. Her first teacher—Eulalia—"specialized in Man-and-woman cases," and as Zora moves through successive initiations, the principal cases that come before her teachers are brought by women. Communal disharmony, malaise, and sickness seem metonymically represented by the troubles these various women bear. And the very efficacy of conjure seems to be reflected in the retributive justice and restored harmony effected by successful negotiations with two-headed doctors. Conjure is restorative in the sense both of a cure and of a renewal of diminished passions and compassion.

The various rites enacted—upon suitable payment ranging as high as $250—by the conjurer represent a combination of sympathetic and homeopathic magic, bringing into the conjurer's act both physical items (such as hair or fingernails) and performative items (such as dolls and miniature coffins). Hurston notes at a number of instances that the entire wisdom of whatever doctor she is working with cannot be placed in *Mules and Men*. Nonetheless, she provides enough details of her own learning, of her successful communication with the Spirit and confident manipulation of spells and rites to convince us that she does, indeed, carry power.

At the commencement of her sojourn in New Orleans, she discovers a certain body of women whom she describes as follows: "I found women reading cards and doing mail order business in names and insinuations of well known factors in conjure. Nothing worth putting on paper." Unlike this company of spurious businesswomen, Hurston, when she makes her way to the house of Kitty Brown, has acquired much that is "worth putting on paper." The wisdom she is able to transmit, in fact, is that of an entire vernacular community and its conditions of both disharmony and possible cure. That such a community has faith in the conjure wisdom, the hoodoo power, the Spirit work that she carries is attested by the attention devoted to such an audience in *Mules and Men*'s penultimate chapter.

"Before telling of my experience with Kitty Brown," writes the narrator, "I want to relate the following conjure stories which illustrate the attitude of Negroes of the Deep South toward this subject." Zora, who has assumed the role of collector throughout the narrative, takes on the function of vernacular storyteller in part 2's chapter 6. What she relates are stories that demonstrate the presence of conjure as a process in everyday African American life and the efficacy of conjure in overcoming arrogant power and outgoing violence—like that of the "wealthy planter of Middle Georgia" who is undone by a black man's hoodoo. Her third story shows that malevolent works are possible when conjure falls into the wrong hands. Each of the tales implicitly speaks of a religion of conjure in black life. Rather than demonstrating the poetics of conjure, chapter 6 captures the sociology of the poetic image. It illustrates the nature and function of conjure as an agency in Afro-American life. And we remember that the bearer of the spiritual legacy in "modern" African American—indeed, one might say, modern African diasporic—life was not a king like Solomon, but a queen, priestess, or Mambo like Marie Leveau.

Womanly spiritual agency is certainly what one infers from the description of Kitty Brown that opens the final chapter of *Mules and Men:*

> Kitty Brown is a well-known hoodoo doctor of New Orleans, and a Catholic. She liked to make marriages and put lovers together. She is squat, black and benign. Often when we had leisure, she told funny stories. Her herb garden was pretty full and we often supplied other doctors with plants. Very few raise things since the supply houses carry about everything that is needed. But sometimes a thing is wanted from from the ground. That's where Kitty's garden came in.

"Fresh from the ground" we find the productive *garden*, like Walker's discovered place of our mothers. In *Mules and Men*, the garden is equivalent to a pharmacy; it is a place from which healing roots and magical herbs of conjure derive. And Kitty—in her squat black benignity—has the character of a deceptively droll African religious sculpture. Her tremendous powers among a congregation of vernacular believers is masked by her unremarkable posture. Surely, however, it is because she, like Zora, is a carrier of the Black Cat Bone that she traverses the earth with her powers unseen. A storyteller and a uniter of lovers, a woman who has syncretized Western religion and African cultural traditions to ensure powers of retribution, redress, reward, and renewal, she provides a model of conjuring that the entire text of *Mules and Men* prepares us for. She is the intimate *home*, the imagistic habitation or poetic space of the spirit in which works of mythomanic transmission can take place.

The fact that Zora takes on Kitty's function—dancing as her substitute in a strenuous conjure ritual—while Kitty bears the suffering of spiritual initiation for Zora, suggests a relationship of identity between the narrator and the New Orleans two-headed doctor. Zora, in effect, inhabits Kitty's *conjure woman* as spiritual space. Kitty, in turn, says, "In order for you to reach the spirit somebody has got to suffer. I'll suffer for you because I'm strong. It might be the death of you." What the final initiation into conjure seems to imply is the narrator's arrival at a point of cultural intimacy, a spiritual space that enables her body to be a mere vehicle for the spirit's passage. Her being as a whole seems to be bonded in womanist ways to a root worker who likes "to make marriages and put lovers together."

The rituals that Zora conducts in partnership with Kitty Brown include, first, a dance for the death of a treacherous "John Doe" who has taken Rachel Roe's money and used it to lure a young girl to his bed. Next, she assists in a set of procedures designed to fulfill Minnie Foster's desire to have, keep, and rule her man. Five days after the dance calculated to end John Doe's life he deserts his young lover and returns to Rachel. And in the penultimate paragraph of *Mules and Men*, we overhear Kitty's recital to Minnie of a formula designed to change her man's mind "about going away."

Hurston's camaraderie with the vernacular community represented by inhabitants of the Florida sawmill seems to come to fullness in her final hoodoo partnership. Having made her way in the first three-quarters of *Mules and Men* through various spaces of the Afro-American vernacular, she at last achieves the power of a two-headed doctor. Her final appearance as a hoodoo healer locates her within a *community of women* who have the powers on their side.

In her appropriation of a corner in the house of conjure, Zora becomes a source of renewal, perpetuation, and harmony for the strong-willed community represented in chapter 6 through 10. Issues of narrative authority and gender are decisively resolved in the image of the conjure woman. There is no room for debate where Kitty Brown's powers are concerned. When she conducts hoodoo rites designed to change the philandering ways of bodacious men, they have no choice but to return to a faithful domesticity. Furthermore, the bonding between Zora and Kitty that provides enabling conditions for curing philanderers testifies to an achieved and trustworthy alliance between women. The absence of such camaraderie is, of course, a primary reason for the disruptions in the concluding chapters of part 1. Finally, the rites of conjure allow a petitioner like Minnie Foster to achieve a hoodoo or conjure brew that is strong enough to control the axe-twirling energies of a Gabe Staggers. When Minnie expresses her fear that Gabe's migratory employment with a construction gang might take him away forever, Kitty reassures her with a conjuring formula:

> "Oh, alright Minnie, go do like I say and he'll sure be back. Write the name of the absent party six times on paper. Put the paper in a water glass with two tablespoons full of quicksilver on it. Write his or her name three times each on six candles and burn one on a window sill in the daytime for six days."

The formula works. Gabe returns with love in his eyes.

The powers of conjure to provide guidelines, controls, motivation, and remedies for a black vernacular community grow out of the ancient, authentic African origins of its practices. These powers are mightily enhanced, however, by the poetic image of conjure in Afro-American culture. That image is most scintillating and liberating when it appears as the Mambo, priestess, or conjure woman rising—ascending like Marie Leveau with the light of wisdom glowing from her head and the brilliance of her works of hand illustrated by votive candles. Narrative authority is sonorously captured in the words of Luke Turner: "Whatever she say, it will come so."

By inference, one might suggest that whatever Zora Hurston projects in terms of the vernacular community that she has so creatively explored must "come so." The two separate domains of her subtitle for *Mules and Men—Negro Folktales and Voodoo Practices in the South*—come together in the concluding postures of her narrative. "Negro folktales," or harmonious cultural discourse that provides and seeks such tales as reference, are contingent upon "voodoo practices" as regulators of Afro-American communal life. Withoout the outlaw religion of conjure and its powers to cure and ensure bonding, there could be no tales. In a sense, the energies of Jim Allen and Big Sweet coalesce in the space of conjure. Zora Hurston—a storyteller of part 2's chapter 6 and as two-headed doctor of chapter 7—combines the roles of bearer of cultural wisdom and woman with the "law in her mouth." One might, in fact, invoke the praise song of Joe Willard and say that Hurston as conjurer is "noble"; she is "uh whole woman and half a man." For her strictly womanly conjuring authority enables her to displace the quotidian narrative energies of Jim Allen by the time we arrive at part 2. She not only tells stories in her own right, but also relates stories that have to do with the most profound spiritual practices of a vernacular community. Rather than an engaging lay narrator, she is a spiritual griot seeking her authority in doctrines and practices that have ancient spiritual roots. By inhabiting the image of *conjure*, one might say, the narrator assumes not merely a power to "change things around" through storytelling, but an ability to "make" an emergent nation of Africans in America. Rather than a "sordid" and "quaint" collection of fugitives, the towering figures of the Everglades Cypress company are inhabitants of a diasporic community whose history has not been invented. Hurston is their uncompromising historian, presenting an unromantic picture of their hard-pressed striving. She also demonstrates, in powerfully poetic terms, however, that their lore and lives, rather than helpless prey to random violence and disorderly rivalry, are subject to the severe codes of conjure. And the space of conjure—both historically and in the narrative frames of her corpus—is most fully defined by women.

> One of the first things we conjure-doctors have to do is to diagnose the case, tell the person whether he is conjured or not . . . and to find out who "layed de trick." The "trick" (charm) must be found and destroyed and the patient cured. If the patient wishes we must also be able to turn the trick back upon the one who set it.

What Hurston discovers in the Everglades Cypress sawmill camp is an image of American enterprise captured by the double-.45 carrying quarter boss who commands the labor and leisure of a group of "outlaw" laborers. The vision is not far removed from a picture of American slavery. The community of the mill has been enslaved, as it were, by the "trick bag" of a dominating society. They have been subjugated to exploitative conditions through the sorcery of white America. Their escape is only through the wisdom of words. When Big Sweet, Joe Willard, or Ella Wall claim to have the "law in their mouths," they are indicating the power of their healing and liberating words to change their status from passive victims to heroic molders of poetic wisdom, indeed, to the role of hoodoo historians of a nation whose history has not yet been invented. They are all possibility in their poetry. The introduction of "voodoo practices" among them means that they can "turn the trick back upon the one who set it."

In *Mules and Men,* the verbal or narrative turning of the trick can be seen in the final storytelling of the narrator. If we remember that she is a full-fledged inhabitant of the Afro-American space of conjure, we shall have no trouble coding the vernaular and radical dimensions of her tale. For in her concluding role Hurston demonstrates the intense and powerfully fine trickery that she realizes as a function of womanly communitas in the house and garden of Kitty Brown.

Mules and Men ends with the story of Sis Cat, who one day catches a rat and sits down at the table to eat her prey. The rat cunningly asks: "Hol' on dere, sis Cat! Ain't you got no manners atall? You going set up to de table and eat 'thout washing yo' face and hands?" When Sis Cat returns from her ablutions, the rat is of course gone. The next time she catches a rat, however, ole Sis is wiser. When asked about washing and manners, she responds: "Oh, Ah got plenty manners. But Ah eats mah dinner and washes mah face and uses mah manners afterward."

The last line of *Mules and Men* delivered by Zora is: "I'm sitting here like Sis Cat, washing my face and usin' my manners." The sentence signifies the full performative or mythomanic possession by spirit of a person who knows she has undone the traditional manners (and means) of accomplishing a classic. She knows at the close of her work that she has refused to craft a compendium of "Negro Folktales and Voodoo Practices" that would satisfy dry, scholarly criteria of anthropology. Hence, she tacitly slips the yoke that even the eminent Franz Boas seems to put on her efforts in a preface that invokes Uncle Remus as the prototype of the Afro-American taleteller. (One witnesses in this preface, of course, a relationship of similarity between Chesnutt's Julius and Boas's Remus. Both are displaced by Zora's hoodoo woman appearing in Zora's own person.) But Zora has not merely slipped the yoke or "turned the trick" on a limited anthropology by the conclusion of *Mules and Men*,[26] for, surely, she has also reclaimed the *whole* soul of the human enterprise for her conjure. She has rectified the theft of the "soul-piece" and become her own patron's superior through initiation into a world that practices arts different from what she calls "the American pharmacopoeia."

At the end of the general text of *Mules and Men*, Zora may be among the "unwashed," but she is also among the culturally well fed. She had dined on the spirit, on the manna of black culture, and knows that she has power to manipulate such manna in significant ways. The glossary and appendix of *Mules and Men*, as a kind of initial demonstration of her power, offer an alternative "pharmacopoeia" that ironically instantiates the *work* and workings of the spirit rather than "glossing" them. The *gloss*, as it were, is the *work*, containing remedies and healing words for those who would transmit the spirit of a *sui generis* Afro-American culture.

Hence, Hurston's work is both a chronicle of the journey *to* roots, and a *pharmakon* of root work. In his essay "Plato's Pharmacy," Jacques Derrida explicates Plato's *Phaedrus* in terms of the controlling metaphor of the *pharmakon*.[27] He defines the *pharmakon* as a phenomenon that serves variously as a drug, a poison, a medium, a technical innovation, a gift, a supplement, an *aide-mémoire*, an occult and "illegitimate" birth, writing, graphemic record, etc. Drawing on Egyptian mythology, he designates Thoth (the presenter of the *pharmakon* to a disapproving Pharoah who seeks to reject and suppress it) as a "god-doctor-pharmacist-magician . . . [who] sews up . . . wounds and heals . . . mutilation."

With *Mules and Men*, Zora Hurston has astutely defied King Boas and Queen R. Osgood Mason in the invention of a *pharmakon* conceived as the script or spirit work of black creativity. She has also, of course, achieved the healing status—the ability to sew up wounds and correct old mutilations—that accompanies a proper knowledge of the pharmacy's resources. The *pharmakon*, as poison, may well be deemed Hurston's contamination of the formal discourse and terms of the anthropology of her own era—an era in which womanist concerns such as those of Ruth Benedict, Margaret Mead, and Elsie Clews Parsons were proliferating. *Mules and Men* in a sense kills the kingly script of a mentor's and a patron's power, undoing the official mode of fieldwork through a kind of cultural autobiographical pharmaceutics. Aware of and capable of employing an official disciplinary language and perspective, *Mules and Men* also speaks (or writes) a radically alternative, vernacular, and black autobiographical set of polluting formulas that enable the conjured passage of spirit. Hurston's Thoth is a root worker of extraordinary linguistic ability and multiple names whose legacy for Afro-American intellectual history is, at least, a type of double writing that effectively negotiates both formal and vernacular worlds.[28]

Having set a classic model of creative black woman as hoodoo worker or conjurer—"rain bringer," "candle lighter," "striker of straight licks with a crooked stick"—Zora can well afford to sit back like Ole Sis Cat. She not only has come with *Mules and Men* to inhabit the space of an Afro-American classic, but also has provided our present era's point of reference for an African woman's creativity in America. (What Eliot would have termed the "presence" of the past for black women writers.) *Mules and Men* is the space in which we must judge and comprehend such appearances in recent black women's writing as Sister Madelaine of Alice Walker's *The Third Life of Grange Copeland* (1970).[29] Sister Madelaine is a businesswoman, fortune-teller, and two-headed doctor rolled into one. She is a woman whose son enrolled at Morehouse College tells her that "witch-riding" and "witches" have been displaced by Freudian dream theory and modern sleep research. But it is the dollars earned by Sister Madelaine that produce a college-bred son who becomes a leader of the campaign for civil rights. The impulse of the spirit toward liberation, as I have suggested, works in myriad ways. Toward the conclusion of *The Third Life*, we learn that Madelaine's son "had spent much of his childhood ashamed that his mother was a fortuneteller, but by the time he left Morehouse and joined the [Civil Rights] Movement he was as proud of how she earned her living as his best friend was that his father was a surgeon. His mother had faced life with a certain inventiveness, he thought, and for this he greatly respected her." A filial respect akin to that expressed by Madelaine's son is accorded by Toni Morrison's Ajax to his mother in the novel *Sula* (1973).[30] Ajax's mother—who sits "in her shack with six younger sons working roots"—is the most interesting woman Ajax has ever met. She inspires thoughtfulness and generosity in all her sons. The narrator of *Sula*, with the understated irony of one who admires fully what she seems to condemn, says of Ajax's mother: "She was an evil conjure woman . . . [who] . . . knew about the weather, omens, the living, the dead, dreams and all illnesses and made a modest living with her skills." With her teeth restored and a straightened back, the woman would have been "the most gorgeous thing alive." She has paid, however, for the weight of her vast pharmacy of "hoary knowledge."[31]

From his mother, Ajax gains a love of airplanes. I shall provide an extended discussion of *Sula* in the next chapter, but for the moment I want simply to emphasize that in the novel the conjure woman and flying are coextensive. And in Morrison's *oeuvre*, Ajax's love of airplanes seems to give birth to Solomon, the Flying African, and his skyward aspiring clan in *Song of Solomon* (1977). The cultural connection between Milkman Dead and Ajax's conjuring mother is, of course, mediated through Pilate, who is *Song of Solomon*'s true medium. She is the person who has the power of communicating with spirits of the dead, and who is (in apt lexical play) a most excellent spirit of the Deads. In one of the eerier thanatotic moments in the narrative, she manifests a long knowledge of the Bible (chapter and verse), a furious reverence for the sanctity of dead men's bones, and a transformative ability (akin to Papa Legba of hoodoo provenance or Leibert Joseph of Paule Marshall's *Praisesong for the Widow*)[32] that bring her into harmony with the best of a two-headed sorority.

When we witness the forceful expressive cultural succession of Zora's conjure woman found in works like those of Walker and Morrison, we know that the creator of *Mules and Men* did, indeed, accomplish the foremost task of the authentic Afro-American cultural worker. To seek a habitation beyond alienation and ancient disharmonies in a land where Africans have been scarred and battered, shackled in long rows on toilsome levees, is the motion of such cultural work. The home that marks the journey's end or theoretical return is the poetic image conceived as a classical space in which one institutes the type of locational pause that Bachelard might have called *eulogized place*—a revered site of culturally specific interests and values. *Conjure* is, to borrow a title adopted for his nationalistic work by Amiri Bakara, the *Spirit House* of black women's creativity. Its efficacy does not consist in its material presence nor in its genteel reconciliation of opposites such as form and content, context and meaning. Rather, it is an improvisational pause, a riff in a mighty orchestration, a nonce solo in which notes or objects at hand are combined to turn the trick on identifiable adversaries.

Red flannel, lodestone, anvil filings, roots, bones, rocks, dust tracks, snake skins, rabbit's feet, photographs, hairpins, brimstone—anything at hand can serve the conjurer as *bricoleur*, enabling her to escape oppressively overdetermined meanings or the agonies of alienated affection. We listen as a conjure woman of Algiers speaks of her improvisation: "Sometimes I take a small piece of lodestone, or at other times a little dirt corked up in a bottle [explained to be "graveyard dirt"], at other times the foot of a rabbit, at times a wishbone of a chicken, or, if I have time, I just make up a package sewed neatly in a red flannel covering."[33]

The secret of the conjurer's trade is imagination, which can turn almost anything into a freeing mojo, a dynamic "jack," or a cunning conjure bag. Quoting from a recent popular song, one might say the trick of spirit work is to "move in space with minimum waste-maximum joy."

The work to be accomplished is not only classically literary or expressive, but also generally healing in a manner captured by the conflation of conjure with the witch as image. In a suggestive study entitled *Witches, Midwives, and Nurses*,[34] Barbara Ehrenreich and Deirdre English write:

> Women have always been healers. They were the unlicensed doctors and anatomists of western history. They were pharmacists, cultivating healing herbs and exchanging secrets of their uses. They were midwives, travelling from home to home and village to village. For centuries women were doctors without degrees . . . They were called "wise women" by the people, witches or charlatans by the authorities.[35]

In Afro-America, the richest cultural wisdom resides in what Derrida calls the resources of a pharmacy—a space in which mythomania works. African women in America have been wise workers of this space. Embroidering, improvising, troping on a standard pharmacopoeia, they have transmitted the soul or spirit of a culture with rainbringing energy. If their work has sometimes been labeled "women's work" as an act of condescension, we know such a label is more than the gesture of thievish, envious kings seeking control. For the labors of black women have always been coextensive with those of Thoth. Like all classical spaces, their *conjure* has possessed the merits of a gift—the powers of a culturally specific pharmacopoeia. One must not conclude a discussion of *conjure* as poetic image, however, with anything approaching the static or the material. The trick, it would seem in light of what has been said so far, is to end not with a pharmacy but with pharmacokinetics—the healing spirit in motion.

Commenting in his autobiography, *The Big Sea*, on a college classmate's insistence that the only way to get material rewards from whites in order to build material buildings for blacks is to compromise black dignity, Langston Hughes says, "I began to think back to Nat Turner,

Harriet Tubman, Sojourner Truth, John Brown, Fred Douglass—folks who left no buildings behind them—only a wind of words fanning the bright flame of the spirit down the dark lanes of time." The force of conjure's image is not caught, nor is black dignity preserved, in material buildings secured by compromise. Its spirit is caught, instead, in bright words such as those that Zora (reverberating with the vernacular energies of Big Sweet and Ella Wall) uses to describe her stature toward the end of *Dust Tracks on a Road*.[36] Her words are pharmacokinetics par excellence; they provide a fitting space in which to conclude the present chapter.

> I have given myself the pleasure of sunrises blooming out of oceans, and sunset drenching heaped-up clouds. I have walked in storms with a crown of clouds about my head and the zigzag lightning playing through my fingers. The gods of the upper air have uncovered their faces to my eyes. I have found out that my real home is in the water, that the earth is only my stepmother. My old man, the Sun, sired me out of the sea. Like all mortals, I have been shaped by the chisel in the hand of Chance, bulged out here by a sense of victory, shrunk there by the press of failure and the knowledge of unworthiness. But it has been given to me to strive with life, and to conquer the fear of death. I have been correlated to the world so that I know the indifference of the sun to human emotions. I know that destruction and construction are but two faces of Dame Nature, and that it is nothing to her if I choose to make personal tragedy out of her unbreakable laws.

We live in *conjure* when we are warmed by such words. Combining the various meanings of "conjure," black women creators have thrust oppressive kings from state, exercised potently magical and occult influence, and performed liberating "tricks" with words. Their acts, surely, have fanned a quintessentially African spirit down dark lanes of time.

And their reverberant pauses—their sonorous moments of locational value in this transport—have left us unique places of esteem as well as conjuring spaces. If these *places* are not physical buildings, they are, nonetheless, building places: places that imagistically give consciousness to place in Afro-American women's expressive traditions. It is the task of the following chapter to extend our poetics to Afro-American women's place.

Notes

1. Gaston Bachelard, *The Poetics of Space*, trans. Maria Jolas (Boston: Beacon Press, 1969), p. 220.
2. By "trope" I mean an unusual rhetorical figure or the pressing into figural service of a type or form from a general cultural repertoire. The "signifying monkey," who is the folk verbal trickster of Afro-American folklore, serves as an analytical trope for the critic Henry Louis Gates, Jr., in his essay "The

Blackness of Blackness: A Critique of the Sign and the Signifying Monkey." In Gates, ed. *Black Literature and Literary Theory*, New York: Methuen, 1984. I use the Afro-American *blues* as such an analytical trope in my book *Blues, Ideology, and Afro-American Literature*, Chicago: University of Chicago Press, 1984. A defining site for tropological criticism is: Hayden White, *Tropics of Discourse*, Baltimore, Johns Hopkins University Press, 1978.

3. Minneapolis: University of Minnesota Press, 1977.
4. New York: Parennial Library, 1970.
5. In *Selected Essays* (New York: Harcourt, Brace, 1950), pp. 3–11.
6. Defined as a compulsion to embroider the truth, to exaggerate, to tell lies.
7. In *Pathologie de l'imagination et de l'emotivite*, Paris: Payot, 1925. Dupre's work first alerted me to the possibilities of the term "mythomania." I discovered Dupre through the work of Louis Mars.
8. In *The Crisis of Possession in Voodoo*, Berkeley, CA: Reed, Cannon, and Johnson, 1977.
9. Ibid., pp. 46–47.
10. In *God's Trombones* (New York: Viking, 1955), pp. 17–20.
11. Hayden's poem is found in *Selected Poems* (New York: October House, 1966), pp. 75–77. Professor Traylor delivered her insights on the poem at a conference for the Institute for the Black World in Atlanta, Georgia, in 1981.
12. Hayden, p. 75.
13. *Invisible Man*, New York: Vintage, 1972. Bledsoe is the chief adversary in the southern college episodes of the novel found in Chapter 2.
14. Marcel Mauss, *The Gift*, trans. Ian Cunnison, New York: Norton, 1967.
15. Charles W. Chesnutt, *The Conjure Woman*, Ann Arbor: The University of Michigan Press, 1969.
16. John Blassingame, *The Slave Community* (New York: Oxford University Press, 1972), p. 45.
17. (Chicago: Encyclopedia Britannica, Inc., 1951) Vol. 23, p. 254.
18. In Newbell Niles Puckett, *Folk Beliefs of the Southern Negro* (Chapel Hill: University of North Carolina Press, 1926), p. 183.
19. Michel S. Laguerre, *Voodoo Heritage*. Beverly Hills, CA: Sage, 1980.
20. *Op. cit.*
21. Mr. Blockson is the curator of the Blockson Collection at the Temple University Library of Philadelphia, Pennsylvania. His remarks on Prosser occurred during a personal conversation in the summer of 1985.
22. Harry M. Hyatt, *Hoodoo, Conjuration, Witchcraft, Rootwork: Beliefs Accepted by Many Negroes* and *White Persons These Being Orally Recorded Among Blacks and Whites*, memoirs of the Alma Egan Hyatt Foundation, 5 volumes, Washington, D.C.: Distributed by the American University Bookstore, 1970.
23. Berkeley, CA: Turtle Island, 1983.
24. Puckett, *op. cit.*, p. 189.
25. Hyatt, *op. cit.*, epigraph to Vol. I.
26. My colleague Roger Abrahams, who made a personal, extensive, and generous response to the present discussion greatly enhanced my knowledge of Franz Boas and his pluralistic, liberal, indeed, revolutionary work in establishing a rigorous discipline of folklore in the United States. My account of Hurston's practice is not an attempt to break faith with such fine scholarly human activity, but to maintain a faithful scrupulosity with respect to *Mules and Men*'s textuality and status as a medium of transmission of the image "conjure." Earlier than Abrahams, Professor Sue Lanser expressed concern about the negotiations of the terms "Jew" and "Jewish" in the present discus-

sion. Again, my circulation and attention to the terms is textually determinate. Still, there is always the question of critical tone, and on that score I think Zora Hurston's circulation of the terms is tonally consonant with the historical problematics of Afro-American/Jewish relations in the United States. There are, one knows, myriad affective and cognitive blindspots in the eyes of both parties to these relations. But Hurston was scarcely an anti-Semite, or ungrateful for the gigantic efforts on her behalf of Boas. Nonetheless, she was also a genius who understood the propensity of a dominant, scholarly elite—as Ellison's Bledsoe puts it—to "give orders" and to assume expertise vis-a-vis "other" cultures. The project of the Afro-American spirit worker is always, then, in double jeopardy of white disapproval and Afro-American rejection. A kind of "nativism" on the part of dominant culture scholars hopes that "native scholars" will never become more "complex" than the material of their group would seem—to the dominant culture—to warrant. There are, for example, folklorist and anthropologists of the dominant culture who believe that a postmodernist or theoretical attention is a *mishandling* of black culture. Similarly, there are Afro-American scholars who claim that such theoretical attention invalidates, *tout a fait*, any claim to genuine cultural knowledge of the *real* or *actual* lore. I think this situation could be called the "Hurstonian pinch." That Zora "signifies" on it in *Mules and Men* provides, if nothing else, an occasion for a reprise on the Afro-American scholar's situation. Given the history of colonialism in our our era, it seems a paradoxical situation, indeed, when scholars of the dominant (colonizing) traditions accuse the native of a misappropriation of either *soul* or *souls*.

27. In *Dissemination* (Chicago: University of Chicago Press, 1981), pp. 61–171.
28. I am indebted to Dominick LaCapra for his suggestions that Hurston's mastery consists in her ability to move inside both the formal, disciplinary and the vernacular discourses. I am grateful to Professor Barbara Babcock for word of the women anthropologists who surrounded Boas in the 1920s and 1930s.
29. New York: Harcourt, Brace, Jovanovich, 1970.
30. New York: Alfred A. Knopf, 1974.
31. New York: Alfred A. Knopf, 1977.
32. New York: G. P. Putnam's Sons, 1983.
33. Puckett, *op. cit.*, p. 239.
34. Old Westbury, NY: The Feminist Press, 1973.
35. Langston Hughes, *The Big Sea*, New York: Hill and Wang, 1963.
36. Urbana: University of Illinois Press, 1984.

Essayists

HOUSTON A. BAKER, JR., is the Albert M. Greenfield Professor of Human Relations at the University of Pennsylvania. His many books include *Afro-American Poetics: Revisions of Harlem and the Black Aesthetic; Blues, Ideology, and Afro-American Literature; The Journey Back;* and *Workings of the Spirit: The Poetics of Afro-American Women's Writing.*

CYNTHIA BOND has been the Research Director of the Black Periodical Fiction Project at Cornell University. She is the compiler, with Jean Fagin Yellin, of *This Pen Is Ours: A History of Writings by and about African-American Women.*

HENRY LOUIS GATES, JR., is the W. E. B. Du Bois Professor of the Humanities at Harvard University, and the chair of the Afro-American Studies Department at Harvard. His books include *Figures in Black, The Signifying Monkey,* and *Loose Canons: Notes on the Culture Wars.*

KARLA HOLLOWAY is a professor of English at North Carolina State University in Raleigh. Her works include *The Character of the Word: The Texts of Zora Neale Hurston* and *Moorings and Metaphors: Figures of Culture and Gender in Black Women's Literature.*

LILLIE HOWARD is an Associate Vice-President for Academic Affairs and a professor of English at Wright State University in Dayton. She is the author of *Zora Neale Hurston.*

BARBARA JOHNSON is a professor of English and comparative literature, as well as chair of the Women's Studies Department, at Harvard University. Her books include *The Critical Difference* and *A World of Difference.*

GAYL JONES is a novelist and critic. Her works include *Corregidora, Eve's Man,* and *Liberating Voices: Oral Tradition in African American Literature.*

FRANCOISE LIONNET-McCUMBER is an assistant professor of comparative literature and French at Northwestern University. She is the author of *Autobiographical Voices: Race, Gender, Self-Portraiture.*

DEBORAH E. McDOWELL is a professor of English at the University of Virginia, Charlottesville. She is co-editor, with Arnold Rampersad, of *Slavery and the Literary Imagination,* the author of numerous essays, and editor of the Beacon Press Black Women Writers series.

ERIC J. SUNDQUIST is the Gertrude Conaway Vanderbilt Professor of English at Vanderbilt University. He is the author of *To Wake the Nations: Race in the Making of American Literature, Faulkner: The House Divided,* and *Home As Found: Authority and Genealogy in Nineteenth-Century American Fiction.*

CHERYL A. WALL is a professor of English at Rutgers University. She is the editor of *Changing Our Own Words: Essays on Criticism, Theory, and Writing by Black Women.*

MARY HELEN WASHINGTON is a professor of English at the University of Maryland, College Park. She is the editor of several books, including *Black-eyed Susans: Classic Stories by and about Black Women* and *Memory of Kin: Stories About Family by Black Writers*.

SUSAN WILLIS is an associate professor of English at Duke University. She is the author of *Specifying: Black Women Writing the American Experience* and *A Primer for Everyday Life*.

MARIA TAI WOLFF is an attorney in San Francisco, California.

Chronology

1891? 1901?	January 7: Born Zora Neale Hurston in Eatonville, Florida, an all-black town. Daughter of John Hurston, a preacher, carpenter, and mayor of Eatonville, and Lucy (Potts) Hurston, a seamstress.
1915	Joins traveling theatrical group, working as a maid and wardrobe girl. Works for a white woman who arranges for her to attend high school in Baltimore.
1918	Graduates from Morgan Preparatory School.
1919–24	Attends Howard University. Studies under Lorenzo Dow Turner and Alain Locke.
1920	Receives Associate Degree from Howard University.
1921	"John Redding Goes to Sea" published in *Stylus* (first published story).
1924	"Drenched in Light" published in December *Opportunity*.
1925	Receives scholarship to Barnard College (first black student). "Spunk" published in June *Opportunity*.
1926	"Muttsy" published in August *Opportunity*. "Sweat" published in *Fire!!*, a short-lived magazine created by Hurston, Langston Hughes, and Wallace Thurman.
1927	Marries Herbert Sheen. "The First One" published in *Ebony and Topaz*. Goes to Alabama to do research, fieldwork for Carter G. Woodson and the Association for the Study of Negro Life and History. Interviews Cudjo Lewis, an ex-slave. The subsequent article "Cudjo's Own Story of the Last African Slaves" is published in the *Journal of Negro History;* much of the article is boldly plagiarized from Emma Langdon Roche's *Historic Sketches of the Old South* (1914).
1928	Receives BA from Barnard in anthropology.
1930	"Dance Songs and Tales from the Bahamas" published.
1931	Divorced from Herbert Sheen. "Fast and Furious" (musical play) also by Clinton Fletcher and Tim Moore published in *Best Plays of 1931–1932*. "Mule Bone: A Comedy of Negro Life in Three Acts" (done with Langston Hughes) published. "Hoodoo in America" published.
1932	Writes and stages "The Great Day" on Broadway.
1933	"The Gilded Six Bits" published in *Story Magazine*. Instructor in drama at Bethune-Cookman College, Daytona Florida (1933–34).
1934	*Jonah's Gourd Vine* (novel) published. Receives Rosenwald Fellowship.

311

1935   Begins graduate studies in anthropology at Columbia University; studies with Franz Boas. *Mules and Men* (folklore) published with introduction by Franz Boas.

1936   Awarded a pair of Guggenheim Fellowships (1936 and 1938). Undertakes fieldwork in the West Indies.

1937   *Their Eyes Were Watching God* (novel) published. Collects folklore in Jamaica, Haiti, and Bermuda (1937–38).

1938   *Tell My Horse* (nonfiction) published. Conducts field research in Florida for Works Progress Administration (1938–39).

1939   *Moses, Man of the Mountain* (novel) published. Marries Albert Price III.

1941   Works as staff writer for Paramount Studios in Hollywood.

1942   *Dust Tracks on a Road* (autobiography) published. "Story in Harlem Slang" published in *American Mercury*.

1943   "The Pet Negro System," "High John de Conquer," and "Negroes without Self-Pity" published. Receives Howard University's Distinguished Alumni Award. Receives Annisfield-Wolf Book Award for *Dust Tracks on a Road*. Divorces Albert Price III.

1944   "Black Ivory Finale" and "My Most Humiliating Jim Crow Experience" published.

1945   "Beware the Begging Joints" and "Crazy for This Democracy" published. Suffers from recurring gall bladder and colon infections.

1946–48   Collects folklore in Honduras.

1948   *Seraph on the Suwanee* (novel) published. Arrested for allegedly molesting a 16-year old retarded boy in violation of "moral" codes; the spurious charges were later dropped. Works as drama instructor at North Carolina College for Negroes (now North Carolina Central University).

1950   "The Conscience of the Land" published. "What White Publishers Won't Print" published in the *Saturday Evening Post* and *Negro Digest*. Works as a maid in Miami.

1951   "I Saw Negro Votes Peddled," "Why the Negro Won't Buy Communism," and "A Negro Voter Sizes up Taft" published. Moves to Eau Gallie, Florida.

1955   Opposes the Supreme Court's decision in the landmark 1954 *Brown v. Board of Education* case, which ended segregation in the public school system.

1956–57   Works as a librarian at Patrick Air Force Base in Florida.

1958–59   Works as a writer for *Fort Pierce Chronicle* and as a part-time teacher at Lincoln Park Academy in Front Pierce, Florida. Suffers a stroke in 1959 and enters St. Lucie County Welfare Home.

1960   January 28: Dies in St. Lucie County Welfare Home in Fort Pierce, Florida. Buried in an unmarked grave in the Garden of Heavenly Rest, the segregated cemetery in Fort Pierce.

1973   Alice Walker marks (with approximation) Zora Neale Hurston's grave with a gravestone.

Bibliography

Abbott, Dorothy. "Recovering Zora Neale Hurston's Work." *Frontiers: A Journal of Women Studies* (1991): 174–81.

Academic Conference of the Zora Neale Hurston Festival of the Arts (1990, Eatonville, Florida). *All About Zora: Views and Reviews by Colleagues and Scholars*, (ed. by Alice Morgan Grant. Four-G: Winter Park FL, 1991.

Alps, Sandra. "Concepts of Selfhood in *Their Eyes Were Watching God* and *The Color Purple.*" *Pacific Review* (Spring 1986): 106–112.

Awkward, Michael. "'The inaudible voice of it all': Silence, Voice, and Action in *Their Eyes Were Watching God.*" In Weixlmann, Joe and Houston A. Baker, Jr., eds., *Black Feminist Criticism and Critical Theory* (Penkevill: Greenwood, FL, 1988): 57–109.

———. *Inspiring Influences: Tradition, Revision, and Afro-American Women's Novels.* Columbia University Press: New York, 1991.

———, ed., *New Essays on Their Eyes Were Watching God.* (Cambridge University Press: Cambridge, 1990): 29–49.

Benesch, Klaus. "Oral Narrative and Literary Text: Afro-American Folklore in *Their Eyes Were Watching God. Callaloo* (Summer 1988): 627–35.

Bethel, Lorraine. "'This Infinity of Conscious Pain': Zora Neale Hurston and the Black Female Literary Tradition." In Hull, Gloria and Barbara Smith, eds. and introds.; Patricia Bell Scott, ed.; Mary Berry (foreward), *All the Women Are White, All the Blacks Are Men, but Some of Us Are Brave: Black Women's Studies.* (Feminist Press: Old Westbury, NY, 1982): 176–188.

Bloom, Harold, ed. *Zora Neale Hurston.* Chelsea, New York, 1986.

———., ed. *Zora Neale Hurston's Their Eyes Were Watching God.* Chelsea: New York, 1987.

Boi, Paola. "Moses, Man of Power, Man of Knowledge: A 'Signifying' Reading of Zora Neale Hurston (Between a Laugh and a Song). In Diedrich, Maria, and Dorothea Fischer-Hornung, eds., *Women and War: The Changing Status of American Women from the 1930's to the 1950's.* (Berg: New York, 1990): 107–26.

Bone, Robert. *The Negro Novel in America.* Yale University Press: New Haven, 1958.

Borders, Florence Edwards. "Zora Neale Hurston: Hidden Woman." *Callaloo* (May 1979): 89–92.

Bray, Rosemary. "Now Our Eyes Are Watching Her." *The New York Times Book Review* (Feb. 25, 1990): 11.

Brock, Sabine and Anne Koenen. "Alice Walker in Search of Zora Neale Hurston: Rediscovering a Black Female Tradition." In Lenz, Gunter H. ed., *History and Tradition in Afro-American Culture* (Campus: Frankfurt, 1984): 167–80.

Brown, Lloyd W. "Zora Neale Hurston and the Nature of the Female Perceptions." *Obsidian* (1978): 39–45.

Burke, Virginia M. "Zora Neale Hurston and Fannie Hurst as They Saw Each Other." *CLA Journal* (June 1977): 435–47.

Bus, Heiner. "The Establishment of Community in Zora Neale Hurston's *The Eatonville Anthology* (1926) and Rolando Hinojosa's *Estampas del Valle* (1973)." In Febre, Genevieve ed., *European Perspectives on Hispanic Literature of the United States.* (Arte Publico: Houston, 1988): 66–81.

Bush, Trudy Bloser. "Transforming Vision: Alice Walker and Zora Neale Hurston." *The Christian Century* (Nov. 16, 1988): 1035–40.

Byrd, James W. "Zora Neale Hurston: A Negro Folklorist," *Tennessee Folklore Society Bulletin.* (June 1955): 37–41.

Byrd, James W. "Black Collectors of Black Folklore: An Update on Zora Neale Hurston and J. Mason Brewer." *Louisiana Folklore Miscellany* (1986–87): 1–7.

Callahan, John F. "'Mah Tongue Is in Mah Friend's Mouf': The Rhetoric of Intimacy and Immensity in *Their Eyes Were Watching God.*" In Bloom, Harold ed., *Zora Neale Hurston's Their Eyes Were Watching God* (Chelsea: New York, 1987): 87–113.

Cantrow, Ellen. "Sex, Race and Criticism: Thoughts of a White Feminist and Kate Chopin and Zora Neale Hurston." *Radical Teacher* (Sept. 1978): 30–33.

Carby, Hazel V. "The Politics of Fiction, Anthropology, and the Folk: Zora Neale Hurston." In Awkward, Michael ed., *New Essays on Their Eyes Were Watching God* (Cambridge University Press: Cambridge, 1990): 71–93.

Carr, Glynis. "Storytelling as Building in Zora Neale Hurston's *Their Eyes Were Watching God.*" *CLA Journal* (Dec. 1987): 189–200.

Christian, Barbara. *Black Women Novelists: The Development of a Tradition 1892–1976.* Greenwood Press: Westport CT, 1980.

Coleman, Ancilla. "Mythological Structure and Psychological Significance in Hurston's 'Seraph on the Suwanee.'" *Publications of the Mississippi Philological Association* (1988): 21–27.

Crabtree, Claire. "The Confluence of Folklore, Feminism, and Black Self-Determination in Zora Neale Hurston's *Their Eyes Were Watching God.*" *Southern Literary Journal* (Spring 1985): 54–66.

Dance, Daryl C.. "Zora Neale Hurston." In Duke, Maurice; Jackson R. Bryer, and M. Thomas Inge, eds., *American Women Writers: Bibliographical Essays.* (Greenwood: Westport CT, 1983): 321–51.

Davis, Jane. "*The Color Purple:* A Spiritual Descendant of Hurston's *Their Eyes Were Watching God.*" *Griot* (Summer 1987): 79–96.

Deck, Alice. "Zora Neale Hurston, Noni Jabavu, and Cross-Disciplinary Discourse." *Black American Literature Forum* (Summer 1990): 237–57.

Dickerson, Vanessa D. "'It Takes Its Shape from de Shore It Meets': The Metamorphic God in Hurston's *Their Eyes Were Watching God.*" *Lit: Literature Interpretation Theory* (1991): 221–30.

duCille, Ann. "The Intricate Fabric of Feeling: Romance and Resistance in *Their Eyes Were Watching God.*" *The Zora Neale Hurston Forum* (Spring 1990): 1–16.

DuPlessis, Rachel Blau. "Power, Judgment, and Narrative in a Work of Zora Neale Hurston: Feminist Cultural Studies." In Awkward, Michael ed., *New Essays on Their Eyes Were Watching God* (Cambridge University Press: Cambridge, 1990): 95–123.

Fannin, Alice. "A Sense of Wonder: The Pattern for Psychic Survival in *Their Eyes Were Watching God* and *The Color Purple.*" *The Zora Neale Hurston Forum* (Fall 1986): 1–11.

Faulkner, Howard J. "Mules and Men: Fiction as Folklore." *CLA Journal* (March 1991): 331–40.

Ferguson, SallyAnn. "Folkloric Men and Female Growth in *Their Eyes Were Watching God.*" *Black American Literature Forum* (Spring-Summer 1987): 185–97.

Flores, Toni. "Claiming and Making: Ethnicity, Gender, and the Common Sense in Leslie Marmon Silko's *Ceremony* and Zora Neale Hurston's *Their Eyes Were Watching God.*" (*Frontiers:* 1989): 52–58.

Foreman, Gabrielle. "Looking Back from Zora, or Talking out Both Sides My Mouth for Those Who Have Two Ears." *Black American Literature Forum* (Winter 1990): 649–67.

Fox-Genovese, Elizabeth. "To Write My Self: The Autobiographies of Afro-American Women." In Benstock, Shari, ed., and Stimpson, Catharine R. intro, *Feminist Issues in Literary Scholarship* (Indiana University Press: Bloomington, 1987): 161–80.

———. "My Statue, My Self: Autobiographical Writings of Afro-American Women." In Benstock, Shari ed., *The Private Self: Theory and Practice of Women's Autobiographical Writings* (University of North Carolina Press: Chapel Hill, 1988): 63–89.

———. "Myth and History: Discourse of Origins in Zora Neale Hurston and Maya Angelou." *Black American Literature Forum* (Summer 1990): 221–36.

Freeman, Alma S. "Zora Neale Hurston and Alice Walker: A Spiritual Kinship." *SAGE* (Spring 1985): 37–40.

Giovanni, Nikki. "Sisters, Too; Great Women in African-American History." *The Black Collegian* (Jan.–Feb. 1992): 60–64.

Glassman, Steve and Kathryn Lee Seidel, eds., *Zora in Florida*. University of Central Florida Press: Orlando; University Presses of Gainesville, Florida, 1991.

Grant, Alice Morgan. *Jump at the Sun: Zora Neale Hurston and Her Eatonville Roots: A Guide for Teachers*. Association to Preserve Eatonville Community: Eatonville, FL, 1991.

Hemenway, Robert. *The Harlem Renaissance Remembered*. ("Zora Neale Huston and the Eatonville Anthropology") ed. by Arna Bontemps. Dodd, Mead and Co., New York, 1972.

———. "Folklore Field Notes From Zora Neale Hurston." *Black Scholar* (1976): 39–46.

———. *Zora Neale Hurston: A Literary Biography*. University of Illinois Press: Chicago, 1977.

———. *Dust Tracks on a Road: An Autobiography*, 2nd ed. University of Illinois Press: Urbana, 1984.

———. "The Personal Dimension in *Their Eyes Were Watching God.*" in Awkward, Michael ed., *New Essays on Their Eyes Were Watching God*. (Cambridge University Press: Cambridge, 1990): 29–49.

Hite, Molly. "Romance, Marginality, Matrilineage: Alice Walker's *The Color Purple* and Zora Neale Hurston's *Their Eyes Were Watching God.*" *Novel* (Spring 1989): 257–73.

Holloway, Karla F.C. *The Character of the Word: The Texts of Zora Neale Hurston*. Greenwood Press: New York, 1987.

hooks, bell. "Zora Neale Hurston: A Subersive Reading." *Matatu* (1989): 5–23.

Howard, Lillie P. "Marriage: Zora Neale Hurston's System of Values." *CLA Journal* (Dec. 1977): 256–68.

———., *Zora Neale Hurston*. Twayne Publishers: Boston, 1980.

Hudson, Gossie Harold. "Zora Neale Hurston and Alternative History." *MAWA Review* (Summer-Fall 1982): 60–64.

Hughes, Carl Milton. *The Negro Novelist*. (Citadel Press: New York, 1953): 172–78.

Hurst, Fannie. "Zora Neale Hurston: A Personality Sketch." *Yale University Library Gazette* (1960): 17–22.

Johnson, Barbara. "Metaphor, Metonymy, and Voice in *Their Eyes Were Watching God*." In Gates, Henry Louis, Jr., ed., *Black Literature and Literary Theory* (Methuen, New York, 1984): 205–19.

Johnson, Lonnell E. "The Defiant Black Heroine: Ollie Miss and Janie Mae—Two Portraits from the 30's." *The Zora Neale Hurston Forum* (Spring 1990): 41–46.

Jones, Kirkland C. "Folk Humor as Comic Relief in Hurston's *Jonah's Gourd Vine*." *The Zora Neale Hurston Forum* (Fall 1986): 26–31.

Jordan, Jennifer. "Feminist Fantasies: Zora Neale Hurston's *Their Eyes Were Watching God*." *Tulsa Studies in Women's Literature* (Spring 1988): 105–17.

Jordan, June. "On Richard Wright and Zora Neale Hurston: Notes Toward a Balance of Love and Hatred." *Black World* (Aug 1974): 4–8.

Kalb, John D. "The Anthropological Narrator of Hurston's *Their Eyes Were Watching God*." *Studies in American Fiction* (Fall 1988): 169–80.

Kim, Myung Ja. "Zora Neale Hurston's Search for Self: *Their Eyes Were Watching God*." *The Journal of English Language and Literature* (Fall 1990): 491–513.

King, Sigrid. "Naming and Power in Zora Neale Hurston's *Their Eyes Were Watching God*." *Black American Literature Forum* (Winter 1990): 683–97.

Kitch, Sally L. "Gender and Language: Dialect, Silence, and the Disruption of Discourse." *Women's Studies* (1987): 66–78.

Krasner, James. "The Life of Women: Zora Neale Hurston and Female Autobiography." *Black American Literature Forum* (Spring 1989): 113–27.

Kubitschek, Missy Dehn. "'Tuh de Horizon and Back': The Female Quest in *Their Eyes Were Watching God*." *Black American Literature Forum* (Fall 1983): 109–15.

Lenz, Gunter H. "Southern Exposure: The Urban Experience and the Re-Construction of Black Folk Culture and Community in the Works of Richard Wright and Zora Neale Hurston." *New York Folklore* (Summer 1981): 3–39.

LeSeur, Geta. "Janie as Sisyphus: Existential Heroism in *Their Eyes Were Watching God*." *The Zora Neale Hurston Forum* (Spring 1990): 33–40.

Lewis, Vashti Crutcher. "The Declining Significance of the Mulatto Female as Major Character in the Novels of Zora Neale Hurston." *CLA Journal* (Dec. 1984): 127–149.

Lindroth, James R. "Generating the Vocabulary of Hoodoo: Zora Neale Hurston and Ishmael Reed." *The Zora Neal Hurston Forum* (Fall 1987): 27–34.

Love, Theresa R. "Zora Neale Hurston's America." *Papers on Language and Literature* (Fall 1976): 422–37.

Lowe, John. "Hurston, Humor, and the Harlem Renaissance." in Kramer, Victor A. ed., *The Harlem Renaissance Re-Examined*. (AMS: New York, 1987): 283–313.

Lupton, Mary Jane. "Zora Neale Hurston and the Survival of the Female." *Southern Literary Journal* (Fall 1982): 45–54.

————. "Black Women and Survival in Comedy: American Style and *Their Eyes Were Watching God*." *The Zora Neale Hurston Forum* (Fall 1986): 38–44.

MacKethan, Lucinda H. "Mother Wit: Humor in Afro-American Women's Autobiography." *Studies in American Humor* (Spring-Summer 1985): 51–61.

Marks, Donald R. "Sex, Violence and Organic Consciousness in Zora Neale Hurston's *Their Eyes Were Watching God*." *Black American Literature Forum* (Winter 1985): 152–57.

Matza, Diane. "Zora Neale Hurston's *Their Eyes Were Watching God* and Toni Morrison's *Sula*: A Comparison." *MELUS* (Fall 1985): 43–54.

McCredie, Wendy J. "Authority and Authorization in *Their Eyes Were Watching God*." *Black American Literature Forum* (Spring 1982): 25–28.

McKay, Nellie. "'Crayon Enlargements of Life': Zora Neale Hurston's *Their Eyes Were Watching God* as Autobiography." In Awkward, Michael Ed., *New Essays on Their Eyes Were Watching God* (Cambridge University Press: Cambridge, 1990): 51–70.

Mikell, Gwendoly. "When Horses Talk: Reflections on Zora Neale Hurston's Haitian Anthropology." *Phylon* (Sept 1982): 218–30.

Nathiri, N. Y. *Zora! Zora Neale Hurston, a Woman and Her Community*. Sentinel Communications Co.: Orlando, 1991.

Naylor, Carolyn A. "Cross-Gender Significance of the Journey Motif in Selected Afro-American Fiction." *Colby Library Quarterly* (March 1982): 26–38.

Neal, Carry. "Eatonville's Zora Neale Hurston: A Profile." In *Black Review* Vol. 2 William Morrow Publishers: New York, 1972.

Newson, Adele S. "'The Fiery Chariot': A One-Act Play by Zora Neale Hurston." *The Zora Neale Hurston Forum* (Fall 1986): 32–37.

———. *Zora Neale Hurston: a Reference Guide*. G. K. Hall: Boston MA, 1987.

Olaniyan, Tejumola. "God's Weeping Eyes: Hurston and the Anti-Patriarchal Form." *Obsidian II* (Summer 1990): 30–45.

Paquet, Sandra Pouchet. "The Ancestor as Foundation in *Their Eyes Were Watching God* and *Tar Baby*." *Callaloo* (Summer 1990): 499–515.

Plant, Deborah G. "The Folk Preacher and Folk Sermon Form in Zora Neale Hurston's *Dust Tracks on a Road*." *Folklore Forum* (1988): 3–19.

Pondrom, Cyrena N. "The Role of Myth in Hurston's *Their Eyes Were Watching God*." *American Literature* (May 1986): 181–202.

Raynaud, Claudine. "Autobiography as a 'Lying' Session: Zora Neale Hurston's *Dust Tracks on a Road*." In Weixlmann, Joe and Houston A. Baker, Jr., eds., *Black Feminist Criticism and Critical Theory* (Penkevill, Greenwood, FL, 1988): 111–38.

Rayson, Ann L. "The Novels of Zora Neale Hurston." *Studies in Black Literature* (Winter 1974): 1–11.

Reich, Alice. "Pheoby's Hungry Listening." *Women's Studies* (1986): 163–69.

Robey, Judith. "Generic Strategies in Zora Neal Hurston's *Dust Tracks on a Road*." Black American Literature Forum (Winter 1990): 667–83.

Robinson, Wilhelmena. *Historical Negro Biographies*. (Publisher's Co.: New York, 1967): 208–10.

Roemer, Jule. "Celebrating the Black Female Self: Zora Neal Hurston's American Classic *(Their Eyes Were Watching God)*." *English Journal* (Nov. 1989): 70–73.

Rosenblatt, Jean. "Charred Manuscripts Tell Zora Neal Hurston's Poignant and Powerful Story." *The Chronicle of Higher Education* (June 5, 1991): B4.

Ryan, Bonnie Crarey. "Zora Neale Hurston—A Checklist of Secondary Sources." *Bulletin of Bibliography* (March 1988): 33–39.

Sadoff, Dianne F. "Black Matrilineage: The Case of Alice Walker and Zora Neale Hurston." *Signs* (Fall 1985): 4–26.

Saunders, James Robert. "Womanism as the Key to Understanding Zora Neale Hurston's *Their Eyes Were Watching God* and Alice Walker's *The Color Purple*." *The Hollins Critic* (Oct. 1988): 1–11.

Schmidt, Rita T. "The Fiction of Zora Neale Hurston: An Assertion of Black Womanhood." *Ilha do Desterro* (1985): 53–70.

Schwalbenberg, Peter. "Time as Point of View in Zora Neal Hurston's *Their Eyes Were Watching God*." *Negro American Literature Forum* (Fall 1976): 104–108.

Sheffey, Ruthe T. "Zora Neale Hurston's *Moses, Man of the Mountain:* A Fictionalized Manifesto on the Imperatives of Black Leadership." *CLA Journal* (Dec. 1985): 206–20.

Smith-Wright, Geraldine. "Revision as Collaboration: Zora Neale Hurston's *Their Eyes Were Watching God* as Source for Alice Walker's *The Color Purple.*" *SAGE* (Fall 1987): 20–25.

Sollors, Werner. "Of Mules and Mares in a Land of Difference; or, Quadrupeds All?" *American Quarterly* (June 1990): 167–167–191.

Speisman, Barbara. "A Tea with Zora and Marjorie: A Series of Vignettes Based on the Unique Friendship of Zora Neale Hurston and Marjorie Kinnan Rawlings." *Rawlings Journal* (1988): 67–100.

St. Clair, Janet. "The Courageous Undertow of Zora Neale Hurston's 'Seraph on the Suwanee.'" *Modern Language Quarterly* (March 1989): 38–57.

Stadler, Quandra Prettyman. "Visibility and Difference: Black Women in History and Literature: Pieces of a Paper and Some Ruminations." In Eisenstein, Hester ed. and introd.; Jardine, Alice ed. and pref., *The Future of Difference* (Hall, Boston, 1980): 239–46.

Stetson, Erlene. *"Their Eyes Were Watching God:* A Woman's Story." *Regionalism and the Female Imagination* (1979): 30–36.

Story, Ralph D. "Patronage and the Harlem Renaissance: You Get What You Pay For." *CLA Journal* (March 1989): 284–95.

Thomas, Marion A. "Reflections on the Sanctified Church as Portrayed by Zora Neale Hurston." *Black American Literature Forum* (Spring 1991): 35–42.

Thornton, Jerome E. "'Goin' on de Muck': The Paradoxical Journey of the Black American Hero" (notes) *CLA Journal* (March 1988): 261–80.

Turner, Darwin. *Minor Chord: Three Afro-American Writers and Their Search for Identity.* Southern Illinois University Press: Carbondale, 1971.

Urgo, Joseph R. "The Tune is the Unity of the Thing: Power and Vulnerability in Zora Hurston's *Their Eyes Were Watching God.*" *The Southern Literary Journal* (Spring, 1991): 40–55.

Wald, Priscilla. "Becoming 'Colored': The Self-Authorized Language of Difference in Zora Neale Hurston." *American Literary History* (Spring 1990): 79–100.

Walker, Alice. "In Search of Zora Neale Hurston." *Ms* (March 1975): 74–82.

———, and Mary Helen Washington, *I Love Myself When I Am Laughing . . . and Then Again When I Am Looking Mean and Impressive: A Zora Neale Hurston Reader.* (Feminist Press: New York, 1979.

———. "Looking for Zora." In Ascher, Carol; Louise DeSalvo, and Sara Ruddick, eds., *Between Women: Biographers, Novelists, Critics, Teachers, and Artists Write about Their Work on Women* (Beacon Press: Boston, 1984): 431–47.

Walker, S. Jay. "Zora Neale Hurston and *Their Eyes Were Watching God*: Black Novel of Sexism." *Modern Fiction Studies* (Winter 1975): 519–27.

Wall, Cheryl A. "Mules and Men and Women: Zora Neale Hurston's Strategies of Narration and Visions of Female Empowerment." *Black American Literature Forum* (Winter 1989): 661–80.

Welsh-Asante, Dariamu. "Dance as Metaphor in Zora Neale Hurston's *Their Eyes Were Watching God.*" *The Zora Neale Hurston Forum* (Spring 1990): 18–31.

Wilentz, Gay. "White Patron, and Black Artist: The Correspondence of Fannie Hurst and Zora Neale Hurston." *Library Chronicle of the University of Texas* (1986): 20–43.

————. "Defeating the False God: Janie's Self-Determination in Zora Neale Hurston's *Their Eyes Were Watching God.*" In Kessler-Harris, Alice and William McBrien, eds., *Faith of a (Woman) Writer* (Greenwood: Westport CT, 1988): 28.

Williams, Delores S. "Black Women's Literature and the Task of Feminist Theory." In Atkinso, Clarissa W. and Constance H. Buchanan, eds. and prefs., Miles, Margaret R. ed., pref., and intro., *Immaculate and Powerful: The Female in Sacred Image and Social Reality* (Beacon Press: Boston, 1985): 88–110.

Williams, Sherley Ann, Ruby Dee, and Jerry Pinkney, *Their Eyes Were Watching God.* University of Illinois Press: Urbana, 1991.

Willis, Miriam DeCosta. "Folklore and the Creative Artist: Lydia Cabrera and Zora Neale Hurston." *CLA Journal* (Sept. 1983): 81–90.

Acknowledgments

"Darktown Strutter." Review of *Jonah's Gourd Vine* by Martha Gruening from *The New Republic* (11 July 1934), ©1934.

Untitled review of *Jonah's Gourd Vine* by Estelle Felton from *Opportunity* (August 1934), ©1934 by the National Urban League. Reprinted with permission.

Untitled review of *Jonah's Gourd Vine* by Emily E. F. Skeel from *The Crisis* (July 1934), ©1934 by the National Association for the Advancement of Colored People. Reprinted with permission.

"Real Negro People." Review of *Jonah's Gourd Vine* by Margaret Wallace from *The New York Times Book Review* (6 May 1934), ©1934 by The New York Times Co. Reprinted with permission.

"Big Old Lies." Review of *Mules and Men* by Henry Lee Moon from *The New Republic* (11 December 1935).

Untitled review of *Mules and Men* by Lewis Gannett from the *New York Herald Tribune Weekly Book Review* (11 October 1935), ©1935 by the New York Herald Tribune Co. Reprinted with permission.

"The Full, True Flavor of Life in a Negro Community." Review of *Mules and Men* by H. I. Brock from *The New York Times Book Review* (10 November 1935), ©1935 by The New York Times Co. Reprinted with permission.

"Between Laughter and Tears." Review of *Their Eyes Were Watching God* by Richard Wright from *New Masses* (5 October 1937).

Untitled review of *Their Eyes Were Watching God* by Alain Locke from *Opportunity* (1 June 1938), ©1938 by the National Urban League. Reprinted with permission.

Unitled review of *Their Eyes Were Watching God* by Lucille Tompkins from *The New York Times Book Review* (26 September 1937), ©1937 by The New York Times Co. Reprinted with permission.

"Luck is a Fortune." Review of *Their Eyes Were Watching God* by Sterling Brown from *The Nation* (16 October 1937), ©1937 by Nation Associates, Inc. Reprinted with permission.

"Vibrant Book Full of Nature and Salt." Review of *Their Eyes Were Watching God* by Sheila Hibben from the *New York Herald Tribune Weekly Book Review* (26 September 1937), ©1937 by the New York Herald Tribune Co. Reprinted with permission.

"You Can't Hear Their Voices." Review of *Their Eyes Were Watching God* by Otis Ferguson from *The New Republic* (13 October 1937).

"Witchcraft in the Caribbean Islands." Review of *Don't Tell My Horse* by Elmer Davis from *The Saturday Review* (15 October 1938), ©1938 by the Saturday Review Associates. Reprinted with permission.

"Old Testament Voodoo." Review of *Moses, Man of the Mountain* by Louis Untermeyer from *The Saturday Review* (11 November 1939), ©1939 by the Saturday Review Associates. Reprinted with permission.

Untitled review of *Moses, Man of the Mountain* by Percy Hutchison from *The New York Times Book Review* (19 November 1939), ©1939 by The New York Times Co. Reprinted with permission.

"Zora Hurston Sums Up." Review of *Dust Tracks on a Road* by Phil Strong from *The Saturday Review* (28 November 1942), ©1942 by the Saturday Review Associates. Reprinted with permission.

"Zora Hurston's Story." Review of *Dust Tracks on a Road* by Beatrice Sherman from *The New York Times Book Review* (29 November 1942), ©1942 by The New York Times Co. Reprinted with permission.

"Freud in Terpentine." Review of *Seraph on the Suwane* by Frank G. Slaughter from *The New York Times Book Review* (31 October 1948), ©1948 by The New York Times Co. Reprinted with permission.

Untitled review of *Seraph on the Suwanee* by Worth Tuttle Hedden from the *New York Herald Tribune Weekly Book Review* (10 October 1948), ©1948 by the New York Herald Tribune Co. Reprinted with permission.

"'The Drum with the Man Skin': *Jonah's Gourd Vine*" by Eric J. Sundquist from *The Hammers of Creation: Folk Culture in Modern African-American Fiction* by Eric J. Sundquist, ©1992 by the University of Georgia Press. Reprinted with permission.

"The Emergent Voice: The Word within Its Texts" by Karla Holloway from *The Character of the Word* by Karla Holloway, ©1987 by Karla F. C. Holloway. Reprinted with permission.

"Zola Neale Hurston: Changing Her Own Words" by Cheryl A. Wall from *American Novelists Revisited*, edited by Fritz Fleischmann, ©1982 by Cheryl A. Wall. Reprinted with permission.

"'I Love the Way Janie Crawford Left Her Husbands': Hurston's Emergent Female Hero" by Mary Helen Washington from *Invented Lives: Narratives of Black Women 1860–1960* by Mary Helen Washington, ©1987 by Mary Helen Washington. Reprinted with permission.

"Wandering: Hurston's Search for Self and Method" by Susan Willis from *Specifying: Black Women Writing the American Experience* by Susan Willis, © by The Board of Regents of the University of Wisconsin System. Reprinted with permission.

"Thresholds of Difference: Structures of Address in Zora Neale Hurston" by Barbara Johnson from *Critical Inquiry* 12 (Autumn 1985), ©1985 by the University of Chicago. Reprinted with permission.

"Breaking Out of the Conventions of Dialect" (originally entitled "Breaking Out of The Conventions of Dialect: Dunbar and Hurston") by Gayl Jones from *Présence Africaine: Revue Culturelle du Monde Noir/Cultural Review of the Negro World* 144 (4th Quarterly 1987), ©1987 by Revue Présence Africaine. Reprinted with permission.

"*Their Eyes Were Watching God:* Hurston and the Speakerly Text" (originally entitled "Zora Neale Hurston and the Speakerly Text," chapter 5 of *The Signifying Monkey*) by Henry Louis Gates, Jr., ©1988 by Henry Louis Gates, Jr. Reprinted with permission.

"Language, Speech, and Difference in *Their Eyes Were Watching God*" by Cynthia Bond, ©1987 by Cynthia Bond. Printed with permission.

"Listening and Living: Reading and Experience in *Their Eyes Were Watching God*" by Maria Tai Wolff from *Black American Literature Forum* 16, No. 1 (Spring 1982), ©1982 by Indiana State University. Reprinted with permission.

"Lines of Descent/Dissenting Lines" by Deborah E. McDowell from *Moses, Man of the Mountain* by Zora Neale Hurston, ©1991 by Deborah E. McDowell. Reprinted with permission.

Index

This is one of six volumes of literary
criticism launching the
AMISTAD LITERARY SERIES
which is devoted to literary fiction
and criticism by and about African Americans.

◆

The typeface "AMISTAD" is based
on wood and stone symbols
and geometric patterns seen throughout
sixteenth-century Africa. These hand-carved
motifs were used to convey the diverse
cultural aspects evident among
the many African peoples.

◆

Amistad typeface was designed
by Maryam "Marne" Zafar.

◆

This book was published with the
assistance of March Tenth, Inc.
Printed and bound by Haddon Craftsmen, Inc.

◆

The paper is acid-free
55-pound Cross Pointe Odyssey Book.